——————— • ———————

MYSTICAL VERTIGO:
CONTEMPORARY KABBALISTIC HEBREW POETRY
DANCING OVER THE DIVIDE

——————— AUBREY L. GLAZER ———————

CONGREGATION
בֵּית שָׁלוֹם
BETH SHOLOM

301 14th Avenue • San Francisco • California • 94118

This book is here for you to read, contemplate and
share in the meditation space of *Makom Shalom*.
Should you like a personal copy, please inquire at the
front desk.

New Perspectives in Post-Rabbinic Judaism

Series Editor
Shaul Magid (Indiana University)

ACADEMIC
STUDIES
PRESS

MYSTICAL VERTIGO

CONTEMPORARY KABBALISTIC HEBREW POETRY

DANCING OVER THE DIVIDE

—— AUBREY L. GLAZER ——

Boston
2013

Library of Congress Cataloging-in-Publication Data :
The bibliographic data for this title is available from the Library of Congress.

ISBN 978-1-61811-166-1 (cloth)
ISBN 978-1-61811-375-7 (paperback)
ISBN 978-1-61811-188-3 (electronic)

Book design by Olga Grabovsky
On the cover: "Sacrifice 1," by Elyssa Wortzman.

Published by Academic Studies Press in 2013
28 Montfern Avenue
Brighton, MA 02135, USA
press@academicstudiespress.com
www.academicstudiespress.com

CONTENTS

Preface:
Shaul Magid ix

Acknowledgements xiii

1. TOUCHING GOD:
Vertigo, Exactitude and Degrees of *Devekut* 21

2. WHY CONTEMPORARY JEWISH MYSTICISM NEEDS POETRY
From Kosman's "Our God" to ben Yitzhak's
IntegrEL Divinity "of All Worlds" 71

3. *DISSEMINATION* OF *DEVEKUT*:
HOW CULTURE CAN CONNECT DEEPER
Agi Mishol's "Woman Martyr" and "Transistor Muezzin" 81

4. CONTRITION AS A RETURNING TO *DEVEKUT*
Binyamin Shevili's Cycle "Contrition" 94

5. OPENING SECRECY: IS THERE DUPLICITY IN *DEVEKUT*?
Schulamith Hava HaLevy's "Strange Fire" and "Impregnation" 119

6. CAUGHT IN THE INFINITY CATCHERS:
DEVEKUT AS A WEB OF DISCOURSE
Shai Tubaly "Come Here," "I Came to God," and "Infinity Catchers" . . 145

7. AUTO-EROTIC COSMOGENY AS *DEVEKUT*:
Rebirthing God as Self in Haya Esther's My Flesh Speaks G!d 154

8. *(HIT)DEVEKUT* AS *DURÉE* OF THE GODLOVER
Disentangling Intuitive Time in Binyamin Shevili's "HomosexuELity" . . 177

9. PARABLES AND PRAYERS OF LOVE AND RAPE:
    Devekut as Depth and Flow of Self in
    Tamar Elad-Appelbaum's "Psalms for Jerusalem" 200

10. SCENT OF DARKNESS:
    A SYNESTHETIC DISSOLUTION INTO *DEVEKUT*
    Yonadav Kaploun's cycles "Scent of Darkness"
    and "A Window of Opportunity" 210

11. I ALMOST VOWED TO TOUCH YOU:
    BREAKING THROUGH DOUBT TO DAILY *DEVEKUT*
    Zelda Schneerson Mishkovsky's "On that Night" 240

12. REBIRTHING *DEVEKUT* FROM DARKNESS TO LIGHT:
    Haviva Pedaya's "Gently Please," "The Golden Molten Stream,"
    "Sun-space," "Crack the Sun," and "Majesty Manacled" 250

13. CODA:
    Gross, Subtle and Secret Moments of *Devekut* 262

Afterword:
Elliot R. Wolfson 267
Bibliography 274
Index 291
Short Bio 304

PREFACE

In the past decade the study of Jewish mysticism has taken a decidedly contemporary turn. Scholars of the kabbalistic tradition fully trained in the languages and nomenclature of classical Kabbalah have in some sense subverted the thesis of the great master Gershom Scholem, who argued that secularism and secularity have made authentic Jewish mysticism all but impossible today. Scholarly essays and books have begun exploring the subterranean cloisters of Jerusalem's *haredi* (ultra-Orthodox) neighborhoods where Kabbalah not only serves the banal function of being part of Israel's *haredi* civil religion but is a living and breathing art that thrives and flourishes among young adepts in search of the life the texts describe.

This new kabbalistic activity is not an isolated phenomenon but part of a larger realignment of *haredi* Judaism toward the world around it. It is part of a move "inward" that is also outward, taking tentative yet also courageous steps outside a world whose imaginary (and concrete) walls no longer protect it from the Zionist project and the secular spiritual renaissance that has seeped into the noisy study-halls and dimly-lit apartments of Jerusalem neighborhoods such as *Tel Arza, Geulah,* and *Meah Shearim.* Many members of these largely closed circles come from, or have connections to, the outside world. Increasing numbers of *haredim* in Israel dwell outside the Hasidic Eastern European binaries of religious and secular that informed both camps (the *haredim* and the secular) for generations. This does not necessarily manifest itself as tolerance. Yet even the more rigid and intolerant world we sometimes see in the news speaks to a new development that has largely cut its ties with its European past.

This book is not a study of that world, but uses one dimension of these shifting sands to make a larger point about the ways in which "New *Haredism*" is making a contribution to a mystical renaissance in Israel.

Aubrey Glazer's interests are not anthropological but metaphysical. For him, culture veils a more internal movement where different worlds are unwittingly getting closer, not farther apart. He uses this new phenomenon to explore the metaphysics of what has thus far largely been examined through cultural analysis. More significant, however, is the way he confronts the relationship between mysticism and poetry in a way few have done before.

Scholars of mysticism have often commented on the apparent symmetry between mysticism and poetry; the phenomenological symbiosis and the shared temperament between the mystic and the poet. Poets themselves recognize this, and mystics often try their hand at poetry, assuming their vocation bleeds naturally into the other. The success of this endeavor, or more often the lack thereof, notwithstanding, the poet and the mystic indeed share a common psychic space. Both poet and mystic attempt to express the subtleties of human experience and the excess of human emotion through language with full knowledge that the only tools at their disposal, words, ultimately fail to adequately illustrate the vicissitudes of the inner world they seek to describe. From Dante to Rilke to Whitman, poets view the mystical as some kind of home, however elusive and however strange. And mystics from Eckhart to Rumi to Rabbi Abraham Isaac Kook view poetry as an expressive form that they feel coheres with their project of communicating transcendence through immanence. The mystic and the poet are failures, but in that failure emerges a precious gift for us; a guide to the very margins of dualism where we can, perhaps, gaze over the precipice (or witness them gazing over the precipice) where the many and the one, or the real and the imagined, or the corporeal and the nothingness, converge. All this has little to do with belief and even less to do with doctrine. The categories and life of normative religion are left in the villages. The mystics and poets prefer the forest and the desert.

Glazer's protagonist in this book is a young enigmatic *haredi* rabbi named Yitzhaq Maier Morgenstern, almost unknown even among scholars of Kabbalah. For many years he published his work anonymously under the title *Yam ha-Hokhma* (*Sea of Wisdom*). He was raised in England in a *haredi* community and immigrated to Israel as a young man. For Glazer, Morgenstern represents a figure on the margin, one who remains deeply embedded in the traditional world of his upbringing, yet one for whom the search for the mystical life, and not merely the study of mystical texts, has brought him to yet another precipice, one that overlooks the horizons of the universal mystical quest. While Morgenstern does not venture far beyond the classical texts he reads and his knowledge of other mystical traditions is not openly discussed in his writings, in this reading of him, Glazer pulls him beyond the confines of the study hall and situates him in the changing world of contemporary Israel. While Morgenstern would hardly recognize himself as a "post-Zionist," Glazer illustrates how the mystical quest takes us beyond the confines of the Zionist project, to a place beyond ethnicity, nationalism, and the opaque borders of collective identity. Glazer sees Morgenstern as an example of how contemporary *haredi* spirituality is contributing, however unwittingly, to a new sense of communal self-fashioning that can potentially move us beyond the binaries of "us" verses "them" (religious/secular, Jew/Arab, Zionist/Diasporist) and into a "politics" of non-dualism that may turn us away from the cliff we seem unable to avoid. On this path, Morgenstern, or perhaps Glazer's Morgenstern, meets some unexpected travelers along the way, individuals who live in his own back yard, strangers he knew nothing about but, when they meet in these pages, between these pages, he (and they) realize they know each other intimately.

The real contribution of this book lies in this unpredicted, and unpredictable, meeting. After situating Morgenstern as a part, albeit somewhat marginal, in the spiritual revolution of new kabbalism in Israel - a renaissance Morgenstern largely views through the narrow lens of his own *hevraya* (spiritual community)—Glazer introduces his readers to figures many have never heard of, even those who reside in Israel. Contemporary Israeli poets such as Admiel Kosman, Avraham ben Yitzhak, Benjamin Shevili, Tamar Elad-Appelbaum, Haya Esther, among others. Some are religious, some are secular, some are both, some are neither. But they are all Hebrew poets, they all breath the Hebrew language, they all draw from the fictive, mythic, imaginary tradition that Morgenstern and his disciples live in as if it were as tangible as a fresh persimmon from the *shuk* on Friday afternoon. In these pages, through sometimes labyrinthine and often illuminating readings of their poetry, these heretics, blasphemers, subversives, and denigrators of all that is holy meet a middle-aged Hasidic mystic in the very place where they all make their home, on the Cliff of the Many that overlooks the vastness of the One, or the nothing, or Nothing, that stretches past the horizon. In the Holy Land that cries the tears of exile. Glazer himself is a kind of participant-observer, a lonely traveler between these two worlds; a *shadkhan* (matchmaker), a *meturgemon* (translator), a *mezayer milin* (painter of words).

This book may leave some scholars scratching their heads and it may leave spiritual seekers barely treading water in the long scholarly footnotes and academic jargon. Perhaps some scholars need to consider that there is also important work to be done beyond delineating context and tracing influence, and seekers need to realize that none of this comes easy. This is a challenging book not only because its content—the mystical, the poetic and what lies between—is elusive, but also because the meetings on these pages, the juxtapositions between a *haredi* mystic and atheistic ones who can't help writing about a God they don't believe in, are not obvious. But isn't that the point of poetry and mysticism? They are not obvious, they both stretch language far beyond language's own comfort zone. Most of us never do get past the "many" to whatever, if anything, lies beyond. But we are inspired by those who try nonetheless. Perhaps it is in that very act of trying that we as humans continue to grow.

Shaul Magid
Bloomington, Indiana

ACKNOWLEDGEMENTS

I am grateful to the editor of this series in *Post-Rabbinic Thought*, Shaul Magid, for encouraging the publication of this study with Academic Studies Press. Through the years, Magid has been thoughtful, critical, and encouraging of this project in the diverse settings of academic conferences, reviews and in the endless dialogue of *devekut* from Fire Island to Harrison. His patience, provocation and companionship through the thinking and experimentation of these studies remain an invaluable inspiration.

I am also grateful to Elliot R. Wolfson, whose support and insight, both critical and poetic, has indelibly marked every page.

Over the past decade, I have been fortunate to receive the generosity of time and spirit of some of the very Hebrew poets changing the scene in Israel. My first foray into this poetic landscape was possible thanks to the generosity of the *Charles and Andrea Bronfman Research Fellowship* during my doctoral work at University of Toronto. The Hebrew poets, Yonadav Kaploun, Admiel Kosman, Tamar Elad-Appelbaum, and Schulamith Chava HaLevy, each have been generous with time and reflection on their poetry and the process in general. I am indebted to my doctoral advisor, Harry Fox (University of Toronto) who introduced me to many of these poets, as well as to Melila Hellner-Eshed (Hebrew University, Jerusalem) who has been open to the dialogue between Jewish mysticism and Hebrew poetry, singlehandedly sharing with me some of the most important and provocative voices on the contemporary Israeli scene.

I also extend gratitude to the following organizations for invitations and opportunities to develop earlier versions of the following chapters:

Chapter 1: Professor Yoni Garb remains boundless in his generosity of spirit and through his pioneering scholarship that so eloquently framed the teachings of R. Yitzhaq Maier Morgenstern. Garb's ongoing critique of my readings as well as his ability to refocus on the nuances of R. Yitzhaq Maier Morgenstern's thinking and praxis remains invaluable. An earlier version of this chapter was first presented as a paper, entitled, "~~Touching~~ God: Degrees of *Devekut* in Contemporary Israeli Kabbalah," (Washington: AJS, Dec. 23, 2008), with thanks to chair, Don Seeman (Emory University), and clarifying questions posed by Menahem Kallus (Haifa University) and Matt Goldish (Ohio State University). That paper evolved into the essay, entitled, "~~Touching~~ *God:* Vertigo, Exactitude, and Degrees of *Devekut* in the Contemporary Nondual Jewish Mysticism of R. Yitzhaq Maier Morgenstern," *Journal of Jewish Thought and Philosophy*, 19.2 (2012) and benefited from the anonymous readers provided by the journal. Thanks to managing editor, Dana Hollander (McMaster University) and editor-in-chief, Elliot R. Wolfson (NYU).

Chapter 2: An earlier version of this chapter was presented as a paper, entitled, "From ELoheinu to SpirEL Dynamics: An Evolution of God-consciousness in Contemporary Jewish Mysticism," (Los Angeles: AJS, Dec. 20, 2009). Special thanks to chair Elliot Ginsburgh (University of Michigan), who read this paper in my absence, when I was showed in.

Chapter 4: An earlier version of this chapter was presented as a paper, entitled "Degrees of *Devekut* in Contemporary Kabbalah and Poetics: Mystical Rapture as Judeo-Sufi Contrition in the Hebrew poetry of Binyamin Shevili," (Boston: AJS, Dec. 21, 2010); special thanks to chair, David Siff (Rutgers University) as well as panelist Nathan Hofer (Emory University), whose paper, "How 'Sufi' Were the Jewish Sufis?" on Sufism helped to clarify some aspects of my presentation.

Chapter 5: An earlier version of this paper entitled, "Poetics of *Anusim* & Impregnation in the poetry of Schulamith Chava Halevy," was first presented at the *Association for Canadian Jewish Studies* (London: University of Western Ontario, May 29, 2005). Harry Fox (University of Toronto) first introduced me to this poetry, and to the poet herself. I am grateful to Schulamith Chava Halevy for her generosity of spirit in supporting my inquiries into her work and writing process. Most of this afterword on Halevy grows out of shared reading, reflection, and conversation with Elyssa N. Wortzman, who also acted as research assistant. This entire study on secrecy was inspired by numerous seminars on Jewish mysticism taught masterfully by Elliot R. Wolfson (New York University). Wolfson's great generosity of spirit and critical thinking continues to inspire much of my research.

Chapter 7: An earlier version of this chapter was published as an essay, entitled, "Auto-erotic Cosmogenies: The Poetry of Haya Esther after Walt Whitman," and appeared in *Hebrew Studies* 46 (2005): 279-299. I am grateful to Melila Hellner-Eshed for her generosity of spirit and intellect that introduced me to the poetry of Haya Esther while attending her Zohar seminar in Jerusalem. Harold Bloom continued to engage me in the conversations surrounding Whitman and the boundaries of canon. Further gratitude is extended to the anonymous readers from *Hebrew Studies* as well as the insightful critique of Ziony Zevit. A preliminary version of this study was first presented at *Limmud Canada*, York University (Nov. 21, 2004).

Chapter 8: An earlier version of this chapter appeared as an essay, entitled, "*Durée, devekuth*, & re-embracing the Godlover: *involution of unio mystica* via collocative homosexu*EL*ity," in *Vixens Disturbing Vineyards* (Boston: Academic Studies Press, 2010), 505-553. This essay was part of *Festschrift* in honor of teacher and friend, Harry Fox, with special thanks to co-editors, Myriam Segal and Justin Yaron Lewis, especially Tzemah Yoreh who assisted with the Hebrew poetry.

Chapter 10: An earlier version of my translation of "Scent of Darkness" appeared in *Poetry International*, with special thanks to Yonadav and Uriel Kaploun for their input on the translation.

PERMISSIONS

Grateful acknowledgement to the following publishers for permission to both translate and reproduce the original Hebrew poetry as follows:

The Bialik Institute and Hakibbutz Hameuchad Publishing House for Agi Mishol's "Woman Martyr" and "Transistor Muezzin" which appeared in *Selections and New Poems* [Hebrew] (Jerusalem:, Jerusalem, 2003), pp. 47, 284. With special thanks to Devorah Levinger and Lisa Katz.

Carmel Publications for Ḥaya Esther's *My flesh speaks G!d*, [Hebrew], (Jerusalem: Carmel, 2001), pp. 7, 8, 11, 145, 147, 160-161, 174-175, 183, 184, 186, 188.

Carmel Publications for Binyamin Shevili's "Contrition" in *Shebo Journal*.

Schocken Publishing House for Binyamin Shevili's *A new Dictionary of Affliction* (2004), pp. 52, 62; *Poems of the Grand Tourist* (1999), pp. 47, 61, 68, 69, with special thanks to Liat Karat.

Schulamith Hava HaLevy for selected unpublished poems.

'Eked Publications for Schulamith Hava HaLevy's "Strange Fire" and "Impregnation" from *Inner Castle: Poems about Being and Being Coerced* (1998).

Carmel Publications for Schulamith Hava HaLevy's "Secret of Impregnation," *Breath Sign* [Hebrew] (2003).

Keter Publications and The Bialik Institute for Yonadav Kaploun's cycle "Scent of Darkness" in *You Are Still Writing* (2004), with special thanks to the poet and Avigayil.

Sifriat Poalim—Hakibutz Hameuchad Publishers for Zelda Schneerson Mishkovsky's "On that night" [Hebrew], *The Poetry of Zelda* (1985), pp. 13-15, with thanks to Avram Kantor as well as to Varda Koch Ocker for her translation.

Sifriat Poalim—Hakibutz Hameuchad Publishers for Admiel Kosman's "Our God," with special thanks to the poet and Avram Kantor.

Gavanim Publishing for Shai Tubali's "Come Here," "I Came to God," and "Infinity Catchers" in *Infinity Catchers* (2009), pp. 2-3, 11, 37.

Mashiv haRuah Journal for Tamar Elad-Appelbaum's "Psalms for Jerusalem" in no. 24, Fall 2007, pp. 9, 11, 15, with special thanks to the poet.

Finally, I am grateful to the generousity of my teacher, Reb Moshe Aaron Krassen, whom I thank for opening this doorway of thinking and praxis through ongoing study in contemporary Jewish Mysticism through the lens of Jean Gebser.

SYSTEM OF TRANSCRIPTION

Special attention should be applied to distinguishing the *he'* (*h*) and the *'heth* (*ch*), and representing the *dagesh* by double consonants (*tiqqun* and not *tikun*).

HEBREW	LATIN TRANSCRIPTION
א	inverted comma facing left
ב	b
ב	b̲
ג	g
ד	d
ה	h
ו	v
ז	z
ח	ch (or h̲)
ט	t
י	y
כ	k
כ	k̲
ל	l
מ	m
נ	n
ס	s
ע	inverted comma facing right
פ	p
פ	f
צ	z
ק	q
ר	r
ש	sh
ת	t

בָ ,בַ ,בּ	a
בֶ ,בֵ ,בֱ	e
בִ	i
בֻ	u
בֹ ,בׂ	o
בְ	ə

I would believe only in a God who could dance.
    —Friedrich Nietzsche, *Thus Spoke Zarathustra*

...dance is governed by the perpetual renewal of the relation between vertigo and exactitude.
    —Alain Badiou, *Dance as a Metaphor for Thought*

CHAPTER I

~~TOUCHING~~ GOD
VERTIGO, EXACTITUDE, AND DEGREES OF *DEVEKUT*

1.0 MYSTICAL APPERCEPTION AND SUBJECTIVITY: ON THE POSSIBLE IMPOSSIBILITY

Is touching God possible? Namely, if touching the *untouchable* is possible, what kind of vertigo ensues? Through the ages, Judaism does more than merely suggest its possibility—it exults in the glory of this divine-human encounter.[1] As the human is in pursuit of the limitless light of the Infinite One, the mind races and restrains itself while the body trembles as it is washed over by an "oceanic feeling" quivering beneath the membrane of consciousness.[2] The mystic remains entranced in this preconceptual dance of *unio mystica* or what the Jewish mystics called *devekut*[3]—that state of reaching but *not reaching*, hovering but *not hovering*, touching but *not touching*. This "oceanic feeling" can shift between ebb and flow, between overflow and retraction, between hyperattention or disattention, between kataphasis and apophasis.[4]

[1.] For example, see most recently Benjamin D. Sommer, *The Bodies of God and the World of Ancient Israel* (Cambridge: Cambridge University Press, 2011); Elliot R. Wolfson, *Through a Speculum That Shines* (Princeton: Princeton University Press, 1997); Howard Eilberg-Schwartz, *God's Phallus: And Other Problems for Men and Monotheism* (New York: Beacon Press, 1995); Peter Schäfer, *The Hidden and Manifest God: Some Major Themes in Early Jewish Mysticism*, trans. A. Pomerance (Albany: SUNY Press, 1992).

[2.] The sensation of *unio mystica* as an "oceanic feeling" that opened a pioneering conversation between mysticism and psychoanalysis is found in Freud's correspondence with Romain Rolland, see most recently, William B. Parsons, *The Enigma of the Oceanic Feeling: Revisioning The Psychoanalytic Theory of Mysticism* (New York: Oxford University Press, 1999), 109-139.

[3.] On becoming entranced and entering into trance states within *unio mystica*, see most recently the work of Jonathan Garb, *Shamanic Trance in Modern Kabbalah* (Chicago: University of Chicago, 2011), 26, 37, 54, 62, 80, 105.

[4.] T. M. Luhrman, *When God Talks Back: Understanding the American Evangelical Relationship with God* (New York: Knopf, 2012), 187, 348n54. Luhrman makes note of an emerging trend in anthropological study of Jewish mysticism that is more attuned to the

Such a crossing-over of psychic realms leads to states of consciousness filled with conundrums, cataclysms, and conjunctions. The challenge remains—how can language render cogent the ineffable and articulate this form of touching which *is not touching* that remains so pervasive in Jewish mysticism? Does it suffice to contain the cognition and perception into apperception of this experience in a term like *devekut*? If there are degrees of *devekut* that have been overlooked,[5] then *vertigo* and *exactitude* will serve to redress and guide a rediscovery of a neglected but nuanced experience so central to contemporary nondual Jewish mysticism and one of its prime exemplars, Rabbi Yitzhaq Maier Morgenstern.

In stretching to the limit to touch something desirable, one remains forever at a loss, inevitably on the "gilded side of loss."[6] The object of desire remains beyond reach. Otherwise how could it remain an endless source of desire?[7] Such a dynamic moment in motion is captured by

psychological aspect of the experience, especially pronounced in the research of Yoni Garb, Yoram Bilu and Michel Kravel-Tovi, ibid., 379.

5. Scholem is careful in his study on *devekut* to limit the implications of this unitive experience to an androcentric perspective concerned solely with the role of the human in community:

"I have said that communion, for all its depth and importance, is not union... But the self within the divine mind... pieces through this state on to the rediscovery of man's spiritual identity. He finds himself because he has found God. This, then, is the deepest meaning of *devekut* of which Hasidism knows, and the radical terms should not blind us to the eminently Jewish and personalistic conception of man which they still cover. After having gone through *devekut* and union, man is still man—nay, he has, in truth, only then started to be man, and it is only logical that only then will he be called upon to fulfill his destiny in the society of man."

See Gershom Scholem, "*Devekut*, or Communion with God," in *The Messianic Idea in Judaism* (New York: Schocken Press, 1971), 222, 227. For an important corrective to Scholem, see Moshe Idel, "Universalization and Integration: Two Conceptions of Mystical Union in Jewish Mysticism," *Mystical Union in Judaism, Christianity and Islam: An Ecumenical Dialogue*, ed. M. Idel & B. McGinn (New York: Continuum Press, 1989), 33-50, esp. 42-43; and Moshe Idel, "Mystical Techniques," in *Essential Papers on Kabbalah*, ed. L. Fine (New York: NYU Press, 1995), esp. 454-462. For a nuanced hermeneutic reading of *devekut*, see Elliot R. Wolfson, *Language, Eros, Being: Kabbalistic Hermeneutics and Poetic Imagination* (New York: Fordham University Press, 2005), 32, 35, 39, 122, 209, 237, 267, 288, 354, 377. Consider also "Introduction: Kabbalah and Modernity," in *Kabbalah and Modernity*, ed. Boaz Huss, Marco Pusi, and Kocku von Stuckrad (Leiden: Brill, 2010), 1-12.

6. Alain Badiou, "Dance as a Metaphor for Thought," in *Handbook of Inaesthetics*, trans. A. Toscano (Stanford: Stanford University Press, 2005), 70.

7. R. Tzaddok haCohen of Lublin, *Peri Tzaddik, Parshat Ha'azinu* (Jerusalem: Mechon Mesamkhai Lev, 1999), 346n10.

"cleaving"—meaning, to adhere as well as to split. This veritable dance of reaching but *not reaching*, touching but *not touching* is intended to deepen the desire for human and divine consciousness to merge. Therefore, as will be shown shortly, to *touch* or to *be so touched*—that is the question surrounding a mystical experience called *devekut*.

Whether one utilizes extroversive/introversive models or some further hybrid, this process of a soul touching the fullness of its origins, and so being transformed, is itself undergoing transformation in the twenty-first-century cultural matrices of the world in general, and of Israel in particular. I argue from context to effect, namely, that to navigate the effect of post-Zionism on contemporary mysticism evolving in Israel, it is useful to proceed from a general to a particular philosophical context. Once the contours of self after postmodernity are outlined in general terms, only then will the hybrid forms of mystical subjectivity emerging in the particular cultural context of Israel and its iterations of contemporary Jewish mysticism be seen in their entire splendor. It is through this path of context-effect that one remarkable exemplar of contemporary nondual Jewish mysticism, R. Yitzhaq Maier Morgenstern, will be explored, with his specific focus on *devekut* in mind.

1.1 Subjectivity and Self after Postmodernity and Post-Zionism

A vexing problem at the cusp of exploring any facet of subjectivity is the very nature of the subject after the death of God and the demise of the human subject. The problem is even more complex when dealing with mystical apperception. This ruptured context of postmodernity is described most succinctly by American phenomenologist Calvin O. Schrag as a "crisis of concepts relative to matters pertaining to the human self understood as subject and agent in discourse and action."[8] This means that perception itself is altered, going so far as expanding the parameters of what is perceived. If perception itself amidst this ruptured context now "testifies a transcendence-within-immanence,"[9] then should not language itself suffice to convey mystical apperception? Experience and what is perceived from it is more complex. While language may attempt to subtly convey one's own

---

[8.] Calvin O. Schrag, *The Self after Postmodernity* (New Haven: Yale University Press, 1997), 2-3.

[9.] Ibid.

subjective experience, there are also experiences beyond the self. These are encounters with exteriority, experiences that take one beyond and before one's own language—to encounter the *other*.

What is beyond and before my own subjectivity challenges the very contours of my own sense of self. Being aware of the *other* beyond my own self, but implied in relation to my own existence, means that there is "also a radical sense of transcendence that is coupled with an alterity."[10] Traces of this encounter are present in much of daily life, or what Schrag calls "intramundane forms of transcendence."[11] It is in this coupling of the everyday and the beyond that there is "possibly a pivotal role in the drama of self-constitution, in the attestation of the self as constituted in and through its relation to the radically transcendent."[12] The looming question facing the evolution of nondual Jewish mysticism—whether grounded in the East or West—is whether the grammar of the Western philosophical tradition, which continues to contextualize the metaphysical within the mystical, is still necessary or sufficient.

1.2 Dual versus Nondual Mystical Apperception

A further challenge in exploring mystical apperception is the textured context of its discourse. For most modernists, the unity of experience, its cognition, and its perception are taken for granted, whereas for postmodernists, such unity is problematic. Such disunity affects contemporary mystical apperception, insofar as a new perspective on transcendence[13] then becomes necessary if nondualism is to be more than an illusion, or what philosophers often refer to as an "ontological fairy tale."[14] To get beyond the illusion

---

10. Ibid., 113.
11. Ibid.
12. Ibid., 114.
13. Ibid., 127.
14. See the useful summation of scholarly disagreement by L. Stafford Betty, "Towards a Reconciliation of Mysticism and Dualism," *Religious Studies* 14 (1978): 291-303. On the claim that nondual mysticism is nothing more than an "ontological fairy tale," see the Israeli scholar, Ben-Ami Scharfstein, who claims that "there is no compelling non-personal reason for believing that a superlative first cause can be grasped, weakly or strongly, by direct experience." Ben-Ami Scharfstein, "How to Justify Reductive Explanation of Myths: Mystical Experience, Exemplified by Krishna Worship, in the Light of Psychoanalysis,

that any cognitive reflection on Being can lead towards the apperception of its capacity to unify all existents within it, such a "reinterpretation and redescription of the conditions for unification" demands a real "pruning [of] the criteria of modernity's demands for universality, necessity and identity."[15]

Such fleeting unity in this ruptured context is recovered through Schrag's introduction of *transversality* as metaphor. This metaphor will prove critical later on in our exploration of the hybridity emerging in contemporary mystical apperception. What motivates this philosophic shift to transversality is the ability of such a metaphor to encapsulate "convergence without coincidence, conjuncture without concordance, overlapping without assimilation, and union without absorption."[16] In redescribing consciousness as achieving a unification of its transversal function, what is then gained is an extension "across past moments of consciousness without solidifying into an identification with any particular moment."[17] This is crucial in situating contemporary mystical apperception after postmodernity, in that "the grammar of transversality replaces that of universality,"[18] and so the metaphysical quagmires no longer obstruct the journey to nondualism.

In what follows, I argue that Schrag's invaluable phenomenological insight can be readily applied to thinking about mystical apperception after postmodernity and after post-Zionism. Transversal unification is so crucial precisely because it "illustrates a dynamic and open-textured process of unifying."[19] This dynamic process of unifying "allows for plurality and difference and neither seeks the metaphysical comforts of stable beginnings and universal telic principles nor displays an epistemological enchantment with zero-point epistemic foundations."[20] What becomes apparent, then,

---

Symbolic Anthropology and the Naive Desire to Know the Truth," in *Myths and Fictions*, ed. S. Biderman & B. A. Scharfstein (Leiden: Brill, 1993), 113-140, esp. 113; Ben-Ami Scharfstein, *Ineffability: The Failure of Words in Philosophy and Religion* (Albany: SUNY Press, 1993), esp. 83, 87, where experience is circumscribed by the content of language after Heidegger and Gadamer.

15. Schrag, *The Self after Postmodernity*, 127.
16. Ibid., 128.
17. Ibid., 127-128.
18. Ibid., 128.
19. Ibid., 129-130.
20. Ibid.

is the degree to which *devekut* is a process of unification moving "beyond the constraints of the metaphysical oppositions of universality versus particularity and identity versus difference."[21] Such a dynamic and open-textured process of unifying also helps to address differentiated culture spheres—East, West, and beyond—that are encountered in the unique case of contemporary mysticism in Israel.[22]

A common line in the sand of mystical discourse tends to be drawn over reified boundaries of Eastern versus Western thinking and devotional practice, notwithstanding the reality that neither are unitary wholes but multiplicities.[23] While the latter is portrayed as highly dualistic, whereby existence and nature are separate entities, the former is portrayed as nondual and radically monistic. How should one approach the discourse about thinking and the devotional practice of contemporary mystical apperception originating in Israel? Does it follow the conventions of the East or the West? Is thinking about such mystical apperception *a priori* dual, nondual, or some hybrid? Once such an analysis of the universal shifting into the transversal allows for unification of culture spheres, is there any set of practices that is universally obliging?[24]

When confronting the question of contemporary mystical experience, the fluid nature of culture spheres—or what shall be referred to later as "cultural glimmerings"—cannot be ignored. The more this notion of transversal self-understanding takes place in historical religions, from the East to the West, the more such culture spheres "are called upon to use the resources of transcendence against themselves."[25] Such a subversive affirmation will become evident in the mystical model to follow from the Diaspora.

As a way to cross this East-West divide, aspects of transversal

---

21. Ibid., 133.
22. Jonathan Garb, *The Chosen Will Become Herds: Studies in Twentieth Century Kabbalah*, trans. Y. Berkovits-Murciano (New Haven: Yale University Press, 2009), 7, 73, 80, 98–99, 112, 120. Compare with Boaz Huss, "The Mystification of the Kabbalah and the Modern Construction of Jewish Mysticism," trans. Elana Lutsky, *BGU Review* 2 (2008), http://web.bgu.ac.il/Eng/Centers/review/summer2008/Mysticism.htm.
23. Schrag, *The Self after Postmodernity*, 146-147. Compare with Otto Pöggeler, "West-East Dialogue: Heidegger and Lao-Tzu," *Heidegger and Asian Thought*, ed. G. Parkes (Honolulu: University of Hawaii Press, 1987), 47-78, esp. 75-76.
24. Schrag, *The Self after Postmodernity*, 134.
25. Ibid., 148.

self-understanding have been attempted by scholars of religion[26] and philosophers,[27] yet its nuance in regard to mystical apperception has only recently been fully realized in the masterful study of Elliot R. Wolfson on Habad Hasidism, *Open Secret*.[28] It is through his comprehensive readings of seven generations of Habad Hasidic leaders or *rebbe'im* in constructive dialogue with Mahayana Buddhism[29] that Wolfson reveals the depth of a nondual meontological mysticism operative within Jewish mysticism of the Diaspora. By *meontological*, Wolfson designates a realm beyond Being previously articulated in Habad Hasidism, namely, a meaning that is prior to the ontology of nature. It is this nondual mystical apperception of nature and the world as concealed divinity that reveals the end of concealment whereby all distinctions subside, namely that "there is no more need to distinguish between visible and invisible, external and internal, holy and profane."[30] It is this erasure of distinctions that marks nondual thinking and experience in Habad Hasidism. Such erasure takes place in a conjunctive state of *devekut* that necessarily "culminates in the abrogation of one's being (*bittul meṣi'ut*) and the expiration of the soul (*kelot ha-nefesh*)."[31]

It is precisely in using the resources of transcendence against themselves

---

26. In his eight rubrics for *An Agenda for Hindu-Jewish Dialogue*, first on Katz's list is pursuit of the absolute through comparative praxis leading to mystical apperception; see Nathan Katz, "The Hindu-Jewish Encounter and the Future," *The Fifty-Eighth Century: A Jewish Renewal Sourcebook*, ed. S. Weiner (Northvale, NJ: Jason Aronson Press, 1996), 331–346, esp. 337–338; Nathan Katz, "Buddhist-Jewish Relations throughout the Ages and in the Future," *Journal of Indo-Judaic Studies* 10 (2009): 7-23; Nathan Katz, "How the Hindu-Jewish Encounter Reconfigures Interreligious Dialogue," *Shofar* 16, 1 (1997): 28-42; see Hananya Goodman, ed., *Between Jerusalem and Benares: Comparative Studies in Judaism and Hinduism* (Albany: SUNY Press, 1994). Consider also Rachel Elior, "HaBaD: The Contemplative Ascent to God," in *Jewish Spirituality* II (New York: Crossroad, 1987), 157–205.

27. Scholars of the philosopher Martin Heidegger still claim that his later period of thinking was deeply immersed in overcoming this divide. Heideggerian thinking is beyond Aristotelian categories of predication, beyond causality, and beyond representational or abstractly conceptual approaches; see Joan Stambaugh, "Heidegger, Taoism, and the Question of Metaphysics," in *Heidegger and Asian Thought*, 79-91.

28. Elliot R. Wolfson, *Open Secret: Postmessianic Messianism and the Mystical Revision of Menahem Mendel Schneerson* (New York: Columbia University Press, 2009), 137-138.

29. Ibid., 109-114, 345n237, notwithstanding the sometimes essentialist and oversimplified claims regarding this East-West devotional dialogue, for example, the "respite of the soul" as life-affirming in Judaism whereas in Buddhism it entails the cessation of life.

30. Ibid., 40.

31. Ibid.

that the "the conjunction of the heart (*devekut di-reu'ta de-libba*)"[32] becomes a possible experience. It is this radical nondual meontological mysticism that inspires Wolfson to ascribe to Habad Hasidism a meontological affinity with Mahayana Buddhism.[33] The import of the nondual meontological perspective is just how radical the erasure appears, in that the "essence of the world is the essence of the *Ein Sof*, but the latter has no essence, and hence the former is without essence."[34]

Whether seeing the Limitless as *Ein Sof* or *Tathagata,* in terms of mystical apperception, this nondual meontological language of devotion exists beyond the limitations of any duality. It becomes clear through Wolfson's study that the nondual meontological devotional language in question is searching for the "consummate nil" (*efes gamur*) in order to effectuate "complete unity" (*ha-yihud ha-gamur*).[35] Such nondual meontology exposes the illusion of any duality between subject and object.[36] It is this very similar gesture of transcendence against itself that allows for "the conjunction of the heart" (*devekut di-reu'ta de-libba*) to occur upon re-entry into the physical world. For it is paradoxically at this re-entry point that "one is most fully conjoined to the divinity that transcends the world."[37] This transversal self-understanding as proffered by Wolfson is a lucid way to cross that East-West divide in thinking through and experience of nondual mystical apperception.

1.3 Nondual Mystical Apperception in Israel

The ensuing challenge posed by nondual mysticism is pronounced once it is contextualized within the particularities of a nation-state, especially one consumed with its mystical-apocalyptic responses to regular terrorist

---

32. Ibid., 47-48.
33. For more on the possibility of devotional affinity and an attempt to define its parameters as a spiritual affinity, see Aubrey L. Glazer, "Imaginal Journeying to Istanbul, *mon amour:* Devotional Sociabilities in Beshtian Hasidism and Turkish-Sufism," in *Pillar of Prayer*, trans. M. Kallus (Louisville: Fons Vitae, 2011), esp. 207–245.
34. Wolfson, *Open Secret,* 110.
35. Ibid., 112.
36. Ibid., 114.
37. Ibid., 146.

attacks.[38] This is most striking in terms of a nation-state's unique language, peoplehood, and land. The degree to which this is navigated through the Hebrew language and the constant evolution of its mystical appropriations has been duly reflected upon elsewhere.[39] Given the sublimated mystical underpinnings of Zionism, there remains a strong possibility of nondual mystical apperception within the post-Zionist condition of contemporary Israeli culture.[40]

Granted, there is a chasm separating the awareness of post-Zionism within secular culture from the same within *haredi* culture. But this chasm may be more semantic than real; as Aran points out, within *haredi* culture the "anti-Zionist attitude... has now undergone some change."[41] Notwithstanding the growing "emotional and ideological rapprochement to Israeli individuals and public,"[42] it is inescapable that within these cultures of Israel, the lived reality is more complex than the simple dualism of Zionist/anti-Zionist. Notwithstanding the strong *haredi* impulse to recover and demand cultural separation,[43] one encounters a subversive affirmation through hybridization as its redemptive vision.

To speak of the religion of Judaism as a culture sphere transcending itself sounds shocking *ab initio*, especially within such a hegemonic religious culture as Israel. Yet this impulse is not so new, in that the search for religion *after religion* was already being explored by renowned German émigrés to

---

38. Gideon Aran, "Contemporary Jewish Mysticism and Palestinian Suicide Bombing," in Huss et al., eds., *Kabbalah and Modernity*, 402-404.

39. Aubrey L. Glazer, *Contemporary Hebrew Mystical Poetry: How It Redeems Jewish Thinking* (New York: Edwin Mellen Press, 2009).

40. While the term "post-Zionism" has been frequently used by Israeli New Historians like Tom Segev and Benny Morris, the term was also used early on by revisionist sociologist Uri Ram, with hopes of the formation of a new universalist social agenda in Israel (in contradistinction to the rise of neo-Zionism); see Uri Ram, *Israeli Society: Critical Perspectives* [Hebrew] (Tel Aviv: *Breirot* Publications, 1993). Compare with Tom Segev, *The Seventh Million*, trans. H. Watzman (New York: Hill & Wang, 1993); Benny Morris, *Righteous Victims: A History of the Zionist-Arab Conflict 1881-2001* (New York: Vintage Books, 1999); Benny Morris, *The Birth of the Palestinian Refugee Problem Revisited* (Cambridge: Cambridge University Press, 2004).

41. Aran, "Mysticism and Suicide Bombing," 394.

42. Ibid.

43. Ibid., 405-409.

Israel—for example, Gershom Scholem, especially in his forays through the *Eranos* conferences promoting a perennial philosophy in dialogue with other historians of religion like Mircea Eliade and Henri Corbin;[44] and Martin Buber, in his forays through comparative mysticisms, especially in his conversations with the great Hindu philosopher and holy man, Rabindranath Tagore, about Zionism and its need to retain an affinity for Eastern mysticism rather than succumbing to its Western counterpart of Orientalism.[45]

What continues to emerge from these landmark forays by German Zionists into the radical transcendence of mystical meta-rationalism beyond religion is a shift towards an integral nondualism. While both of the aforementioned scholars were engaged in friendship and protracted debate,[46] their unique readings of Hasidism—whether Buber's legendary and dialogical approach or Scholem's pantheistic and theoretical approach[47]—represent extremes of the interpretive pendulum. But when it came to the degrees of *devekut*, however, there was a certain shared appreciation for expounding upon the experience, cognition, and perception that mysticisms provided, whether particular or general. [48]

Regardless of the degree of integration, there remains a renaissance in this yearning for nondualism not only in Europe but also in Israel. As the exemplar and gatekeeper of the academic study of Jewish mysticism in Israel, from 1941 to 1963, in public Scholem consistently remained skeptical about the possibility of contemporary Jewish mysticism as "real Kabbalah" while allowing for a more universal "Intuitive Kabbalah."[49] Yet

---

44. Steven M. Wasserstrom, *Religion after Religion: Gershom Scholem, Mircea Eliade, and Henri Corbin at Eranos* (Princeton: Princeton University Press, 1999), esp. 21–82.

45. Maurice Friedman, "Martin Buber and Asia," *Philosophy East and West* 26 (1976): 411–426. See also Ella Shohat, "The 'Postcolonial' in *Translation: Reading Said in Hebrew*," in *Paradoxical Citizenship: Essays on Edward Said*, ed. S. Nagy-Zekimi (London: Lexington Books, 2006), 25-48.

46. Moshe Idel, "Martin Buber and Gershom Scholem on Hasidism," *Old Worlds, New Mirrors: On Jewish Mysticism and Twentieth-Century Thought* (Philadelphia: University of Pennsylvania Press, 2010), 205-216.

47. Ibid., 208.

48. See ibid., 213-216 for a thoughtful reflection on *devekut,* read through the lens of Buber and Scholem. Idel argues how both divergent lenses on *devekut* are operative simultaneously, for "it is possible to unite with God because he [*sic*] penetrates all of existence, and this continuing efflux facilitates the mystical encounter," ibid., 215.

49. Boaz Huss, Marco Pusi, and Kocku von Stuckrad, "Introduction: Kabbalah and Modernity,"

this yearning recognizes that the one Existent is both the creator and the substance out of which the creation takes place—that it is all One and the consciousness of the One is implicit in all.[50] Unlike historians and philosophers of religion, like Scholem and Buber, it is precisely in their radical transcendence of mystical meta-rationalism that contemporary universal spiritual masters like Sri Aurobindo (1872–1950) and Mira Alfassa (1878–1973) or Abraham David Salman Hai Ezekiel (d. 1897) and Madame Blavatsky (1831–1891) traverse the East-West divide. Such figures exemplify a boundary crossing mostly ignored by the academic study of mysticism. This hybridity of mystical subjectivity, as Huss has recently shown,[51] is manifest in the crossing over of Kabbalah and theosophy—a cornerstone of mysticism in modernity. Such hybridity that tends towards the universal exemplifies a yearning to deepen an ephemeral discourse of mystical apperception without getting trapped in metaphysical thickets.

Truth be told, however, while this mystical moment of *devekut* has been taking place for centuries, mainly through the constructivist portals of God, Torah, Israel,[52] or other devotional technologies, the residue of

---

1-2. However, Scholem's conversations with Harold Bloom seem to contradict this supposition. Bloom suggested to me this notion of *Intuitive Kabbalah* as drawn from his conversations with Scholem over the years, and it is evident from Scholem's correlations of Whitman and Bucke that *Intuitive Kabbalah* stems from what Bucke referred to as the "intuitions" of cosmic consciousness; see A. Lozynsky, *Richard Maurice Bucke, Medical Mystic: Letters of Dr. Bucke to Walt Whitman and His Friends* (Detroit: Wayne State University Press, 1977), 170. See also R. M. Bucke, *Cosmic Consciousness: A Study in the Evolution of the Human Mind* (Secaucus, NJ: Citadel Press, 1989). Allusions to this more universal and not necessarily Jewish mysticism, *Intuitive Kabbalah*, did however make their way into print. It is worthwhile to compare Scholem's comments on Whitman's friend and executor, Richard Maurice Bucke and Edward Carpenter, as well as Arthur Rimbaud and William Blake as contemporary exemplars of *Intuitive Kabbalah*. See Scholem, "Religious Authority and Mysticism," in *On the Kabbalah and its Symbolism*, trans. R. Manheim (New York: Schocken Books, 1965), 16-17.

50. Sri Aurobindo, "Indeterminates, Cosmic Determinations and the Indeterminable" [1914-1920], *The Life Divine*, Book 2, Part I, Chapter 1 (Twin Lakes: Lotus Press, 1990), 311–338.

51. For a welcome corrective, see Boaz Huss, "The Sufi Society from America: Theosophy and Kabbalah in Poona in the Late Nineteenth Century," in Huss et al., eds., *Kabbalah and Modernity*, 167-193.

52. Such "constructivist portals of God, Torah, Israel" would follow the Constructivists (like Katz, Hick, and Gimello) who see mystical experiences as being constructed by beliefs, expectations, and intentions employed through the social, economic, and religious context of the mystic. For the classic constructivists analyses, see Steven T. Katz, "Language,

the radical transcendence of mystical meta-rationalism remains fragrant throughout contemporary cultural matrices also particular to Israel. This is leading to an evolution of a much more hybridized subjectivity[53] that retains its trans-*haredi* cultural roots. After the waves of Zionism that influenced much of the agenda in literary and devotional circles, there is a cultural shift amidst a post-Zionist context[54] that informs the mystical renaissance taking place now in Israel.[55]

There is much at stake in asserting that both the form and content of *devekut* itself is undergoing transformation through the contemporary cultural matrices of Israel. The Orientalism that was partially responsible for constructing the secular in Zionist discourse is the same dualistic thinking that, by extension, separated the secular from the sacred as distinct categories with the founding of the State of Israel.[56] Amidst

---

Epistemology, and Mysticism," *Mysticism and Philosophical Analysis* (New York: Oxford University Press, 1978), 22-74; Steven T. Katz, "The 'Conservative' Character of Mystical Experience," *Mysticism and Religious Traditions* (New York: Oxford University Press, 1983), 3-60.

53. Such "a hybridized subjectivity" builds on the cross-culturalists (like Stace, Zaehner, and Smart, as well as neo-cross-culturalists like Wainright and Stoeber) who define a limited variety of mystical experiences crossing over cultural and religious lines. See, for example, Michael Stoeber, "Constructivist Epistemologies of Mysticism: A Critique and a Revision," *Religious Studies* 28 (1992): 107–116; Michael Stoeber, "Introvertive Mystical Experiences: Monistic, Theistic, and the Theo-monistic," *Religious Studies* 29 (1993): 169-184.

54. See Amnon Raz-Krakotzkin, "Orientalism, Jewish Studies, and Israeli Society: Some Notes," *Jama'a* 3 (1999): 34–61; Amnon Raz-Krakotzkin, "A National Colonial Theology—Religion, Orientalism and the Construction of the Secular in Zionist Discourse," *Tel Aviver Jahrbuch für Deutsche Geschichte* 30 (2002): 312-326.

55. Garb, *The Chosen Will Become Herds*, 101-102.

56. Recall a visionary monist, like the first chief rabbi of Mandate Palestine, Rav Avraham Yitzhak Kook (1865–1935), whose eclectic *œuvre* easily defies cultural classification. Kook was already challenging his contemporaries both in literary and devotional circles and their tendency to think of sacred/secular as simply the fixed terms of dualism. In *Orot ha-Kodesh*, written while crossing cultural matrices (ca. 1904, Jaffa–1911, Switzerland, England, Jerusalem) while in the throes of his utopian monism, Kook already recognized that resolving the apparent conflict between the worlds of the sacred and the profane is a function of subjectivity; see R. Avraham Yitzhak Kook, *Orot ha-Kodesh*, vol. 2 (Jerusalem: Mossad haRav Kook, 1938), 311n17. Moreover, Kook proffers a resolution of this dualism that pits the sacred against the profane cultures of Mandate Palestine in the following mapping: (1) One must either move horizontally between domains in a graduated fashion (from a state of the elevated sacred to the more mundane sacred, eventually to the elevated mundane, etc.); or (2) one must elevate the profane vertically to be absorbed fully into the sacred. See Kook, *Orot ha-Kodesh*, 311n18. Regardless of which strategy is practiced,

the current fragmentation in the aftermath of such dualism, however, Hebrew cultures in general, and *haredi* cultures in particular, still retain an "organic integration" as systems that flourish through "harmonious interrelatedness."[57] How harmonious such cultural webs are in the contemporary context remains an open question, but the degree to which these webs are challenging and dissolving dualistic thinking bespeaks a growing renaissance in Israel of mystical knowledge and experience.

How the varieties of mystical apperception called *devekut* affect what is meant by subjectivity, culture, and the literatures of such experiences, as well as modernity's demand for "universality, necessity and identity,"[58] will inform our current exploration. The focus will be limited to one

---

Kook sees this regimen of unifications or *yihudim* as taking precedence over all traditional values; see Garb, *The Chosen Will Become Herds*, 77. This is crucial insofar as the nondual mystical apperception being proffered privileges subjectivity. Secondly, there is a cultural matrix at work in religious cultures. A more nuanced view of spiritual evolution inspires Kook's 1910 articulation in "Fragments of Light" of a fourfold cultural matrix that moves towards embracing a nondualism in "the totality of the cultural realm," as (1) *the divine*; (2) *the moral*; (3) *the religious*; and (4) *the national*. The freedom of (1) the divine aspect of culture transcends all knowledge and experience, whereas the yearning within humanity for (2) the moral aspect of culture allows for the emergence of an autonomous vision. The social boundaries which limit the perfection of (4) the national aspect of culture have an adaptive capacity and necessarily appropriate elements from the preceding three cultural realms, edging towards a nondualism. See R. Avraham Yitzhak Kook, "Fragments of Light," *Abraham Isaac Kook: The Lights of Penitence, The Moral Principles, Lights of Holiness, Essays, Letters, and Poems*, trans. Ben Zion Bokser (New York: Paulist Press, 1978), 309. Ultimately, however, as Jonathan Garb astutely notes, the paradox in Kook's thinking remains that "the individual dimension (the inner harmony of the *Tzaddiq*) is inextricably bound up with the national dimension (the rectification of the entire nation by the *Tzaddiq*)"; see Garb, *The Chosen Will Become Herds*, 78. This seeming tension between individual and collective dimensions is more of an oscillation that allows for a high degree of anomianism or personal devotion to mark the journey to mystical apperception. Compare with Jonathan Meir, "Lights and Vessels: A New Inquiry into the 'Circle' of Rav Kook and the Editors of His Works" [Hebrew], *Kabbalah: A Journal for the Study of Jewish Mystical Texts* 13 (2005): 163-248. Regarding the important pre-Israel passage of Rav Kook's subjectivity within his autobiographical theology, see also Yehudah Mirsky, *An Intellectual and Spiritual Biography of Rabbi Avraham Yitzhaq Ha-Cohen Kook from 1865 to 1904* (Ph.D. diss., Harvard University, 2008).

57. Kook, *Fragments of Light*, 309. See Amnon Raz-Krakotzkin, "The Golem of Scholem: Messianism and Zionism in the Writings of Rabbi Avraham Isaac HaKohen Kook and Gershom Scholem," in *Politik und Religion im Judentum*, ed. Christoph Miething (Tübingen: Niemeyer, 1999), 223-238.

58. Schrag, *The Self after Postmodernity*, 127.

exceptional, contemporary exemplar of nondual Jewish mysticism in Israel. In such a decentralized theocracy, whose fragmentation breeds a neo-tribalism committed to restoring collective identity through separation within the cultural landscape,[59] I argue that this emerging articulation of nondual mystical apperception is present in literatures both devotional and poetic.[60] As these devotional and poetic literatures shimmer forth from two seemingly disparate Hebrew cultures in Israel, the dualism reified into categories of sacred/secular and theoretical/devotional begins to dissolve through *devekut* and reconstitute hybrid identities. For this hybridity to be possible, it requires a more thorough transversal self-understanding.

While North America has seen its share of *bricolage*[61] identities within its population of mystical seekers, after Scholem and Buber there is a hybridization of mystical subjectivity developing specifically in Israel that deserves further investigation. A key component of this hybridization of identity[62] is the Hebrew language—a shared doorway further promoting a

---

[59.] Aran's research into *Zaka* volunteers (*Zihuy Korbanot Ason*, literally: "Disaster Victim Identification") and how they are guided at terrorist bombing sites by a popular Lurianic kabbalism sheds much light on a tendency within *haredi* culture to prioritize separation as a central value. As Aran states, "*Zaka* volunteers are intolerant of hybrids, meticulously preserving binary distinctions and various classifications." See Aran, "Mysticism and Suicide Bombing," 407-408. Aran then goes on to cite a plethora of rabbinic prooftexts to buttress this tendency within *haredi* culture to prioritize separation as a central value. Notwithstanding the accuracy of Aran's field research and general claims, by contrast, it is precisely on this point that the innovative devotional teachings of R. Morgenstern challenge the exoteric status quo through his esoterism. Namely, nondual mystical apperception seeks to dissolve binary distinctions to repair the rupture of original unification that comes with devotion to the practice of *devekut*.

[60.] For in-depth reflections on the mystical poetics present in Hebrew poetry, see Glazer, *Contemporary Hebrew Mystical Poetry*.

[61.] The notion of identity as a *bricolage* begins with Claude Lévi-Strauss, referring to any spontaneous action, including the characteristic patterns of mythological thought generated by human imagination based on personal experience. These experiences affect the images and entities generated through "mythological thought" that arise from pre-existing things in the imaginer's mind. It has recently been used to describe the nature of identity as a series of contiguous layers for young adults 18-26 who have returned from life-changing Israel journey experiences, which is perhaps another level of *devekut* as cultural connectivity. See Len Saxe and Barry I. Chazan, *Ten Days of Birthright Israel: A Journey in Young Adult Identity* (Waltham, MA: Brandeis University Press, 2008); see also Claude Lévi-Strauss, *The Savage Mind* (Chicago: University of Chicago Press, 1966).

[62.] I am reappropriating Boyarin's ingenious translation of *min* as "hybrid" here, building upon

softer nondual "organic interrelatedness"[63] in a climate of strong dualism within tribal worlds.[64] Through this shared language, however, subjectivities continue shifting in and out of locales and experiences without any longer being bound by such dualism.

The emerging trend of mystical apperception being traced here points to an experiential state whereby the aspirant unites with a deeper nondual consciousness, transcending a human-divine subjecthood *merging into* and *returning to* nondual consciousness. When subjectivity then reformulates, the human-divine matrix has necessarily changed. Whether this experiential state is articulated through a poetic record of experience or presented as a devotional guidebook for entering that experience, the language used to describe the degrees of *devekut* is undergoing a renaissance in Israel worthy of critical attention.[65] These degrees of *devekut*, between vertigo and exactitude, point to a transversal self-understanding taking place in the diverse spiritual culture spheres of Israel that are capable of using the resources of transcendence against themselves.[66]

1.4 Mystical Conundrum: Why Touching Is ~~Touching~~

Returning to the language of nondual mystical apperception then raises the question of whether or not coherence is possible when writing the word "touching" in that it is necessary but not sufficient. When this question

---

his understanding of borders between religions as having been historically constructed out of discursive acts, and extrapolating it to experiential acts as well. See Daniel Boyarin, *Border Lines: The Partition of Judaeo-Christianity* (Philadelphia: University of Pennsylvania Press, 2006), xii, 15, 132, 208-211, 220.

63. See aboven 42.

64. See aboven 50; Aran, "Mysticism and Suicide Bombing," 407-408.

65. Contemporary Israeli explorations differ from what is going on in North America with Art Green's invaluable remapping of Hasidism or Ira Stone's creative reorientation of *Mussar*. For more on the Israeli situation of *haredi* spiritual regeneration and renewal, see Zvi Mark, review of Jonathan Garb, *The Chosen Will Become Herds: Studies in Twentieth-Century Kabbalah, Kabbalah: A Journal of Mystical Texts* 17 (2008): 88-99.

66. Schrag, *The Self after Postmodernity*, 148. In particular, while the cultural matrices of Rav Kook just reviewed (see n56) have clearly lost their transversal self-understanding as edited and censored by R. Tzvi Yehudah Kook and their proto-messianic political extrapolation into *Gush Emunim*, there is a renewed interest in recovering such a loss. For the republication of these once censored writings, see Rav Kook, *Shemoneh kevatzim mi-ktav kodsho*, 2 vols. (Jerusalem: n.p., 2005). See also Garb, *The Chosen Will Become Herds*, 77, 120, 134n16.

of coherence arises, it then leads to the condition of a word being under erasure, or what Jacques Derrida (1930–2004) called *sous rature*. By printing both the word and its erasure, appearing as ~~touching~~, we preserve the very nuance in reaching *but not reaching*, hovering *but not hovering*, touching *but not touching*. "Experience," writes Derrida, "has always designated the relationship with a presence, whether that relationship had the form of consciousness or not."[67] By offering experience as the absence of a presence through an already absented presence, Derrida reveals not the fullness of the experience, but the aroma of its ~~trace~~.

Not everyone endowed with eyes of sight is ready to behold such a ~~trace~~. It is the outsider already inside who possesses the courage to behold the insight of such a ~~trace~~, especially when the container of the experience is lost or broken. The outsider is intimately aware of the inside, for how else does one reach the outside if not from the inside already taken leave of? Some contemporary exemplars of the outside/insider that have much to contribute to the *in*volution of nondual Jewish thinking have been addressed elsewhere.[68]

The ~~trace~~ as a sign of mystical yearning has been dueling against dualism from post-Temple Judaism until the contemporary moment.[69] A

---

67. Jacques Derrida, *De la grammatologie* (Paris: Les Editions de Minuit, 1967), 89; Jacques Derrida, *Of Grammatology*, trans. G. C. Spivak (Baltimore: Johns Hopkins University Press, 1974), 60. Compare with Wolfson, *Open Secret*, 345n237.

68. For further consideration of the negative dialectics of Theodor W. Adorno (1903-1969) and the rational mystical grammatology of Ludwig Wittgenstein (1889-1951), see Aubrey L. Glazer, *A New Physiognomy of Jewish Thinking: Critical Theory after Adorno as Applied to Jewish Thought* (New York: Continuum Press, 2011). Regarding *in*volution as opposed to evolution as a spiritual process, see Glazer, "*Durée, devekuth,* & re-embracing the godlover: *in*volution of *unio mystica* via collocative homosexu*EL*ity," *Vixens Disturbing Vineyards: Embarrassment & Embracement of Scriptures, Festschrift in Honor of Harry Fox leBeit Yoreh* (Boston: Academic Studies Press, 2010), 515n1.

69. After the catastrophe of the Jerusalem Temple's destruction in 70 CE, the place of non-place takes a central role in the speculative realms of the mystics. One such figure ready to behold such a ~~trace~~ is the consummate outsider who is already inside, Simeon ben Zoma (90-125 CE). Embodiment of this contradictory seeing what *cannot be seen* is Ben Zoma's gift that distinguishes him from his rabbinic colleagues. As one of four sages who enters into the garden of mystical experience, known as *PARDE"S*, Ben Zoma beholds a moment of deep mystical apperception and is "stricken" [*nifgah*]. All that remains of his fleeting experience is the Scriptural trace of his state: "*Have you found honey? Eat only what you can hold, lest you be stuffed with it and spit it out*" (Proverbs 25:16); see b. *hagigah* 14b. Despite the warning of his colleague Akivah—that upon ascent into the upper palaces demarcated by the stones of pure marble one must refrain from exclaiming: "Water! Water!"—ben Zoma is stricken. His taste of honey's pristine sweetness

unifying aspect of the immersion experience into mystical union through the ages is evident in how much that striking encounter with the formless form echoes the union between lover and beloved.[70] Such sweetness beyond the taste of what is sweet comes to be known as *mati ve-lo mati*.[71] The degree to which this desire is an oscillation will be shown shortly in a contemporary exemplar of nondual mysticism. Such oscillation is a function of discrete impulses, akin to vertigo and exactitude. This impulse dances between a moving forward as an *in*volutionary force (*redifah*) versus a more cautionary and withdrawing *de*volutionary force (*me'akev*). A harmonization (*hishtavu'ut*) is possible through the crown of consciousness (*Keter*). Amidst such oscillation, there is a need for an integrating factor (*yishuv ha-da'at*). Without such integration, imbalances in the directional flow of either force become harmful to the mystic.[72]

For the presence of a ~~trace~~ from these oscillating states of *de*volutionary vertigo and *in*volutionary exactitude, there must be tension. But tension is not quite a dialectic awaiting synthesis. It is precisely in the friction and collision that new possibilities are birthed, making innovation possible. The friction between these two poles must first break down the existing order. What emerges as a new order is created out of the possibilities

---

beyond sweet comes to be thus known as *mati ve-lo mati* or מטי ולא מטי.

70. Such erotic language pervades Zoharic Kabbalah and Lurianic Kabbalah. Compare Zohar I:16b, 65a, II:268b, III:164b, etc., with Vital, *Sefer etz ḥayyim* 7:1, 7:2, 38:7; Cordovero, *Pardes rimmonim*, 11:6. Hasidism, however, is willing to go further in crossing the boundaries of this ~~touching~~ than its precursors, as in *Liqqutai Moharan* 24:8–9. I am grateful to Elliot R. Wolfson for sharing his reflections on this expression. Compare with Maria Eva Subtelny, "The Tale of the Four Sages Who Entered the "Pardes": A Talmudic Enigma from a Persian Perspective," *Jewish Studies Quarterly* 11, 1-2 (2004): 3-58.

71. Dancing behind the veil of this expression of מטי ולא מטי or *mati v'lo mati* in Aramaic and at home in its zoharic contexts, is the Hebrew expression *nogai'a ve-eno nogai'a* or ואינו נוגע. Such a peculiar expression, so difficult to render, traces back to its conjunctive usage in biblical idiom of hovering as *merakhefet* or מרחפת, compared with hovering as an eagle sheltering her birdlings; see *t. ḥagigah* 2:2; *y. ḥagigah*, 9a.

72. R. Yitzhaq Maier Morgenstern, *Yam ha-ḥokhmah* (Jerusalem: Mechon Yam ha-ḥokhmah, 5770/2010), 32, esp. 639b-640a:

...ב' כחות הפכיים המשמשים בו בערבוביא, והם המעכב וכח הרדיפה, דמצד אחד רדיפה דמחשבה למירדף אבתריה, דהמוחין רודפין להשיג זה האור, וזהו נקרא כח הרדיפה, מאידך כלול בו עוד כח הנקרא כח המעכב, שהוא המעכב את המוחין מלהשיג אור הכתר הנעלם בסוד כתר לי זעיר המורה על ההמתנה... ושני כוחות אלו משמים בכל עת בבת אחת, ודייקא על ידי צירוף שניהם [כח הרדיפה והמעכב] זוכה האדם להשיג אור הכתר בבחינת מטי ולא מטי, ור"ל, מטי על ידי כח הרדיפה, ולא מטי על ידי כח המעכב...

that arise when an existing order shatters. Through such shattering, the creation of new vessels to hold light allows for this very apperception of ~~touching~~ the infinite light. The spherical expressions of these new vessels inhere in the spiral realm, albeit limited by what is referred to as first-tier consciousness. In the process of shattering, a shift is taking place between what Jean Gebser (1905–1973) called *first-* and *second-tier consciousness.* The probability that one truth can exist concurrently with another truth-claim multiplies with ascent into each tier. That shift is critical for the overflow of this dance to take shape, by embodying the quality of knowing that is *un*knowing.[73] This dance remains a hallmark of mystical apperception.

While this *second-tier consciousness* is perspectival, knowledge itself in that tier is now *a*perspectival.[74] What is critical in terms of the *in*volution of consciousness in this regard is a further oscillation between egotism and egolessness.[75] Through cultivation of a deeper sense of the various temporal forms all pointing in return to origin, the adept then has the capacity to realize greater self-transparency. This self-transparency is realized by attachment to those experiences "of timelessness in the union of conjugal love, the timelessness of nightly deep-sleep, the experience of rhythmic complementarity of natural temporicity which unites [one] in every heart-beat and rhythmic breath with the courses of the universe."[76] This interconnectivity of existence through such intramundane forms of transcendence allow for immersion into unitive consciousness. Such immersion affects the sense an individual holds of self within the greater temporal whole.

Temporal awareness, by extension, plays an important role in disclosing a certain messianic consciousness. Such consciousness facilitates experiences of true divinity through a return to the Limitless with deeper vessels and ~~vessels~~. It is only through the ~~vessels~~ of ~~touching~~ as one that there is a possibility of beholding the Holy One of Blessing. Such a temporally expansive act of envisioning is a rectification of that shattering that

---

[73.] Morgenstern, *Yam ha-ḥokhmah,* 5770/2010, 640b. Compare with R. Nahman of Bratzlav, *Liqqutai MoHaRa"N,* 1:24.

[74.] Jean Gebser, *The Ever-Present Origin* [1949, 1953], trans. N. Barstad and A. Mickunas (Athens: Ohio University Press, 1985), 528-533.

[75.] Ibid., 532.

[76.] Ibid., 531.

now enables the adept to see more light, to touch more of the divine.[77] However, such messianic consciousness must still be grounded in the ego, notwithstanding the oscillation between egotism and egolessness.

This seeming eruption into expansive consciousness then returns the adept to a necessary articulation of such mystical apperception as erasure or *sous rature*. Erasure (*makha*) has its own texture of joy (*semaikhim*) in ascent from the ground of Being while entering into ~~being~~, and in the process of ascent through ~~being~~, there is then ~~touching~~.[78] There is a certain reinvigorating *jouissance*, moreover, that comes out of the immersion experience of touching, for in touching a non-differentiated state of existence is reached. Paradoxically, in the return outwards into being—in that moment of coming back into self—is where an experience of joy is possible. In the experience of deep touching, however, that kind of total immersion is actually beyond joy. It is precisely what Badiou deftly describes as the "inscription as if on the gilded edge of loss" that comes into play here: joy is the erasure of Being entering ~~being~~ and then resurfacing.

It is this subtle but constant oscillation in between realms that is key to appreciating the transformative power of mystical apperception. The power such an oscillation exerts not only influences the experience itself, but also touches both thought and poetry ensuing from such mystical experiences. ~~Touching~~ God points to the experiences embedded in the *jouissance* of ~~touching~~ that is touching itself. Returning to this brilliant phrasing of "vertigo and exactitude"[79] guides the articulation of such ~~touching~~, thereby developing an appreciation of the subtle degrees of *devekut* that coexist within every experience. Entry and preparation into unitive consciousness are one when the degree of *devekut* encountered is in constant oscillating motion.[80]

---

77. Morgenstern, *Yam ha-ḥokhmah* (5768/2008), 539.

78. Attributed to the Kotznitzer Maggid, *Ner Yisrael* [1820] (Jerusalem: R. Amram Opman Publicationsnd.), 172n29, as quoted in Morgenstern, *Yam ha-ḥokhmah*, 5770/2010, 644a:

ומעין זה דרש המגיד הק' מקאז'ניץ בסוד הפסוק שמחים בצאתם, דקai אבחינת מטי, ושמחים מלשון מחה, שנמחים ומתבטלים מקיומם ובאים לאפיסה, ועי"ז ושׂשׂים בבואם, כי "כשעולים לכתר נאמר והיתה לבער, כי נכללו באין ואפיסה וכמעט בטלים ממעלתם, ונקראים לגבי העולמות ולא מט[י] וכו' וזהו שמחים בצאתם, היינו כשיותצאים ממקומם לעולם העליון וכו', ועליו אמרו מה שיהיה ימית אדם שיהיה ימית עצמו ומטי אין, ועל ידי הלא מטי ויהיה אח"כ שׂשׂים בבואם", עיש"ב.

79. Badiou, *Dance as a Metaphor for Thought*, 70: "dance is governed by the perpetual renewal of the relation between vertigo and exactitude."

80. R. Tzaddok haCohen of Lublin, *Kuntrus et le-okhel* (Jerusalem: Mechon Mesamkhai Lev,

This constant motion is the oscillation embodied in the pinnacle form of the arts—namely *dance*. The texture of this embodied oscillation in dance "would therefore demonstrate the strange equivalence not only between quickness and slowness, but also between gesture and non-gesture."[81] Even though every genuine thought depends on an event, dance serves well here as a metaphor for more than thought: it articulates the oscillation between presence and absence, between the taking place and the non-place of the event of mystical apperception itself. The event of such a moment of touching is nothing but its own disappearance; "[n]evertheless, an inscription may detain the event, as if on the gilded edge of loss. The name is what decides upon the having taken place. Dance would then point toward thought as event, but before this thought has received a name—at the extreme edge of its veritable disappearance; in its vanishing, without the shelter of the name."[82]

It is on this "gilded edge of loss" that mystical immersion then takes place. What emerges from that "vanishing without the shelter of the name" is a nuanced language, both venerated by the mystic and sung by the poet. Furthermore, as contemporary mystics like R. Yitzhaq Maier Morgenstern subtly note, the very separation of t̶o̶u̶c̶h̶i̶n̶g̶ does not in any way contradict the depth of unification; rather it becomes the ornamentation of futurity. Such messianic futurity is enshrouded in the mystery of the simple, twofold, threefold, fourfold song[83]—namely, poetry.

1.5 Renaissance in Devotional Hebrew Cultures

A remarkable exemplar of devotional Hebrew cultures can be found within the hybrid networks of *haredi* worlds in Israel today. In these worlds,

---

1999), 403a-b, n 5.

81. Badiou, *Dance as a Metaphor for Thought*, 61.

82. Ibid., 61.

83. Attributed to R. Nahman of Bratzlav, *Liqqutai MoHaRaN* 2:2; 42; see Morgenstern, *Yam ha-ḥokhmah*, 5767/2007, 21-23, 719, esp. 23:

אלא הענין הוא כמו שביאר רבינו ז"ל (לקו"מ ח"ב ב') שהתכלית היא שיתגלה האחדות הפשוט מתוך
פעולות המשתנות דייקא...וזהו האור הוא בסוד מטי ולא מטי...היינו שבח' הפירוד אינו סותר לעמקות
היחוד, זה בח' הקישוט שמתגלה לעתיד לבוא, שמתגלה מעלת היחוד ביתר שאת, בסוד שיר פשוט
כפול משולש מרובע...

there is a growing interest in, and regeneration of, the contemporary exploration of mystical apperception through *devekut,* as already noted in the pioneering studies of Garb, Huss, and Meir.[84] The mystic to be now

---

84. See Jonathan Garb, *The Chosen Will Become Herds,* esp. 1-10; Jonathan Garb, *Yehidai ha-segulot yehiyu le-adarim: Iyunim be-Kabalat ha-Meah ha-Esrim* (Jerusalem: Carmel, 2005), esp. 224-225; Jonathan Garb, "Ramah gevohah me'od shel intensiviot ruḥanit," *Eretz aḥeret* no. 41 (2008); Jonathan Garb, "Mystical and Spiritual Discourse in the Contemporary Ashkenazi Haredi Worlds," *Journal of Modern Jewish Studies* 9 (2010): 17–36; Jonathan Garb, "The Modernization of Kabbalah: A Case Study," *Modern Judaism* 30 (2010): 1-22. See also Jonathan Garb, "The Spiritual-Mystical Renaissance in the Contemporary *Haredi* World," paper presented at the conference *Kabbalah and Contemporary Spiritual Revival: Historical, Sociological and Cultural Perspectives,* The Israel Science Foundation and The Goren-Goldstein Center for Jewish Thought (Ben Gurion University: May 20-22, 2008), http://pluto.huji.ac.il/~jogarb/Events.html. In this lecture, Garb raises the issue as to whether there is any longer a macro-vision of Israeli society, given all of its fragmentation during this time of tribalism.

See Huss et al., "Introduction: Kabbalah and Modernity," 1-13; Boaz Huss, "The Mystification of the Kabbalah and the Modern Construction of Jewish Mysticism," trans. Elana Lutsky, *BGU Review* 2 (2008), http://web.bgu.ac.il/Eng/Centers/review/summer2008/Mysticism.htm; Boaz Huss, "The New Age of Kabbalah: Contemporary Kabbalah, the New Age and Postmodern Spirituality," *Journal of Modern Jewish Studies* 6 (2007): 107-125.

Another important part of this creative renewal is the challenge for *haredim* in finding the continuity of the relationship between God and the people of Israel in a post-*Shoah* context. This becomes extremely charged in terms of exclusionary visions of contemporary mystics who see Zionists as belonging to the *sitra aḥra* (other side); see Marc Gopin, *Between Eden and Armageddon: The Future of World Religions, Violence, and Peacemaking* (New York: Oxford University Press, 2000), 119-124. Compare with the Habad mystic, Rabbi Yitzhak Ginsburgh, whose spiritual authority for many in the settler movement inspired his apologetic pamphlet, *Baruch HaGev*er ("Blessed Is the Man"), praising Baruch Goldstein, the Jew who murdered over thirty Muslims in a mosque on Purim 1994. On Goldstein as "redeemer" amidst the aforementioned slaughter, see Aran, " Mysticism and Suicide Bombing," 391-392.

See also Jonathan Meir, *Imagined Hasidism: Satire, Reality, and Concept of the Book in the Anti-Hasidic Writing of Joseph Perl/Sefer Megale Temirin* (Ph.D. diss., Hebrew University of Jerusalem, 2010); Jonathan Meir, "The Imagined Decline of Kabbalah: The Kabbalistic Yeshiva Sha'ar ha-Shamayim and Kabbalah in Jerusalem in the Beginning of the Twentieth Century," in Huss et al., eds., *Kabbalah and Modernity,* 197–220; Jonathan Meir, "Mikhael Levi Rodkinson—Between Hasidism and *Haskalah*" [Hebrew], *Kabbalah: A Journal for the Study of Jewish Mystical Texts* 18 (2008): 229-286; Jonathan Meir, "The Revealed and the Revealed within the Concealed: On the Opposition to the 'Followers' of Rabbi Yehuda Ashlag and the Dissemination of Esoteric Literature" [Hebrew], *Kabbalah: A Journal for the Study of Jewish Mystical Texts* 16 (2007): 151-259; Jonathan Meir, "Wrestling with the Esoteric: Hillel Zeitlin, Yehoshua Zeitlin, and Kabbalah in the Land of Israel," *Judaism, Topics, Fragments, Faces, Identities: Jubilee Volume in Honor of Professor Rivka Horowitz,* ed. Ephraim Meir and Haviva Pedaya (Beer Sheva: Ben Gurion University, 2007), 585-647; Jonathan Meir, "Lights and Vessels: A New Inquiry into the 'Circle'

explored here began publicizing his teachings as anonymously written *sefarim,* with low print runs, advertised merely by word of mouth. Over the past decade, these writings have grown into expansive collections. This most innovative mystical voice is also one of the youngest: R. Yitzhaq Maier Morgenstern, the author of *Yam ha-ḥokhmah, Netiv ḥayyim,* and *De'i ḥokhmah le-nafshekha.*

Why are these works of R. Morgenstern resonating so strongly both inside and outside the *haredi* communities of origin? How is it that his innovative thinking is affecting devotional praxis of *devekut* both inside and outside the unfolding Hasidic networks?[85] While an element of R. Morgenstern's expanding impact may be attributed to his mystical-magical charisma and hypernomian spiritual practice,[86] I argue that it is his innovative, hybridized thinking through key theoretical issues in Kabbalah and Hasidism as they apply to the lived practice of a devotional life of *devekut* that will likely remain his strongest innovation and contribution to contemporary Jewish mysticism.[87]

The degree to which these writings reflect a collective yearning to articulate a language of mystical apperception, steeped in a traditional framework of devotional literature, oscillates beyond its boundaries while remaining ensconced within the practice of tribal culture.[88] As that tribal

---

of Rav Kook and the Editors of His Works," op. cit.

85. Garb, "Mystical and Spiritual Discourse," 23-24.

86. Garb's usage of the term "hypernomian" likely denotes superogatory prayer and devotionality. For more on the nuances of "hypernomianism" in light of Wolfson, see below 140. Also reconsider Garb's claim that "on the scholastic level, Morgenstern's main innovation is a kabbalistic reinterpretation of Talmudic and halakhic texts, the most ambitious project of this nature ever essayed." Garb, "Mystical and Spiritual Discourse," 24.

87. One key theoretical issue in Kabbalah and Hasidism that continues to apply to the lived practice of a devotional life is the imaginality of the dream of prayer as explored in Wolfson's reading of R. Morgenstern in his most recent monograph, see Elliot R. Wolfson, *A Dream Interpreted Within a Dream: Oneiropoiesis and the Prism of Imagination* (New York: Zone Books, 2011), 229-236.

88. While Wolfson has already pointed to what he calls "pietistic transvaluations" whereby the mystic holds the center at the margins, as well as challenging the dichotomy of conservatism/anomianism, the present investigation seeks to build upon this astute observation by suggesting another way of processing the shimmerings of culture and experience. See Elliot R. Wolfson, *Venturing Beyond: Law & Morality in Kabbalistic Mysticism* (New York: Oxford University Press, 2006), 286-316.

culture becomes more trans-*haredi,* the emerging devotional literature inevitably both resists and absorbs aspects of secular culture as well as the global mystical cultures.[89] What interests me here is how these devotional texts and cultures continue to catalyze a rapid linguistic and devotional evolution in the degrees of a hybridized mystical subjectivity, as manifest in the thinking and practice of *devekut.*

In what follows, I trace the contours of these emerging articulations of mystical apperception through some representative (but by no means exhaustive) examples of the devotional teachings on the hybridity of *devekut* by R. Yitzhaq Maier Morgenstern. Beyond a recurring interest in articulating mystical apperception, what unites these efforts is a keen ability to more fully integrate the mystical alongside the philosophical into the poetics of daily devotional life.[90] More than a novel synthesis of past systems and praxis of Hasidic mystical pietism,[91] what emerges in R. Morgenstern's mysticism is a veritable evolution of the spiritual lexicon in the degrees of *devekut.*

By first focusing on one of the most striking contemporary authors of devotional Hebrew literature in Israel, I hope to show that there is a dissolution of the dualism between strictly devotional (i.e., religious) and academic (i.e., secular) studies on *devekut.* My second aim is to see how contemporary explorations of the contours of *devekut* then open the gateways of experiential record to the reader and writer alike, furthering the project of expanding Hebrew cultures and its canons as well as hybridized subjectivity of the spiritual self.

---

89. Garb, "Mystical and Spiritual Discourse," 20.
90. I build here upon the insights of Paul Brunton who has articulated a necessary evolution of the devotional life from the mystical to the philosophical to the ethical. See Paul Brunton, *The Hidden Teaching beyond Yoga* (New York: Weiser Books, 1984); Paul Brunton, *The Quest of the Overself* (New York: Random House, 2003). I am grateful to Moshe Aaron Krassen for bringing Brunton to my attention.
91. Aside from the primary nexus of Habad and Bratzlav Hasidisms, according to Garb, R. Morgenstern in *Yam ha-ḥokhmah* synthesizes many more sources, such as *Kabbalat ha-Rashash,* Komarno, Ramhal, Rav Ashlag, and also the Vilna Gaon tradition, including the *Leshem* (J. Garb, e-mail communication, December 28, 2008). While acknowledging their role in Morgenstern's mystical apperception, I see these precursors as somewhat more minor in relation to his larger project of the evolving spiritual practice of *devekut.*

1.7 Hebrew Cultures: Towards a Shimmering of Cultures

The contemporary renaissance of Hebrew cultures in Israel is causing an interpenetration of previously discreet dualistic realms of discourse and praxis. This shift to the nondual is also happening within the boundaries once separating cultures of devotional literature and spiritualist poetry.[92] As nondualism resurfaces, many religious, sociological, and cultural presumptions of center and margin need to be re-examined, in light of an emerging neo-tribalism in Israel, beyond the kibbutz, *kevutzah*, or *moshav*.[93] That interpenetrating process is one I refer to as a "shimmering of genres,"

[92.] For example, see Glazer, *Contemporary Hebrew Mystical Poetry*.

[93.] See Philip Wexler, *Mystical Interactions: Sociology, Jewish Mysticism, and Education* (Los Angeles: Cherub Press, 2007), esp. 178-179. By re-examining the question of the sociological context of mysticism in Israel today, the question emerges: Is it possible to still uphold the dualistic thinking of center/margin after Eisenstadt? Or are we entering into the realm of neo-tribalism? For the former debate on the center/margin dichotomy in utopian society, see S. N. Eisenstadt, "Martin Buber in the Postmodern Age," *Society*, 34, no. 4 (May/June 1997): 50. In the footsteps of Martin Buber, Eisenstadt is concerned with the sociological construct of utopia, education, and community in the postmodern age. The role of utopian thought in the cultural and institutional dynamics of civilization was key to Buber's thought as Eisenstadt notes: "[Buber] encouraged the search for educational, communal, and even utopian arenas of social interaction in which these tensions could be sustained, resulting in the constant transformation and renewal of culture. I think that is why Buber was so interested in the Hasidic community, in which he saw an inherent potential for renewal through the maintenance of inner tensions. In Israel, he saw a similar potential in the pioneering settlements—the *kibbutz*, the *kvutza*, and the *moshav*—and he looked for it in many other civilizations as well. Notwithstanding his demand for content in dialogue, Buber, unlike many other utopians, was always wary of prescribing specific contents for frameworks of cultural regeneration. This attitude was reflected in his stance on a problem central to the political discourse of his day: the issue of centralization versus decentralization... Buber... asserted that the balance between centralization and decentralization must depend on the historical situation of the moment." S. N. Eisenstadt, "Martin Buber in the Postmodern Age," 50.

On the other hand, this approach is to be contrasted with the neo-tribalism of Michel Maffesoli, who argues that mass culture has disintegrated such that existence today is conducted through fragmented tribal groupings; see Michel Maffesoli, *The Time of the Tribes: The Decline of Individualism in Mass Society* (London: Sages Publications, 1996), 72-103 (Yoni Garb, e-mail communication, December 28, 2008). This is surfacing in many realms of neo-tribal culture, i.e., Burning Man, Rainbow Gatherings, and beyond, to a renewed interest in intentional communities after Havurat Shalom, including Elat Hayyim and more recently to *Adamah Fellows*, based on a Jewish farm. These neo-tribal models are flowing back and forth to Israel as the global village continues expanding.

rather than a Geertzian postmodern "blurring of genres."[94] In light of Schrag's aforementioned transversal self-understanding within unification, I argue for a more symbiotic view of devotional cultures, one that *shimmers* between mystical cognition, perception, and its experience as conveyed and sometimes swerved through that very language. This perspective is being proffered at a time when the academy has excelled at analyzing "the system of meanings embodied in the symbols which make up the religion proper" but has historically been more dualistic in "relating these systems to social-structural and psychological processes."[95] Such dualism continues even in exemplars of current scholarship.[96]

1.8 Reframing Devekut from Psychology to Metaphysics

To reframe this investigation, it is necessary to return to the existent presumptions of culture and its analyses of Jewish mysticism. On the one hand, Scholem was the first to delimit touching or *devekut* as a socio-psychological "communion" rather than the possibility of utter metaphysical "union."[97] Necessary revisionism followed with Idel's sobering call for "a more balanced view of Jewish mysticism as not only a system of

---

94.   This possibility of a "shimmering of genres" rather than a postmodern "blurring of genres" has become more clear in the course of this investigation thanks in part to the questions posed to me by Philip Wexler and Matt Goldish at the Association of Jewish Studies meeting in Washington, DC, on December 23, 2008. While beyond the scope of this investigation, Wexler's project of exploring mystical sociality and its cultural implications after Geertz deserves much more sustained reflection in light of Garb's current research. For the preliminary contours of that larger project, see Wexler, *Mystical Interactions*, esp. 16-20, 175. Wexler's locution of a "circulation of energy that requires... interpenetration, for the actualization of mystical interactions" further clarifies one trajectory of cultural "shimmerings"; Wexler, *Mystical Interactions*, 179.

95.   Clifford Geertz, "Religion as a Cultural System," *The Interpretation of Cultures* (New York: Basic Books, 1973), 125.

96.   For example see Mark's critique of Garb's current research, which hinges on the center and peripheries of the Hasidic and *haredi* community; see Mark, review of Garb's *The Chosen Will Become Herds*, 98-99.

97.   See n. 1 above. Most remarkable is how most Western religions appear to shy away from the experiential possibility of "communion-union-identity" according to Ken Wilber, "The One Two Three of God" (Boulder: Sounds True, 2006). While this is the case with exoteric, legal traditions, it is my contention that is not so with all of esoteric Judaism, especially as concerns *devekut*.

theosophical symbolism, abstract speculations, and 'moderate communion' but as a full-fledged mystical phenomenon."[98] More recently, however, Pachter suggests a further nuance in a typological reading of *devekut* as correlated to a given experience within one of a series of literary genres of sixteenth century Safed.[99] While the period of our analysis is contemporary, the influence of these earlier genres, for the most part constructivist in nature, still needs to be noted:

(1) *Homiletical writings* that portray *devekut* as a path through Torah that enables the human soul to return to its origins in God; [100]

(2) *Ethical manuals* that anchor personal experiences (whether ascetic or ecstatic) as the actualization of *devekut*; [101]

(3) *Systematic theosophies* that allow *devekut* to shift focus from the psychological to the metaphysical, that is, from human experiences arising from this state of clinging to God more towards the divine reaction arising from this unitive state within the divine self.[102]

On the other hand, there are literary critics, such as Reuven Tsur, who see a kind of mystical union in the transcendence of the ultimate boundaries of language, akin to a transcendence of the boundaries of self.[103] Other literary critics, including Hamutal bar-Yosef,[104] see the literary texts themselves actually facilitating a universal "mystagogic" experience, capable of transforming the spiritual state of its readers,

---

98. Idel, "Mystical Techniques," 478.

99. Mordechai Pachter, *Roots of Faith and Devekut: Studies in the History of Kabbalistic Ideas*, vol. 10, ed. Daniel Abrams (Los Angeles: Cherub Press, 2004), 7-337.

100. Ibid., 236–264.

101. Ibid., 265–288.

102. Ibid., 288–316.

103. Reuven Tsur, *On the Shore of Nothingness: A Study in Cognitive Poetics* (Exeter: Imprint Academic, 2003), 86.

104. Hamutal Bar-Yosef, "An Introduction to Mysticism in Modern Hebrew Literature," *Kabbalah: Journal for the Study of Jewish Mystical Texts* 11 (2004): 375n33; Hamutal Bar-Yosef, *Mysticism in 20th Century Hebrew Literature* (Boston: Academic Studies Press, 2010).

regardless of allegiance or connection to any religious culture.[105] From Tel Aviv to Jerusalem, amidst divergent academic approaches, there are other voices—channeling devotional inspiration—that come to exemplify many of the burning questions surrounding a complete immersion within the divine essence or *devekut be-atzmut ha-boreh*.[106] Namely, how can a human being fulfill this yearning to touch God if the journey itself is delimited solely by human community, the human condition, and the language of ~~touching~~? Are there degrees of mystical apperception that will challenge our assumptions about the transformation of human-divine consciousness and the subjectivity of devotional cultures? Moreover, why is it that so much of the Jewish discourse about unitive experiences remains steeped in embarrassment and blocked by metaphysical impasses? These questions will be explored in the degrees of the nondual mystical apperception of *devekut*.

1.9 Degrees of Devekut: A Roadmap

Through immersion, *devekut* seeks to overcome the tension between the human experience of divine consciousness between a filling pleroma (*melo kol ha-aretz kevodo*) and encircling pleroma (*sovev kol almin*), between descending and ascending consciousness, between interior experiences of unity (*penimiyut*) and those on the exterior (*ḥiṣoniyut*), between immanence and transcendence.[107] Such an introductory classification presumes and acknowledges the pre-existent articulation within Hasidism of the degrees of *devekut* as follows:

1. Exteriorized fervor;
2. Interiorized stillness;
3. Enrapturing ascent.

---

105. Hamutal Bar-Yosef claims that mysticism is a universal human desire which need not be conditioned "by an established religion or a specific culture"; see Hamutal Bar-Yosef, *Mysticism in 20th Century Hebrew Literature*, 14.
106. Morgenstern, *Yam ha-ḥokhmah*, 5767/2007, 551a-556b.
107. Morgenstern, *Yam ha-ḥokhmah*, 5768/2008, 608b.

2.0 *DEVEKUT* AS DEVOTIONAL EXPERIENCE
IN R. Y. M. MORGENSTERN

A most compelling exemplar of nondual Jewish mysticism within the *haredi* cultural regeneration in Israel through the Hebrew language is encountered in the prolific devotional studies on *devekut* by (the once anonymous) mystical master in Jerusalem, R. Yitzhaq Maier Morgenstern. Most prominent and impressive amidst his growing corpus of original writings would have to be his voluminous and comprehensive annual proceedings of his academy as *sefarim*, entitled *Yam ha-ḥokhmah* (Sea of Wisdom). These annual teachings are collected mostly from *shi'urim* based in *Torat ḥakham,* given at Mechon Yam ha-Hokhmah between the years 5764–5771/2004–2011.

As an *émigré* in his thirties from Great Britain, educated in a family of Gurer Hasidism,[108] Morgenstern's devotional thinking reveals diverse influences. Such religious diversity reflects Morgenstern's growing transversal self-understanding. R. Morgenstern bears the indelible imprint of studies at the neo-Lurianic *Yeshivat Sha'ar Shamayim* under the auspices of R. Moshe Erlanger, while continuing to maintain close contact with R. Tzvi Maier Zilberberg,[109] as well as deep traces of immersion in Bratzlaver and Lubavitcher Hasidism. This unique breadth of devotional knowledge bodes well as R. Morgenstern continues to dedicate himself to training and deploying a kind of "spiritual elite" in Jerusalem.[110]

While the numbers of attendees at his Sabbath and holiday *tischen* or table-talks are relatively small, R. Morgenstern conducts his seminars in the Tel Azra *haredi* section of Jerusalem, where his influence is spreading vastly. Given that his disciples are mostly *admorim*-in-training, or devotees of diverse Hasidic and kabbalistic lineage undergoing training to take over the mantle of leadership in their given communities, Morgenstern's

---

108. For more on Gurer Hasidism, see Art Green, "Introduction," *The Language of Truth: The Torah Commentary of the Sefat Emet/Rabbi Yehudah Leib Alter of Ger* (Philadelphia: Jewish Publication Society, 1998), xv-lviii. See also Michael A. Fishbane, "Transcendental Consciousness and Stillness in the Mystical Theology of R. Yehudah Arieh Leib of Gur," *Sabbath—Idea, History, Reality,* ed. Gerald G. Blidstein(2004), http://hsf.bgu.ac.il/cjt/ files/Shabbat-Book/Shabbath-English-119-130-Fishbane.pdf .

109. Garb, "Mystical and Spiritual Discourse," 20-24.

110. Mark, review of Garb, *The Chosen Will Become Herds,* 97; see also Garb, "A Very High Level of Spiritual Intensity," 87-90.

influence is becoming felt far and wide. What makes R. Yitzhaq Maier Morgenstern, now in his forties, so unique is his expansive knowledge of Hebrew and Aramaic mystical literatures as well as his integration of experience from diverse cultures, to the point of "transcending and including"[111] his mystical precursors: Lurianic Kabbalah, especially through its neo-Lurianic iterations in the Yemenite Kabbalist R. Shalom Shar'abi (1720–1780, a.k.a *RaSHa"SH*)[112] and Rabbi Yitzchak Isaac Yehudah Yechiel Safrin of Komarno (1806–1874, a.k.a. Komarno Rebbe), as well as classics of Beshtian, Bratzlaver, Lubavitcher, and Gurer Hasidisms. While the expanse of Morgenstern's knowledge and courageous envisioning anew of each tradition warrant in-depth analyses in their own right, recall the purpose of this limited investigation is to appreciate his cogent epistemology for thinking and practicing *devekut.*

Let me be clear: the intention here is to see beyond mere parallels between historical sources[113] and one prominent contemporary Jewish mystic, toward a realization of how this contemporary, nondual mysticism navigates the ambivalence of its post-Zionist condition. The hybridization

---

111. By building on Wilber's idiom of "transcending and including," I am suggesting a different model than one of either discontinuity or continuity. Whereas Garb initially refers to this dynamic within *haredi* worlds and contemporary Kabbalah as one of "continuity and change" and then concludes by describing *haredi* Kabbalah as "innovation and continuity," my emphasis is upon an evolution of spiritual consciousness taking place that requires a process of "transcending and including" perhaps closer to what Garb elsewhere describes as the "ongoing development of mystical modernities," notwithstanding the demise of modernity in light of postmodern spiritualities. See Garb, "Mystical and Spiritual Discourse," 18, 30-31; Jonathan Garb, "The Modernization of Kabbalah: A Case Study," *Modern Judaism* 30 (2010): 17-18. Compare with Ken Wilber, *Integral Spirituality: A Startling New Role for Religion in the Modern and Postmodern World* (Boston: Shambala Press, 2007), 129, 130, 141. For a corrective to Wilber, see Gebser, *The Ever-Present Origin,* esp. 617-621; see also William Irwin Thomson, *Coming into Being: Artifacts and Texts in the Evolution of Consciousness* (New York: St. Martin's Press, 1996), 14. Regarding the strong influence of postmodern spirituality upon contemporary Jewish mysticism, see Boaz Huss, "The New Age of Kabbalah: Contemporary Kabbalah, the New Age and Postmodern Spirituality," *Journal of Modern Jewish Studies* 6 (2007): 107-125, esp. 116-121.

112. Pinhas Giller, *Shalom Shar'abi and the Kabbalists of Beit El* (Oxford: Oxford University Press, 2008), esp. 5-19. See also Jonathan Meir, "The Imagined Decline of Kabbalah."

113. For an elaboration on this methodology for reading Hasidism, see Glazer, "Imaginal Journeying to Istanbul," 209-245.

of Hasidic devotionality,[114] which R. Morgenstern so deftly conceals in its revealment, would have been all but unthinkable in earlier moments of Zionist and Hasidic history. In contrast, the current post-Zionist condition allows for a veritable unravelling of categorical rigidity within this epistemological framework. Yet any letting go is all the while a taking hold, remaining tethered to an expanding trans-*haredi* cultural sphere. [115]

In his brilliant oscillation between Lurianic Kabbalah and Beshtian Hasidism, I argue that R. Morgenstern articulates more than a remarkable compendium of Hasidic hermeneutics; there is also a succinct epistemology for understanding the insights of *devekut* and integrating those very insights into the devotional life. The distilled version of this epistemology of *devekut* is most prominently articulated as an introduction to his commentary on the weekly Torah readings, *De'i ḥokhmah le-nafshekha* (Know Wisdom in Your Soul).[116] To fully appreciate the more expanded version of this epistemology of *devekut* that follows, it is first worthwhile to briefly outline the distilled version preceding *De'i ḥokhmah le-nafshekha*.[117]

If the *raison d'etre* of every existent is for human consciousness to become a vehicle or *merkavah* for divine consciousness, R. Morgenstern can then articulate how *devekut* fulfills this very role of embodying such

---

114. See R. Morgenstern, "Not in the Heavens," *Yam ha-ḥokhmah* (5770/2010), 47-60, where Morgenstern's approach to hybridity distinguishes between Sephardi and Ashkenazi devotional perspectives regarding Halakhah and Kabbalah. While it is forbidden to innovate Halakhah through direct mystical apperception, it is permissible to reconcile halakhic quandaries through mystical apperception; Morgenstern, *Yam ha-ḥokhmah* (5770/2010), 55.

115. While I agree wholeheartedly with Garb's clarion call to scholars of contemporary mysticism to approach their subject with methodologies that are more fluid and subtle in keeping with the fluidity of trans-*haredi* subjectivity, it is curious how the contemporary Israeli context is described. Garb sees the "recession of Zionist self-confidence, marked by the 1973 war and the resultant wave of the newly observant" as what allows for this inner-directed spirituality to emerge. See Garb, "Mystical and Spiritual Discourse," 30-31. Perhaps "the recession of Zionist self-confidence" is a euphemism for the emerging post-Zionist context, which remains a strong catalyst for furthering this hybridization of spiritual identity. In regard to questions of such hybridization, the influence of postmodern spirituality upon contemporary Jewish mysticism however is duly noted; see Boaz Huss, "The New Age of Kabbalah," 116-121.

116. R. Yitzhaq Maier Morgenstern, *De'i ḥokhmah le-nafshekha: Siḥot kodesh* (Jerusalem: Mechon Yam ha-ḥokhmah, 5767/2007), 36-54.

117. Ibid., 40-41.

a matrix of consciousness. *Devekut* is the spiritual glue between elevated states of consciousness that allows for mystical apperception to become a devotional reality.[118]

Traversing the spheres of divine consciousness known as the *sefirot*, R. Morgenstern deftly shows how the exterior kabbalastic underpinnings of the cosmos work simultaneously as the epistemological framework of an interiorized Hasidic devotionality. Tracing the contours from below to above, R. Morgenstern outlines Grounding-*Malkhut* as the receptivity to serve through devotion. This is especially pronounced when the heart is not aroused into a preliminary state of Awe-*Gevurah* and Love-*Hesed*. From this foundation of Grounding-*Malkhut,* an arousal to Love-*ḥesed,* Awe-*Gevurah,* and *Devekut-Tiferet* is then possible. This kabbalistic strategy allows for the transformation of that point of equanimity between Love-*ḥesed* and Awe-*Gevurah* through *devekut*. This reveals how the true pleasure of the unitive moment of consciousness through *devekut* comes by way of the connectivity between the One emanating and the one receiving that emanation.[119] From this kabbalistic framework of a deeper awareness within unitive consciousness, there is a subtle shift within *devekut* towards that "gilded state of loss" encapsulated through memory. The next level of manifestation mirrors Love-*ḥesed* and Awe-*Gevurah* through *devekut* in a gilded state of loss as the residual Memory of Love-*Netzaḥ*, Memory of Awe-*Hod*, and Memory of *Devekut-Yesod.*

This subtle shift in manifestation evinces the degree to which the revelation of illumination becomes more concealed through its traces of Memory of Love-*Netzaḥ*, Memory of Awe-*Hod*, and Memory of *Devekut-Yesod.*[120] Within the recurring "trace of the holy" or *reshimu de-kedusha* there is embedding within the subconscious layer of each level of manifestation. Especially during deep moments lacking such connectivity, *devekut* is that trace of memory in a gilded state of loss that wires the circuitry of this eternal oscillation.

The more expanded version of this epistemology, not only for understanding, but more importantly for integrating the insights of *devekut*

---

118. Ibid., 40.
119. Ibid., 41.
120. Ibid.

into the devotional life, is found throughout R. Morgenstern's annual teachings at the institute *Mechon Yam Ha-ḥokhmah,* hosted at the academy *Yeshivat Torat Hakham* in Jerusalem. At the same time as R. Morgenstern is delivering these consecutive, intensive *shi'urim* on *devekut* at Yeshivat Torat Hakham, which will be explored shortly, he is also teaching and constructing a further hybrid *gnosis* on Zion and Jerusalem.

2.1 Hybrid Imaginalities of Zion and Jerusalem

Thinking, practicing, writing and teaching in Israel as a mystic, R. Morgenstern inevitably has to contend with the place of Zion and Jerusalem in his devotional life, all the while—in predominant *haredi* fashion—boycotting Israeli political life.[121] While until recently, R. Morgenstern has rarely focused any of his formal written teachings explicitly on Zion and Jerusalem,[122] there are recurring hybridized mystical motifs of Zion and Jerusalem that indelibly mark his teachings as they impact contemporary devotional life.

R. Morgenstern does actually begin to address the dialectical role of Israel-Diaspora, in a recent introduction to *Yam ha-ḥokhmah,* in terms of its impact on the devotional imaginality. One might expect some sort of insight of mystical theodicy, for example, as a way of at least processing the suffering that ensues as a result of the ongoing threat of terrorism, as is the case with Aran's insights to *Zaka's* constantly evolving theosophy in the face of daily terror.[123] However, R. Morgenstern's response is embodied in his devotional practice of teaching on the Sabbath's third meal, which is intended to serve as a spiritual strategy of hastening messianic consciousness. The mystic intends this to be realized by connecting to the *Shekhinah* as

---

[121.] According to Garb's field research, R. Morgenstern has "joined the growing movement to boycott Israeli political life"; see Garb, "Mystical and Spiritual Discourse," 31.

[122.] R. Morgenstern makes frequent references to the religious realities of living a devotional life in the holy city of Jerusalem. On the walls of Jerusalem, see Morgenstern, *Yam ha-ḥokhmah* (5768/2008), 282; Morgenstern, *Yam ha-ḥokhmah* (5769/2009), 442; Morgenstern, *Yam ha-ḥokhmah* (5770/2010), 465. On the rabbinic authorities of Jerusalem and related rulings or customs, see Morgenstern, *Yam ha-ḥokhmah* (5767/2007), 51; Morgenstern, *Yam ha-ḥokhmah* (5768/2008), 32, 33, 42, 289; Morgenstern, *Yam ha-ḥokhmah* (5770/2010), 91.

[123.] See aboven 56.

She hovers between the Galilee and the Western Wall of Jerusalem[124] by cracking through the negative spiritual energies of Esau and Ishmael. These negative energies known as *Qelippot* are likely allusions here to the felt presence of radical Islam within Israel.[125] While these tropes are invoked, R. Morgenstern continues to read them through a hybridized lens, which allows for his mystical apperception to dislocate the requisite connection points of divine presence with messiainic consciousness to be site-specific to the Land of Israel. Rather, the matrix remains highly spiritualized in every thing and every place, especially within the inner depth of the heart, for this non-dual mystical apperception. [126]

Such a tendency to spiritualize Zion can be seen as R. Morgenstern deftly builds on Talmudic sources that speak to this dialectic of "controversy-insight" [*R"iv-R"avi*][127] as well as culling inspiration from R. Nahman of Bratzlav's oral teachings which unambiguously state "my true place is the Land of Israel, so when I travel I only go to the Land of Israel, notwithstanding for now I am a shepherd in Bratzlav and elsewhere [in the Diaspora]."[128] As an émigré to Israel from England, clearly R. Morgenstern cannot completely negate the value of diasporic insight. Yet by deftly re-orienting this dialectic of "controversy-insight," its mystical realization takes place in the "integration of thinking in the secret of Peace, which is the Land of Israel." [129] The degree to which R. Morgenstern's non-dual mystical

---

124. Morgenstern, "Author's Introduction," *Yam ha-ḥokhmah* (5764/2003)np. see third page, where Morgenstern explicitly invokes *Bamidbar Rabbah* no. 11 whereby "the *Shekhinah* never moves from the Western Wall."

125. Morgenstern, "Author's Introduction," *Yam ha-ḥokhmah* (5771/2010), 37-38; Morgenstern, "Author's Introduction," *Yam ha-ḥokhmah* (5769/2008), 39; Morgenstern, "Author's Introduction," *Yam ha-ḥokhmah* (5767/2006), 17-19; Morgenstern, "Author's Introduction," *Yam ha-ḥokhmah* (5766/2005): 15n1-3, Morgenstern, "Author's Introduction," *Yam ha-ḥokhmah* (5765/2004), 9; ibid., *"Be'ur Torah no. 5: Liqqutai Moharan Tinyana,* 125n11; Morgenstern, "Author's Introduction," *Yam ha-ḥokhmah* (5764/2003)np. see first page.

126. Morgenstern, "Author's Introduction," *Yam ha-ḥokhmah* (5764/2003)np. see third page, where Morgenstern explicitly invokes the adage of the Sages that "the *Shekhinah* never moves from the Western Wall" and goes on to interpret it esoterically to mean that although the Western Wall is the site, the divine presence actually is found in all places one searches, especially in darkened places given the deep divine withdrawals into absence which still bring forth the residue of presence.

127. bSanhedrin 24a.

128. Morgenstern, *Yam ha-ḥokhmah* (5772/2011), 55-60.

129. Ibid., 57-59.

apperception influences his interpretative strategy here returns ultimately to a re-integration of this Diaspora-Zion dialectic of "controversy-insight" within the spiritualized imaginality of the Land of Israel.

To appreciate this most recent articulation of the place of Zion and Jerusalem in R. Morgenstern's devotional life, perhaps a moment of contrast is necessary. Whereas a subversive affirmation of Jerusalem becomes the imaginal messianic site through which the entire exterior world is transformed into the Land of Israel for the seventh Lubavitcher rebbe of the Diaspora, R. Menahem Mendel Schneerson,[130] by contrast what will become clear is that for R. Yitzhaq Maier Morgenstern these imaginal motifs of Zion and Jerusalem reflect an interiorized nondual mystical perspective of *devekut*. Whereas the imaginality of Jerusalem, for R. Schneerson, may reorient its center at 770 Eastern Parkway in Brooklyn to emanate its messianic mission to the world, for R. Morgenstern, by contrast, the imaginality of Jerusalem is a deeply contemplative state of spiritual consciousness whose expansiveness transcends and includes the topography of Israel without being limited to a given address in the Tel Azra *haredi* section of Jerusalem. In contrast to the hyper-physical spiritualization of Brooklyn as a microcosm of the universe that is even rebuilt in Israel, for Morgenstern there is a limitation to the degree of spiritualizing the physicality of Zion and Jerusalem beyond the borders of the mystic's heart and mind.

Jerusalem is more than the sum of its parts, especially in its current state of desolation and destruction, which still permeates the Temple Mount. The shift from the real geographic site of this desolation to its imaginal counterpart is of chief concern insofar as it affects the mystic's devotional life and pulsations of *devekut*. Zion and Jerusalem are then utterly spiritualized as *ruhaniyut*[131]—a directly interiorized experience

---

130. Wolfson, *Open Secret*, 133-134.

131. For Jerusalem as direct spiritual experience, see Morgenstern, *De'i hokhmah le-nafshekha* (5767/2007), *Parshat Terumah*, 254, 255. For the plethora of references to Zion as direct spiritual experience, see Morgenstern, *De'i hokhmah le-nafshekha* (5767/2007), *Parshat Ve'ethanan*, 473; *Parshat Devarim*, 467; *Parshat Masai*, 453; *Parshat Korah*, 411; *Parshat Shelakh lekha*, 394; *Parshat Be-ha'alotekha*, 388; *Parshat Nasso*, 379; *Parshat Be-Har-Be-hukotai*, 355; *Parshat Kedoshim*, 338; *Parshat Tazria-Mezora*, 327; *Parshat Va-yikra*, 303, 307; *Parshat Terumah*, 263; *Parshat Shemot*, 200; *Parshat Va-yehi*, 188; *Parshat Me-kez*, 164; *Parshat hayyai Sarah*, 110.

of mystical apperception. This is described as an eye-to-eye experience of unmediated supernal illumination,[132] even imagined as a rainbow of holiness.[133] This interior plane of Zion and Jerusalem serves as site for the rebuilding of a wholly spiritualized Third Temple within the mystic.[134] Given the remaining possible violent counter-narratives within the national-religious worlds of Israel that have become at once more radicalized (in the small remnant) and more despairing since the disengagement of Gaza (the growing remnant), there is a need for a more "quietistic"[135] sweetening of the judgment that surrounds the desolation that is the Temple Mount.[136] Critical for this imaginal rebuilding of the

---

132. Morgenstern, *Yam ha-ḥokhmah* (5770/2010), 801; Morgenstern, *Yam ha-ḥokhmah* (5768/2008), 27; Morgenstern, *Yam ha-ḥokhmah* (5767/2007), 27.

133. Morgenstern, *De'i ḥokhmah le-nafshekha: Siḥot kodesh, Parshat Noaḥ*, 80.

134. R. Morgenstern, *She'airith Ya'akov: Hiddushim v'Beurim 'al Massechet Megillah* (Jerusalem: Mechon Yam ha-ḥokhmah, 5759/1999), esp. 128b-136b; 219a-220a; 340a-341a; 359b-360a ; 370a-371a; 372b-373a. The site of Jerusalem even becomes spiritualized as that cultivated state of consciousness described as *Yeru-Shalem=Yirah-Shalem/Shelaima* or Integral Transparency. I am grateful to Yoni Garb for bringing the *She'airith Ya'akov* to my attention.

135. R. Morgenstern's approach to Zion and Jerusalem could be seen as a continuation of a stream of early Hasidic devotional practice that is much more quietistic than zealous; see Rivka Schatz Uffenheimer, *Quietistic Elements in Eighteenth-Century Hasidic Thought* [Hebrew] (Jerusalem: Magnes Press, 1968), esp. 9-31. Compare with R. Morgenstern's call for a different kind of spiritualization of the land, and at its core is a spiritualized inner war of Armegeddon rather than a policial, exteriorized war of Armegeddon, see Morgenstern, *She'airith Ya'akov: Hiddushim v'Beurim 'al Massechet Megillah* (5759/1999), esp. 131b, 132a-b. R. Morgenstern explicity rejects what he refers to as "the contaminated Zionist ideology and their ridiculous messianic project," see ibid., 136a-b. Morgenstern goes so far as to mark 1896 as the moment of contamination of devotional thinking by Zionist ideology (i.e. when Theodor Herzl writes *The Jewish State* which articulates the vision of political Zionism to solve anti-Semitism through the founding of a nation-state). R. Morgenstern's spiritualized approach to Zion and Jerusalem finds fleeting moments in which devotional convergence with the political categories of anti-Zionist or post-Zionist appears plausible, but remain ultimately ambivalent.

136. Morgenstern, *Yam ha-ḥokhmah* (5770/2010), 827, 829; Morgenstern, *Yam ha-ḥokhmah* (5768/2008), 446. The case of zealous settlers known as the Jewish Underground was discovered in the 1980s; their hyperliteral reading of rebuilding the Third Temple envisioned blowing up the Dome of the Rock as a kabbalistic drama. See Aran, "Mysticism and Suicide Bombing," 409-413. Even the more mainstream religious Zionism of *Gush 'Emunim* for R. Morgenstern is actually based on faulty assumptions due to misreadings of archaeology, and consequently its implications for spiritual history are dire; see most recently, Morgenstern, *De'i ḥokhmah le-nafsheikha* (5772/2012), *Parshat Bamidbar*, 3-33, esp. 14-18.

demarcated sites of Zion and Jerusalem, as well as the Third Temple, is the efficacy of *devekut* during experiences of prayer and study.[137] Rebuilding such a ruptured interworld—bridging of reality and imagination—requires an awareness of every moment as pregnant with *devekut* so long as nondual consciousness informs the practice itself.[138] The true interiority of this imaginal rebuilding process is itself a spiritual rectification of the rupture between the mystic and the *Shekhina* or Neighboring Divine Presence that once hovered over the Holy of Holies in the Jerusalem Temple.[139] It is that yearning within this very rupture that becomes most pronounced for the mystic amid nondual mystical apperception in Jerusalem.

Juxtaposed with the reality of Jerusalem's brokenness is its constant potential for rectification by way of the aroma of redemption and messianism. Regarding redemption, the rejoicing that catalyzes it has imaginal implications, specifically in the realm of divine spheres of consciousness known as *sefirot* and *parṣufim*. By rereading the rabbinic narratives of rejoicing with the Daughters of Jerusalem,[140] or the Sons of Zion,[141] through the Fifteenth of Av as well as on the Festival of Water Drawing[142] around the Temple and through the streets of Jerusalem, a manifestation of the non-manifest takes place. This happens through dance, specifically shifting from linear to rounded, spiral formations.[143] The purpose of such oscillations between linearity and circularity is to allude to an arousal of deeper spiritual consciousness that must be manifest in order for redemption to take place.[144] That process of making the non-manifest manifest is experienced through the subtle qualities of speech/song succinctly symbolized through the duality of *Torah/Tefillah,* mirrored through the divine spheres of consciousness known as *Malkhut/*

---

137. Morgenstern, *Yam ha-ḥokhmah* (5770/2010), 431, 827, 829.

138. Ibid., 826.

139. Morgenstern, *Yam ha-ḥokhmah* (5768/2008), 381; Morgenstern, *De'i ḥokhmah le-nafsheikha* (5766/2006), *Parshat Mishpatim*, 250.

140. Morgenstern, *Yam ha-ḥokhmah* (5767/2007), 679.

141. For *Bnai Ṣion*, see Morgenstern, *Yam ha-ḥokhmah* (5767/2007), 652, 653; for *Avilai Ṣion*, see ibid., 548, 549.

142. Morgenstern, *Yam ha-ḥokhmah* (5768/2008), 510.

143. Morgenstern, *Yam ha-ḥokhmah* (5770/2010), 826.

144. Ibid.

Yesod.[145] Circling back to a fuller experience of dance, the real rejoicing with the Daughters of Jerusalem refracts through the sphere of *Malkhut*,[146] while the Sons of Zion are channeled through *Keter*.[147] Arousal of the imaginal rejoicing within the celestial dance itself is embodied in Zion and Jerusalem[148]—all the while gilded on the edge of loss.

This perennial sense of loss awaiting imminent redemption is at the heart of Zion and Jerusalem.[149] The yearning for deeper discernment—amidst such a dance gilded on the edge of loss—is manifest through a real need for cultivation of the sphere of *Binah*. The gaping hole inside the heart of Zion and Jerusalem is that birthing power to break through the womb of delusion that delays complete redemption.[150] Such a yearning for greater discernment and understanding courses deeper through the conflict-ridden streets and personages of Jerusalem. By reorienting another classic oscillation in Lurianic Kabbalah, that of the competing divine personae or *parṣufim* of the matriarchs, Leah and Rachel,[151] R. Morgenstern brings newfound equanimity to an all-too common perception of never-ending tension that typifies Jerusalem as an imbalanced religious center overrun by hyper-legalistic zealots. Such an imbalance is a product of dualistic thinking, whereby religion (*Halakhah*)

---

145. Morgenstern, *Yam ha-ḥokhmah* (5768/2008), 669.

146. Morgenstern, *Yam ha-ḥokhmah* (5767/2007), 679.

147. Ibid., 652, 653.

148. Morgenstern, *Yam ha-ḥokhmah* (5768/2008), 673, 686.

149. When loss is perennial, it approaches the precipice of ritualization, as explained to me by Harry Fox, beginning with the lament of Tammuz as described in Ezekiel 8: 14, as well as in the post-Temple midnight vigil of *Tiqqun Hatzot* still performed in Jerusalem, see Shaul Magid, "Conjugal union, mourning and *Talmud Torah* in R. Isaac Luria's *Tikkun Hazot*," *Daat* 36 (1996), xvii–xlv.

150. Morgenstern, *Yam ha-ḥokhmah* (5764/2004), 64; Morgenstern, *Yam ha-ḥokhmah* (5768/2008), 291, 601, 605; Morgenstern, *Yam ha-ḥokhmah* (5769/2009), 426.

151. There are three *parṣufim* that emerge from the Minor Persona [*Zeir Anpin*]: Rachel, Jacob, and Leah. Rachel and Leah are both aligned with the Feminine of the Minor Persona [*Nuqbah de-Zeir Anpin*]. Rachel, however, is considered to be the true partner of Jacob, seeing that she is the tenth point of the World of Points [*Olam ha-Nequdim*] that encompasses the World of Unification [*Olam ha-Atzilut*]. Rachel is conjoined with Jacob back to back, whereas Leah has the capacity to ascend above Jacob for greater illumination; see Hayyim Vital, *Otzrot ḥayyim, Sha'ar Tiqqun ha-nuqbah*, ed. Frisch, vol. 2, ch. 1, fol. 44b (Jerusalem: Mechon Da'at Yosef, 5769/2009), 306–318; ibid., *Sha'ar Ya'aqov ve-Leaḥ*, vol. 2, ch. 1, fol. 45b, 319–335.

stands in opposition to spirituality (*Kabbalah*). Such a dualism tends to then separate the terrestrial from the celestial Jerusalem.[152] To rectify this dualistic chasm, R. Morgenstern then reorients the map of Jerusalem. The perceived dualism is then masterfully dissolved in repositioning the imaginal topography of Jerusalem and her residents. This allows for a stratified reality to become spiritualized into a constructive oscillation; the people of Jerusalem and her walls now symbolize the divine persona of Leah, while the saints of Jerusalem and the expansion of her streets symbolize the divine persona of Rachel.[153] Wholeness amidst the rupture dissolves this dualism into the possibility of *devekut* through its nondual mystical apperception.

This daring repositioning of the imaginal topography of Jerusalem and her residents also provides a window into the operative networks of *haredi* culture within Jerusalem, and how a quietistic but messianic mystic like Morgenstern resolves these competing forces through his uniquely transversal approach of hybridity. Take, for example, the walls of Jerusalem, which for R. Morgenstern now symbolize the stringent rule of law emanating from the *Beit Din Tzedek* or Rabbinical High Court, while the expansion of Jerusalem's streets symbolize that messianic impulse overflowing through hypernomian cultivation of nondual mystical apperception. A key insight that translates hypernomian[154] practice back

---

152. Morgenstern, *Yam ha-ḥokhmah* (5767/2007), 73. Compare with Zion symbolizing the seal of *Yom Kippur* and Jerusalem symbolizing the seal of *Hoshanna Rabba*; see Morgenstern, *Yam ha-ḥokhmah* (5768/2008), 207.

153. Morgenstern, *Yam ha-ḥokhmah* (5768/2008), 262; *Yam ha-ḥokhmah* (5767/2007), 608.

154. The term "hypernomian" has been reflected upon extensively by Elliot R. Wolfson to indicate a law *beyond the law*, a law wherein permissible and forbidden are no longer distinguishable; see, for example, Wolfson, *Open Secret*, 55-56, 164-165, 180, 322n129; Wolfson, *Venturing Beyond*, 14, 109, 186, 235-237, 240, 249, 260, 262-263, 272-273, 284, 304, 315; Wolfson, "*Open Secret* in the Rearview Mirror," *AJS Review* (forthcoming). While in the latter study Wolfson refers to R. Schneerson's locution of *le-ma'lah mi-torah u-miṣvot*, in the case of R. Morgenstern, I am suggesting that hypernomian coincides with his *penimiyut ha-halakhah*, which is nondual mystical union. Hypernomianism for the latter is that state in which the law becomes lawless by virtue of its perceived duality of interiority/exteriority dissolving in the experience of *devekut*. Through such *devekut* experiences, a hybrid subjectivity emerges and Halakhah itself appears to also undergo involution. In both cases, as Wolfson notes, the devotional stance is "transmoral as opposed to immoral"; Wolfson, *Venturing Beyond*, 262. See also Morgenstern, *Yam ha-ḥokhmah* (5770/2010), 47-60, where he dedicates a responsum, "Not in the Heavens" to exploring the role of Kabbalah in revealing the concealed truth

into hybridized thinking for R. Morgenstern is how this kind of nondual mystical apperception is only possible through playful oscillation amid the dualistic personae of Leah and Rachel. Such perceived dualism is only an illusion; nondual mystical apperception is realized in penetrating this illusory reality through devotional practice that recalibrates the system to its original state of unification, regardless of its present state of rupture. Jerusalem, then, is the roadmap for redemption, but only insofar as its dualistic thinking can be dissolved by its quietistic, messianic, indigenous mystics dwelling within her. What this example of reorienting mystical symbols of the divine personae shows is the need for constant oscillation between religion (Halakhah) and spirituality (Kabbalah) through nondual mystical apperception.

To resolve such tensions on the intellectual plane of *pilpul* or casuistry alone is insufficient. Instead, R. Morgenstern proffers a devotional practice that translates this hybridity of Jerusalem and Zion into a living spiritual reality. In-depth spiritual practices vary, from intense yogic breath work[155]

---

of Halakhah after the talmudic polemic over the Oven of Akhnai (*b. Baba Meṣia* 59b, *b. Temura* 16a) which ultimately is reconciled through nomian rabbinic authority rather than with mystical inspiration from heavenly voices. The general structure of *Yam ha-ḥokhmah* is to begin each volume with a *Dvar halakhah* [word on the law] and then progress to *Penimiyut ha"Shas* [interiority of Talmud]. This may reflect a strategy of *moving beyond the law* by *moving through* the interiority of the law in its source and precedent. For a full-length halakhic response on the question of mystical apperception in legal decisions, see Morgenstern, *Shu"Tim* (Jerusalem: Mechon Yam ḥa-ḥokhmah, 5770/2010). Regarding the Sabbatean residue of hypernomianism, R. Morgenstern reiterates that while it is forbidden to "innovate" [*le-ḥadesh ḥidushim*] Halakhah through mystical apperception, it is permissible to "reconcile" [*le-bakhria*] halakhic quandaries through mystical apperception. This distinction between innovation and reconciliation is necessary, given that for centuries halakhic decisors were battling against the perception that Sabbateanism justified antinomian behavior through mystical apperception alone, leading to a denigration of all hypernomianism; see Morgenstern, *Yam ha-ḥokhmah* (5770/2010), 56. Regarding *teshuvah* as a commandment requiring transgression as a prototype for the debate over hypernomianism in Yaakov Yosef of Polonoyye, and the ensuing contradictions unresolved by Pierkaz, see Glazer, "Imaginal Journeying to Istanbul," 210-211n6.

155. For example, see Morgenstern, *Yam ha-ḥokhmah* (5767/2007), 665-668. For implicit parallels in Patanjali's yoga sutras that refer to this technique of breath control as *pranayama*, see for example Swami Hariharananda Aranya, trans., *Yoga Philosophy of Patanjali* (Albany: SUNY Press, 1981), *Sutra* 1:34, 78-80. Part of Morgenstern's draw in the contemporary hybrid spiritual culture of Israel, as Garb astutely notes, is "the growing presence of alternative medicine and Far Eastern meditation techniques in the spiritual

as an authentic form of Jewish meditation subtly articulated through a multi-part study called *Derekh ha-Yihud*,[156] to devotional intentions, known as *kavvanot*, for deepening the ongoing spiritual practice of Reb Nahman's vigil cycle of psalms, known as *Tiqqun ha-Kelali*.[157]

Consider briefly the imaginal hybridity of Jerusalem within the aforementioned devotional practice of Jewish meditation. While the question remains whether his choice not to explicitly reference Patanjali's devotional practice of *astanga yoga* betrays a "resistance to the growing presence of alternative medicine and Far Eastern meditation techniques in the spiritual landscape of many *haredi* worlds,"[158] R. Morgenstern still manages to deftly translate a comparable devotional effect of *pranayama* by reclaiming or "rediscovering" it through a hybridized kabbalisitic-yogic spiritual practice. As he articulates it, the Jewish form of this embodied spiritual practice focuses on cultivating inner awareness by expansion and restraint of the breath through different *sefirot* of the body, from *Malkhut* to *Keter*.[159] The journey through the *sefirot* embodied in the meditator then cycles through *perishut ve-harhakah* (withdrawal), to *hasagah* (effortless inner awakening), reaching *yihud ve-devekut* (unitive bliss). This clearly parallels the journey through the *chakras* embodied in the meditator through *pratyhara* (withdrawal), *jayanna* (effortless inner awakening), and *samadhi* (unitive bliss). Here, once again, a dissolution of perceived duality separating the devotional forms of yoga and Kabbalah reveals itself to be a more subtle oscillation through nondual mystical apperception.

---

landscape of many *haredi* worlds"; see Garb, "Mystical and Spiritual Discourse," 24.

[156.] This teaching on cultivating unitive consciousness through Jewish meditation is in three parts. See Morgenstern, *Yam ha-hokhmah* (5766/2006), 305-352; Morgenstern, *Yam ha-hokhmah* (5767/2007), 659-706; *Yam ha-hokhmah* (5769/2009), 803-840.

[157.] The preponderance of (re)printing of the *Tiqqun ha-kelali* for seven consecutive volumes of *Yam ha-hokhmah*, accompanied by nuanced reflection for cultivating deeper spiritual intentionality during the vigil suggests that this is part of an ongoing core practice (not just for Bratzlav Hasidim); see Morgenstern, *Yam ha-hokhmah* (5764/2004), 91-103; Morgenstern, *Yam ha-hokhmah* (5765/2005), 183-208; Morgenstern, *Yam ha-hokhmah* (5766/2006), 547-558; Morgenstern, *Yam ha-hokhmah* (5767/2007), 707-737; Morgenstern, *Yam ha-hokhmah* (5768/2008), 691-724; Morgenstern, *Yam ha-hokhmah* (5769/2009), 878-881; Morgenstern, *Yam ha-hokhmah* (5770/2010), 867-886.

[158.] Garb, "Mystical and Spiritual Discourse," 24.

[159.] For example, see Morgenstern, *Yam ha-hokhmah* (5767/2007), 665-668.

2.2 Hybridity of Spiritual Self: An Epistemology of the Soul

There is considerable ingenuity on the part of R. Morgenstern in providing an epistemological framework to think through these given spiritual practices, recalling *ta'amai ha-miṣvot* literature which explains the thinking behind a given practice, along with lessons on the *locus classicus* of Habad Hasidism, R. Shneur Zalman of Lyadi's *Tanya*.[160] In his epistemological framework for spiritual practice, one encounters R. Morgenstern's tendency toward innovative hybridization most prominently in his recent book-length study, *Netiv ḥayyim* (Path of Life).[161] A certain hybridity is required for the contemporary seeker in a post-Zionist context, which is subconsciously acknowledged by R. Morgenstern. He realizes *Netiv ḥayyim* can effectively serve as a hybridized introduction to an epistemology and devotional practice of Hasidism. It is composed of comprehensive teachings delivered by R. Morgenstern in his desire to carry forward the Komarno Rebbe's *Netiv miṣvhoteikha* and R. Hayyim Vital's *Otzrot ḥayyim*—thus this hybrid title of *Netiv ḥayyim*. What emerges is a seemingly familiar hybrid of Lurianic Kabbalah and Beshtian Hasidism as already reconciled by one of its foremost practitioners, the Komarno Rebbe. Thus *Netiv ḥayyim* offers its comprehensive reorienting introduction to "those seeking to enter the gateways of a pristine spiritual devotion by way of Hasidism bequeathed by the Besht,"[162] all the while retaining its kabbalistic rigor in search of a nondual mystical apperception.

2.3 Hybridity of Spiritual Self: Nondual Consciousness

Within this comprehensive context of spiritual thinking and practice, R. Morgenstern also devotes considerable resources to the thought and experience of *devekut*. It is noteworthy that almost every edition of *Yam ha-ḥokhmah* is generally structured according to a progression of topics, beginning with Halakhah, progressing to Kabbalah, and culminating with Hasidism. It

---

[160.] Morgenstern, *Yam ha-ḥokhmah* (5765/2005), 103-148; Morgenstern, *Yam ha-ḥokhmah* (5766/2006), 201-247.

[161.] The first iteration collects eight lessons see Morgenstern, *Yam ha-ḥokhmah* (5771/2011), 339-434; for the more complete iteration which collects the fuller twenty-two lessons, see Morgenstern, *Sefer netiv ḥayyim* (Jerusalem: Mechon Yam ha-ḥokhmah, 5771/2011).

[162.] Morgenstern, *Yam ha-ḥokhmah* (5771/2011), 339.

is instructive that one such subsection is devoted to a hybrid called "Interiority of Kabbalah and Hasidism," where R. Morgenstern provides a lengthy exposition of *devekut* in the fifth branch of "Threefold Holiness" (*Ma'amar kedushah meshuleshet*).[163] It is this collection of teachings that stands as a remarkably innovative reflection on unitive consciousness. Ultimately there is more than merely an anthologizing or synthesizing of historic teachings of these diverse Hasidic masters at play here; rather, there is a subtle involution taking place in the language of unitive consciousness in *devekut*.

In attempting to articulate what he calls "the Truth in the condition of degrees of *Devekut*," R. Yitzhaq Maier Morgenstern delimits his apperception to the three aforementioned degrees of *devekut*:[164]

(1) descent or immanence;
(2) ascent or transcendence;
(3) endless essence or oceanic undifferentiation.

These paradigmatic unitive experiences are exemplified for R. Morgenstern by the spiritual personnae of Ba'al Shem Tov and the Mittler Rebbe, also known as Rabbi Dov Ber of Lubavitch (1773–1827).[165] By delimiting the degrees of mystical apperception within this matrix, R. Morgenstern continues parsing out mystical experience as a subtle oscillation, rather than succumbing to any apparent dualism. This oscillation recurs between the interiority of ascent in *Hokhmah* and the exteriority of descent in *Binah*. Immanence, transcendence, and unitive consciousness are thus the common filters correlating a dynamic appreciation in the flow of *devekut* through three symbiotic degrees. By repositioning these records of mystical apperception as genres of transformative subjectivity, R. Morgenstern is innovating this lexicon of tradition. It is by no means intended as a hierarchy of *devekut*; rather, it is a way of seeing the complex interrelations as spiraling oscillations within this constellation of mystical

---

163. Morgenstern, *Yam ha-ḥokhmah* (5768/2008), 551-640.
164. Ibid., 608b:מלא כל הארץ כבודו, סובב כל עלמין, עצמות אין סוף.
165. R. Dov Ber of Lubavitch or the *Mittler Rebbe* (Yiddish, literally "the Middle Rebbe"); Rabbi Dov Ber of Lubavitch (1773-1827), the second Habad Rebbe, son and successor of the Alter Rebbe (Yiddish, literally "the Older or First Rebbe"), and uncle and father-in-law of the Tzemach Tzedek.

experiences. The recorded subjective experiences of spiritual masters can be used as a heuristic to reposition how one reads and experiences nondual mystical apperception.

2.4 The First Degree of Devekut: Exteriorized Fervor

The first degree of *devekut,* conveyed as a complete divestment from corporeal embodiment, is found in the spiritual persona of the Ba'al Shem Tov or the Besht.[166] In the reported throes of his unitive experience of *devekut,* the Besht embodies what he describes as an *aliyat ha-neshamah,* that is, a complete ascension of the soul, no longer contained within or connected to the limitations of the body. Rather, all that remains of this soul in the peak of its ascent into unitive experience with divine consciousness is a *reshimu* or trace still concatenating within embodiment. By prefacing his ascent with a prayer to mend what remains in the lower realm, the Besht simultaneously straddles two states.[167] The higher one ascends into this *aliyat ha-neshamah,* the more present and aware one becomes of the lower world in ascent, without entirely abandoning it. The soul at this highest and most present moment, for R. Yitzhaq Maier Morgenstern, is considered to be both on the cusp of death while being also "intertwined in the web of life."[168] This is a degree of immersion within unitive consciousness whereby embodiment can no longer inhibit or veil this true "communion and interpenetration."[169] So intense is this interpenetration that even if one's limbs were removed it would not impede the flow of light.[170]

---

166. Morgenstern, *Yam ha-ḥokhmah* (5768/2008), 608a. See also Hayyim Vital, *Sha'ar ha-Yehudim* (Lemberg: n.p., 1865), chap. 4, fol. 4a, which was a very influential text in early Hasidism, although there appear to have been various psycho-physical contexts in the Besht's experiences of *devekut.* Special thanks to Menahem Kallus for bringing this text to my attention.

167. Compare with Morgenstern, *Yam ha-ḥokhmah* (5768/2008), 610b, where Reb Nahman's articulation builds on the Besht: "Only when the two are one, above and below, can there be a whole world." See *Liqqutai MoHaRaN,* 1:68.

168. Morgenstern, *Yam ha-ḥokhmah* (5768/2008), 608b: צרורה בצרור החיים

169. Ibid., 608b: הדביקות והתכללות הזאת האמיתית. For more on this translation of *hitkalelut* as the "interpenetration" of two elements involved in a process by which there emerges a different entity, see Idel, "Universalization and Integration," 33-50, esp. 42-43.

170. Morgenstern, *Yam ha-ḥokhmah* (5768/2008), 608b.

2.5 The Second Degree of Devekut: Interiorized Stillness

The next degree, by contrast, is a *devekut* encapsulated in the spiritual typology of the Mittler Rebbe, either through exteriorized fervor or interiorized stillness.[171] When the Mittler Rebbe and his father, the Ba'al ha-Tanya (1745–1812)[172] were together at a wedding with the Berditchever Rebbe, the Mittler's interiorized stillness stood in relief from the Berditchever's exteriorized fervor. Only once the heart—the seat of rapture—was under complete control, could the Mittler then pray with such deeply interiorized stillness.[173] It is in this very "interpenetration of cognition into the heart" where one discovers the true meaning of the sphere of Wisdom [*Koaّh Maّh*].[174] R. Morgenstern is suggesting that these degrees of *devekut* are a necessary part of a nondual oscillation process, whereby an energetic renewal takes place. That lens returns in the interplay between <u>Hokhmah</u> and *Binah*: the former as the arc of ascent, where the natural mind apprehends divinity in every experience and the pleasure of excitation caused by recurrence;[175] and the latter as the arc of descent, where the natural mind discerns the expansiveness of humanity returning to nest in the divine womb.

2.6 The Third Degree of Devekut: Enrapturing Ascent

In that infinitesimal moment prior to the interpenetration of ascent and descent, <u>Hokhmah</u> catalyzes holiness, while *Binah* catalyzes purification. Both filters are necessary for a deepening of unitive consciousness that is at once above and below. What is striking, however, is how central a role is played by cognition in reaching that ultimate point of control over the interiority of the heart; only then is "integral holiness" possible.[176] Through such a union, whereby the projected light is integrated into its source, when the *knower* and *known* are unified, then any framing of reality

---

171. Ibid., 611a-b.
172. R. Schneur Zalman of Lyadi (1745-1812), founder and first rebbe of the Habad branch of hasidism, known also as the Alter Rebbe, the Rav, and as Ba'al ha-Tanya.
173. Morgenstern, *Yam ha-ḥokhmah* (5768/2008), 611a-612a.
174. Ibid., 12a-b: אז המוח שֶׁל יט על פנימיות הלב... חכמה = דמי שזוכה לגילוי עצמות כח מ"ה
175. Ibid., 623b.
176. Ibid., 623a-b: עיקר שֶׁל ימות הקדושה

necessarily changes[177]—something Scholem could not countenance with his suspicions about *devekut*.[178]

So the journey through these degrees of *devekut* allows the mystic to recalibrate an equanimity between the agency of holiness (*Hokhmah*) and the agency of purification (*Binah*).[179] Without such ongoing recalibration of the degrees of *devekut*, unitive consciousness is shallow and short-lived. In mapping out these three degrees of *devekut*—exteriorized fervor, interiorized stillness, and enrapturing ascent—R. Yitzhaq Maier Morgenstern articulates a more nuanced line of transition as a shimmering between the manifest and the non-manifest, between cognition and emotions, between mind and heart.[180] Only when such an oscillation is truly porous can the deeper ascent into *devekut* take place.

That truth is encapsulated in the trope of "shimmerings"[181] introduced by R. Morgenstern above. Within the intellectual-historical arc of kabbalistic ideas, *sahsahot* would be rendered as the myriad-upon-myriad levels above the deepest level of unitive consciousness that begin the World of Emanation (*Aztilut*). This primordial process of shimmerings—at once reachable yet *beyond reach*—commonly refers to a universe of flashings, splendors, or sparklings.[182] The further one reaches by stretching to the limit of consciousness to touch God, the more that desire is aroused to deepen the touch, even if it remains beyond touch as ~~touching~~.

---

177. Ibid., 623a-b.
178. See Scholem aboven 1.
179. Morgenstern, *Yam ha-hokhmah* (5768/2008), 625b.
180. Ibid., 630a-b.
181. *Sahsahot* [צחצחות].
182. For example, see Zohar I: 113b-114a, I:141a, I:224b, II:97a, II:142b, II:210b, and compare with Matt's translation of *sahsahot* as "radiances" (from the root *shh*, "to gleam"). Matt builds his understanding from the literal meaning of *sahsahot* as "parched regions" or "thirst"; Daniel C. Matt, *Zohar Pritzker Edition*, vol. 3 (California: Stanford University Press, 2006), 349n256, 352n268. Kaplan's translation is less helpful in rendering *sahsahot* as "Universe of Splendors"; see Aryeh Kaplan, *Innerspace: Introduction to Kabbalah, Meditation, and Prophecy*, ed. A. Sutton (Jerusalem: Moznaim Publications, 1991), 111. Compare with Cordovero, *Pardes Rimonim*, 5:4, 8:1, 11:4, 11:7, 23:18, where every soul has its own sparkling desire, and thus all souls that come forth from *Binah* have a great sparkling quality, each according to their capacity. See R. Nahman of Bratzlav, *Liqqutai MoHaRaN*, no. 24:8: "For these lights are the *sahsahot*, they are higher than the *sefirot*. Fortunate is one who is worthy of having his mind race to grasp these insights—even though it is not within the power of the intellect to attain them, for they do not make themselves attainable or known." Compare with R. Natan of Nemirov, *Liqqutai halakhot, Hilchot Rosh hodesh* 6:7; *Hilchot Kibud av va-em*, 2:16.

These illumined shimmerings are the thinnest of lines dancing between the manifest and the non-manifest, necessary at every moment of awakened existence, despite being reachable *yet not quite reachable*.[183] Such awakening takes place when a deepening interpenetration occurs between self-immersion into one's devotional identity and experience of deep delight.[184] Notice how mystical apperception, privileged by the divergent neo-Lurianic strains in the contemporary Hasidism of R. Morgenstern, can be correlated, thereby unveiling deeper degrees of *devekut*. The aspirant deepens that delight, which animates worlds of consciousness by further immersing itself into a state of unknowing. By rejoicing in this epistemological limit as to what remains tangible, the constitution of human consciousness, as well as the possibility of enrapturing ascent, then both become unified.[185] In other words, at the deepest point of *devekut*, there is no longer a difference between cognition and emotion.

Of great interest to the perceptions and cognitions of contemporary mysticism is R. Yitzhaq Maier Morgenstern's reading of *saḥsaḥot,* and how every action is intimately linked with consciousness through this deepening desire for touching God. What that crowning moment of insight or delight (*Keter*) allows for is an interplay between touching and t̶o̶u̶c̶h̶i̶n̶g̶. For without the restraint of that crowning moment (*Keter*), cognition would ascend to its source in the Light of the Infinite One and never descend back into the world of language and ideas. This interplay of racing and restraining, of manifest and non-manifest, is necessary for the vitality of such *jouissance* that is nourished through this divine-human matrix of consciousness. It is from this very interplay of the epistemological and the emotional that one takes hold of this shimmering transition between mystical experiences recorded in diverse literary cultures of devotionality. Articulating mystical apperception as such an interplay means that when a mystic or poet seeks out and records their unique degrees of *devekut*, those degrees may once again be experienced and reached. This is how the experience of reading and writing can be "mystagogic" with a capacity of transforming spiritual states through the nuance of such interpenetrating shimmerings.

---

183. Morgenstern, *Yam ha-ḥokhmah* (5768/2008), 639b.
184. Ibid., 634a–b: מסירת נפש ותענוג
185. Ibid., 631a–b.

2.7 Conclusion: Devekut as the Shimmering of Mystical Cultures

In light of this reflection on the degrees of *devekut,* the question remains: Why must a deeper yearning for union looming in language always accentuate the dualism separating the soul from its source? Such reticence and embarrassment about nondual mystical union stems from the fear of loss. There is fear over the loss of selfhood in relation to the *other,* lest it lead to an abandonment of the ethical, but only if that self was disconnected *a priori* from an ethical foundation. There is fear over the loss of dignity, lest it is replaced by deformity within the form of the union itself. Yet, when that infinitesimal distance separating dualistic conscience from its nondual origin is upheld, it reveals more about a given subjectivity than the possibility of the given experience.[186] When dualistic categories like dignity/deformity or sacred/secular rule the conscious mind, these categories impact upon the possibility of entering into the nondual experience of *devekut* in its various degrees. Seeing someone else or their experience as deformed, ugly, strange, or profane really mirrors one's own lack and rupture from nondual consciousness.[187] Such a rupture exemplifies *devekut* as a *first tier* shimmering of cultures.

While the freedom of the divine aspect of culture transcends all knowledge and experience, the yearning within humanity for the moral aspect of culture allows for the emergence of an autonomous vision.[188] That vision, now emerging with contemporary Hasidic nondual mystics like R. Yitzhaq Maier Morgenstern is not, however, necessarily a function of the moral aspect of culture alone. Rather, R. Yitzhaq Maier Morgenstern appears to be part of what Garb sees as the "growth of a group of new *'Admorim* (Hasidic rabbis) who are not related to the

---

186. For more on such dualism, see Marjorie O'Rourke Boyle, *Senses of Touch: Human Dignity and Deformity* (Leiden: Brill, 1998).

187. See *Toldot Ya'akov Yosef, ḥayye Sarah,* trans. Jonathan Slater (New York: Ateres Publishing, 2001), 212a:

> Even when you see something ugly or unbecoming in another person, you should turn your heart to thinking that the Holy One dwells there, too, since there is no place devoid of Him.

> For a more sustained reflection on the challenges intrinsic to the dualism of beauty/ugly, see Harry Fox, "Poethics: How Every Poet is a Jew," *Contemporary Hebrew Mystical Poetry,* i-xxxiv.

188. Returning to the fourfold Kookian model of culture; see n. 47 above.

particular Hasidic courts and whose influence derives from an exceptional mystical charisma."[189] When we consider the case of R. Yitzhaq Maier Morgernstern,[190] it is important to realize how that lineage has in no way predetermined the trajectory of his mystical teachings. On the contrary, R. Yitzhaq Maier Morgenstern exemplifies a transversal self-understanding in transcending and including Bratzlaver, Lubavitcher, and Gurer Hasidisms, only to continue evolving his own unique nondual language and practice of *devekut*. That regeneration of language through diverse mystical experiences has been possible precisely because of the narrow social boundaries so typical of the *haredi* world is unprecedented in Jewish history. Israel's growing trans-*haredi* cultures shift the playing field: devotional expression of nondual mystical apperception dissolves the separation of dualisms. At the same time, those social boundaries limiting the perfection of the national aspect of culture not only adapt and appropriate elements from the preceding three cultural realms,[191] but the shimmering *to and fro* between devotional cultures allows a further involution to take place. Such a shimmering of culture that typifies the regeneration of language and experience of *devekut* in R. Yitzhaq Maier Morgenstern is no longer limited to or by one specific devotional culture, rather, its contemporary manifestation is a true hybrid.

So, through whichever doorway one enters the nondual mystical apperception of *devekut*, what our preliminary remarks here point to is a deeper symbiosis of a nuanced reality in mapping out these three spirally interrelated constellations of *devekut*:

(1) exteriorized fervor through the vitality of *Binah;*
(2) interiorized stillness through the calm of *Hokhmah;*
(3) enrapturing ascent in the oscillating integration of *Keter.*[192]

Mystic and poet, as well as literary critic and scholar of Jewish mysticism, are all to some degree yearning for the articulation of a more nuanced line of

---

189. Mark, review of Garb, *The Chosen Will Become Herds,* 97.
190. Ibid., esp. 97-99.
191. Kook, "Fragments of Light," 309.
192. Morgenstern, *Yam ha-hokhmah* (5767/2007), 572a-b.

transition shimmering between the manifest and the non-manifest, between cognition and emotion, between mind and heart.[193] This is a hybrid level of *devekut* as a shimmering culture evolving and expanding itself.

Thus, while the insufficiency of mapping out *devekut* as merely socio-psychological communion (after Scholem and Geertz) is being somewhat redressed, the metaphysical texture of union is only recently finding its voice. That process has begun in earnest with Wolfson's "thick description" of the radical nondual meontological Jewish mysticism of the late Lubavitcher Rebbe, based in the Diaspora of Crown Heights notwithstanding its devotional implications reaching the entire globe, of course, includes Israel.

In the case of nondual mystical apperception in Israel, such a contemporary context of decentralized, fragmented Hebrew cultures in the wake of Orientalism requires an interpretive shift, away from dualistic thinking towards a hybridized shimmering of genres and experiences. It is precisely this "new era of plural *haredi* worlds" that allows for a deeper degree of fluidity within devotional micro-identities of Hasidism. What sets R. Yitzhaq Maier Morgenstern apart, however, is the degree to which his thinking and practice embrace this religious pluralism to construct and envision an authentic nondual mystical apperception within the hegemony of exoteric rabbinic culture in Israel. Such mystical apperception transcends and includes a swath of seemingly opposing tributaries within the devotional life—from Beshtian, Lubavitcher, Bratzlaver, and Gurer Hasidisms of Ashkenazi religious culture to the Lurianic Kabbalah of RaSHa"SH within the Sephardic cultural framework. This phenomenon in early twenty-first century Jerusalemite mysticism is surely facilitated by "an eclectic attitude among some contemporary Israeli kabbalists, who combine the *kavvanot* of the RaSHa"SH with the tradition of the Vilna Gaon and the Hasidic movement."[194] Such an innovation of hybridized mystical self would be less likely to take place without such a deep shimmering of cultures in Israel.

I have argued how the very form of mystical apperception known as *devekut* is undergoing transformation and involution in terms of its

---

193. Morgenstern, *Yam ha-ḥokhmah* (5768/2008), 630a-b.
194. Meir, "The Imagined Decline of Kabbalah," 207.

cognition and perception through a symbiosis of practical experience and its written word. There is a shimmering of mystical cultures taking place in Israel, ironically being catalyzed with great effect by R. Yitzhaq Maier Morgenstern, a Diaspora *émigré*.[195] As nondual mystical apperception shimmers between the cognitive and emotive realms, between theory and praxis, the subjectivity of reader, writer, and aspirant also undergoes transformation. Only when these degrees of *devekut* are seen and experienced as truly porous, symbiotic, and engendering a hybrid identity can a return to the vertigo of ~~touching~~ take place.

[195.] It could be argued by this logic that R. Yitzhak Ginsburg, also an American émigré, achieved similar mystical apperception through his thinking, writing, and activism in Israel. Given Ginsburg's proclivity to elide the mystical and the political, however, any innovations he realized were more damaging than insightful and thus caught in a deeply dualistic view of *self* separated from *other* that became his reality. See Aran, "Mysticism and Suicide Bombing," 390-392.

CHAPTER II

WHY CONTEMPORARY JEWISH MYSTICISM NEEDS POETRY:
FROM ADMIEL KOSMAN'S "OUR GOD"
TO AVRAHAM BEN YITZHAK'S
INTEGREL DIVINITY "OF ALL WORLDS"

וְהֵן לְכָל הָעוֹלָמִים אַתָּה נָתוּן.–.–

...וּמְצָאוּךְ הַדְּבָרִים הָרְחוֹקִים וְהַקְּרוֹבִים–

וְדָרְשׁוּ נַפְשֶׁךָ.

And you're given to all worlds.
... as things both distant and near find you,
And call for your soul.[1]

Poetry reveals "interbeing"[2]—an interconnectivity of all sentient beings. But can this truth of poetry still be heard? Is it still possible for the concretion of the spiritual that takes place through poetry to be heeded? If the soul is to evolve through *involution*, then contemporary Jewish Mysticism needs poetry. The hybridity of non-dual mystical apperception previously discussed, affects the degrees of *devekut* experienced. These degrees bring into relief the texture of the journey that remains grounded in subjectivity while transforming it. To address this evolutionary challenge, I will extrapolate a theoretical-critical framework from thinker Jean Gebser (1905-1973) to suggest what an involution of god-consciousness crucial for contemporary non-dual Jewish Mysticism might look like.

Mystical Vertigo necessarily builds upon the opening foray into the non-dual Jewish mystical apperception in the trans-*haredi* culture of R. Yitzhaq

---

[1] Avraham ben Yitzhak, "Psalm," *Collected Poems*, trans. Peter Cole (Jerusalem: Ibis Editions, 2003), 36/37.

[2] By "interbeing" I mean the interconnectivity of all souls, or *tzror ha'hayyim*, see R. Tzaddok haCohen Rabinowitz of Lublin, *Peri Tzaddik*, vol. 1, *Parshat VaYeshev*, no. 6, s.v. *bamidrash bercho b'or panav shel adam* (Lublin: n.p., 1934), 128a.

Maier Morgenstern, by now shifting the contours of the journey to another form of mystical record—poetry. Since it is poetry that provides a real concretion of the spiritual, the ensuing chapters will each include brief analyses of a few discrete Hebrew poems. In shifting from nondual Jewish mystical apperception in the hybridity of trans-*haredi* culture towards the hybridity in mystical Hebrew poetry, my intention is to trace the contours of contemporary Jewish mysticism being revealed in Israel. Hebrew poetry, as I have argued elsewhere,[3] has the potential to redeem Jewish Thinking—without an appreciation of the prophetic impulse hovering within strong Hebrew poetry, Jewish Thinking remains bereft of its visionary capacities. In this chapter, we will focus on the analysis of two discrete Hebrew poems, one by Admiel Kosman (b. 1957) and the other by Avraham ben Yitzhak (1883-1950). These poems bring into relief the texture of that integral step towards the involution of consciousness, redressing the non-dual experience of God through names.

The poetry being discovered now, especially in Israel, is being written from within the vast decline in civilization beginning in the first decade of the twentieth century, which includes but is not limited to the *Shoah*.[4] It is precisely from this sense of decline that Gebser foresees a crisis in need of redressing as restructuration.[5] Consciousness structures are a universal way to observe and overcome the inner divisions of the very rational mind that has caused much of this century's decline. These fivefold "turnings of consciousness" [*Bewusterdungs Prozess*] throughout the various ages and civilizations,[6] reveal how human perception is evolving in its spiritual potential, each structural stage including and transcending what preceded it. In the "turnings" themselves, called *wandlung*, certain qualities, expressions and articulations emerge that are intrinsic to each structural stage of perception.

The question that then emerges in the nexus of mysticism and poetry is: how does one navigate that shift from God as allegory and method to

---

3. Aubrey L. Glazer, *Contemporary Hebrew Mystical Poetry: How It Redeems Jewish Thinking* (New York: Edwin Mellen Press, 2009).

4. Jean Keckeis, "*In memoriam Jean Gebser*," *The Ever-Present Origin* (Athens: Ohio University Press 1985), xx.

5. Keckeis, "*In memoriam Jean Gebser*," xix.

6. Ibid., xx.

God as a Diaphanous Divinity? Amidst contemporary rational habits of discursive thought, any concretion of divinity that is more transparent and multivalent remains a challenge for an evolution of structure and quality.[7] Each of these structures and qualities is related to a divine name[8] as evinced in this mapping of the evolution of consciousness:

STRUCTURE:	QUALITY:	NAME:
1. Archaic	Dominance	*EL Shaddai/Elyon*[9]
2. Magical	Authority	*YHVH*[10]

[7.] For example, rather than posit three different sources resulting from three divergent concepts of God (J, E, P), it is more accurate to see three kinds of theophanies (i.e. corporeal revelation/J; dreams and night visions/E; verbal revelation/P) which are not necessarily mutually exclusive, see Umberto Cassuto, *The Documentary Hypothesis: Eight Lectures*, trans. I. Abrahams (Jerusalem: The Magnes Press, Hebrew University, 1961), 57-59. This sensitivity to the diverse perspectives of the One is especially needed when reading the ensuing fivefold mapping.

[8.] The range of divine names prevalent in Ancient Israel, including those names naturalized from the Phoenician pantheon is beyond the scope of the present investigation. While the "diversity among Israelites regarding the number of deities in various pantheons..." has been duly noted, Zevit, suggests that "[m]etaphorically, [the Israelites] appear to have worked from a small menu rather than a smorgasbord. Contemporary scholarship, however, is unable to determine the principles underlying the selection or how those selected constituted a logical diet at any given time or place," see Ziony Zevit, "The Names of Israelite Gods," *The Religions of Ancient Israel: A Synthesis of Parallactic Approaches* (New York : Continuum, 2001), 609n99.

[9.] Regarding the antiquity of *El Elyon* as ranging between eighth to sixth century B.C.E. as corroborated by extra-biblical sources, see Nahum Sarna, Excursus 7: *El Elyon*, Genesis 14:18-20, 22, *The JPS Commentary to Genesis* (Philadelphia: JPS, 1989), 381. Sarna suggests that given the fossilized nature and usage of *El Elyon,* it came to be replaced by *YHVH Elyon.* The antiquity of *El Elyon* parallels that of *El Shaddai,* which according to extra-biblical references thus dates the usage of *Shaddai* as pre-Mosaic *circa* fourteenth century B.C.E. The name *El Shaddai* is found mostly in biblical poetry, see ibid., Excursus 11: '*El Shaddai,* Genesis 17:1, 384-385.

[10.] Placement of the name *YHVH* before *Elohim* is influenced by Wright's hypothesis that *YHVH*-worshipping people from the South eventually merged with *El*-worshipping people to the North in Ancient Israel, to create a unified alliance. This is borne out by historical evidence like the Merenptah Stele attesting to the Egyptian's extermination of the Israelites (their "seed is not"). This gives rise to a likely alliance between the Israelites and the people of Shasu, a nomadic tribe with historic antagonism against the Egyptians ("*Yhw* [in] the land of the Shasu"). Wright argues that sharing the common enemy of the Egyptians is what leads to the merger of peoples, evolving into their "crafting of a shared narrative of divine deliverance from Egyptian torment," see Robert Wright, *The Evolution of God* (New York: Little, Brown & Co, 2009), 114-115. Regarding the name

STRUCTURE:	QUALITY:	NAME:
3. Mythical	Justice	*Elohim*[11]
4. Mental	Representation	*Eloheinu*
5. Integral[12]	Participation[13]	*EL*[14]

Despite the challenge in absorbing the shifts of perspective intrinsic to such transitional moments, seeking out the divine through its naming continues to take place through poetry.

YHVH, Cassuto argues that "...*YHVH* is a proper noun, the specific name of Israel's god, the God whom the Israelites acknowledged as the Sovereign of the universe and as the Divinity who chose them as His people..." The innovation of the Biblical literature is in its identifying the specific God of Israel as the universal god of the entire earth. Midrashic and talmudic literature is noticeably lacking in any usage of *El, Elohah* and *Elohim*, as the rabbis preferred replacing it solely with national form of the faith through *YHVH*. The main difference at stake here is between a personal, direct, immanent relationship (*YHVH*) as opposed to a metaphysical, transcendental relationship (*Elohim*). See Cassuto, *The Documentary Hypothesis*, 18-19, 25, 28, 30, 31. Compare with Jeffrey Tigay, Excursus 4: "The Lord," *The JPS Commentary to Deuteronomy* (Philadelphia: JPS, 1989), 431-432. Dating for the usage of *YHVH* composed in the southern kingdom of Judah falls between 922-722 B.C.E., see Richard Elliott Friedman, *The Bible With Sources Revealed: A New View Into the Five Books of Moses* (New York: HarperCollins, 2003), 3. Friedman emphasizes "that different sources have a different idea of when the name YHVH was first revealed to humans. According to J, the name was known since the earliest generations of humans... But in E and P it is stated just as explicitly that YHVH does not reveal this name until the generation of Moses." Moreover, "[t]he E and P sources identify God as El or simply as 'God' (Hebrew *Elohim*) until the name is revealed to Moses. After that they use the name YHVH as well." Ibid., 10. Building on this line of thinking, there is a necessary evolutionary stage at which each name can be fully revealed and perceived by humanity.

11. Regarding the name *Elohim*, Cassuto argues that in many instances: "... *Elohim* was originally a common noun, an appellative, that was applied to both the One God of Israel and to the heathen gods..." In other instances, the precedence given to *Elohim* over *YHVH* is "... indicative of progress and a higher religious outlook." See Cassuto, *The Documentary Hypothesis*, 18, 26. Dating for the usage of *Elohim* composed in the northern kingdom of Judah falls between 922-722 B.C.E.; see Friedman, *The Bible With Sources Revealed*, 4.

12. Jean Gebser, *The Ever-Present Origin* (Athens: Ohio University Press, 1985), see Synoptic Tables, 617-621.

13. The recasting of this column for *Quality* can be found in William Irwin Thomson, *Coming into Being: Artifacts and Texts in the Evolution of Consciousness* (New York: St. Martin's Press, 1996), 14.

14. Cassuto argues that the usage of EL often follows "... the non-specific *El* of the Gentile Sages and their One God, and following the literary practice of the wise men of other nations, they, too, frequently employed the generic terms *El, Eloha, Elohim*, preferring them to the national Name, *YHVH*." See Cassuto, *The Documentary Hypothesis*, 24.

* * *

Poetry is uniquely positioned within all other forms of writing to make space for touching God. This partially because poetry is "aperspectival." Poetry expresses an evolution in god-consciousness through "the emerging consciousness of time as an immeasurable and mentally inconceivable world constituent."[15] The poet's "concern is not primarily with the merely ponderable (or mental), nor with conceptualizing the non-mental (or mythical) but rather with the perceiving and imparting 'in truth' of the 'perpetual plentitude,' the whole or integrity which is permeated by the spiritual energy of origin that is only obscured by the image-world of the psyche and restricted by thinking." [16] If "there is no longer heaven or hell, this world or the other, ego or world, immanence or transcendence,"[17] then one of the main tasks of contemporary Jewish Mysticism is to awaken the soul to its integral origin as a perceptible whole beyond dualism. In turning to the intricate implications within the Hebrew poetry at hand, a transparency of the "praeligio(n)" reveals the spirit into perception.[18]

* * *

Such yearning for the evolution of god-consciousness marks the journey of a poet like Admiel Kosman, born in 1957, hailing from Haifa. Initially exposed to religion in the *yeshiva* world, then the world of the spirit through aesthetics at *Bezalel Academy of Art* in Jerusalem, finally Kosman served in the Israeli Defense Force, which partially explains why his poetry is supple enough to explore the tension between religious forms and the spiritual journey. At the heart of the convergence between religion and spirituality, Kosman zeroes in on the petitionary prayer particle known as "Our God" [*Eloheinu*]:

---

15. Gebser, *The Ever-Present Origin*, 528.
16. Ibid., 320.
17. Ibid., 543.
18. Ibid., 529, 543.

"אֱלֹהֵינוּ"

הֶעָרַת הַמְבָאֵר בִּכְתָב יָד עַתִּיק שֶׁל סִדּוּר נֻסַח אַשְׁכְּנַז

אֱלֹהֵי הָאֲפִיסָה שֶׁל הַדְּבָרִים,
אֱלֹהֵי הַשּׁוּם דָּבָר וֶאֱלֹהֵי הַכְּלוּם,
וֶאֱלֹהֵי הָאַיִן, אֱלֹהֵי הַגּוּרְנִישְׁט, אֱלֹהֵי
הַזְּבַּנְג, וְהַפִצּוּץ הַקָּר, וֶאֱלֹהֵי הַבּוּם.

וֶאֱלֹהִים גָּדוֹל, שֶׁלֹּא יָדַע לְאַיֵּת
אֶת הָעוֹלָם, וֶאֱלֹהִים הַבַּעַר,
אֱלֹהִים הַבּוּר, אֱלֹהִים אַנַאלְפָבֵּית,
אֱלֹהִים הַפָּיְיפֶן, וְהַגּוּרְנִישְׁט, שׁוּם דָּבָר,
זֶה אֱלֹהִים גָּמוּר.

אַךְ דַּע כִּי רַק הוּא;
רַק הוּא "אֱלֹהֵינוּ" -
הַנִּזְכָּר וְהָאָמוּר.[19]

Our God
An explanatory note on a manuscript of an Ashkenazi Prayerbook

God of the zero sum of things,
god of nothing at all and god of nothing,
& god of No-thing, god of the *gurnesht*, god
of the slam-bang, & the ruthless explosion, & god of the boom.
& great god, who doesn't know to spell
out the world, & the stupid god,
ignoramus god, illiterate god,
god that's broken, & the *gurnesht,* No-thing,
this is god absolute.

But know, there is only One;

Only this One is "our God"—
The One referred to & the One spoken of.

---

19. Admiel Kosman, "Our God" [Hebrew], *Proscribed Prayers: Seventy One New Poems* (Tel Aviv: *HaKibbutz Hameuchad,* 2007), 119.

Apparently concealed within the marginalia of a prayer book, Kosman uncovers his demand for an evolution of god-consciousness. Inside the poem itself, meanwhile, the poet unveils a real theological quandary. The poem struggles in shifting from the tribal vision of "Our God" into allegory and method, then to a more Diaphanous Divinity. Shifting from God as an Unmoved Mover to a Most Moved Mover, from the slang of the I.D.F. to Israel's mean streets is what allows for an expansion from *Eloheinu* to Integr*EL* Divinity.[20] The greatest leap in the evolution of god-consciousness happens from the Mental to the Integral level, from perceiving God as volitional to realizing the integral truth of divinity as *EL*. Although Kosman's poem has yet to complete the full integral turn, such a turning towards non-dual consciousness is possible when there is no longer any binary distinction between the "god that's broken, & the *gurnesht*, No-thing," and the absolute infinite.

* * *

There is an evolution of god-consciousness, however, permeating the prophetic, pre-World War I poetry of Avraham Sonne (1883-1950). Born in the Galician city of Przemysl, this poet transforms himself and his name into Avraham ben Yitzhak upon emigrating to Israel in 1938 just as the Nazis storm Vienna. Avraham ben Yitzhak's eleven poems precede his withdrawal into silence from writing altogether. A poetry that is at once prophetic and highly modern,[21] the watch-hands of Avraham ben Yitzhak's poetry showed not only the specific Jewish time, but the hour for world literature[22] as it could open to a concretion of the spiritual:

לֵילוֹת כִּי יַלְבִּינוּ

בְּאֵלֶּה לֵילֵי הַחֲלוֹם הַלְּבָנִים
שֶׁיָּחֲלַם עוֹלָם עָיֵף,
יָדֹם יַקְשִׁיב הַזְּמַן אֶל דָּפְקוֹ,
בְּהַרְנִין מַעְיָנוֹת

---

20. Gebser, *The Ever-Present Origin*, xxix.

21. H. N. Bialik, *Letters of Haim Nahman Bialik* [Hebrew], vol. II, 1906-1923, ed. P. Lachover (Tel Aviv: n.p., 1938), 190.

22. Leah Goldberg, *Encounter with a Poet,* [Hebrew] (Tel Aviv: Sifriat Poalim, 1988), 57.

רַנַּת עַצְמוּתָם.
וְעָבָר וְעָתִיד יַשְׁתַּלְּמוּ
שְׁלָוַת נְצָחִים בַּהוֹוָה—
בִּדְמִיַת חַיֶּיךְ
יִשְׁקְטוּ כוֹכָבִים,

וְרוּחַ מִנְּצָחִים תְּפַכֶּה—

—עֵינֶיךְ תִּרְחַבְנָה—

When Nights Grow White

In these white nights of the dream
dreamed by a dreary world,
time grows still and listens
for its pulse in the fountains,
singing their song of self.

Past and future come to terms,
the present holds the calm of eternity—
quiet stars
in your life's stillness,
and a spirit from eternity blows—
as your eyes grow wide.

To shift from seeing the world asleep to taking it all in utterly awakened, from a passive to an aroused aperspectival temporality, from *Eloheinu* to Integr*EL* Divinity, is nothing short of wondrous that it is accomplished in two stanzas by Avraham ben Yitzhak. Such unitive moments reveal a new self intertwined in a process of whitening the soul, searching for greater transparency. Intertwined with the echo of the prophetic call to understanding[23] is the poet's vision of the night that grows white, of darkness transforming into light. In opening to the depth of time, where "the present holds the calm of eternity," a deepening awareness of the stillness births a new aspect of self.

This revelation of a new layer of self, neither egotistic nor egoless, reaches a level of transparency of ego-freedom. It is a luminous moment

---

23. After the verse: "Though your sins are like crimson, they can turn white like snow..." (Isaiah 1:18).

where "your eyes grow wide" so there is then a newfound capacity to envision more expansively. This "transparency of space and time as well as of light, of matter and of soul" is what Gebser refers to as a diaphaneity.[24] The next structural stage in the evolution of consciousness—moving from Mental to Integral—is the dissolution of the dialectic between "ego or world, immanence or transcendence."[25] It is in such deep transparency—diaphaneity—that a new "spirit from eternity blows," now perceiving the soul awakening to its integral origin in the whole.

* * *

In traversing structural stages in the evolution of consciousness from *Eloheinu* to Integr*EL* Divinity, the degree to which each wave is a critical part of all subsequent waves becomes clearer. But none of these aforementioned "first-tier" turnings (i.e. Archaic; Magical; Mythical; Mental) fully appreciate the existence of other turnings beyond their own level, always instead falling into the trap of perceiving its worldview as the best perspective. This is what impedes so many subjects from evolving beyond the Mental level. Getting beyond a lashing out against other waves is possible through "second-tier thinking"—namely, an integral consciousness attuned to the interior stages of development. Poetry is one of the greatest modes of attunement to this interiority.

For such attunement to be possible, a reshaping of perception must take place. Reshaping time consciousness happens by stepping back and seeing the whole, shifting from the "every day" to the "all (i.e. universal) day,"[26] from the weekday to a redemptive day that is "all-Sabbath."[27] Precisely this aperspectival approach to time consciousness evolves beyond obsessing over any one level. Rather Integr*EL* Divinity means a certain consciousness is ready "to be given to all worlds,"[28] that is, to the overall spiral of existence.

---

24. Gebser, *The Ever-Present Origin*, 542.

25. Ibid., 543.

26. Ibid., 533.

27. For example, see R. Tzaddok haCohen Rabinowitz of Lublin, *Sefer Peri Tzaddik*, vol. 5, *VaYelekh-Shabbat Shuvah*, no. 2, s.v. *'Od b'midrash Tanhuma* (Lublin: n.p. 1934), 189a.

28. Avraham ben Yitzhak, "Psalm," *Collected Poems*, trans. Peter Cole (Jerusalem: Ibis Editions, 2003), 36/37.

A contemporary Jewish Mysticism of Integr*EL* Divinity seeks out contexts to embrace, include, and integrate separate systems into holistic spirals. From relativism to holism, from pluralism to integralism, from *Eloheinu* to Integr*EL* Divinity, "...as things both distant and near find you,/and call for your soul"[29] so does the evolution of spiritual consciousness become possible. Poetry is one such lost link of attunement, making possible the concretion of the spiritual, opening each soul to once again touch God within mystical vertigo.

---

29. Ben Yitzhak, "Psalm," 36/37.

CHAPTER III

DISSEMINATION OF *DEVEKUT*: HOW CULTURE CAN CONNECT DEEPER
AGI MISHOL'S "WOMAN MARTYR" AND "TRANSISTOR *MUEZZIN*"

How deeply can both citizen and stranger connect through culture? How deep of a connection between intersecting cultures, both global and local, is even possible? Can this depth of connection bring salvation, or does it merely perpetuate the strange cultural survival of the fragmented people that composes a nation? Recently, philosophical and political responsibility has called into question what we mean by "minority" and "ethnicity" within the construct of the nation. This responsibility, as cultural theorist, Homi K. Bhabha sees it, for conceiving of "minoritization and globalization" as being quasi-colonial, calls for a thinking beyond boundaries. Post-colonial theorists like Bhabha question whether there is a location of culture beyond typical dialectical polarizations of the local and the global, the center and the periphery, or indeed, the citizen and the stranger? Through a process he calls *DissemiNation* of meaning, time, peoples, cultural boundaries and historical traditions, Bhabha is suggesting that it is possible for the radical alterity of a national culture to create new forms of living and writing.[1] In what follows, I will reconsider how the deeper connectivity of *devekut* to these new forms of living and writing Hebrew culture through the lens of *DissemiNation* of Israel is possible through its poetry.

To begin this process of reconsidering how contemporary Hebrew culture thinks through its own constructions of identity, we return to one of the earliest plays on "minoritization" of ethnicity within the canon of scripture, known as *The Song of Songs*. Amidst the imperialism of the Roman rule of Palestine, those Jewish readers of the Song flourished "by

---

[1]   Homi K. Bhabha, "DissemiNation: Time, narrative and the margins of the modern nation," *The Location of Culture* (London: Routledge Classics, 1994), 199-244.

fostering local particularisms while partly co-opting provincial grandees"[2] problematizing the boundaries of "minoritization" altogether. If Palestinian Jews reading the Song in the third and fourth centuries had already "become full participants in the Roman provincial system,"[3] then its literature of "minoritization" was nothing short of subversive. Already in the first chapter, the Song portrays the beloved in her own terms. She is aware how easy it is to be judged by her Cushite complexion as *other,* so she quickly beckons her lover not to turn away. Despite his initial lust for her, the lover might be tempted to turn away from this beloved because she appears as a stranger to the citizen, all the while remaining part of an integrated minority culture:

שְׁחוֹרָה אֲנִי וְנָאוָה בְּנוֹת יְרוּשָׁלָם
כְּאָהֳלֵי קֵדָר כִּירִיעוֹת שְׁלֹמֹה
אַל תִּרְאוּנִי שֶׁאֲנִי שְׁחַרְחֹרֶת
שֶׁשְּׁזָפַתְנִי הַשָּׁמֶשׁ[4]

I am dark, daughters of Jerusalem
And I am beautiful!
Dark as the tents of Kedar, lavish
as Solomon's tapestries.

Do not see me only as dark:
The sun has stared at me...

While this kind of erotic Hebrew language in contemporary poetry echoing from the *Song* is not foreign to the modern Israeli, its language still manages to evoke a kind of foreignness. This sense of foreignness comes through in the coloring of the beloved, drawing so excessively on metaphor that it reaches the radical anti-metaphor of her beauty. By overwhelming the lover with metaphors, the beloved nearly destroys through such a fantasy the very act that makes metaphor possible. This

---

[2.] On the question of whether the Ancient Jews were indeed a distinct and unique Mediterranean society, and to what degree such a community was integrated, see Seth Schwartz, *Were the Jews a Mediterranean Society? Reciprocity and Solidarity in Ancient Judaism* (Princeton: Princeton University Press, 2010), 173-175.

[3.] Schwartz, *Were the Jews a Mediterranean Society?*, 174.

[4.] *Song of Songs* 1:5-6.

desired beloved becomes an object of loss written across the body of the people. How does this happen? Focusing on this brief description of the beloved as black, she draws her identity from fragments of the nomadic experience of the Bedouins, whose tents of Kedar are woven from the wool of black goats. The synecdoche of Kedar invokes opulence while playing with what it really can mean to be dark and black.[5] Curiously, Solomon's curtains appear, once, as a *hapax* only here in the Song, making this complexion all the more precious. These veils refer to royal splendor that hide the beloved from the lover. The lover's tendency, like all citizens, to be judged by their own standards rather than seeing the hybridity of the stranger, holds a strong dialectic of center and periphery. Yet clearly the *Song* is invoking the depth into the darkness yet to be plummeted which reveals a different texture of "minoritization" of this dark, black and beautiful beloved. Just as Solomon admonishes one not to see wine as simply sparkling red, that is, focusing only on the superficial color while ignoring its intoxicating powers,[6] so the black beloved is admonishing the lover not to overlook her intoxicating power in getting distracted by the apparent foreignness of her color. This brief poetic passage stands as a remarkably daring example of how Hebrew poetry in the early scriptural canon already challenges its connections to foreignness as a mark of "minoritization."

Take the challenge one step further moving forward centuries into the complex cultural mosaic of contemporary Israel, where connecting foreignness as a mark of "minoritization" takes place in the quotidian. The ruling Hebrew culture determined the boundaries of citizenship and homeland. Despite all good intentions apparent in the necessary founding of the State of Israel and its rebirthing as a Jewish democracy, this strange hybrid of a Middle Eastern nation-state continues to come under critique. The challenge remains to balance the need for a Jewish sanctuary in the world in the aftermath of the genocide of the *Shoah* while ensuring this modern nation-state structure remains a democracy

---

5. Such opulence is echoed in Isaiah 21:16, 60:7, Jeremiah 49:28-29, Ezekiel 27:21; see *The Song of Songs: The World's First Great Love Poem*, trans. C. Bloch and A. Bloch (New York: The Modern Library, 1995), *s.v.* 'oholey qedar, 140.
6. For parallel, see Proverbs 23:31.

of all its citizens. This complexity is already evinced in Israel's Declaration of Independence, which envisions *Eretz Yisrael* as the spiritual, religious and political birthplace of Jewish identity. "Here they first attained to statehood, created cultural values of national and universal significance and gave to the world the eternal Book of Books. After being forcibly exiled from their land, the people kept faith with it throughout their Dispersion and never ceased to pray and hope for their return to it and for the restoration in it of their political freedom..."[7] So far this narrative preamble of the Declaration expresses a need to normalize the diasporic existence of Jews through the ages. In praying, hoping and seeking to normalize their spiritual, religious and political identity already formed in this same space is what perennially guides the people in their return to the Land of Israel, spawning its rebirth. Notice, however, the primary role of culture in this rebirthing. The act of creating cultural values of national and universal significance is what gives the world the eternal Book of Books. Turning back to Bhabha, we see in this narrative of the Declaration how the location of culture is both temporal and textual. What happens when an historic "minoritization" is displaced into the majority ruling culture, to the point where it now determines citizenship by color-coded markings on passports and license plates? Such a rebirth of political freedom in an ancestral homeland only addresses the past, but what about the future of those who seek to exercise the right of return? Is the transition then possible from "minoritization" to inter-cultural political existence, all the while holding fast to its ethical imperatives?

Ensuring complete equality and rights to all inhabitants irrespective of religion, race or sex is an ideal of "minoritization," but on the ground, this reality of a more inter-cultural political existence rubs up against ethical imperatives. To what degree are ethical imperatives still ethical when they severely limit the guaranteed freedom and complete equality of the Declaration? The poetics of alterity embodied by the beloved resonates in the contemporary social fabric of Israeli culture. How much does color affect the equality and rights of all inhabitants, irrespective of race or sex? This ideal of "minoritization" even faces challenges for the diverse

---

7. Maas Boertien, *Israel's Declaration of Independence* (Jewish Council in Israel for Interreligious Consultations, 1970.)

tabula of Jews who are *other* within Israel. The tension created by the first wave of North African Jews, with their Arab culture masked in dark complexions, coming into a predominantly Ashkenazic Israeli culture, only reinforces the more recent tensions that Ethiopian Jews continue to face in acculturating within the larger, elite Ashkenazic *émigré* population. The Ashkenazic hegemony over "minoritization" and their normalization through most governmental agencies, creates an identity that is at once stranger and citizen within the homeland. This identity is made more complex by the cultural masks of Europe and the Orient that brought them to this place to begin with. Taken one step further is the situation of the Israeli Arab or even the Palestinian within Israeli society. Once we explore how Hebrew poetry serves the role of *DissemiNation* of *devekut*, a more nuanced mosaic of culture that can connect more deeply to identity construction is possible.

This exploration will be limited to two contemporary poems by Israel's living poet laureate, Agi Mishol (b. 1947). Both poems to be explored, "Woman Martyr" and "The Transistor *Muezzin*" challenge assumptions about the location of culture and the responsibility for conceiving of "minoritization and globalization" as being quasi-colonial. Is this relocation of culture through these two poems then an exemplification of a "heterological tradition"?[8] Namely, do these poems manage to remain deeply suspicious about categorical closure of thought and being,[9] preferring to rediscover the *other* as authorized by the *other*, or is Mishol as poet violating this authorization through her subversive critique of the *other*? In her process of sifting through the remains and the fragments on the shelves of our mundane, collective experiences, I argue that Mishol is a Hebrew poet writing about a most provocative and challenging form of *devekut* deeply located in culture. Mishol is seeking ways to continue touching God as she moves through the mosaic that binds every woman in Israel together through her own mystical vertigo.

---

8.   Michel de Certeau, *L'Absent de l'Histoire* (Paris: Mame, 1973), 153-180.

9.   Wlad Godzich, "The Further Possibility of Knowledge," *Heterologies: Discourse on the Other*, trans. B. Massumi, Theory and History of Literature, vol. 17 (Minneapolis: University of Minnesota Press, 1986), vii-ix.

שאהידה

הָעֶרֶב מִתְעַוֵּר
וְאַתְּ רַק בַּת עֶשְׂרִים
(עֶרֶב שֶׁל שׁוּק, אלתרמן)

אַתְּ רַק בַּת עֶשְׂרִים
וְהַהֵרָיוֹן הָרִאשׁוֹן שֶׁלָּךְ הוּא פְּצָצָה.
מִתַּחַת לַשִּׂמְלָה הָרְחָבָה אַתְּ הָרָה חֹמֶר נֶפֶץ,
שְׁבָבִים שֶׁל מַתֶּכֶת, וְכָךְ אַתְּ עוֹבֶרֶת בַּשּׁוּק
מִתְקַתֶּקֶת בֵּין הָאֲנָשִׁים עַנְדְּלִיב תַּקָאטְקָה.

מִישֶׁהוּ שִׁנָּה לָךְ בָּרֹאשׁ אֶת הַהֶבְרָגָה
וְשִׁגֵּר אוֹתָךְ לָעִיר,
וְאַתְּ שֶׁבָּאת מִבֵּית לָחֶם, בָּחַרְתְּ לָךְ דַּוְקָא
מַאֲפִיָּה. שָׁם שָׁלַפְתְּ מִתּוֹכֵךְ אֶת הַנִּצְרָה
וּבְיַחַד עִם חַלּוֹת הַשַּׁבָּת
הַפֶּרֶג וְהַסּוּמְסוּמִים
הֶעֱפַתְּ אֶת עַצְמֵךְ לַשָּׁמַיִם.

בְּיַחַד עִם רִבְקָה פִּינְק עַפְתְּ,
וְיָלָנָה קוֹנְרֶיֶב מְקַוְקַז,
נִסִּים כֹּהֵן מֵאַפְגָנִיסְטָן
וְסוּהֵילָה חוּשִׁי מֵאִירָאן,
וְגַם שְׁנַיִם סִינִים גְּרַפְתְּ אִתָּךְ
אֶל מוֹתֵךְ.

מֵאָז כִּסּוּ עִנְיָנִים אֲחֵרִים
אֶת הַסִּפּוּר שֶׁלָּךְ
שֶׁעָלָיו אֲנִי מְדַבֶּרֶת וּמְדַבֶּרֶת
מִבְּלִי שֶׁיִּהְיֶה לִי מַשֶּׁהוּ לְהַגִּיד.

Woman Martyr

The evening goes blind,
and you are only twenty.
(*"Late Afternoon in the Market," Nathan Alterman*)

You are only twenty
and your first pregnancy is a bomb.
Under your broad skirt you are pregnant with dynamite

and metal shavings. This is how you walk in the market,
ticking among the people, you, Andaleeb Takatka.

Someone loosened the screws in your head
and launched you toward the city;
even though you come from Bethlehem,
The Home of Bread, you chose a bakery.
And there you pulled the trigger of yourself,
and together with the Sabbath loaves,
sesame and poppy seed,
you flung yourself into the sky.

Together with Rebecca Fink you flew up
with Yelena Konre'ev from the Caucasus
and Nissim Cohen from Afghanistan
and Suhila Houshy from Iran
and two Chinese you swept along
to death.

Since then, other matters
have obscured your story,
about which I speak all the time
without having anything to say.[10]

In contextualizing the locus of culture for this poet, it is worth remembering that Agi Mishol was born to Hungarian Holocaust survivors making *aliya* to Israel by the age of four. She and her husband still live on a *moshav* farm in *Kfar Mordechai* in Gedera, Israel. Schooled in Hebrew literature at Hebrew University in Jerusalem, Mishol serves as writer-in-residence at Tel Aviv University, as well as teaching creative writing at Alma College in Tel Aviv— two of the many loci of Hebrew cultural renaissance taking place today in Israel. After having won every major Israeli poetry prize, she has also been awarded the first Yehudah Amichai Prize in 2002, which solidified her status as poet in the contemporary Hebrew canon. From inside the deep quiet of her contemplation of the natural world, her poetry bursts forth with the chaos of life. To unpack the location of "minoritization" culture and how this

---

10. Agi Mishol, "Woman Martyr," *Look There: New and Selected Poems*, trans. Lisa Katz (Minnesota: Graywolf Press, 2006), 6.

connects to a deeper *devekut* of cultural identity in Israel means beginning with the poem's title, "*Shaheeda*" [שאהידה].

The title alone is a shocking roadblock to most Hebrew readers, freezing them in their tracks. Calling someone a "martyr" in Israel today locates that person within the culture of radical Islam, a culture of self-sacrifice to kill other infidels all motivated by a flawed, literalist misreading of a theological metaphor. That missed metaphor comes as a just dessert for the typically unmarried, adolescent *shaheed* who has reserved place in heaven at a banquet with seventy virgins. What is striking here is not only that Mishol uses the taboo referent of *shaheed*, but then expands this terrifying category to a woman, entitling her poem, "*Shaheeda.*" How dare a Zionist poet open her first words by locating it in the discourse of that culture of terror? But such daring is what strikes the reader at first blush as an outright heterology, that is, Mishol appears already connected to the *other* as a means of constructing a discourse authorized by the *other*. That authorization comes through the use of the term *Shaheeda,* rather than "homicide bomber."

Yet the daring does not stop with the title, as Mishol positions this poem further into the pandemonium by juxtaposing *Shaheeda*, Andaleeb Takatka, with renowned Zionist poet, Nathan Alterman (1910-1970). Although it seems that Mishol has so much to say about this young woman, the *Shaheeda's* story remains unsayable. By contrast, Alterman's story needs no elaboration and can remain unsaid. This repositioning of cultures, between the unsayable edging towards ineffability, and the unsaid, is a powerful means of pointing to what Bhabha calls an "inter-cultural political existence and ethical imperative." Considering Alterman's cross-cultural journey from Poland to settle in Tel Aviv, from 1925 until his death there in 1970, his *aliya* points to a *DissemiNation*. Trained in agronomy in France, Alterman worked as a translator for Hebrew newspapers, publishing his first poems in 1931. Alterman was a regular contributor of political poetry to the daily *Ha'aretz*, where, decades later, this very poem by Mishol was first published on the Sabbath of the aftermath of the tragedy. Alterman was a poetic spokesman for the national struggle, to the point where many of his poems were banned by the British Mandate authorities, eventually being passed from hand to hand by an eager public. After 1948 social and political themes became the dominant feature in Alterman's lucid and urgent public verse.

It is this same lucidity and urgency which Mishol draws upon to set as the first bookmark in the unpacking of her Hebrew pastiche of Alterman and Andaleeb, glued together by the remains of her victims to serve as another bookend.

No matter how dark the world may appear, this poet yearns to find equilibrium between self and world, allowing her to remain, as critic Dan Miron calls her, the Comic Sybil.[11] Her dark humor is already evident in choosing the Alterman epithet for "A Woman Martyr." Alterman appears to be a poetic precursor of Mishol, someone who also believed in the power of a humorous glance at the world so as to rebalance it. "A Woman Martyr" presents a biting irony to readers of Ha'aretz as they mull over the Sabbath literary supplement where it first appeared with wounds still fresh in the public sphere. By titling her poem "*Shaheeda*," Mishol explodes every Zionist poetic predisposition. The most agonizing moment, just as the poem begins, is a tearing into Alterman's love poem, "Late Afternoon in the Market." From his collection, *The Dove City (Ir Ha'yonah)* Alterman's love poem to Jerusalem depicts a young beauty of barely twenty years in the market place:

> The evening goes blind
> And you are only twenty
> As the saw's teeth cry out in the market place,
> Your beauty overtaking them all.

Knowing that most Israeli readers are in the midst of enjoying the respite Hebrew culture provides with *Ha'aretz* Sabbath supplement on the kitchen table and Alterman on the bookshelf, the poet leaves the closing image of this stanza unsaid. She establishes an allusion to those cries of laborers for love, cries which grow even stronger when they return in Alterman's sixth stanza, albeit with a slight variation:

> The evening goes blind
> While you illumine faces.
> Your charm in the market breaks
> The hearts of shopkeepers.

---

11. Dan Miron, "Afterword: The Comic Sybil," *The New and Selected Works of Agi Mishol*, [Hebrew] (Tel Aviv: *Hakibbutz Hameuchad*/Bialik Press, 2003), 293-443.

What Mishol manages to do by only including the first half of the verse is to transform those cries of laborers for love into cries of fleers from death. As Alterman's paean to love and labor appears as a shard in Mishol's opening verse, it is then blown away by the bomb of this next beauty. Suddenly the leering love for a beauty in the marketplace undergoes a surreal inversion. The "screws are loosened" within this lover's head as the *shaheeda* is launched into Bethlehem. Not only is she called by her martyr's name, canonizing her homicide bombing as a religious rite in fundamentalist eyes, but she is also named as a person. The poet attempts to lament the loss of the another human *qua* human, as Andaleeb Takatka, a nanosecond before she dehumanizes herself by turning into an object, giving over her life to the love of death. Her objectification is deepened by further irony as the young woman from Beth-lehem (the City of Bread) blows herself up in a bakery. Again objects celebrating life, like the Sabbath loaves, are juxtaposed with this woman-as-bomb pulling the trigger of herself. The remains are no longer of a human subject, but those of a merging with "sesame and poppy seed" all flying high into the sky. The homicide bomber's ascent into this phantasmagoric "Paradise" for Mishol takes place as object and not as subject. The next stanza separates the object of woman-as-bomb from the subject of innocent-bystander-whom-she-murders. Each of the bystanders' names is recited along with their country of origin. Here Mishol is enacting her own *DissemiNation* of Israel, interweaving dispersed lives flung into sudden death hailing from all over the globe to be in this mosaic moment. Émigrés are subjects hailing from the USA, Caucasus, Afghanistan, Iran and even China who make up the multicultural fabric on the shelf of Israel's bakery of ethnicities.

The poet challenges the limits of "minoritization" culture and how this connects to a deeper *devekut* of cultural identity in Israel. At the limits, this poem presents four images of women, more object rather than subject. Those typologies are of the pregnant martyr, victims at the bakery, and the seductress at the market; each of these typologies is intertwined with, albeit in vulgar form and language, and juxtaposed to the poet herself. The poet does not want to succumb to the cultural *devekut* of Alterman's seductress at the marketplace, nor does the poet want to be a victim at the bakery. Both typologies are disempowering and objectifying, yet what more can she achieve through language as a poet?

The innocence of the seductress in the marketplace is corroded as the screws are loosened by a radical theology of martyrdom. Despite the contrasts, both women succumb to a similar fate of dissolving as objects into the world around them. The lament of the poet is that she is talking as much as the martyr is ticking, yet both women are accomplishing precious little. Is the poet more effective than the martyr at galvanizing a "minoritization" culture into a deeper *devekut* of cultural identity in Israel? The challenge remains open as the poet struggles with cultivating a deeper connectivity amidst disconnection, and overcoming the sense that her words may even be read as destructive as the martyr's bomb itself.

What rises into the pleroma of poetic consciousness is the chief concern here, and the poet has turned to the bookshelf of Israeli experience, whether the canonical Zionism of Alterman, or *Ha'aretz*, the daily site of Hebrew culture. Mishol seeks to wake up the dormant lovers of life and death to offer another more elegant but complex poem to explore this tension.

[מוֹאזין הטרנזיסטור]

מוּאָזִין הַטְרַנְזִיסְטוֹר עוֹלֶה בַּמַטָּע—
חָסָן יָחֵף וּמְחֻבָּר לְאַדְמָתִי
לָשׁ אֶת בְּצֵק הָעֶרֶב מִקֶּמַח יְהוּדִי
יוֹתֵר מִדַּי עָדִין יָא חָאגִ'י—אֲנִי,
שֶׁכְּבָר עָצַמְתִּי אֶת עֵינֵי הַמְדַמְיָנוֹת אַחֲרֵי יוֹם קָטִיף
שְׁפוּפָה אִתּוֹ מֵעַל לָאֵשׁ שֶׁהוּא מַבְעִיר.

אֲנַחְנוּ מְתַכְנְנִים אֶת הָאֶפְּרְסְקִים שֶׁל מָחָר
עַל "אֵירוֹפָּה" וְסִיגַרְיָה בֵּיתִית.
יָא חָאגִ', כָּכָה מְגִיחָה אֲנַחְתוֹ הָעַרְבִית
נִתְמֶכֶת עַל עֲצוּרֵי שְׁמֵי הַהוּנְגָּרִי הַמְסֹרָס.

בְּדִמְדּוּמֵי הַפוֹטוֹסִינְטֶזָה הָאֵלֶּה רָצוֹת
יָדָיו מֵעַל הַפַּח
עוֹשׂוֹת בַּפַּתָּה כְשָׁפִים.
חָסָן מְאַרְמֵן לִי אֲגָדוֹת
אֶלֶף לַיְלָה וְלַיְלָה מֵעַזָּה,
גּוּפוֹ שְׁפִיפוֹן גָּמִישׁ
עֵינָיו תְּשׁוּבָה לָאֵשׁ.

[The Transistor Muezzin]

The transistor muezzin rises in the orchard—
Hussein barefoot and bound to my land
kneads the evening dough from Jewish flour
"*Ya Hagi* too fine,"—I
who already closed my sorting eyes after a day of harvest,
crouch with him over the fire he kindles.

We're planning the fruit of tomorrow
over *Europa* and home-made cigarettes.
"*Ya Hagi*," his Arab sigh slithers forth
supported on the consonants of my castrated Hungarian name.

In these photosynthesis twilights his hands
run over the tin
casting a spell with pita.
Hussein castles me legends
a thousand and one nights from Gaza,
his body a supple viper
his eyes an answer to the fire.[12]

Pondering what Hebrew poets are for, one can remain in the world of theory or enter the world of praxis. What the critic attempts is to unpack the library of experience. Just as critic Walter Benjamin (1892-1940?) encountered a newfound aura between the cracks of light shining upon familiar texts in a new setting in unpacking his library, so decades later Homi Bhabha asks whether the order of reshelving his books determines his location of cultural identity on the shelves of life experience.[13] How we order ethnicity within our own waking experience is often a function of how we connect one experience with the next. *Devekut* moments of deeper connectivity, which also dissolve the boundary between self and other, challenge the stark dichotomies of wakefulness. This connectivity takes place in moments of both *eros* and *thanatos*, in moments of love and death. Exploring further what Benjamin calls that "dialectical tension between the poles

---

12. Agi Mishol, "Transistor Muezzin," *The Defiant Muse: Hebrew Feminist Poems From Antiquity to Present*, trans. Linda Zisquit (New York: The Feminist Press at CUNY, 1999), 206-207.
13. Homi K. Bhabha, "Unpacking My Library...Again," *The Post-Colonial Question: Common Skies/Divided Horizons*, ed. I. Chambers and L. Curti (London: Routledge, 1996), 199-211.

of disorder and order,"[14] this second Mishol poem appears to be more about the *eros* connected with the love of life in contrast to the martyr's embrace of death. The poet knows how deceiving appearances can be, and thus unveils its truth through the eyes of the other.

Here the poet's Hebraicized Hungarian name sticks to the tongue of the other, Hussein, who calls out her Hebrew name with an Arabic drawl. By having Hussein, the Palestinian farmhand, call out to the Israeli farmer, a calling out to the poet within her own poem—Agi Mishol inscribes herself as farmer and poet of the other, in relation to this other with whom she yearns to merge. That erotic attraction is what teaches each of them what it means to hear the land's music and see its fire. As an Israeli landowner, all she can bring to the encounter is the fire of cheap *Europa* cigarettes, along with some other tobacco they likely rolled together. Ultimately, the poet learns from Hussein everything she lacks from the land even though she owns it. Hussein brings the music of living on the land through his transistor *muezzin*, and in walking barefoot he is bound to the land, using fire to bake her bread. The innuendo of bread-making as intercourse is renowned,[15] but Hussein's act of love-making is fired by a more primal heat that emanates from the conflicted earth upon which they both stand. The embodied nature of the other stands in contrast to the farmer who is deeply disconnected from feeling her own plot of farm land. Their encounter is important as it holds out a hope, albeit cynical, of how the sharing of each person's experience of "minoritization" culture may connect to a deeper *devekut* of cultural identity in Israel. Hussein trains and guides her through this land, and by renaming her Hagi, he also accepts her as his *other* transforming her into the *same*. In an inversion from the Garden of Eden, here in the orchard this farmhand Adam renames the farmer Eve and entices her to leave her garden for a more embodied life in the orchard. Is he seducing her to leave the garden of Zionism behind in the hope of embracing the orchard of liberal democracy? Such a merging however cannot be complete; it remains the lingering question. Once each person has shared their subjective experience as *other* in "minoritization" culture, a deeper *devekut* within the mosaic of identity in Israel awaits a new name.

---

14. Watter Benjamin, "Unpacking my Library," Selected Writings 1931-1934, (Cambridge: Belknap, 2004), 487.
15. For example, see bNedarim 90b, *ad. loc. Shitah Mekubetzet.*

CHAPTER IV

CONTRITION
AS A RETURNING TO *DEVEKUT*
BINYAMIN SHEVILI'S CYCLE "CONTRITION"

1.0 MYSTICAL APPERCEPTION THROUGH CONTRITION OF HEBREW CULTURES

By word and experience, both poet and mystic seek to overcome the yearning that separates every human being from the divine. It is that very tantalizing trace of divine consciousness, always almost within reach, that gives way to this deeper yearning to re-ascend after descending into disconnectedness from the divine. That point of reuniting in unitive consciousness is called *devekut*. Recall the subtle degrees of *devekut* through poetic and mystic exemplars following Morgenstern's matrix in the opening chapter of: (1) Exteriorized fervor; (2) Interiorized stillness; (3) Enrapturing ascent. The present investigation will focus on how descent impels a deeper ascent, and how contrition, as understood by both mystic and poet, fuels that re-ascent into *devekut*.

1.1 Yearning for Mecca in Jerusalem: The Poetry of Binyamin Shevili

After waves of Zionism influencing much of the agenda in literary and even some devotional circles, there is a seismic cultural shift taking place now in Israel. What interests me then is how contemporary Hebrew cross-cultural webs, subjectivities, and these new portals of experience are crossing boundaries to transform the nature of mystical apprehension. As ideological divisions and binary thinking let go, there is a more seamless *to and fro* between diverse religious cultural matrices, lo and behold even between Judaism and Islam in Israel.

There is a growing migration to the Far East, as young adults complete their I.D.F. service. Upon their return home, there is a renaissance in

Israel of a yearning for mystical knowledge and experience that challenges the hegemony of the exoteric rabbinate. One of the true boundary crossers in this renaissance project is poet, novelist, and critic, fifty-six year old Binyamin Shevili. Akin to this migratory generation searching for spiritual treasures in faraway lands, born in 1956 as a Jerusalemite from Yemin Moshe, Shevili remains a liminal figure, taking mystical journeys to Greece and Turkey to write veritable travelogues of the soul, exploring spiritual affinities of Jewish mysticism with Islamic Sufism and Zen Buddhism.[1] Is it so unusual then that this Hebrew poet's boundary-crossing creations—despite being criticized as anti-intellectual,[2] hermetic,[3] reclusive,[4] ecstatic[5] and erotic[6]—have been awarded the *Prime Minister's Prize for Creativity* 5758?

Binyamin Shevili was part of a minor wave of literature in Israel in the 1990s, dedicated to mystical explorations through the media of poetry and prose, publishing the creative records of their discoveries in a journal called *Mirrors,* or *Mar'ot.*[7] The journal first appeared in 1990, lasting for only four issues, but in that time, the mystical streams seen through these "looking glasses" could be classified in one of two ways: (1) the prophetic-mystical dimension;[8] (2) the nihilistic-critical dimension. Binyamin Shevili and Daniel Sutbosky (a.k.a. Daniel Ben Yosef) were the dominant voices in the prophetic-mystical dimension. Hailing from that artistic inter-world nestled between East and West Jerusalem, Yemin Moshe,[9] Shevili was

---

1. Yoram Meltzer, "Looking at the world and finding himself," [Hebrew] *Ma'ariv: Literature & Books* (October 6, 2010), 26.

2. Beni Tzipor, "Novel: Books that Disjoint," [Hebrew] *Ha'Aretz: Culture & Literature* (December 30, 2005), 5.

3. Adina Mor-Hayyim, "Poetry Arousing Conventions," [Hebrew] *Maariv: Literature Supplement* (March 16, 1990): 6.

4. Mordechai Goldman, "Solitude of the Writer," [Hebrew] *Ha'Aretz: Culture & Literature* (May 8, 1998), 4ד

5. Amir Or, "The Way to Mecca," [Hebrew] *Ha'Aretz* (April 9, 1993), 9ב

6. Moshe Zinger, "What is a Jewish Poem?" *Ha'Aretz* (May 21, 1993), 9b; Hayyim Nagid, "*Erotica and Mysticism,*" [Hebrew] *Yediot Ahronot: Sabbath Supplement* (July 2, 1992), 32.

7. Jill Amuyel, "There Is Also a Different Love," [Hebrew] *Dimui* vol. 10 (Jerusalem: 1996): 26-29, 81.

8. Nili Gold, "'Merciful Father Abraham': The mystical poetry of Binyamin Shvili," in *Religious Perspectives in Modern Muslim and Jewish Literatures,* ed. G. Abramsen and H. Kilpatrick (London: Routledge, 2006), 71-89.

9. Ibid., 27.

dedicating much of his spiritual journey after completing his I.D.F. service to studying the Jewish mystical path, through Kabbalah,[10] Hasidism, as well as through Agnon's recast mystical legends into *Hebrew Belles Lettres*,[11] and even scouring through Sabbetean and Frankist mysticisms (thanks to Scholem's legacy still reigning during Shevili's studies at Hebrew University), finally branching out to contemplate the spiritual constitution of human identity through universal mystical symbols.[12]

It is this final universal branch of the spiritual journey that struck readers and critics of Shevili's Hebrew poetry as most unusual with the 1992 publication of *Poems of Yearning for Mecca* [*Shirai Ga'aguim L'Mecca*].[13] The provocative and decadent dimensions in this collection push their formative Sufi mystical influences (like Ibn al-Arabi, Musa ibn al-Rass, Jelaludin Rumi, and Abraham ibn Adam)[14] beyond the pale of their religio-cultural referents, edging closer back to origins.[15] For a journey that begins immersed in the Jewish mystical sources of Kabbalah and Hasidism, branching off into an exploration of the Islamic mysticism of Sufism, Shevili's poetry bespeaks an unquenchable yearning to re-unite the universal human need for intimacy in the divine Without End—all in Hebrew.

Unlike his spiritualist precursors in *Hebrew Belle Lettres* like Shai Agnon (1888-1970) and Pinhas Sadeh (1929-1994), Shevili unveils the origins of this burning desire by translating Sufism into Hebrew, and in so doing, he

---

10. According to Amuyel, Shevili was dedicating time to studying the Cordoverean Kabbalah through the writing of Scholem's student. See Yosef ben Shlomo, *Doctrine of Divinity in R. Moshe Cordovero* (Jerusalem: Mossad Biailik, 1965). This book in turn influenced a poem written by Shai Agnon, and Agnon was also a figure of great influence for Shevili, especially the mystical resonances in the Zohar about the dog named, Balak in Agnon's "Yesterday, Day Before" [Hebrew].

11. Amuyel, "There Is Also a Different Love," 27. When asked to chose a piece of literature that best represented the poet's own style, Shevili chose Agnon's short story, "'Till here,'" in which an architect is commissioned to build a palace for the king. Agnon remained a formative influence for the way Shevili learned how to amass ancient mystical lore and legends, and interweaving them into his own poetic voice as high literature.

12. Amuyel, "There Is Also a Different Love," 26-27.

13. Ibid., 28. See Binyamin Shevili, *Poems of Yearning for Mecca* [Hebrew] (Tel Aviv: Tamuz Publications, 1992).

14. Binyamin Shevili, "Journeying to Mecca in the wake of Ibn al-Arabi," *Poems of the Grand Tourist* (Tel Aviv: Schocken, 1999), 113; Shevili, "Hymn of Musa ibn al-Rass that sought my face," *Poems of the Grand Tourist* [Hebrew], 114.

15. Amuyel, "There Is Also a Different Love," 28.

remains a lone voice[16] transforming the very contours of the seeker's path to divine truth as a more universal human need. Poetry, for Shevili, is a realm for journeying between realms both pure and impure, sacred and profane, material and spiritual, immanent and transcendent, integrated by a *coincidentia oppositorium*.[17] It is this coincidence of opposites which lays the groundwork for the latest poetry cycle, called, "Contrition" [*Harata*]:[18]

חרטה

אֲנִי מְפַחֵד מְפַחֵד מְאֹד מֵהַמַּחֲלוֹת וּמֵהָעֵיסְפוּת מֵהָרְאִיָּה שֶׁנֶּחֱלָשֶׁת מֵהַסְּחַרְחוֹרוֹת בַּפַּחַד שֶׁלִּי יֵשׁ חַדּוּת הוּא חַד כְּמוֹ תַּעַר. אֲנִי מַרְגִּישׁ כְּמוֹ צִפּוֹר שֶׁשָּׁבְרוּ לָהּ אֶת הַכְּנָפַיִם בִּמְעוֹפָהּ. הַפַּחַד יוֹצֵא לִי מֵהַפֶּה טַעְמוֹ מַר. אֲנִי מְפַחֵד שֶׁהָאֲנָשִׁים יְגַלּוּ מַה מִּסְתַּתֵּר מִתַּחַת לַהַבָּעָה שֶׁעַל פָּנַי. מַשֶּׁהוּ רַע מַשֶּׁהוּ מַפְחִיד. אֲנִי עוֹלֶה בָּרְחוֹב אַךְ יוֹרֵד לַמַּצְלוּלוֹת מִשְׁתּוֹקֵק לִפְתֹּחַ אֶת סֵפֶר שִׁירָיו שֶׁל רוּמִי אַךְ אֵין לִי כֹּחַ. אֲנִי מְנַסֶּה לִשְׂמֹחַ אַךְ הַשִּׂמְחָה לֹא בָּאָה מֵהַלֵּב אֶלָּא מֵהַמֹּחַ. הַלֵּב הוּא הַמָּקוֹם שֶׁל הַדְּאָגוֹת וַאֲנִי אוֹמֵר: 'דְּאָגָה בְּלֵב אִישׁ יְשַׁחֶנָּה'. אֲנִי מְנַסֶּה לְדַבֵּר עִם הַמֶּלֶךְ דָּוִד.

בַּחוּרָה פָּסְעָה בַּמּוֹרָד רָחוֹק מִמֶּנּוּ נִבַּט הַיָּם. שִׂמְלָתָהּ שְׁחֹרָה חָלְצָה לְבָנָה. אָן מָרִי שִׁימֵל כָּתְבָה סֵפֶר עַל הַשִּׁירָה הַמִּיסְטִית בָּאִסְלָאם הִבַּטְתִּי בַּשִּׁירָה שֶׁיָּרְדָה בָּרְחוֹב כְּשֶׁהִיא נִצְמֶדֶת לַקִּיר צְנוּעָה יָפָה לְבָנָה וּמְדַכְּאָה.

אֲנִי הִיא זוֹ שֶׁאֹהַב וְזֶה שֶׁאֹהַב הוּא אֲנִי.

חָמֵשׁ פְּעָמִים בַּיּוֹם הֵם מִתְפַּלְּלִים עַכְשָׁו כְּשֶׁהַכַּדּוּר הַקָּדוֹד שֶׁבְּתוֹךְ הַמַּרְאָה שֶׁמֵּעָלַי נוֹפֵל הַמּוּאַזִּין מְבָרֵךְ אֶת אֱלֹהִים בְּקוֹל שֶׁל פְּלָדָה וַאֲנִי יוֹרֵד מֵהַגֶּשֶׁר.

הַחַיִּים אוֹמֵר אֶבֶן אָל חוּסַיְן סוּלְמִי אֶפְשָׁר שֶׁיִּהְיוּ מְבֻסָּסִים עַל יְדַע שֶׁהָאָדָם מְקַבֵּל מֵאֲחֵרִים... שֶׁיּוֹתֵר אוֹ אוּלַי פָּחוֹת יוֹדְעִים מִמֶּנּוּ אֶפְשָׁרוּת נוֹסֶפֶת טוֹבָה יוֹתֵר שֶׁהַחַיִּים יִהְיוּ מְבֻסָּסִים עַל הַנִּסָּיוֹן אַךְ הַטּוֹב מִכֹּל הוּא כְּשֶׁהַחַיִּים מְבֻסָּסִים עַל הַחַיִּים כְּמוֹ מַיִם שֶׁצּוֹלְלִים בְּמַיִם.

הַכָּחֹל נִמְצָא בְּתוֹךְ הָעַיִן הָעֲנָנִים אֵינָם כְּבֵדִים כְּמוֹ שֶׁהֵם נִרְאִים הַסִּירוֹת מַמְתִּינוֹת. כָּתֵף אַחַת שֶׁלִּי כּוֹאֶבֶת עַיִן אַחַת שֶׁלִּי חַמָּה וְיָגֵעָה מְלֵאָה דְּאָגוֹת. הַדֶּרְוִישִׁים לֹא נָסְעוּ כְּדֵי לִבְלוֹת הֵם הִשְׁתַּכְּנוּ בְּמִלּוֹנוֹת הֵם קָמוּ עִם שַׁחַר וְהִתְפַּלְּלוּ תְּפִלָּה רִאשׁוֹנָה אַחַר כָּךְ לָמְדוּ נָתְנוּ צְדָקָה כְּמוֹהֶם עָלַי לַעֲזֹב אֶת הַדֶּרֶךְ בָּהּ הָלַכְתִּי עַד עַתָּה.

16. Ibid., 81.
17. Ibid., 28.
18. Binyamin Shevili, "Contrition," *Carmel*, vol. 13 (Jerusalem: 2010): 35-39.

הַכֹּחַל מַבְלִיט אֶת הָאֵין צֶבַע הוּא פֶּרְגּוֹד שֶׁנִּפְתָּח אֶל הַמְּאוֹם. מָה אֲנִי יָכוֹל
לַעֲשׂוֹת וְעוֹד לֹא עָשִׂיתִי כְּדֵי שֶׁמְּעַט אוֹר יִכָּנֵס לְתוֹךְ הַחֹשֶׁךְ בּוֹ אֲנִי נִמְצָא.
תָּמִיד נִמְלַטְתִּי מֵהַכְּנִיעָה לְאֵין אֱלֹהִים וְעַכְשָׁו אֲנִי רֵיק כִּי אֲנִי יוֹדֵעַ שֶׁאֱלֹהִים
כָּל כָּךְ הָיָה בִּי תָּמִיד בְּלִי לִהְיוֹת. עָלַי לַעֲבֹר אֶת הַחֹשֶׁךְ מָה אֶעֱשֶׂה וְאֵינִי יוֹדֵעַ
אֵיךְ לְהַדְלִיק אוֹתוֹ.

סֵפֶר   פַּעַם בֶּן הָאָדָם דִּבֵּר עַכְשָׁו הִגִּיעַ אֵלַי הַקּוֹל שֶׁלּוֹ.
אֲנִי הֶעָנָן שֶׁמְכַסֶּה אֶת הַשָּׁמַיִם שֶׁלִּי. כְּשֶׁתִּזְרַח הַשֶּׁמֶשׁ יִמַּסוּ הַמִּלִּים שֶׁכָּתַבְתִּי.
זֹאת הִיא הַצְּעָקָה שֶׁצּוֹעֶקֶת הַשֶּׁמֶשׁ הַשּׁוֹקַעַת בִּי.

כְּשֶׁאֲנִי כּוֹתֵב וּמְנַסֶּה לִשְׁכֹּחַ כַּמָּה אֲנִי בּוֹדֵד זֶה הַוִּתּוּר עַל הַחֹשֶׁךְ. הָאוֹר בַּחוּץ
לֹא מְרֻמֶּה מִישֶׁהוּ שָׁר שָׁם שִׁיר גַּעְגּוּעִים וְהָאֹזֶן מַקְשִׁיבָה וּמַאֲמִינָה לְתַעֲתוּעָיו
שֶׁל הָאִישׁ חֹשֶׁךְ.

אֵיךְ אֶמְצָא אֶת הֶחָבֵר הַגָּדוֹל שֶׁל דָּוִד הַמֶּלֶךְ, אֶת הַלֹּא יְהוּדִי, אֶת אֶלְוָה הָאֹזֶן.

עֶבְדּוּלָה אִבְּן מַרוּוַאן הַשָּׁלִיט פַּעַם בְּשִׁגְגָה מָטְבֵּעַ לִבְאֵר מְזֹהֶמֶת מִיָּד אַחַר כָּךְ
הָלַךְ וְשִׁלֵּם שְׁלוֹשָׁה עָשָׂר דִּינָרֵי זָהָב כְּדֵי שֶׁיֵּשְׁבוּהוּ לוֹ כְּשֶׁנִּתְבַּקֵּשׁ לְהַסְבִּיר אֶת
מַעֲשֵׂהוּ הַמּוּזָר אָמַר כִּי שְׁמוֹ שֶׁל אַלְלָה חָקוּק הָיָה עַל הַמַּטְבֵּעַ לָכֵן מִתּוֹךְ
כָּבוֹד וְיִרְאָה הִרְגִּישׁ חוֹבָה לְהוֹצִיאָהּ מֵהַבְּאֵר בְּכָל מְחִיר.

פַּעַם פָּנְתָה רַבִּיעַ אֶל אַדְוִיָה לֵאלֹהִים וְאָמְרָה: 'כָּל חֲפָצַי בָּעוֹלָם הַזֶּה הוּא
לִזְכֹּר אוֹתְךָ וּבָעוֹלָם הַבָּא לְהַבִּיט בְּךָ בִּנְגוֹעַ לְכָל שְׁאָר הַדְּבָרִים עֲשֵׂה בִּי
כִּרְצוֹנְךָ'.

אַהֲבָה   כְּשֶׁהָעִוֵּר אוֹמֵר לְזֶה שֶׁעוֹדֶנּוּ רוֹאֶה אֵינֶנִּי רוֹאֶה אֲנִי רַק חוֹלֵם בְּלִי לִרְאוֹת.

כְּשֶׁאֵינִי אוֹהֵב אֵין לִי מָקוֹם לָלֶכֶת אֵלָיו אֲבָל אֲנִי בְּכָל זֹאת הוֹלֵךְ הֲלִיכָה בְּלִי
הֲלִיכָה אֲנִי הוֹלֵךְ וּמְבַקֵּשׁ אֶת שֶׁאָבְדָה נַפְשִׁי.

אֵיךְ אוּכַל לְהָנִיחַ לְעַצְמִי מֵאֱלֹהִים בְּלִי לָדַעַת מִי אֲנִי בִּשְׁבִילוֹ. אִם לֹא אֵדַע
אֶת אֱלֹהִים לֹא אֵדַע מִי הוּא לֹא. לֹא אֵדַע אוֹתָנוּ.

לְאִמָּא שֶׁלִּי סַבָּא שֶׁלִּי קָרְאוּ בָּבוֹ. פַּעַם אָבִי לָקַח אוֹתִי אֵלֶיהָ לִשְׁכוּנַת
הַבּוּכָרִים הִיא גָּרָה בְּחֶדֶר דּוֹמֶה לְכוּךְ שֶׁל נְזִירָה פָּחַדְתִּי מִבִּגְדֶּיהָ הַשְּׁחוֹרִים
וּמֵעֵינֶיהָ הַסּוֹמוֹת שֶׁהִבִּיטוּ לְמָקוֹם אֶחָד בִּלְבַד... אֶל קוֹלְקִיס וְגִזַּת הַזָּהָב לְשָׁם
אֲנִי רוֹצָה לְהַגִּיעַ. אֲנִי הוּא זֶה שֶׁעָלָיו לַהֲפֹךְ אֶת הַתּוֹרָה וְלִכְתֹּב לְךָ לֶךְ לְךָ
מֵאַרְצְךָ וּמִמּוֹלַדְתְּךָ אֶל בֵּית אָבִיךָ.

כְּדֵי לִכְתֹּב יָצָאתִי מֵהַבַּיִת. אִי אֶפְשָׁר לִכְתֹּב בַּבַּיִת עַל כָּךְ שֶׁאֵין בַּיִת. כְּדֵי

לִבְנוֹת בַּיִת צָרִיךְ לְהַחֲרִיב בְּאֵיזֶשֶׁהוּ מָקוֹם... בַּיִת. הַבַּיִת בְּקוֹלְכִיס חָרֵב מִזְּמַן אֵינֶנִּי נוֹסֵעַ כְּדֵי לִבְנוֹת אוֹתוֹ. אֲנִי נוֹסֵעַ לְגַלּוֹת כַּמָּה אֲנִי חָרֵב. יוֹשֵׁב בְּאִיסְטַנְבּוּל וְקוֹרֵא שִׁירִים שֶׁל רוּמִי מֵבִיט בָּעוֹבְרִים וְשָׁבִים שֶׁנִּרְאִים כְּמוֹ זֶה עַתָּה נוֹלְדוּ וּכְבָר הֵם מֵתִים.

מִי שֶׁמְּשַׁקֵּר יוֹדֵעַ לְסַפֵּר אֶת הָאֱמֶת. זֶה שֶׁמְּדַבֵּר אֱמֶת לֹא יוֹדֵעַ לְסַפֵּר שְׁקָרִים כָּךְ מַפְסִידִים הַיְּהוּדִים אֶת הַמַּתָּנָה שֶׁנִּתְּנָה לָהֶם הָאָמָנוּת.

אֲנָשִׁים חוֹלְפִים עַל פָּנַי וַאֲנִי לֹא מוֹצֵא אֶת עַצְמִי. רוּמִי מְסַפֵּר כִּי פַּעַם אַחַת לִפְנוֹת בֹּקֶר יָצָא מֻלָּא נָאסְרָאדִין מִן הַטַּבֶּרְנָה וְשׁוֹטֵט חֲסַר מַטָּרָה בָּרְחוֹבוֹת שׁוֹטֵר עָצַר אוֹתוֹ וְשָׁאַל מַדּוּעַ הוּא מְשׁוֹטֵט בְּשָׁעָה כָּזֹאת הֵשִׁיב לוֹ מֻלָּא נָאסְרָאדִין שֶׁלּוּ יָדַע לַעֲנוֹת עַל שְׁאֵלָתוֹ הָיָה שׁוֹכֵב כְּבָר בְּבֵיתוֹ לִפְנֵי שָׁעוֹת רַבּוֹת.

יֵשׁ לָנוּ חָבִית גְּדוֹלָה שֶׁל יַיִן/וְגָבִיעַ אַף לֹא אֶחָד/טוֹב לָנוּ כָּךְ/כָּל בּוֹקֶר לוֹהֲטִים אָנוּ/ וּבָעֶרֶב שׁוּב אָנוּ/לוֹהֲטִים/הֵם אוֹמְרִים שֶׁאֵין לָנוּ תַּקָּנָה הֵם צוֹדְקִים/אַךְ לָנוּ זֶה כְּלָל לֹא אִכְפַּת.

הַקְּרִיאָה וְהַכְּתִיבָה הֵן הַנֵּר שֶׁמֵּאִיר בְּפַחַד.

אֲנִי רוֹצָה לַחֲזֹר אֶל הַיַּלְדוּת הַזְּקֵנָה שֶׁל תְּמִימוּתִי וּלְהַאֲמִין שֶׁאֱלֹהִים נִמְצָא גַּם בַּפֶּרַח הַשּׁוֹתֵק שֶׁל הַפֶּה.

הַכּוֹכָבִים מְשַׁקְּרִים דַּוְקָא כְּשֶׁהֵם אוֹמְרִים אֱמֶת... כְּבָר אֵינֶנּוּ קַיָּמִים.

הֵן יוֹשְׁבוֹת וּמְעַשְּׁנוֹת נַרְגִּילָה מְשׂוֹחֲחוֹת בְּשֶׁקֶט וּמְשַׂחֲקוֹת שֵׁשׁ בֵּשׁ לֹא מְעַנְיְנוֹת לִפְנוֹת מַעֲרָבָה לְכָל הַיּוֹתֵר מוּכָנוֹת לָשֵׂאת לְשָׁם מַבָּט כְּמוֹ אָתָאתוּרְק. עִם הַשֶּׁקֶר הֵן הוֹלְכוֹת לְשָׁם בְּלִי לָזוּז. יְכוֹלוֹת לְהָבִין אֶת בְּיָאזִיד מֻבַּסְטָאם שֶׁיָּדַע לְשַׁקֵּר זְמַן רַב לִפְנֵי שֶׁלָּמְדוּ אֶת זֶה הַתֻּרְכִּים.

אִיסְטַנְבּוּל דְּגֵי הַכֶּסֶף שֶׁלְּךָ שׂוֹחִים בַּשָּׁמַיִם כְּשֶׁבַּלֵּב שֶׁלִּי דּוֹלֶקֶת אֵשׁ/כֹּה רַבִּים זִכְרוֹנוֹתַיִךְ מֵהַחֹשֶׁךְ שֶׁל הַיּוֹם/מֵהַיָּם הַמַּר שֶׁל מַרְמָרָה/מֵאַלְלָה שֶׁהָלַךְ וְהַמּוּאַזִּין קוֹרֵא לוֹ כַּמָּה הוּא גָדוֹל/אֲנִי יוֹשֵׁב עַל הַגַּג וּמַבִּיט בָּאֳנִיָּה הַנּוֹצֶצֶת שֶׁעוֹבֶרֶת מֵעַל.

הַנָּשִׁים שֶׁאָבְדוּ דַּרְכָּן אֶל הַיַּיִן לְבוּשׁוֹת כְּאִלּוּ אֵין גּוּף לְלִבּוֹ שֶׁל רוּמִי כִּי לְפִי שֶׁל הָעוֹר אֵין חֵשֶׁק לְהִגָּלוֹת. אֲנִי צָמֵא לַיַּיִן שֶׁל הָאֶסְקְלָאם לַנָּשִׁפִים שֶׁהִצִּיעוּ בְּשִׁירָם כִּי הַיַּיִן בְּכָל אֲנִי רוֹצָה לְהַשְׁפֵּךְ מֵהַגָּבִיעַ לַקְּעָרָה מִמֶּנָּה שׁוֹתֶה הֶחָבֵר שֶׁלָּנוּ הַגָּדוֹל שֶׁתָּמִיד שִׁכּוֹר מֵתַי נָבִין שֶׁאֵין דֶּרֶךְ לָבוֹא אֶל הָאֱלֹהִים מִלְּבַד כָּל דַּרְכְּךָ.

קַח מֵאִתָּנוּ אֶת הַזְּמַן הֵם אוֹמְרִים אֵין לָנוּ צֹרֶךְ בּוֹ יוֹשְׁבִים עַל שְׂרַפְרַפִּים
וּמְשַׂחֲקִים בְּקֻבִּיּוֹת. עוֹפוֹת הַמַּיִם צוֹרְחִים צִפּוֹר שְׁחֹרָה מְקַפֶּצֶת מֵעָנָף לְעָנָף
וְנִשְׁאֶרֶת בְּאוֹתוֹ עֵץ עֲנָנִים מְסָרְבִים לָנוּעַ אוֹטוֹבּוּס רוֹמִי חוֹזֵר עַל עַצְמוֹ
אֵינוֹ מְעַיֵּף וְאֵינוֹ מִתְעַיֵּף מְעוֹרֵר גַּעְגּוּעִים לְגַעְגּוּעִים. דָּבָר לֹא יִמָּחֵק לַמְרוֹת
שֶׁהַכֹּל יַחֲלֹף כִּי מַה שֶׁהָיָה תָּמִיד יִשָּׁאֵר תָּמִיד הָיָה. הַבָּחוּר מְסוֹכְנוּת הַנְּסִיעוֹת
אוֹמֵר שֶׁשְּׁנֵי נְהָרוֹת נִפְגָּשׁוּ רוֹמִי וְשַׁמְסִי טַבָּרִיז אוֹקְיָנוֹס גָּדוֹל סָעַר בִּי
כְּשֶׁפָּגַשְׁתִּי אֶת שְׁנֵי הַנְּהָרוֹת הַצִּפּוֹר הַשְּׁחֹרָה שֶׁדִּלְּגָה מֵעָנָף עַל הָעֵץ
הֵכִּיר הִבִּיטָה בִּי וְשָׁאֲלָה 'לָמָּה לֹא תִּלְמַד לְקַפֵּץ גַּם אַתָּה?'

לֹא טוֹב לִי מְנֻסָּה שֶׁיִּהְיֶה לִי טוֹב וְאֵינִי יָכוֹל מַרְגִּישׁ מְלֻכְלָךְ. הַסְּפָרִים לֹא יְנַקּוּ
אוֹתִי אוֹמְרִים שֶׁהֵם עֲרֻמִּים יוֹתֵר מֵחַיַּת הַשָּׂדֶה מַבְטִיחִים כָּל פַּעַם מֵחָדָשׁ
שֶׁהִנֵּה מַמָּשׁ בַּקָּצֶה מֵעֵבֶר לָהֶם אֶמְצָא אֶת אִיתָקָה.

אֵלֶּה שֶׁאֵינָם יוֹדְעִים בְּאֵיזוֹ דֶּרֶךְ לָבוֹא אֶל הַדֶּרֶךְ אֵינָם יוֹדְעִים שֶׁאֵת הַיַּיִן שֶׁל
רוֹמִי הֶחְלַפְנוּ מִזְּמַן בְּסֵכָר.

יֵשׁ בִּי אֶת הָרַעַל וְגַם אֶת הַתְּרוּפָה. הַדֶּרְוִישִׁים הִרְבּוּ לְהַבִּיט בַּנְּעָרִים שֶׁעַל
פְּנֵיהֶם עוֹד לֹא צָמַח זָקָן בְּיָפְיָם וּבְרַצְחוּתָם הֵם רָאוּ אֶת גַּשְׁמִיּוּת הָאֵל. טִפּוֹת
שֶׁל גֶּשֶׁם טִפְטְפוּ הַבַּטְתִּי בְּאַיָּלָה יָפָה וּבְדִמְעוֹת שֶׁעַל חַלּוֹן הַטַּבְּרָנָה כְּשֶׁחָלְפוּ
הָעֲנָנִים וְהַשֶּׁמֶשׁ זָרְחָה רָאִיתִי אֶת מִזְדָּהּ שׁוֹתָה מִן הַשָּׁמַיִם כּוֹכָבִים.

אֲנִי עֲדַיִן מְפַחֵד אֲבָל פָּחוֹת. מַה רָאֲתָה אָז בְּבוֹ בְּפָנַי עֵינֶיהָ הַסּוֹמוֹת הִיא
שֶׁבָּאָה מִקּוֹלְכִיס שֶׁפַּעַם קָרְאוּ לָהּ גּוֹרְגוֹנָה וְצִפְעוֹנִים צָמְחוּ עַל רֹאשָׁהּ אֲנִי עֲדַיִן מְפַחֵד
מֵעֵינֶיהָ הָרֵיקוֹת שֶׁמְּסֻגָּלוֹת עַד כָּאן לִרְאוֹת.

מֵדֵיאָה   הַבֶּגֶד שֶׁלָּבַשְׁתְּ שָׁם יִשְׂרֹף אוֹתָךְ אִם תִּלְבַּשׁ אוֹתוֹ כָּאן.

הַפַּחַד בָּא וְהוֹלֵךְ כְּמוֹ גַּלִּים מָתְנַי כּוֹאֲבִים אֲנִי זָקוּק לְפֶה רָחָב כְּמוֹ שָׁמַיִם כְּדֵי
שֶׁאוּכַל לוֹמַר אֶת כְּאֵבוֹ שֶׁל הֵלָא מְאֹהָב. אוּלַי זֶה הַחֹם שֶׁבָּא לְחוֹלָה מִן הַקֹּר.
אַבּוּ יָאזִיד מִבִּיסְטָאם הִתְפַּשֵּׁט כְּנָחָשׁ הַמַּשִּׁיל אֶת עוֹרוֹ הִבִּיט בְּעַצְמוֹ וְאָמַר
'אֲנִי הָיִיתִי הוּא'.

נָחָשׁ   הַשָּׁלְיָה שֶׁקָּרַעְתִּי מִגּוּפִי כְּדֵי לְהִוָּלֵד.

הַכַּלָּה עָלְתָה בְּמַדְרֵגוֹת הַגָּלְטָאסְרַי עִם מְלַוִּים וּמְלַוּוֹת נָשִׁים בְּבִגְדֵי פְּרִישׁוּת
מְטֻפָּחוֹת רֹאשׁ וְעוֹד מִינֵי מִכְסִים שֶׁכָּחוּ שֶׁגַּם הֵן הַיּוֹם כֻּלּוֹת אֱלֹהִים נוֹתֵן יֳפִי
כְּרָאוֹת עֵינָיו וּמֵעַל פֶּרַח הַשַּׁחַף בִּצְחוֹק אַכְזָר.

כָּל צַעַד שֶׁלִּי הוּא תְּפִלָּה קִינָה שֶׁבַח חֶלְצָהּ שֶׁל אִשָּׁה הִיא טַלִּית חֲגוֹרָה הִיא
תְּפִלִּין הַכּוֹבַע הוּא כִּפָּה כִּי הָעֵינַיִם רוֹאוֹת מֵעֵבֶר לָאוֹר שֶׁאֵין אֱלֹהִים.

אַיָּלָה   חֲרֵדָה מְדֻלְגֶּת וּמְקַפֶּצֶת בָּרְחוֹבוֹת מְחַפֶּשֶׂת דֶּרֶךְ לְהִמָּלֵט מֵהַצַּיָּדִים

הַפֶּרַח נִפְתַּח כְּשֶׁהוּא אוֹמֵר שֶׁהוּא נִפְתַּח כָּל הַשְּׂפוֹת הֵן נְהִיָּה לַבַּיִת הַהוּא
שֶׁאֵין לוֹ קִירוֹת לַשָּׂפָה שֶׁלִּי יֵשׁ רַק חָבֵר אֶחָד זוּג אָזְנַיִם שֶׁגָּרוֹת מֵעַל.

בְּתוֹךְ הָאַהֲבָה הַזֹּאת מוּת/דַּרְכְּךָ מַתְחִילָה בְּצַד אַחֵר/הֱיֵה שָׁמַיִם/קַח גַּרְזֶן
אֶל כָּתְלֵי הַכֶּלֶא/הִמָּלֵט/צֵא וְלֵךְ כְּאֶחָד שֶׁלְּפֶתַע נוֹלַד/עֲשֵׂה זֹאת עַכְשָׁו/
כְּשֶׁאַתָּה עָטוּף בְּעָנָן דַּק/הִמָּלֵט הַצִּדָּה מוּת/וְהֱיֵה שֶׁקֶט שְׁקֵטוּת הִיא הַסִּימָן/
שֶׁמַּתָּ/חַיֶּיךָ הַקּוֹדְמִים הָיוּ מְנוּסָה מְטֹרֶפֶת/מֶהָשֶּׁקֶט/הַיָּרֵחַ הַמָּלֵא חֲסַר
הַמֶּלֶם/יוֹצֵא עַכְשָׁו.

כְּשֶׁעָלִיתִי מִגֶּשֶׁר הַגָּלֶאטָה לְאִיסְטַנְבּוּל בִּקֵּשׁ מִמֶּנִּי מְצַחְצֵחַ נַעֲלִים שֶׁאֶתֵּן
לוֹ סִיגַרְיָה שֶׁקֵּרַרְתִּי וְאָמַרְתִּי שֶׁאֵין לִי יָכֹלְתִּי לָתֵת לוֹ אַחַת אֵיךְ אוּכַל לָמוּת
אִם אֲנִי כָּל כָּךְ רוֹצֶה לִחְיוֹת.

בִּשְׁבִיל לָמוּת לֹא מַסְפִּיקוֹת מִלִּים אֲנִי רוֹצֶה לָמוּת. יֵשׁ לִשְׁקֹעַ בְּלִי צֹרֶךְ בְּאוֹר
גַּם בְּלֹא לְהָאִיר. בְּבוֹ כִּבְתָה אֶת מְאוֹר עֵינֶיהָ וּמֵתָה לִפְנֵי שֶׁמֵּתָה כְּדֵי לָמוּת
לִפְנֵי שֶׁתִּחְיֶה.

אֲנִי שֶׁאֶפֹּלוּ אֶחָד הוּא הַכֹּל בִּשְׁבִילוֹ נִפְרָד מֵהָעִיר בַּת שְׁנֵים עָשָׂר מִילְיוֹן.

אֵיפֹה נִמְצָא הַיָּם הַשָּׁחֹר אוּכַל לִרְאוֹתוֹ רַק כְּשֶׁהַשָּׁחֹר יַפְצִיעַ וְיָבִיא עִמּוֹ אֶת הַפֶּצַע.

[1]

I am afraid, really afraid of the ailments, exhaustion and vision that weaken with
the dizziness of my fear. There is a sharpness to it as subtle as a razor. I feel
like a bird whose wings have been broken from their flight. Fear froths forth
from my mouth and it tastes bitter. I am afraid that men will uncover what is
concealed beneath my facial expression. Something evil, something terrifying.
I ascend to the street but descend into the abyss, yearning to open a book of
Rumi's poetry,[19] but I have no strength. I try to rejoice but joy no longer comes
from my heart rather from my mind. The heart is the site of fear, so I say, "Care
in the heart of a man makes it glad."[20] I am trying to speak with King David.[21]

---

19.   This is the thirteenth century sufi poet, Jelaludin Rumi (1207-1273), a.k.a. Melvana Jalal
ad-Din Muhammad Rumi, or Mawlana Jalal-ad-Din Muhammad Balkhi. Born in Balkh
(present day Afghanistan) and died in Konya, Turkey.

20.   The full verse reads as follows: "Care in the heart of a man bows it down; but a good word
makes it glad." (Proverbs 12:25). The poet is misreading the verse as "Care in the heart of a
man ~~bows it down; but a good word~~ makes it glad." It is unclear whether Shevili is quoting
from King David the Builder's *Hymns of Repentance* [გალობანი სინანულისანი,
galobani sinanulisani], see below.

21.   While Shevili the poet is attempting to channel the spirit of King David, author of

[2]

A young woman stepped down the slope of the street, to peer at the sea. Her blouse—black, her dress—white. Annemarie Schimmel wrote a book on Islamic mystical poetry,[22] meanwhile I glanced at the poetry descending into the street form-fitting to the wall, beautifully modest, white and oppressed.

[3]

I am she, the one who is loved and the one who is loved is I.

[4]

Five times a day do they pray. Now that the darkening globe in the mirror above me falls, the *Meuzzin* calls forth prayer to God in the metallic voice, and I descend from the bridge.

---

the Hebrew Bible's Psalms, there is a more likely allusion that unfolds in the course of this poem. Shevili is also trying to channel the poetic voice of King David the Builder (Georgian: დავით აღმაშენებელი, *Davit Aghmashenebeli*) (1073-1125) a.k.a. H.M. The Most High King David, son of George, by the will of our Lord, King of Kings of the Abkhazians, Kartvelians, Ranians, Kakhetians and the Armenians, Shirvanshah and Shahanshah of all the East and West, Sword of the Messiah. This King David was buried at the Gelati Monastery, whereby entry into the academy requires a direct confrontation with his tomb, positioned beneath the first stone of the gatehouse. The Gelati Academy was considered by King David's historian to be: "a second Jerusalem of all the East for learning of all that is of value, for the teaching of knowledge—a second Athens, far exceeding the first in divine law, a canon for all ecclesiastical splendors." This medieval King David the Builder sees himself as the reincarnation of the Biblical David, notwithstanding the Christian cult of the Mother of God. See Donald Rayfield, *s.v.* "Davit II," *Reader's Encyclopedia of Eastern European Literature*, ed. Robert B. Pynsent, S. I. Kanikova, HarperCollins New York 1993, 82. Although the Kingdom of Georgia had been a tributary of the Seljug Turkish Empire, King David IV sought to centralize governance and restore order. His attacks disrupt Turkish trade throughout the region, reaching a climax with the unlikely defeat of Sultan Mahmud II and his troops. Upon capturing the city of Tbilisi, King David eventually relented in his harsh treatment of the Muslims of Tbilisi, extending more compassion to them than would Muslim rulers. King David the Builder was also a messianic poet, who upon liberating Armenian lands from the Turks was given the title "Sword of the Messiah." He is known to have written his *Hymns of Repentance* [გალობანი სინანულისანი, *galobani sinanulisani*] as a series of eight free-verse psalms. King David the Builder was canonized by the Georgian Orthodox Church. See http://georgianwines.blogspot.com/2008/06/david-builder-defeats-turks-ushers-in.html

22. Part of Shevili's remark here refers to the tension between experience and knowledge. The erotic typology of woman here is troped as intellectual versus sensual. Schimmel's book explores the question of whether Persian lyrical poetry should be interpreted as mystical or as erotic. See Annemarie Schimmel, "The Rose and The Nightingale: Persian and Turkish Mystical Poetry," *Mystical Dimensions of Islam* (North Carolina: University of North Carolina Press, 1975) 287-344.

[5]

It is possible that life, says Ibn al-Husayn al-Sulami,[23] is based upon the knowledge that one receives from others... that more or less one knows from them an additional possibility for good that life is based upon tribulations, but the greatest good is when life is based upon life, like water that delves into water.

[6]

The blue within the eye, the clouds appear to alight as ships at bay. One shoulder of mine is aching, one eye is hot, and touch is full of anxiety. The dervishes would not travel to be amused, nor stay in hotels, rather they would arise with dawn and pray the first prayer, then study, give alms, like them I must leave the path I have traversed until now.

[7]

The blue emphasizes non-color, the veil opening to the abyss. What can I do that I have not yet done so that a bit of light will enter this darkness I find myself in. I've always fled from submission to no-God, and now I am empty for I know that God was very much with me without being. I must overcome this darkness, what shall I do, as I know not how to illumine it.

[8]

Book Once the human being spoke, now that voice has reached me.

[9]

I am the cloud that veils my heavens. When the sun shall rise, the words I've written shall dissolve. This is the cry that the setting sun cries out to me. When I write and try to forget how much I wander, it is a relinquishment over the darkness. The light outside does not deceive, someone sang songs of yearning there, the ear listens and believes the deceit of the dark-man.

[10]

How will I find the great friend of King David, the non-Jew, aloe of the ear.

[11]

Once Abdullah ibn Maruvan[24] mistakenly cast a coin into a wretched well.

---

23. This is the tenth century Turkish sufi, Ibn al-Husayn al-Sulami (936-1021), a.k.a. Abu 'Abdul-Rahman Muhammad ibn al-Husayn ibn Muhammad ibn Musa ibn Khalid ibn Salim ibn Rawia al-Sulami (325-412)

24. This is the ninth century Kurdish theologian and convert to Islam century, Abdullah ibn Maruvan a.k.a. Muhammad ibn Abdullah ibn Mihran Dinawari. This name also recalls the Arab general, Maruvan ibn-Muhammad, who in 737-738 mercilessly destroyed the village

Immediately afterwards he went on to pay thirteen gold dinars to have the coin returned to him. When asked to explain his strange actions, he said the Name of Allah was inscribed on the coin, thus out of respect and awe he felt obliged at all costs to recover the coin from the well.

[12]

Once Rabia Al-'Adawiyya[25] turned to God and said: "My desire in this moment is to remember you, and in the time-that-is-coming only to gaze upon you; with regards to everything else, do with me as You desire."

[13]

Love When the blind man says to it that we still see, I cannot see, rather I only dream without seeing.

[14]

When I do not love, I have no space to approach him, nevertheless I walk the path without walking, I walk and seek that which has my soul has lost.

[15]

How will I allow myself to rest from God without knowing what I am to God. If I cannot know God, I cannot know what God is not. I will not know us.

[16]

My great grandmother was called Bebo. Once my father took me to see her in the Bukharian neighborhood, she lived in a room that resembled a nun's alcove. I was afraid of her black garb and her blind eyes that looked to one place only... there towards Colchis and the golden shearings, that is the place I want to reach. I am the one who must invert the Torah and write, Go forth from your land and from your nativity toward your father's home.

[17]

In order to write I left the house. It is impossible to write in the house when there is no *Beit*. In order to build a house, one needs to expand in some place... the house in the Colchis has been destroyed for some time, I am not traveling to build it. I am traveling to reveal how much I am destroyed.

---

of Nokalakevi, in Colchis. He is known to the Georgians as Maruvan the Deaf, seeing that he ignored their pleas for mercy throughout his rampage of Georgia.

25. This is the eighth-ninth century Iraqi sufi poet, Rabia Al-'Adawiyya, a.k.a Rabia of Basra, Rabia al-Basri (717-801). She remained an ascetic saint who refused to marry given the intensity of her intimacy with God (*shatahat*).

Sitting in Istanbul and reading Rumi's poetry, gazing at passersby that appear as though they have just been born and are already dying.

[18]
One who lies knows how to tell the truth. One who speaks the truth does not know how to tell lies. This is how Jews lose the gift given to them by art.

[19]
People pass before me so I cannot find myself. Rumi tells how once before daybreak Mullah Nussradin[26] came out from the tavern stumbling around without any direction in the streets. A policeman stopped him and asked why he was stumbling around at this hour. Mullah Nusaradin answered the officer that if only he knew how to respond to his question, he would already be at home asleep many hours ago.

[20]
We have a great barrel of wine/and even a chalice/it suits us fine/every morn we are inflamed with passion/and at night still/ we are burning/those who say we have no remedy are right/but for us it makes no difference.

[21]
Reading and writing are the candle that illumines in moments of fear.

[22]
I want to return to the aging childhood of my naivete and to believe that God is found in the silencing flower of the mouth.

[23]
The stars actually lie when they speak the truth...they no longer exist.

[24]
They sit and smoke a pipe, whispering silently and playing backgammon, not interested in turning westward, as much as they are ready to cast a glance there like Attaturk. They walk there with the lie without moving. They can understand Byazir of Bistam who for some time knew how to lie before the Turks taught them.

---

26. Nassrudin (ca. 1209 CE—ca. 1275/6 or 1285/6 CE) allegedly lived in Anatolia, Turkey. Referred to as the Mullah Nassrudin, he was born in Hortu Village in Sivrihisar, Eskişehir and then settled in Akşehir, and later in Konya (where Rumi lived). His teachings are recorded as a pithy folk wisdom and favored by many Sufi masters, including Rumi.

[25]

Istanbul, your silver fish swim in the sky, while in my heart a fire is lit/how great are your memories from the darkness of the day/from the bitter sea of Marmara/from Allah that took leave and the *Meuzzin* calling out after this one of his grandeur/I sit on the roof and gaze at the sparkling ship that passes over yonder.

[26]

The women lost their way to the wine dressed, as if there is no body, the heart of Rumi, for the beauty of the skin has no desire to be revealed. I am parched for the wine of Islam, for the balls expressed in their poetry, for the wine is in all, I want to cause it to spill from the serving cup to the bowl, and from it our great friend drinks who is always drunk, when will we understand that there is no path to God except every path.

[27]

Take time away from us, they say, we have no need for it, sitting on the stools and playing dominoes. Bird fowl screeching, a black bird jumping from branch to branch, remaining in the same tree, clouds refusing to wander, a bus parking, Rumi repeats himself, he is not tiresome and does not exhaust himself, arousing yearnings to yearnings. Nothing will be erased, even though it all shall fade, for what always was shall remain. The young man from the travel agencies says that two rivers intersect, Rumi and Shams of Tabriz, a great ocean erupted inside of me when I met these two rivers, the black bird skipped from branch to branch upon the giant tree gazing at me and asked, 'Why don't you also learn how to jump?'

[28]

Things are not good for me, but I try to make it alright, and when I cannot I feel filthy. The books will not cleanse me, they say they are more sly than wild animals, assuring themselves each time anew, for behold at this edge beyond them shall I find Ithaca.[27]

[29]

Those who do not know which path to take towards the path do not know that we switched out Rumi's wine with sugar.

[30]

I have within me both the poison and the cure. The Dervishes would frequently gaze at young men whose beards had yet to grow in, through

---

[27].   The destination of Odysseus' journey throughout *The Odyssey* to reunite with his beloved Penolope is Ithaca. By contrast, Shevili is in search of the Beloved in Istanbul and Colchis but will ultimately return home to Jerusalem.

their beauty and their ruddiness they beheld the embodiment of the god. Droplets of rain dripped, I gazed at the beautiful gazelle and at the tears upon the tavern's window, as the clouds have passed and the sun has risen, I saw *Mazda,*[28] as she was drinking stars from the heavens.

[31]

I am still afraid but less so. What did Bebo see at that moment in the blinded eyes of the one who came from the convent Colchis,[29] that was once called Gorgona and vipers grew upon her head,[30] I am still afraid of her empty eyes that are fit to see until here.

[32]

Medea.[31] The garment that you wore there will burn you if you wear it here.

[33]

Fear comes and goes like waves, my thighs ache, I deserve a mouth as wide as the heavens so I can speak about the sufferings of one who is not beloved. Perhaps it is the fever that comes to the afflicted from the cold. Abu Yazid of Bistam[32] stripped like a snake strips its skin, gazed at himself and said: 'I was He.'

---

28. *Mazda,* god of the Zoroastrian pantheon. Zarathustra's unique name for his God, *Ahura Mazda,* means "Wise Lord" or "Lord of Wisdom." *Mazda* also signifies "Wisdom" as a feminine noun (like the Greek *Sophia*), but *Ahura* (literally "High Being") is masculine. Zarathushtra uses this recurrent theme throughout the *Gathas,* namely, that God is both feminine and masculine. In the *Gathas,* the two names are either used separately but most often together as *Mazda Ahura* (Wise Lord), see http://www.zoroastrianism.cc/mazda_ahura.html

29. Colchis is the old kingdom of Georgia, known as the Land of the Golden Fleece, see Medea below n. 31. The actual site of this legendary kingdom remains in dispute but the Greeks still remained inspired by the Colchis region of Georgia and the River Phasis running through it. Colchis is a journey of approximately under two days from Istanbul.

30. This is Medusa, chief of the three Gorgons.

31. *Medea* (Greek: Μήδεια, *Mēdeia,* Georgian:მედეა, *Medea*). In Greek mythology, she was the daughter of King Aeëtes of Colchis (the old kingdom of Georgia), the niece of Circe, the granddaughter of the sun god, Helios, and later wife to the hero, Jason, with whom she had two children: Mermeros and Pheres. The garment being referred to in the poem is the golden fleece that King Aeëtes promises to Jason upon his return from Iolcus to Colchis to reclaim the throne. Medea falls in love with Jason, promising to assist him on the condition that he marry her if he succeeds in his mission. After many trials, Jason sails away with Medea, giving her the fleece as promised. Aphrodite blinds Medea in her mad love for Jason to the point that she kills her brother, Absytrus, to distract her father to ensure safe passage with Jason.

32. This is the Persian sufi, born in Bastam, Iran, named Abu Yazid of Bistam (804-874), a.k.a. Bayazid Bastami, Tayfur Abu Yazid al-Bustami. His grandfather was a Zoroastrian convert to Islam. Abu Yazid is considered to be the first "intoxicated" sufi, who upon achieving

[34]
Snake The placenta I tore from my body in order to give birth.

[35]
The bride ascended the stairs of the Gelati Monastery[33] with male and female processionals, women in habits, with veils and other kinds of coverings, they forgot that today they are also the brides of God who endows beauty just as his eyes see and from the seagull above that leaped forth with a cruel laughter.

[36]
Every step of mine is prayer, lament, praise, a woman's blouse is a prayer shawl, a belt is phylacteries, the hat is head covering, for the eyes see from beyond the light that there is no God.

[37]
Gazelle Trembling, skipping, jumping in the streets, seeking a path to escape from the hunters.

[38]
The flower is opened when it says it is opened, all languages become that home without walls, my language only has one friend, a pair of ears that reside above.

[39]
Within this love, death/your path begins as an other side/be heavens/grab an axe to the prison walls/escape to the side! death/get out and go like one who is suddenly born/do this now/when you are enshrouded like a thin cloud/escape the hunt/and the sign is deep silence/that you died/your previous life was tried and debauched/ from the silence/the moon fills the absence of words/take leave now.

---

annihilation of self proclaimed open (and heretical) intimacy with God (*shatahat*).

Exemplary sayings of this *shatahat* echoing "I was He" in the poem, include: "Moses desired to see God; I do not desire to see God; He desires to see me" and "I am I; there is no God but I; so worship me!" See John Walbridge, "Suhrawardi and Illumination," *The Cambridge Companion to Arabic Philosophy*, ed. Peter Adamson, Richard C. Taylor, Cambridge University Press, 2005. 206; Ritter, H. "Abū Yazīd (Bāyazīd) Tayfūr B. Īsā B. Surūshān al-Bistāmī." Encyclopaedia of Islam, Second Edition, ed. P. Bearman, Th. Bianquis , C.E. Bosworth, E. van Donzel and W.P. Heinrichs. Brill, 2009. Brill Online. see http://www.brillonline.nl/subscriber/entry?entry=islam_SIM-0275

33. The Gelati Monastery was built in the twelfth century by King David the Builder, also responsible for founding the Gelati Academy of philosophy. King David consolidated Eastern and Western Georgia.

[40]

As I ascended from the Gelati bridge to Istanbul, a man shining shoes asked
me for a cigarette, I lied to him and told him that I couldn't give him one,
how will I die if I don't want to live.

[41]

The words 'I want to die' do not suffice to really die. One needs to needlessly
sink into light without leaking illumination. Bebo extinguished the light
of her eyes and died before she died, in order to die before she would live.

[42]

I, for whom even one is all, for him I have taken leave of this city of twelve
million.

[43]

Where is the black sea to be found, I'll see it once the black punctures bring
on the wound of dawn.

1.2 Contrition as Mystical Connection of Devekut

Contrition, as Shevili reiterates, is an oftentimes overlooked form of
mystical connection. Cultivating contrition [*haratah*] is a prerequisite for
returning to a deeper consciousness of intimacy in the divine [*teshuvah*],
such that this spiritual station has been a perpetual focus in Jewish
spirituality through the ages. Already a spiritual station within the *Tahanun*
liturgy recited twice daily, contrition [*haratah*] is what opens the flow of
Divine Compassion.[34] Building on the earlier medieval philosophical and
ethical foundations of contrition [*haratah*],[35] each mystical stream—from
the external cosmic spiritual drama of Lurianic Kabbalah[36] to the internal

---

34. See for example, *Sod haYihud: Siddur Ramhal* (Jerusalem: Ramhal Institute, 2007), 177-
   178n94, where the 13 Attributes of Compassion are aroused through contrition. Unless
   this spiritual journeying takes place, *Vidui* is not possible nor is *Teshuva* efficacious.
35. See for example, R. Saadia haGaon, *Sefer Emunot veDeot*, 5:2; R. Joseph Albo, *Sefer
   haIkarim*, 4:27; *Sefer haHinukh*, Command no. 406. It is noteworthy that, already in the
   Talmudic mind, God has contrition for certain creatures of creation, see bSukkah 52b.
36. Some exemplars of Lurianic Kabbalah on *harata* include: Hayyim Vital, *Sefer Shaarai Kedushah*
   1:6; Shalom Sharabi, *Sefer Nahar Shalom* 39a; Israel Horowitz, *Shenai Luhot haBrit* 7:17 s.v.
   b'asara ma'marot; Moshe Hayyim Luzzatto, *Mesilat Yesharim* 4, s.v. *k'niyat ha'zerizut*.

psychical practice of Hasidism[37]—serve as a refining agent for that process of returning to deeper divine consciousness [*teshuvah*].

This return to a more intimate connection of *devekut* takes place through concrete steps in Hasidism, which deserve a brief elucidation to appreciate the poem at hand by Shevili. On the one hand, there is Reb Shneur Zalman of Lyadi, who articulates a path of *Zebrukhenkeit*; that is composed of: (1) heart-rending contrition, (2) spiritual accounting of transgression and (3) confession; (4) followed by a newfound devotion to practice.[38] Contrition is ultimately viewed as one of the greatest spiritual evolutions [*tiqqun*] possible within the framework of a commanded existence.[39] Awakening to the transformative power of contrition as connection is an important step in the spiritual evolution of both mystic and poet.

On the other hand, Reb Nahman of Bratzlav's articulation of this spiritual condition is already alluded to by the title of Shevili's *Poems of Longing for Mecca*.[40] It is the experience of *ga'aguim*[41] or that deep longing, for Reb Nahman, that can return one back into a deeper state of *devekut*. What then is the fine line that differentiates such spiritual longing from manic depression? Whereas the manic depression of *marah shehorah*[42] is

---

37. Some exemplars of Hasidism on *harata* include: Ze'ev Wolf of Zhitomir, *Me'or Eynaim*, *s.v. VaYetze*; Abraham Heschel of Apt, *Ohev Yisrael*, *s.v. Zakhor v'Purim*; R. Tzaddok haCohen Rabinowitz of Lublin, *Tzidkat haTzaddik*, no. 238.

38. HaBa"D Hasidism has devoted extensive thinking to the role of contrition (*harata*) in the process of catalyzing systematic return (*teshuvah* which then is further divided into supernal and terrestrial return). For example, see R. Shneur Zalman ben Baruch of Lyadi, *Liqqutai Amarim Tanya b'zeruf Marai Makomot, Liqqutim Perushim v'Shinui Nushaot*, *s.v. u'mitharet u'mevakesh mehila v'seliha* 11:225; ibid., *Liqqutai Amarim Tehorim*, ed. Yissachar David ben Yehushua, vol. 2, *s.v. b'haftarah, Shabbat Shuvah*, 61:152; ibid., *Liqqutai Amarim Tehorim, Vayikrah: Be'Har*, 90; *Liqqutai Amarim (Mahadura Kama)*, 11:26: 93; 16, etc.

39. Sustained reflection on contrition as a modality of connection is found in numerous sources, especially *Sefer Orhot Tzadikim*, Gate 11, Gate of Contrition.

40. Amuyel, "There is also a different love," 28.

41. See for example, Reb Nahman of Bratzlav, *Liqqutai MoHaRaN (Mahadura Kama)*, no. 155; ibid., *Liqqutai MoHaRaN (Mahadura Batra)*, no. 78; ibid., *Shivhai MoHaRaN*, no's 29, 33; ibid., *Sihot MoHaRaN*, no. 24; ibid., *Liqqutai Eitzot*, *s.v. Emeth v'Emunah, Eretz Yisrael, Tzaddik*.

42. See for example, Reb Nahman of Bratzlav, *Liqqutai MoHaRaN (Mahadura Kama)*, no's 23, 30, 282, ; ibid., *Liqqutai MoHaRaN (Mahadura Batra)*, no's 9, 10; ibid Reb Natan of Nemirov, *Liqqutai Tefillot* II:9; II:21; ibid., *Sihot MoHaRaN*, nos. 43, 155, 197; ibid., *Liqqutai Eitzot*, *s.v. Brit, Pegamo v'Tikkuno*.

a longing born of deep suffering without any trace of estrangement from divinity, *ga'aguim* are always imbued with traces of divine presence, even in the feeling of remoteness—that is what fuels the reconnection of *devekut*.[43]

As a devotional poet, Shevili channels this deep longing in his estrangement from the divine by searching for a way to express this as his own authentic spiritual truth[44] through a mystical path[45] in Hebrew. How? By hearing the voice of the Psalmist, King David, and the Sufis that followed his ecstatic path in his own epic poem.[46] The Hebrew poet yearns for that same intimacy, again with God, but must strive to ascend again through a heart-rending connection of contrition. This process of emerging from the descent is a kind of "chiseling" and "scratching away" at the outer layers of self as expressed in the literal root of contrition itself [*HaRaTa*][47] once it is rendered reflexive. As I have explored elsewhere,[48] those who traversed this path in Istanbul searching for the voice of King David include none other than Shabbetai Tzvi (1626-1676), the Ba'al Shem Tov (1698-1760), and Reb Nahman of Bratzlav (1772-1810). I would argue that Binyamin Shevili [*B"Sh*] likely sees himself as a reincarnation of peripatetic mystic, the Ba'al Shem Tov [*Be"ShT*], as both are seeking the direct connection with King David—the mystical persona who penned the Psalms. Shevili then takes this one step further by seeking to channel the spirit of a Davidic reincarnate, King David the Builder (1073-1125).[49]

---

43. I am indebted to R. Moshe Aaron Krassen for clarifying this nuance between the *ga'aguim* of R. Nahman and the *zebrukhenkeit* of R. Shneur Zalman.

44. Goldman, "Solitude of the Writer (2)," *Ha'Aretz: Literature & Culture* (May 8, 1998), 41

45. See for example, Moses Ḥayim Luzzatto, *Mesilat Yesharim*, Ch. 4, *Derekh Kinyat haZehirut; Sefer Ḥareidim*, Ch. 9, 47, 63; etc.

46. Recall how King David decries in Psalm 139:21: "And do not I strive with those that rise up against/for You?"

47. *HRT* denotes chiseling, scraping as related to the formation of the Golden Calf, see *Midrash Tanhuma, Ki Tissa* 14. Whereas *HRT* in the reflexive form of *hitpa'el* denotes scratching oneself, it then comes to connote that very feeling of regret that happens when the outer surface of self is scratched away.

48. See Aubrey L. Glazer, "Imaginal Journeying to *Istanbul, mon amour*: Devotional sociabilities in BeSH"Tian Hasidism & Turkish-Sufism," *Spiritual Affinities* (Kentucky: *Fons Vitae*, 2011).

49. While Shevili the poet is trying to channel the spirit of King David, author of the Hebrew Bible's Psalms, there is a more likely possibility that unfolds in the course of this poem. Shevili is trying to speak with King David the Builder (Georgian: დავით აღმაშენებელი, *Davit Aghmashenebeli*) (1073-1125) a.k.a. H.M. The Most High King David, son of George, by the will of our Lord, King of Kings of the Abkhazians, Kartvelians, Ranians, Kakhetians and the

Aside from channeling such Jewish messianic avatars, this Jerusalemite poet desires to expand the horizon of his mystical apperception, thus his turn to the deeply immanent mysticism overflowing in Sufi poetry. What Shevili discovers in this stream of the journey are mystics who practice anomianism. This entails subjecting oneself to public reproach by appearing to disregard the rules of proper behavior, even the outward rites of religion, which is a defining feature of an Islamic Sunni sect of dervishes, known as the Malamiyyah.[50] Their only sign was poverty, humility, trustworthiness, and beneficence.[51] Good deeds are discounted privately, while the world's disapproval and anger is sought to publicly battle and refine one's ego.[52] This heroic attitude for a peaceful life is secured by interior purity and overcoming the commanding self.[53] Letting go of any over-reliance upon the technologies of prayer (i.e. coat, rosary, prayer rug) becomes a defining way of this anomian rediscovery of true self.

Self-humiliation as critique by these Sufis demands that the formalities of the prayer life give way to a more informal, and thus direct access to divine consciousness. This yearning for direct access means challenging conventional prayer technologies and fixed liturgies, reflected in the flow of free verse in Shevili's poetic cycle. In Sufism, reaching contrition is the mystical moment known as "the Station of No Station," and it assumes one has already traversed and evolved from the path of earlier typologies: (1) from the worshippers [al-'ubbad]; (2) to the Sufis; (3) then reaching the People of Blame [malami]. Whereas the worshippers "purify their inward dimensions from every blameworthy attribute which has been blamed by the Lawgiver,"[54] the Sufis are imbued with good character [khuluq] and chivalry [futuwwa], and see all acts as selflessly belonging to the divine.[55] Only the People of Blame [malami] see their acts as emanating from the One, so they

---

Armenians, Shirvanshah and Shahanshah of all the East and West, Sword of the Messiah.

50. The *Malamiyyah* enters its second phase in Turkey during the fourteenth and fifteenth centuries with the saint Hajji Bayram Wali and his disciple, Amir Siqqini. See Shaikh Tosun Bayrak al-Jerrahi al-Halveti, *Inspirations: On the Path of Blame Shaikh Badruddin of Simawna* (Vermont: Threshold Sufi Classics, 1993), 44, 57-62. I am grateful to Shaikh Tosun Bayrak for sharing the *Malamiyyah* sources with me.

51. Shaikh Tosun Bayrak, *Shaikh Badruddin of Simawna*, 62.

52. Ibid., 44.

53. Ibid., 47.

54. William C. Chittick, *Ibn al-'Arabi's Metaphysics of Imagination: The Sufi Path of Knowledge* (New York: SUNY Press, 1989), 373a.

55. Ibid., 373b.

allow self-blame and criticism all to evoke contrition. Blaming of self as spiritual practice comes from being completely at one with God, then taking blame for the failure for the One not to be manifest in existence.[56] Through Shevili's epic poem of "Contrition" the poet absorbs the Sufi devotion to imagine becoming a Jewish *malami*. To achieve this, Shevili must journey from Jerusalem to Istanbul and back again. In light of an emerging mystical subjectivity of boundary-crossing from Jewish to Islamic mysticism and back again, Shevili's epic poem can now be opened for deeper reading.

1.3 The Journey of Contrition through Shevili's Poetic Cycle

The journey into truly understanding the constitution of self is affected by its own dissolution in the face of the other. That process of dissolution of self begins with a fear of the impending fallenness and deep disconnection. By scratching away at the surface of self, the poet realizes that the yearning for his soul to soar is hampered by the sharpness of this fear. The anxiety deepens for the poet in questioning whether this fear is over falling into depression or a deeper state of unquenchable yearning as Shevili begins this journey into "Contrition" remarking:

> I am afraid, really afraid of the ailments, exhaustion and vision that weaken with the dizziness of my fear. There is a sharpness to it as subtle as a razor. I feel like a bird whose wings have been broken from their flight. Fear froths forth from my mouth and it tastes bitter. I am afraid that men will uncover what is concealed beneath my facial expression. Something evil, something terrifying. I ascend to the street but descend into the abyss, yearning to open a book of Rumi's poetry, but I have no strength. I try to rejoice but joy no longer comes from my heart rather from my mind. The heart is the site of fear, so I say, "Care in the heart of a man makes it glad." I am trying to speak with King David.

> A young woman stepped down the slope of the street, to peer at the sea. Her blouse—black, her dress—white. Annemarie Schimmel wrote a book on Islamic mystical poetry,[57] meanwhile I glanced at the poetry descending into

---

56. Ibid., 375a.
57. See Annemarie Schimmel, "The Rose and The Nightingale: Persian and Turkish Mystical Poetry," *Mystical Dimensions of Islam* (North Carolina: University of North Carolina Press, 1975), 287–344. Part of Shevili's remark here refers to the tension between experience and knowledge. The erotic typology of woman here is troped as intellectual versus sensual.

the street form-fitting to the wall, beautifully modest, white and oppressed.

I am she, the one who is loved and the one who is loved is I.

From Rumi to King David, from the erotic body descending into the street to the mind of a scholar reflecting on it, what is evident in these three free verse stanzas is how much the emotion of fear is intertwined with the emotion of love. By claiming an intimate interlinking of fear in love (so common to Hasidic spirituality, yet deftly remaining *unsaid*), Shevili is revealing an emotional pattern that will resonate throughout this cycle. Catalyzed by fear, the descent into contrition moves into tremors of yearning for lost love. The masculine self yearns for reunion with the feminine, and ultimately reabsorbs her. Therein arises the realization that even in this moment of disconnection there is a connection through being beloved.

This sense of yearning which is being aroused through descent continues to build as some of Shevili's strongest Sufi exemplars are then evoked and translated into Hebrew a few stanzas later:

> Once Abdullah ibn Maruvan[58] mistakenly cast a coin into a wretched well. Immediately afterwards he went on to pay thirteen gold dinars to have the coin returned to him. When asked to explain his strange actions, he said the Name of Allah was inscribed on the coin, thus out of respect and awe he felt obliged at all costs to recover the coin from the well.

> Once Rabia Al-'Adawiyya[59] turned to God and said: "My desire in this moment is to remember you, and in the time-that-is-coming only to gaze upon you; with regards to everything else, do with me as You desire."

This turn to Abdullah ibn Maruvan and Rabia Al-'Adawiyya again reveals the poets yearning to emerge, and re-ascend from his unfolding

---

Schimmel's book explores the question of whether Persian lyrical poetry should be interpreted as mystical or as erotic.

58. This is the ninth century Kurdish theologian and convert to Islam century, Abdullah ibn Maruvan a.k.a. Muhammad ibn Abdullah ibn Mihran Dinawari.

59. This is the eighth-ninth century Iraqi sufi poet, Rabia Al-'Adawiyya, a.k.a Rabia of Basra, Rabia al-Basri (717-801). She remained an ascetic saint who refused to marry given the intensity of her intimacy with God (*shatahat*).

descent. This foreseen surfacing back into deeper desire is again intimately intertwined with the depth of the fall. What Abdullah ibn Maruvan's parable shows is the degree to which the divine is always inscribed and even more deeply encountered in the descent itself. Thus the shift from Abdullah ibn Maruvan to Rabia Al-'Adawiyya is a shift in the stations of desire, from descent as apparent disconnection from the divine to a deeper ascent into desire for divine consciousness within the constitution of self.

> People pass before me so I cannot find myself. Rumi tells how once before daybreak Mullah Nussradin[60] came out from the tavern stumbling around without any direction in the streets. A policeman stopped him and asked why he was stumbling around at this hour. Mullah Nussaradin answered the officer that if only he knew how to respond to his question, he would already be at home asleep many hours ago.

> *We have a great barrel of wine/and even a chalice/it suits us fine/every morn we are inflamed with passion/and at night still/ we are burning/those who say we have no remedy are right/but for us it makes no difference.*

> Reading and writing are the candle that illumines in moments of fear.

Recall how the poet began his descent by claiming that even Rumi's ecstatic poetry could not rouse him back to joy as the dark night of the soul begins clouding over. Yet Shevili now returns to Rumi for assistance in making ascent from the descent through the satirical parables of Mullah Nusaradin. This parable about wandering is integral for understanding both the particularity of Shevili's current ascent through the descent of contrition as well as the larger trajectory of his poetic travelogue for the soul. The poet must wander in order to find his way home; in the wandering itself, a purpose for the soul is recovered. In this liminal state of unknowing, the soul can continue its ascent into deeper consciousness, and without this wandering it would be trapped in stasis. A shift from the solitary voice to a collective one is then marked through the laughter

---

60. Nassrudin (ca. 1209 CE—ca. 1275/6 or 1285/6 CE) allegedly lived in Anatolia, Turkey. Referred to as the Mullah Nassrudin, he was born in Hortu Village in Sivrihisar, Eskişehir and then settled in Akşehir, and later in Konya (where Rumi lived, see above, n.57). His teachings are recorded as a pithy folk wisdom and favored by many Sufi masters, including Rumi.

that emerges from Nussradin's tale, opening the poet to an ecstatic moment. That ecstasy is symbolized by overflowing wine, which is the breakthrough of writing itself. Writing for the poet is an ecstatic elixir out of any possible depression that might take hold, spills into into a deeper understanding that the descent being experienced is for the sake of ascent, and that the contrition is for the sake of returning home. With the prospect of a home-coming in the offing, the poet is able to get a grip on the fear and channel it into the contrition that deepens the yearning for reunion:

> Things are not good for me, but I try to make it alright, and when I cannot I feel filthy. The books will not cleanse me, they say they are more sly than wild animals, assuring themselves each time anew, for behold at this edge beyond them shall I find Ithaca.[61]

> Those who do not know which path to take towards the path do not know that we switched out Rumi's wine with sugar.

The next step in this process of descent for the sake of ascent is confession. In confessing what the poet feels and expressing the confidence that he will ultimately make it through this momentary disconnection in the descent, he also has an important realization. Despite the fact that a poet must write, returning to books is not the solution. By turning to the head when it is the heart that yearns for connection is counter-productive to his spiritual journey. Having the strength to make this confession as a poet is cathartic. This is what allows the poet to steer his soul upward in the process of emerging from the descent, almost able to see the homeward trajectory of his journey materializing. Despite the ironic reference to homecoming as Ithaca, the Hebrew poet knows his beloved awaits him in his own Ithaca of Jerusalem. The problem of course being that the consciousness of Jerusalem, *Yirah-shalem* or the true awe he yearns for embodied in that navel of the universe is presently devoid of its contents. The more painful realization that comes forth in the poet's confession is how the wine of ecstatic mystery has been swapped for the sugar of rabbinic hegemony that is Israel. As daring as this realization is for the Hebrew poet, it must

---

61. See above n. 26.

take place for him far away from home. It is this distance from Jerusalem that empowers him with a deeper yearning to return home. This process of return, the final rung of the contrition cycle, is now what will guide the poet home with a more refined spiritual compass.

This realization of a homecoming in the offing would never have dawned upon the poet unless he entered into his peripatetic wanderings to begin with. Now everything is seen in a new light breaking through the dark night of the soul:

> Every step of mine is prayer, lament, praise, a woman's blouse is a prayer shawl, a belt is phylacteries, the hat is head-covering, for the eyes see from beyond the light that there is no God.

By stepping out of his house to write through this poet's experience of the world, everything can be seen as a vessel for channeling the holy.

1.4 Conclusion: Contrition as Devekut of Devotional Cultures

Contrition within devotional cultures is the fear of losing human connection to the divine. What Shevili awakens in his journey through contrition is how the anxiety of disconnecting is overcome by reconnecting through the other's devotional culture only to return back to one's own devotional path. When binary thinking that normally rules the mind melts away, only then can the devotional categories of the other reconnect the seeker through devekut from a place of fallenness.

In traversing boundaries that once separated devotional cultures, Shevili's poem is pointing to a further evolution of consciousness taking place. The very regenerative process in the language of devekut requires an experience of spiritual affinity as evinced throughout Shevili's poetry cycle of "Contrition" [Harata]. The very form of mystical apprehension known as devekut is undergoing transformation by a symbiosis of contrition in word and experience. The more an evolution of mystical apperception is taking place, the more the particular devotional cultures rewrite such universal symbolism as their own, in Shevili's case by translating and rewriting the warp of Sufi lore on the yearning heart through contrition into the woof of his Hebrew poetry cycle. As mystical apprehension requires a foundational moment of contrition, the ascent from descent requires more from the emotive than cognitive realm, more praxis than theory. Only once this process leads to *devekut* of (1) heart-rending contrition, (2) spiritual accounting of transgression and (3) confession, (4) followed by a newfound devotion to practice, can the greatest evolutions of consciousness be re-awakened. The more that mystical experience is truly porous, engendering a hybridity of devotional cultures (in this case between Hasidism and Sufism), the more nuanced the connection through *devekut*. Such a rending of the self through contrition reconnects the heart as below, so above, forever changing the divine-human matrix in the process.

CHAPTER V

OPENING SECRECY: IS THERE DUPLICITY IN *DEVEKUT*?
SCHULAMITH CHAVA HALEVY'S "STRANGE FIRE" AND "IMPREGNATION'S SECRET"

Is there duplicity in the unitive experience of *devekut*? The further one enters into the exploration of the degrees of *devekut* the more each degree appears to be veiled in secrecy. Why is the experience of unitive consciousness so often wrapped in secretive language? If this experience is so deeply yearned for by ensouled beings, then why must this revelation appear so concealed? Notwithstanding the fear of exposing one's innermost vulnerability to judgmental exterior forces, resorting to concealment at the moment of deeper revealment seems to go against the unitive nature of *devekut* itself.

Mystical vertigo suggests a breakdown of boundaries between the human and the divine. This dissolution of domains allows for a merging of interiority and exteriority. Moving beyond the vulnerability arising from such dissolution, there emerges a deeper submission—a giving over of the commanding self to the unitive experience veiled in secrecy. But is the seeker of the secret prone to duplicity? That lurking sense of duplicity layering secrecy may in fact be a necessary oscillation. It is that texture of oscillation—from revealing the concealed to concealing the revealed[1]—that deserves further exploration through strong poetry.

It must first be noted, however, that throughout the history of Jewish mystical literature, there is a turning to secrecy as the site of intimate sharing, the place for revealing *gnosis*. Already in the Hebrew Bible, *sod* meaning "counsel"[2] becomes that which is shared in a circle of intimate

---

1. For an extensive reflection on the role of secrecy and its revealed concealment in contemporary Hasidism, see the masterful study by Elliot R. Wolfson, *Open Secret: Postmessianic Messianism and the Mystical Revision of Menahem Mendel Schneerson* (New York: Columbia University Press, 2009).
2. Lamentations 11:13; Jeremiah 6:11, 23:22; Job 19:19; Amos 3:7.

friends,[3] evolving in Talmudic times into secret counsel that may be revealed to a discrete few.[4] A sharing of a secret with an intimate *other* dissimulates back into the divine.[5] In yearning for such intimacy with the divine, the mystic shares that taste of the limitless experience through the veil of secrecy. The ineffable experience is then conveyed through the confines of language.[6]

Secrecy overflows with paradox. On the one hand, sharing an intimate secret can be delicious, while on the other hand, *saying* an unspoken secret can dangerous—even deadly.[7] Both delicious and deadly, these tropes enshroud and shimmer forth from the self-same secret. The deeper the disclosure of the secret, the greater the proximity to death. The very *thanatos* of secrecy is how its *eros* imbues those who share in the liminal pleasure of such intimacy.[8]

Such apparent paradoxes of secrecy will serve to contextualize the poetic possibilities of secrecy in one of Israel's most important young poets, Schulamith Chava Halevy. As the poet herself dissimulates the open secret

---

3.   Jeremiah 6:11, 15:17, 23:18, 22; Job 15:8, 19:19; Psalm 64:3; Amos 3:7.

4.   Compare the Biblical sources on revealing secrecy in Lamentations 11:13, 20:19, 25:9; Amos 3:7 with the Talmudic strictures of revealing the secret Chariot Visions or *Maase Merkava*, in bHaggigah 12b-14a. See Ithamar Gruenwald, "The Jewish esoteric literature in the time of the Mishnah and Talmud," *Immanuel* 4 (1974): 37-46; see also Daniel Abrams, "A neglected talmudic reference to *Maase Merkava*," *Frankfurter Judaistische Beiträge* 26 (1999): 1-5.

5.   Psalm 25:14; Lamentations 3:32.

6.   The common mystical locution of secrecy is some variation of the following: Zoharic Kabbalah uses *sod razah*, while Lurianic Kabbalah uses *sodai ha-sodot* and *razah*; and *razah de-razin*; for further reflections on the mystical implications of veiling and secrecy, see Elliot R. Wolfson, "Occultation of the Feminine and the Body of Secrecy in Medieval Kabbalah," *Rending the Veil* (New York: NYU Press, 1999), 113-154; ibid., Secrecy, Modesty, and the Feminine: Kabbalistic Traces in the Thought of Levinas," *Journal of Jewish Thought & Philosophy* 14, 1-2 (2006): 193-224.

7.   How deadly, then, is the speaking of ineffable secrets when a master has no choice but to reveal to a given disciple an esoteric teaching? For the hagiographic accounts in *Sefer Toldot haAri* of Luria's obligation to disclose [*mehuyav ani legalot*] the secret, esoteric teaching to Vital has an almost erotic tension to it, see Meir Benayhu, *Sefer Toldot haAri* (Jerusalem: Ben Tzvi Institute, 1967), 197-198.

8.   The more that this disciple, Vital, coaxes his master [*hiftzir harbe ba'rav she'yomar lo oto ha'sod*], the more Luria feels the desire arising to disclose the secret. One week after the secret is disclosed to Vital, however, Luria's son, Moses, dies as a consequence. This insight grows from Elliot R. Wolfson's *Seminar in Lurianic Kabbalah* (New York: NYU, 2002).

of her poetry to be "... my dialogue with God in my poetry, in death, and in love with God there."[9] But why is death inevitable when the secret is revealed? Secrecy brings *jouissance* at the hour of its opening, all the while this revelatory experience of disclosure enshrouds the world of both mystic and poet.

In the poet's collections, whether *The Inner Castle*[10] and *Breath Sign*,[11] Schulamith Chava Halevy points to another way of seeing and experiencing secrecy. This poetic envisioning is ontic rather than ontological[12]—namely, the experience that gives rise to language rather than the concepts which describe it. For both mystic and poet, these experiences are conveyed through language and influenced by its devotional culture.[13]

Interweaving the warp of religious culture and the woof spiritual texture within the poet's formation begins with her ancestry hailing from the *Anusim* of Spain and Portugal. Emigrating to Israel with her family from Switzerland, Schulamith Chava Halevy spent her youth growing up in Poria Ilit, in the Galilee, establishing lifelong friendships with neighboring Bedouin-Israelis and Druzes.[14] Although during the Six Day War in 1967, the Swiss Embassy offered the entire family asylum in Switzerland, her parents decided to cast their children's destiny along with their people in Israel.[15] The family moved from the Galilee to Jerusalem and then back to the Galilee. While in Jerusalem, she balanced out the time she spent as a somewhat reclusive and precocious young poet by volunteering in the local hospitals, even after her required military service. Tending to the wounded exposed her to the vicissitudes of life and the ravages of war.[16] Exposure to the wounds of life came full circle as she struggled in coming to terms with a destructive disease of her own immune system. Like all strong poetry, Halevy's poems reflect on the fleeting nature of time in relation to eternal

---

9.   Conversation with Schulamith Chava Halevy (Tel Aviv: August 17, 2005).
10.   Schulamith Chava Halevy, *Inner Castle: Poems about Being and Being Coerced* [Hebrew] (Jerusalem: 'Eked Publications, 1998).
11.   Schulamith Hava Halevy, *Breath Sign* [Hebrew] (Jerusalem: Carmel, 2003).
12.   Pierre Boutang, *Ontologie du Sécret* (Paris: PUF, 1973).
13.   Schulamith Chava Halevy, "Être poete dans un pays ravagé par la guerre," *Foi & Vie: 33e Cahiers d'etudes juives* n5, trans. G. Toledano & D. Banon (Decembre 2005): 46-76. I am grateful to the poet for sharing this published French translation as well as her Hebrew original.
14.   Ibid., 48-49.
15.   Ibid., 52.
16.   Ibid., 55-56.

temporality. Her perpetual yearning to return to the primordial unity of non-dual consciousness is reflected in this unpublished poem, for example:

מָקוֹם בִּזְמַן

שָׁאֲנִי נָא אֶל הַמַּעֲמַקִּים
הַמַּרְקִיעִים
הַנִּשָּׂאִים
אֶל הַמָּקוֹם
בַּזְּמַן
בְּטֶרֶם
...
אֲזַי אֶהְיֶה זוֹהֲרָה
תִּזְרֵנִי אֶל תּוֹךְ
צְעִיף הָאֵינְסוֹף
אֶל הַנְּהוֹרָה

שׁוּבָה אֵלַי וְאָשׁוּבָה
לְמַה שֶׁהָיִינוּ לִפְנֵי
הַבְּרִיאָה[17]

A Place in Time

Alight me now to the heavenly
depths
delivering
to the place
in time
ere
...
Radiant shall I be
as you scatter me
into the shroud of the Limitless
towards the Light

Return to me and I shall return
to what we were ere
creation

---

17. Halevy, "A Place in Time," Uncollected and unpublished.

How does such a yearning to return to the "ere" [*terem*] of primordial unity relate to secrecy? Is there an unspoken secret self that has been ruptured and torn from its origin of non-dual consciousness of "what we were" that is recovered in her poetry? That lost "we" is a collectivity of forgotten voices, of lost souls, that the poet seeks to channel through her poetry. To a large degree those are the voices of the crypto-Jews or *Anusim*, thousands of whom the poet is continuously in contact with for her ongoing research. Her research explores the ways in which customs and traditions have been secretly preserved amongst those *Anusim* (including priests) who have been coerced into an exterior conformity to Christianity while retaining an inner practice of Judaism. But beyond the academic side of her research on the *Anusim*, as a poet, Halevy's recovery of these hidden stories allows her to reveal how much her own soul is bound up in theirs. Her poetry breaks open these time capsules concealed within the souls of others in the hope of returning to the secret self that has been ruptured and torn from its origin of non-dual consciousness.

So if there is a symbolic constellation of secrecy operative in Halevy's poetry, it is more expansive than an ontology or chain of concepts strewn together to reveal the nature of Being philosophically. Rather, I will argue that the poetic shift from *Inner Castle* to *Breath Sign* is parallel to the shift in Lurianic Kabbalah from *gilgul* to *'ibbur*.[18] Whereas *gilgul* refers to the transmigration of a soul to a given body,[19] *'ibbur* traces the transition of a soul to a different psychic state.[20] Distinguishing the layers of secrecy here is important. Transmigration is an embodied secrecy, whereas impregnation is an ensouled secret.[21] The poet turns from the

---

18. I am grateful to Elyssa N. Wortzman for sharing this insight regarding the shift from *gilgul* to *ibbur* and suggesting its correlation with Halevy's poetics.

19. For a hermeneutic reading of *gilgul* in contemporary Hebrew poetry after Harold Bloom's revisionary ratios, see Aubrey L. Glazer, "Rebirthing Redemption: Hermeneutics of *gilgul* from *Beit Leḥem Yehudah* into Pedaya's Poetry," *Kabbalah: Journal for the Study of Jewish Mystical Texts,* ed. D. Abrams & A. Elqayyam, vol. 11 (2004): 49-83.

20. Menahem Kallus, "Pneumatic Mystical Possession and the Eschatology of the Soul in Lurianic Kabbalah," *Spirit Possession in Judaism,* ed. M. Goldish (Detroit, Wayne State University Press, 2003), 159-185, 385-413.

21. R. Isaac of Acre claims elsewhere that the entire Torah from *Aleph* to *Tav* is the secret of impregnation, see R. Isaac ben Samuel of Acre, *Meirat Einayim, Parshat Bereishith,* 43b-44a, *ad. loc. Yafe Einayimn* 68. The order of impregnation and its secret is exemplified through the case of Cain and Abel and the impregnation of the soul of Seth (son of Cain)

poetics of an interior experience disguised in a dissonant exterior form, toward the poetics of an interior experience that plummets deeper inside its own interiority. In Schulamith Chava Halevy's poetry from *The Inner Castle* and *Breath Sign* in what will be explored is both impregnation as an ensouled secret and transmigration as an embodied secret.

Whether she is evoking the plight of the hidden Jews who converted to Christianity known as *Anusim*—replete with their concealed ritual practice of lighting candles in castles, cathedrals, basements or around walls—or more embodied poems on coitus and impregnation, Halevy's opening of secrecy exceeds the mythic or the ontological.[22] Her poetry's symbolic constellation is expansive enough to oscillate between impregnation as an ensouled secret and transmigration as an embodied secret. Whereas *Inner Castle*, subtitled, *Poems about Being and Being Coerced,* is primarily concerned with the struggle of one's inner soul being coerced to transmigrate into the guise of exterior body, *Breath Sign* turns inwards to explore degrees of the soul's very embodiment.[23] Through the contours of Halevy's symbolic constellations, I shall explore how her poetics resist an *ontology* of secrecy, opening to the secrecy of *ontic* experience itself. This resistance to the coercion of being and being coerced, in turn has implications for the non-dual language of mystical apperception.

In considering these uncollected poems by Schulamith Chava Halevy, what is striking is the degree of oscillation. There is a veritable shimmering

---

into Moses (as alluded to by the letters of Seth/<u>Sheth</u> and Abel/<u>H</u>evel = Moses/<u>MoSheH</u>). For more on R. Isaac of Acre in general, see Eitan P. Fishbane, "Authority, Tradition, and the Creation of Meaning in Medieval Kabbalah: Isaac of Acre's *Illumination of the Eyes,*" *Journal of the American Academy of Religion* 72, 1 (2004): 59-95; on *devekut* in particular, see Eitan P. Fishbane, *As Light Before Dawn: The Inner World of a Medieval Kabbalist* (Stanford: Stanford University Press, 2009), 242-243, 255-257, 272-277, 281; see also, Sharon Faye Koren, "Kabbalistic Physiology," *AJS Review* 28, 1 (2004), 335n95.

22. *Contra* Michael Fishbane's importing of "myth" as a key term of analysis rather than discovering such terms within Jewish Thinking, as per Hindy Najman's suggestion (Chicago: AJS, December 2005), see Michael A. Fishbane, *Biblical Myth and Rabbinic Mythmaking* (New York: Oxford University Press 2003), and contrast his notion of myth with Adorno's usage of "constellation," see Theodor W. Adorno, *Negative Dialectics,* trans. E. B. Ashton (New York: Verso, 1995).

23. This concern is apparent already in the title of the collection, *'Ot Hevel,* which can also be translated *The Sign of Abel.* For the correlation between the impregnation of the soul and Abel/*hevel,* see above n21.

forth from a deeply unitive experience of communion utterly revealed, to a more interiorized experience of impregnation, finally to a deeply concealed revealment in prayer. Each poem embodies the subtle ebb and flow of *devekut* and its playful, often duplicitous, relationship to opening secrecy, as evinced in this first quatrain:

דבקות

בָּאתָ בִּי כְּמוֹ לַפִּיד בִּמְעָרָה נִשְׁכַּחַת
וְהָיִיתִי בּוֹעֲרָה וְהָיִיתִי צוֹרַחַת
כָּךְ חָצִינוּ אֶת לִבַּת לִבּוֹ שֶׁל הָעוֹלָם הַזֶּה
לְפוּתִים וּכְרוּכִים בְּכַף יָד הַבּוֹרֵא[24]

You entered me like a torch in a forgotten cave
And I was aflame, screaming
This is how we halved the inner lava heart of this world
Wrapping and grasping tightly inside the palm of the Creator

Lover and beloved portrayed as the landscape, as in this short quatrain, is perhaps a familiar device in erotic poetry. Yet as the fire of the flame conjoins with the earthiness of the cave, something changes in the world. A volcanic eruption on the outside is giving voice to something deeper taking place on the inside. What is remarkable in this seemingly clichéd imagery is how the poet's evocation of the familiar serves as a pathway to reveal what is concealed.

By letting intercourse give way to communion, lover and beloved are able to reveal deeper layers of existence concealed in this world by halving "... the inner lava heart of this world." As the hearts of these lovers are pierced and then conjoined on the inside, their experience of the outer world changes. This leads to the realization that once the outer world dissolves, or is cut in half like a fruit, then these lovers can finally see into their core—revealing what has otherwise remained concealed. Lovers in communion, at the core, find themselves in mystical vertigo touching God, "Wrapping and grasping tightly inside the palm of the Creator." What this first quatrain captures so effectively is the transformation that takes place

---

24. Halevy, uncollected.

when the concealed spiritual underpinnings of a physical experience are revealed. Once those layers are progressively shed, then there is necessarily a shifting in any perspective of God and the world. The illusion of the world dissolves before lover and beloved in deep communion, but that very unitive experience cannot be separated from the mystical vertigo of touching God.

From this pulsating quatrain that accomplishes so much with so little, we shift to another scene of lovers embracing in a more delimited landscape. This next poem begins by marking time and place as indices of communion.

ט"ו באב, מילופוטמוס

כְּשֶׁהַגֵּאוּת עָבְרָה עָלֵינוּ
הָיִינוּ חֲבוּקִים
יַחְדָּיו עָבַרְנוּ בַּגַּלִּים
צָלַלְנוּ. הָיִינוּ צְלוּלִים
יָרֵחַ מַאֲדִים עָלָה עַל הַמַּיִם
מַדְהִים מֵחָדָשׁ חֲלוּקֵי אֲבָנִים
יַחַד נִלְכַּדְנוּ בְּרֶשֶׁת הַרְדִידִים.
כָּל דָּמַי מִתְנַקְזִים אֶל נְהַר הַשֵּׁנִי
שֶׁנִּצְבַּע עַל מֵימֵי הַיָּם
הָאֶגֶאִי.

בְּדָמַיִךְ יָרֵחַ אֲנַחְנוּ מִתְחַטְּאִים
בְּמֵימַיִךְ כְּבַעֲסִיס רִמּוֹנִים
אֲנַחְנוּ מִתְכַּנְּסִים עַד
שֶׁתָּרוּם וְתַלְבִּין אֶת
הַגַּלִּים וְאֶת כָּל הָעָכוּר בָּנוּ
אָז נַעֲלֶה מִן הַיַּיִן כּוּלָדוֹת
זוֹחֲלִים אֶל חוֹף חָדָשׁ עַל פְּנֵי
הַחֲלוּקִים. 25

15th of Av, Mylopotamos

When the tide ebbed over us
we were embracing
as one, we crossed in the waves

———

25. Halevy, "15th of Av, Mylopotamos," uncollected.

we dove. We were lucid
a reddening moon rose upon the water
astonishing anew rock & slivers
together we were trapped in a net of veins.
All my blood draining to the scarlet river
that was painted upon the water of the Aegean
Sea.

In your blood, moon, we betray ourselves
in your water, as in pomegranate wine
we withdraw within ourselves until
you'll lift and whiten the
waves and whatever is murky within us
then we'll ascend from the filth like newborns
slithering from the water to
the new beach upon
the rocks.

Locating oneself inside of the exterior of this *devekut* experience evokes a sensual memory. Yet entering into spatio-temporal web of communion is wrapped in mystery, beginning from the juxtaposition within the title immediately into the first stanza of the poem. The poet opens a scene already underway that demands a deeper reading of the secret concealed within the Hebrew time of the Fifteenth of Av as marked in the space of the Greek Island, Mylopotamos.

There is a linguistic merging of Hebrew time with Greek space in the juxtaposition within the title itself. What other space but Jerusalem could *Tu B'Av* possibly evoke? Or put another way, how could the experience of *Tu B'Av* really be felt anywhere else outside of Jerusalem? Although concealed in the Island of Mylopotamos where ancient cities like Eleftherna and Axos that may still resonate with their glorious antiquity of thousands of years earlier,[26] this poem is less about recovering that lost site of Homer or Pindar and more about being as far away from Jerusalem as possible. The poet dissolves into the Greek space of the unconscious in Aegean Sea only to be reborn resurfacing on its rocks in Hebrew time at the poem's close. To reveal deeper layers in the temporal texture of this communion,

---

[26.] During the Geometric and Daedalian period (ca. 1100-620 BCE).

it is necessary to clarify the moment of the Fifteenth of Av, known simply as *Tu b'Av*.

Intoxicating from its origins, *Tu b'Av* exemplifies the concealed power of Hebrew temporality revealed. From the time of grape harvest,[27] to the time of wood collection for Temple fires,[28] the intoxication of devotional service still resonates from Jerusalem within this sacred moment in time. More significant to the poem is the legend that connects *Tu b'Av* to the full moon. Like other liminal moments—times where the sacred is revealed at a threshold—the celebration of *Tu B'Shevat*, *Pesah* or *Sukkot*, *Tu b'Av* all begin on the night between the fourteenth and the fifteenth of their respective Hebrew months.[29] Such liminal nights are a full moon in the lunar calendar, linking their waxing and waning with fertility in ancient of hand cultures.[30] The poem at hand is recovering this temporal tissue of fertility in the contemporaneity of this *Tu B'Av* in Mylopotamos.

Yet this context deepens as the tissue of Hebrew temporality further reveals contours of the Israelite's desert wanderings. Doomed by God to die before reaching the Land of Israel, every year on the Ninth of Av, these former slaves seeking liberation from Egypt would dig graves, rest in them and pass the night as if buried below the earth. Upon arising in the morning, each surviving Israelite would then take a head-count to see who had died that year. In the fortieth year of wandering, the ritual was enacted, but no one died. Thinking they had miscalculated the calendar, the Israelites slept in their graves a second night, then a third, and so on. On the seventh night, when the full moon of *Tu B'Av* came out, the people knew the decree had ended–now they could enter the Promised Land.[31] As the stagnation of death ebbs, new life flows into a moment re-embracing lost love. This moment of rebirthing is then truly a Day of the Breaking of the Axe—a day when mortality no longer holds sway, a moment where love really conquers all—even death.

---

27. bTaanit 26b.
28. Known as *Yom Tever Magal* or "Day of Breaking the Axe," see bTaanit 31a
29. *Tu B'Shevat* (fifteenth of Shevat, Jewish Arbor Day); *Pesah* (fourteenth of Nissan, Passover) or *Sukkot* (fifteenth of Tishrai, Feast of Booths), *Tu b'Av* (fifteenth of Av, Jewish Sadie Hawkins Day).
30. I am grateful to Jill Hammer for this insight.
31. *Lamentations Rabbah*, Prologue 13; *Numbers Rabbah* 16:20.

This intimate linking of love and death—each a necessary side on the coin of existence—finds its way into so much strong poetry, be it Hebrew or Greek.[32] Yet the intimate melding of love and death onto that selfsame coin of existence serves to open its expanse into ultimate unity—a condition where the death of death merges with love. Even if that unity is overwhelmingly experienced through love, death as an integral part of this cycle is never far away. Just as buried fruit gives forth new seed, the human soul buried over the ruins of Jerusalem on the Ninth of Av still can be reborn. So too as the newly reborn light of *Tu b'Av's* full moon rises to hover over the lovers on the shore below, there is the realization that a life imbued with love must mark time henceforth.

This deft interweaving by Halevy of the natural world with the lovers on the seashore is more than mere pathetic fallacy. Namely, the natural elements in the poem do not only reflect what the lovers are feeling, rather by the expansion of the very flesh of the lovers' embrace it comes to envelope the natural world, touching God. By having her language ebb and flow in and out of the lover's embrace, the poet evokes the underside of *devekut*—that sense of entrapment in an embodied "net of veins." In feeling the push and pull of the weave in the water, like fish swimming in the net, that unitive experience undulates back from the very water of the Aegean Sea, returning where it began—Mylopotamos.

Greek spatiality, in the poem, is marked by Mylopotamos—a paradise concealed in its own communion of natural elements with glimmering aquamarine waters embracing velvety sands covered in luminous pebbles. For the lover and beloved of the poem, this crossing over the comma delineating Greek space and Hebrew time, allows this moment of "*Tu b'Av,* Mylopotamos" to become a day of new conceptions. It falls forty days before the twenty-fifth day in the month of *Elul*—the day on which all the world (including Mylopotamos) was created[33]—when beloveds are predestined to re-unite with long lost lovers. While *Tu b'Av* began as a

---

32. From "Love is as fierce as death" (Song of Songs 8:6) to a constant rebirthing in Paradise. Every day bodies are buried and rise again with new luminosity in the ancestors dwelling place (Zohar III, 162a-b). *Eros* tends to be paired with *Psyche* in Greek mythology and poetry, but like *Thanatos* is the offspring of *Nyx* and *Erebos*. Both appear as an essential element of existence in Hesiod and Homer.

33. bMoed Katan 18b.

Jerusalemite elixir of match-making, weddings, and ecstatic dancing to sweeten the sting of destruction lingering from the Ninth of Av, this rejoicing conceals the secret being revealed in this moment—the reunion of the divine Beloved conjoining with Her human lover.[34] As the world is continually reborn, the exilic *Shekhinah* is reunited through the ebb and flow of *Tishrei*—a month of new beginnings encapsulating every incipient moment.

Beginning again is also about preparing to love after death. Such loving time following the betrayal of the Jerusalem Temples' destruction is that when both the divine and human partners will return to their lost wholeness. Cycling through the seasons, *Tu B'Av* embodies a day of human and divine rebirth after loss, when love can overpower death. This temporal texture of rebirthing redemption is only possible by allowing the lunar cycle to resurface from its concealment by the Gregorian calendar. This eclipse of Hebrew time through time allows the moon to redeem the sun and for lover to reunite with her beloved. Such redemption needs *devekut* between opposites.

Turning from the eclipsing of exterior elements as signs of inner transformation, this next poem from *Inner Castle: Poems about Being and Being Coerced,* called "Strange Fire," evokes the mystery of "split identity."[35] Such an intertwining of Jewish and Christian ritual and its symbolism points to a self-awareness of the subjective mind,[36] engaged in social and religious dissent.[37] Subjectivity is then enshrouded in the very liminality of longing to belong for the *Anusim*[38]—a poetic predicament that continues "to surpass their time, their faith, their language"[39] into the present of the poem itself:

---

34. R. Tzvi Elimelekh ben Pesah Shapira of Dinov, *B'nei Yissachar, Ma'amarai Hodeshai Tamuz-Av, Ma'amar 4: Betulah b'Mahol,* vol. 1 (New York: n.p., 1946), 108a-110b.

35. This sense of "split identity" is what personifies the socio-religious predicament of the cryto-Jew, see Yirmiyahu Yovel, *The Other Within: The Marranos: Split Identity and Emerging Modernity* (Princeton: Princeton University Press, 2009).

36. Ibid., 88.

37. Ibid., xi, 79, 104, 107, 355, 402,

38. Anita Waigort Novinsky, "Marranos and Marranism: A New Approach," *Jewish Studies* 40 (2000): 7.

39. Novinsky, "Marranos and Marranism," 20.

אש זרה

מְאוּרָה מְכֻתֶּמֶת
זָהָב צְלָמִים.
מֵעֲשָׂרוֹת הַנֵּרוֹת בְּפִנַּת הָרִצְפָּה
אֵשׁ זָרָה זוֹהֶרֶת,
וּלְאוֹרָה,
בִּדְבֵיקוּת עֵינַיִם
גוּפוֹת מִתְנוֹדְדוֹת
עֵינַיִם קְפוּצוֹת
מְמַלְמְלוֹת
קֹרְעֵי תְּהִילִּים
סְגֻלוֹת
קְמֵעוֹת לַחֲשִׁי.[40]

Strange Fire

Illumined, stained
gold of icons.
Candles bunched in the corner upon the floor
strange fire shining,
and in its light
cleaving in wordwhiskers
bodies swaying
eyes darting
mumbling
tearing psalms
talismans,
some secret-scroll whispers.

The act of reading the poem is a kind of encroachment upon the secrecy of a strange fire. Its ritual purpose remains concealed in secrecy throughout the poem. The secrecy of such a strange fire is already echoed in the elliptic narrative of concealment in Leviticus 10. Whatever happened to Aaron's sons, Nadav and Avihu, upon making a deviant offering of strange fire, called an *'esh zarah,* remains shrouded

---

40. Halevy, *Inner Castle: Poems about Being and Being Coerced,* 14.

in mystery. Their fiery ascent continues to dumbfound readers, writers and interpreters—most alarming, of course, is this residue of mystical vertigo in the Hebrew Bible.

Most salient to the poem at hand, however, is the more ambiguous reading which sees Nadav and Avihu as mystics par excellence. These figures are the very mystical precursors to the tension between fidelity to tradition and its heretical dissent. Inspiration from the depths of the soul motivates these iconoclastic Hebrew priests-to-be in the Jerusalem Temple. Their deviant offering expresses a heartfelt yearning to receive a divine blessing in their immolation—a poem of the highest order:

בִּקְרֹבַי אֶקָּדֵשׁ
וְעַל פְּנֵי-כָל-הָעָם אֶכָּבֵד[41]

I am sanctified through those near me
And I am glorified above all the people.

By evoking this mysterious narrative in the title of her poem, Halevy is already writing in secrecy—the nature and experience of this strange fire remains unsaid throughout. Reading takes place from the outside of the experience peeking into what is just beyond reach and perception. The poet embraces an even deeper hermeticism in sketching out the most minimal of details. Such a doubled secret, deliciously ambiguous, can be read from the outside-in or the inside-out.

From the outside-in, this poem evokes women engaged in a deep prayer moment at a shrine. Is it possible that this shrine is the Western Wall in Jerusalem? Seen from a distance, removed from the specificity of its religious culture, such an ingathering of women by a wall is curious. What would motivate women—intrinsically endowed with a connection to the spirit world—with such a need to pray before a wall? Why this yearning for structured enclosure, especially in a patriarchal context? Insofar as the poem portrays experiences of women praying at the Western Wall, it evokes intimacy at a remove. The yearning to connect is strong notwithstanding the sense of exile evoked from the very site of prayer.

[41.] Leviticus 10:3. My translation departs from that of JPS, which renders this verse as follows: "Through those near to Me I show Myself holy,/And gain glory before all people."

Her disconnect begins when the poet encounters parts of this exterior structure leading to the holy that seem to embody the very opposite of holiness. Once the poem reveals that the pathway itself has been painted gold, the dynamism of the yearning becomes stagnant. Suddenly at the gateway to the Holy of Holies, the gate has been mistaken for the heart of the matter. It is here that the outsider yearning to connect on the inside is confused by her religion that has become alien. Is this gateway nothing more than a "cavernous place of superstition"?[42] How could the site of the *Shekhinah*'s exile—an engendered aspect of the divine feminine—become filled with words "praying only to the Father"?[43] Touching the wall, the poet breaks down her view as outsider looking in. What appeared to be idolatry from the outside dissolves into the collective sorrow of thousands on the inside, now washing over her own words. Emanating the wounds of eternal temporality into mundane time, this wall serves as a nexus for the poet's journey through her daily return to the place at the same time. This return unravels another layer of time and its original wound through exile now pulsing through the wall.

From the inside-out, almost every verb used in the poem evokes reminiscences of the *Anusim*, that sense of a group cramming together tightly to share "some secret scroll-whispers" while they are "cleaving in word-whiskers" and their bodies are "swaying" and "mumbling" with their "eyes darting." Such overwhelming suspicion upon being discovered at any moment pervades much of this poem in particular, and in the poetry in this collection, in general. The pervading concern is with the coercion of being and being coerced. Touching the wall in Jerusalem, the poet is anointed with the sweat, tears and misery of her ancestors—namely, the *Anusim*.[44]

Those who remained Jews in secrecy are never referred to by Halevy as *Marranos* or *Conversos*, for it assigns victimhood and implies responsibility not rightly their own.[45] While one is coerced on the outside to be a devout Catholic in terms of fidelity to dogma, catechism, lifestyle, garb and ritual, on the inside these hidden Jews retained the

---

42.	Conversation with Schulamith Chava Halevy (Tel Aviv: August 17, 2005).
43.	Ibid.
44.	Ibid.
45.	Conversation with Schulamith Chava Halevy (Jerusalem: August 7, 2005).

secret identity of their true soul. For women in Spanish Crypto-Judaism, their secret lives found perpetuity through ritual identification.[46] This complex psychological experience "... carries in it a double identity, distressed and eventually creative."[47] Further anxiety of influence from the *Anusim* has been noted regarding the creativity of poets harboring such a double identity in their poetry. This inner conflict—the duplicity of *devekut*—births a creative relation to language while remaining deeply torn from within it.

The hidden spiritual life of the *Anusim* of Spain and Portugal post-1492 gave rise to a bizzare and secret syncretism in the lands of their dispersion all for the sake of survival. Their forgotten memories return through a language of secrecy that defies the appearance of being and its categories. Theirs is a fragmented *saying* that reverberates from "private notes sent secretly by prisoners" and "phrases overheard in the corridors of convents and the hushed conversations that took place in *boticas* (pharmacies), meeting places, for poets, dissidents and social outcasts."[48] Nestling in the secrecy of this marginal status is especially significant when a female poet comes to write under the anxiety of influence of *Anusim*.[49] Through the duplicity of *devekut,* the poet reveals how women bereft of an exterior spoken language continue to retain an interior ritual language of their own—"influencing therefore challenging, liberating therefore changing, and creating therefore threatening"[50]—as is the way of all strong poetry.

[46.] Renée Levine, *Women in Spanish Crypto-Judaism, 1492-1520* (Waltham: Brandeis University, Ph.D. dissertation, 1983), 22-79, esp. 44-45: "Keeping and observing the Sabbath chronologically begins with candle-lighting, and crypto-Jewish women were expressly concerned with keeping this commandment. While the most common accusation was that of having lit lamps, the wording for male suspects often differed."

[47.] Novinsky, "Marranos and Marranism," 7.

[48.] Ibid., 9.

[49.] Ibid., 13. Novinsky refers to the paradigmatic Marranos of Paraíba, illiterate women with a ritual language of their own.

[50.] "And the *marranos* emerge as a leaven of society, influencing, therefore challenging; liberating, therefore changing; creating, therefore threatening, a group that always loses in an atmosphere of reaction, but always helps develop a society that is open and free." See Martin A. Cohen, "Toward a New Comprehension of the Marranos," *Hispanica Judaica: Studies in the History, Language, and Literature of the Jews in the Hispanic World*, Vol. I: History (Barcelona: Puvil-Editor, 1980), 35.

Through the course of this terse, twelve line poem, however, the exact contours of their ritual remains a secret. How can the poem then penetrate the secrecy so deeply rooted, to the point where everything new, progressive or modern has to be "whispered secretly"?[51] Those women gathered in prayer seem to be basking in the light of a strange fire of *candiles limpios* (clean lamps) or lamps with *mechas nuevas* (new wicks)[52] beneath golden crosses, perhaps to welcome the ritual marking of temporality for a Sabbath or Chanuka? Is this a moment taking place in secret in the church or in the synagogue after its hosts have taken leave for the night? The tenor of secrecy is elevated in that whole words cannot even be made out, only "word-whiskers." All that can be discerned are swaying and cleaving motions near the fire. But why this "tearing of Psalms and talismans" that creates those unsayable "secret-scroll whispers"?

Common themes in such secret prayers of guilt and redemption[53] feel inaccessible as, ultimately, the secret remains unsaid in this poem. The reader is only privy to a deliciously ambiguous view, from the outside-in and the inside-out of the secret being shared in this clandestine ritual moment. Along this path, the next poem at hand seeks to deepen the strange fire already aflame in all its secrecy by revealing it, paradoxically, in more explicit ritual terms:

סוד העיבור

כּוֹרַעַת לְצִדֵּי תְלוּלִיּוֹת
חוֹפֶנֶת קַרְקַע שְׁחוֹרָה רְטֻבָּה
אֶצְבָּעוֹת מְבַקְּשׁוֹת שָׁרָשִׁים וּפְקָעוֹת
מְרַקַּחַת רֵיחוֹת כְּמֵהִין וּפְטְרִיּוֹת
אֵזוֹב טָבוּל, בְּנֵי שָׁרָךְ
בְּסִלְסוּל עָבְרִי
עֲשָׂבִים רְמוּסִים וּרְקַב עָלִים

---

51. Novinsky, "Marranos and Marranism," 11. Novinsky here is referring to Father Antonio Vieira's correspondence which she sees as typifying not only the self-image of the Marrano in Portugal but that extends to the Marrano psyche in general.

52. Levine, *Women in Spanish Crypto-Judaism*, 29.

53. Novinsky, "Marranos and Marranism," 15. Other parallel themes in Sabbatean poetry include: "...the resurrection of the dead, the return of the Jews to their homeland, and the hope for redemption," see Jacob Barnai, "Christian Messianism and Portuguese Marranos: The Emergence of Sabbeteanism in Smyrna," *Jewish History*, 7, 2 (Fall 1993): 122.

עִם רְמָזִים שֶׁל פֶּטֶל וְשׁוֹקוֹלָד
לֵאמֹר, בְּכֶרֶס הָאֲדָמָה טְמוּנוֹת
הָאִמָּהוֹת אֲבָל
הַחֹדֶשׁ הַזֶּה אֶפְשָׁר
נִזְכֶּה
לִגְאֻלַּת רַחֲמִים.

קְרַב אֵלַי מִתּוֹךְ הַמִּסְתּוֹרִין
מַה נַּקְרִיב לוֹ? הַיִּרְצֶה
מָר-דְּרוֹר אוֹ לְבוֹנָה זַכָּה?
נְבַקֵּשׁ, נִמְצָא כָאן
תּוּתֵי יַעַר
הַיִּרְצֵם תַּחַת דָּם
צִפֳּרִים
שׁוֹר וָאַיִל?
הֲיִקַּח, מַה יִּקַּח?
מָלֵא בֵּיתֵנוּ תְּפִלָּה
מַה יִּרְקַח בְּבִטְנִי
קָחֵנִי הָאֹהֱלָה
וּקְסָמִים בְּמַטְךָ
אֶל חֵקֶר
סוֹד הָעִבּוּר.[54]

Impregnation's Secret

She's bowing round the knolls
palming black, moistened earth
fingers seeking roots and bulbs
an array of aromas like mushrooms
dipped hyssop, fern
as my fetus curls
crushed herbs and rotten leaves
with hints of raspberry and chocolate
saying, the matriarchs are nestled
in the earth's belly but
perhaps this month
we shall merit
the redemption of mercy.

---

[54] Halevy, *Breath Sign*, 7.

Come closer to me from the mystery
what shall we offer? Will the One desire
myrrh or fine frankincense?
Let's seek, here we'll find
wild berries.
Will the One want them in blood's stead,
birds,
a bull or a gazelle?
Will the One take it, what'll It take?
Fill our prayer places with
what it'll compound in my belly;
take me to the Tent
along with magic from your staff
to unearth
impregnation's secret.

Enshrouded in secrecy, there is a performative language of ritual that imbues this poem. But what is the experience being ritualized? The secrets of the calendar?[55] An ancient fertility rite?[56] An ensoulment ritual seeking signs of life after death?[57] A sublimated trace of a rite remains in this poem—something more than women weeping for *Tammuz* at the north gate of the Temple.[58]

Too often, religion in its received forms is accepted as normative. But beneath these normative forms courses an undercurrent of spiritual evolution in transition. That cataclysmic transition marked a shift early in Near Eastern culture from a pantheon of gendered deities toward a more radicalized patriarchal monotheism.[59] The salient scar of this

---

[55.] Gaonic influence is suggested here in reference to the intercalations for a leap year and other adjustments to the calendar as *sod ha'ibbur*; conversation with Schulamith Chava Halevy (Tel Aviv: August 17, 2005).

[56.] This secret, sublimated past remains under contention. Many arguments have been made for the pre-existence of fertility worship in Ancient Israel, the question being whether this practice was widespread or pre-Semitic, see Elford Higgens, *Hebrew Idolatry and Superstition: Its Place in Folk-Lore* (New York: Kennikat Press, 1893). Regarding fertility rites, Higgens argues for a "prehistoric ritual" that is common to each religion of the soil, Ancient Israel being one of many but not unique, ibid., 29, 74.

[57.] This suggestion was shared with me by Elyssa N. Wortzman.

[58.] Higgens, *Hebrew Idolatry and Superstition*, 54.

[59.] Ibid., 54. Tikva Frymer-Kensky, *In The Wake of the Goddesses: Women, Culture, and the Biblical Transformation of Pagan Myth* (New York: Free Press, 1992), 32.

transition that still surfaces in Hebrew poetry is embodied through the act of centralizing worship. When yearning was local, its embodiment was local, through deities and rites nearby. Relocating this desire to one site (the Jerusalem Temple), and the invocation of one name (the Tetragram, YHVH) requires erasure and sublimation. The sublimation of wandering desire marks a loss. That loss is still felt in the Hebrew language itself—the erasure of local gods and goddesses within the pantheon of Ancient Israel's monaltry. While this sublimation may have run counter to the desires of the Ancient Israelites, as evinced in the prophetic rallying against the worship of Asherah trees,[60] it beckons the question—what lost secret is being recovered in this poem on impregnation?

Embodied impregnation is intimately intertwined with a poetics of the cosmos for Ancient Israel. Impregnation or *'ibbur* in Hebrew poetics is a kind of reliquary—the site and names of the goddesses have been effaced, all the while its residue reverberates. That reverberation rests in a symbol utterly mundane—the Tree of Life. This is no ordinary tree; rather, this symbol is the imaginality of a cosmic tree. It is that ancient, secret, imaginal bridge between reality and imagination, between the terrestrial world and the celestial world that reverberates to be remembered in this poem.[61]

Traces of this spiritual struggle around the tree and her link to cosmic power echo throughout this poem. That struggle returns in the shape of a forgotten form. That form is the ritual of desiccating the earth during the summer to bring forth autumnal rain and fertility, to weep for the goddess *Tammuz*.[62] The prophets condemned women of horticultural

---

60. Deuteronomy 16:1; Judges 6:25, 26, 28, 30; I Kings 1:15, 16, 18; II Kings 13:6, II Kings 18:4, II Kings 21:3, II Kings 23:4, 6, 7, 15; II Chronicles 15:16.

61. Such tree symbolism echoes all the way back from neo-Assyro-Babylonian theosophy in which the deities of the Mesopotamian pantheon map onto the spheres of divine consciousness or *sefirot* of the Kabbalistic tree. The Tree of Life or *Etz Ḥayyim* in Kabbalah that first returns in *Sefer haBahir* as the "Tree-that-is-all" [*ha'ilan she'hakol bo*]; see Daniel Abrams, ed. *The Book Bahir: An Edition Based on the Earliest Manuscripts, Sources and Studies in the Literature of Jewish Mysticism* (Los Angeles: Cherub Press, 1994), 125 n. 14. For a comprehensive and astute analysis on the origin of the "Tree-that-is-all" apart from its more theosophic iteration as the Tree of Life, see Elliot R. Wolfson, "The Tree That Is All: Jewish-Christian Roots of a Kabbalistic Symbol in *Sefer ha-Bahir*," *Along the Path: Studies in Kabbalistic Myth, Symbolism, and Hermeneutics* (New York: SUNY Press, 1995), 63-88, esp. 70-88.

62. Ziony Zevit, *The Religions of Ancient Israel: A Synthesis of Parallactic Approaches* (New York:

heresy,[63] in their planting of small gardens filled with pleasant plants known as *nitai na'amanim* to hasten fertility.[64] Throughout the poem these plants appear as part of the secret ritual performed through the words of the poet-as-alchemist. While the precise choreography is all but forgotten, a form of prostration associated with divination[65] practiced in such ritual moments returns here in the poem.[66] With the casting out of the goddess archetype from the imaginal realm, the secret of birthing has also been forgotten. It is precisely this forgotten realm of an ancient ritual which the poet seeks to recover and reveal anew—a secret of rebirthing, both somatic and cosmic.

The poem also evokes another celebratory foretaste of redemption. Partially, it is through the aroma of the fruit and wine that whisper "with hints of raspberry and chocolate" reminiscent of the Sephardic *Hadas* celebration of birthing.[67] Resonances of typical *Hadas* liturgical-poetry hover with: "*Hadas, Hadas,* good *Hadas* (tidings) should come to you,"[68] echoing through her own verse "perhaps this month/we'll merit/the redemption of mercy." And partially this aroma evokes a faraway vision in

---

Continuum, 2001), 559a; Moshe Weinfeld, "Feminine Features in the Imagery of God in Israel: The Sacred Marriage and the Sacred Tree," *Vetus Testamentum* 46, 4 (1996): 515-529.

63. Isaiah 17:10-11; Ezekiel 8:5-17.

64. Ziony Zevit, *The Religions of Ancient Israel*, 518b-519a. For a correlation of plants and cosmos through the astrological symbolism inherent to plants as belonging to the following categorgizations: (1) Astrological; (2) Zodical; (3) Planetary; see Le R. P. Festugière, "Plantes décaniques," *La Révélation d'Hermès Trismégiste,* vol. I (Paris: Librarie LeCoffre, 1944), "'Astrologie et Les Sciences Occultes,' 139-143; ibid., Plantes zodiacales," 143-146; ibid., "Plantes planétaires," 146-160.

65. Isaiah 28:14, Jeremiah 2:27-28.

66. Zevit, *The Religions of Ancient Israel,* 530-531.

67. Levine, *Women in Spanish Crypto-Judaism,* 181-185. This *Hadas* celebration the night before circumcision had to remain a secret as it becomes evidence in testimonials exposing the secret of many crypto-Jews. For female children there is the liturgical rite that Sefardim call *Zeved haBat,* which envisions the child's nearing embodiment as redemptive by reading her body as the symbolic *topos* of Jerusalem. See Levine, *Women in Spanish Crypto-Judaism,* 181: "Marina González's confession provides the general description that on the eighth night after childbirth, '...some people came to my home and ate and celebrated and said that it was the night of *Hadas.* Similarly did María García admit that relatives came to the house where they received fruit and wine and rejoiced on that eighth night called the night of *fadas'.*"

68. Ibid., 185.

the forest.[69] The aroma of the forest in all its primordiality intoxicates the poet. The intoxication of the imminent is from the very "birthing inside nature."[70] This birthing—an intoxication with imminence—inspires the return to a life imbued with the fragrance of infinity. But does this inner birthing allow for non-dual mystical apperception to take place? Can the apparent dualism of immanence/transcendence be overcome?

The poem's strategy for resolving this dualism is evident in returning to creation itself. The masculine/feminine dualism that saturates so much of the creation narratives within the Hebrew Bible and rabbinic exegesis is now called into question by the poem. By re-imagining woman as the creative force of a Creator[71] "...half-angel/half-human..."[72] the poet is repositioning and rectifying the imaginality. The cycle of creation is interrupted as the poet attempts through words to appease God as she conjoins with her human partner. The divine appetite for sacrifice as part of the creative cycle is sublimated through the love the poet shares with her partner. By questioning the true desire of the divine appetite, the act of true offering returns to its source in the prayerful intimacy of love rather than sacrifice. It is in that very moment of *devekut*, between lover and beloved, that a non-dual mystical apperception of the expansive network of creation becomes possible.

The poem also evokes a season overflowing with eros and redemption. Given the incipience of redemption hovering throughout this poem, it is the month of *Nissan*[73] that is being evoked, especially the time of the Final Passover.[74] Redemption erupts in the spring, a time when the Song of Songs is in the air, intimately intertwining it to the embodied renewal of rebirthing. It is no surprise that the language of this poem's redemptive renewal is partially alchemical. The language of forgotten fertility rites swirls throughout this poem, drawing further linguistic residues of

---

69. This poem was written after a vision in a forest in Cochrelle, France just outside Normandy. Conversation with Schulamith Chava Halevy (Tel Aviv: August 17, 2005).

70. Conversation with Schulamith Chava Halevy (Tel Aviv: August 17, 2005).

71. Halevy, "Creation (according to woman)," *Breath Sign*, 44.

72. Halevy, "Mending," *She'Vo: Journal of Poetry,* vol. 14 (June 2005): 166.

73. *Pirkai d'Rabbi Eliezer* n30.

74. Portrayals of the Last Passover, *Pesaḥ Aḥaron*, are troped as the final celebration marking the coming of a new eschaton, see bBerachot 17a, *Pirkai d'Rabbi Eliezer* n21, etc.

magic bowls and amulets discovered in the Cairo Genizah. Palestinian alchemy—terser like its Talmud—tended to be written on metal, whereas Babylonian alchemy—more prosaic like its Talmud—tended to be written on parchment.[75] The poetics of performativity of these forgotten fertility rites is most intriguing, almost duplicitous. How can rebirthing take place when the experience is forgotten and the only remains are written? The dualism between oral and written text remains with every mystical text and poetic record. The task of the poet though is not only to write but to invoke as alchemist the experience that has undergone erasure.

When read as the written remains of an erased fertility rite, this poem returns all the magical ingredients of the earth for their consecration—root, bulb, dipped hyssop, and fern. The poet recovers their raw power, but just how these natural elements are measured—measuring as the root of all *poesis*–and then performed along with their invocations remain a secret. The poet shifts from invocations of an alchemist to a pregnant mother holding a deep connection to the cult of her ancestors. Rather than turn to a spiritual elder, as is common practice in Jerusalem,[76] the performative poetics swerve away from the expected. Unlike the alchemist, here the poet as spiritual guardian of her fetus invokes the divine through the matriarchs.[77] However, this invocation refrains from invoking the magical power that inheres in

---

75. Lawrence H. Schiffman and Michael D. Swartz, *Hebrew and Aramaic Incantation Texts from the Cairo Genizah: Selected Texts from Taylor-Schecter Box K1, Semitic Texts and Studies 1* (England: Sheffield Academic Press, 1992), 29.

76. Ibid., 29. Susan Starr Sered, *Women as Ritual Experts: The Religious Lives of Elderly Jewish Women in Jerusalem* (New York: Oxford University Press), 22-25.

77. Schiffman and Swartz, *Hebrew and Aramaic Incantation Texts*, 70-75, see TS K1.30: "and to the Holy Names by which I have adjured you./Fulfill all that is written here, so that /a blessing of goodness may befall you. Moreover, I/adjure and decree upon you, all kinds of/ demons and demonesses, lilis and liliths, evil spirits,/male harmful spirits and female spirits, male and female those (composed) of/fire and those (composed) of water, those (composed) of air/ and those (composed) of earth...Get away, get away from her to someplace else, and/do not come near her, by the power of this holy/combination of (letters)... so that she experience/no pain during the period of her menstrual impurity or when she is/ritually pure, so that she may be healthy for all time. Amen./But if you should abrogate this, my adjuration, I will beat/you with the iron rods of those four/holy matriarchs, BILHAH, RACHEL, ZILPAH,/LEAH. Therefore, fulfill this adjuration/so that a blessing of goodness may befall you. Amen."

the specificity of the matriarchs' names.[78] By concealing part of what is being revealed, it is now the impregnated poet rather than the elder through whom language spans the imaginal gap between the ancestors and the performative moment.

While these *sayings* become sublimated into a *said* within much of canonical Hebrew literature, its afterlife in this poem opens a lost secret. Themes common to earlier prayers of coercion and being coerced, of guilt and redemption,[79] as well as formulae of lost fertility rites of recently uncovered inscriptions of "YHVH and his Asherah" at Kuntillat 'Arjud[80]—all inaccessible in the first poem—are now an open secret by the end of this poem's first stanza. Liturgical gestures continue to echo here in the noticeable shift from third person to first person, bridging the first to second stanza, mimicking a common opening mystical intentionality or *kavvanah* of invocation "in the name of [*leshem yihud*]" to close with the secret of *amen*. This poem invites an inward reading to witness a secret ritual moment, opening further by unearthing its mystery, only to replace this revelation with an untold secret by the final verse.

Is it possible that the provocative invocation of impregnation can return the poet to her desired non-dual mystical moment? Is it enough to dissolve the boundaries of binary thinking, of Creator/created; of man/woman; of tribal history/future redemption? For poet as alchemist, rebirthing creative consciousness is a manifold process that moves through evolutionary stages. These stages for the seeker mirror developmental stages of the physiology of a newborn. Given that one engaged in rebirthing creative consciousness is likened to a newborn, it is fitting that developmental stages of physiology are misread by mysticas as spiritual

---

78. Hans-Jürgen Becker, "The Magic of the Name and Palestinian Rabbinic Literature," *The Talmud Yerushalmi and Graeco-Roman Culture III* (2002), 391-407.

79. Levine, *Women in Spanish Crypto-Judaism,* 15. Other parallel themes in Sabbatean poems include: "...the resurrection of the dead, the return of the Jews to their homeland, and the hope for redemption," see Jacob Barnai, "Christian Messianism and Portuguese Marranos: The Emergence of Sabbeteanism in Smyrna," *Jewish History*, Vol. 7, no. 2 (Fall 1993), 122.

80. Weinfeld, "Feminine Features in the Imagery of God in Israel," 515-529. Weinfeld bases his research assumption on Tikvah Frymer Kensky's pathbreaking work but only pursues it as legitimate once the inscriptions discovered at Kuntillat 'Arjit are more widely known and accepted, see above n. 59.

stages. Thus one comprehensive way of misreading this process of creative unfolding to non-dual origins could include: (1) coitus or *zivvug*;[81] (2) impregnation or *'ibbur*;[82] (3) birthing or *leidah*;[83] (4) contraction or *tzimtzum*;[84] (5) jouissance or *sha'ashua*;[85] (6) separation or *nesirah*;[86] (7) nursing or *yeniqah*;[87] (8) weaning or *gemilah*;[88] (9) youth or *qatnut*;[89] (10) mending the feminine or *tiqun denuqbe*;[90] (11) maturity or *gadlut*.[91]

The strangeness of this poem's recovery of a sublimated fertility rite with a deepening of ensoulment between mother and fetus brings us back full circle to the nature of Halevy's secrecy. Whether a strange fire from the outside burning on the inside, or a forgotten fire within that burns deeper with interior illumination—the poet seeks to recover and embody the secret of non-dual consciousness that is beyond binary opposition. Through her opening of unlikely symbolic constellations of secrecy in these poems, Schulamith Chava Halevy reveals how coercion and impregnation point to non-dual mystical apperception. Dissolving the dualism that separates the outside/in and the inside/in opens the secret. This doubling the layers of secrecy is a bold shift in the dualism

---

[81.] For example, see Vital, *Etz ḥayyim* Gate 5: Ch. 3; ibid., Gate 6: Ch. 8; ibid., Gate 7: Ch. 4, etc. This locution occurs over 370 times in *Etz ḥayyim* alone.

[82.] For example, see Vital, *Etz ḥayyim*, Gate 3: Ch. 3; ibid., Gate 5: ibid., Ch. 1; Gate 6: Ch. 2, etc. This locution occurs over 560 times in *Etz ḥayyim* alone.

[83.] For example, see Vital, *Etz ḥayyim*, Gate 20: Ch. 3; ibid., Gate 25: Ch. 4; ibid., Gate 31: Ch. 1; ibid., Gate 39: Ch. 11; ibid., Gate 47: Ch. 3.

[84.] For example, see Vital, *Etz ḥayyim*, Gate 1: Ch. 2; ibid., Gate 1: Ch. 3; ibid., Gate 1: Ch. 4, etc. This locution occurs over 16 times in *Etz ḥayyim* alone.

[85.] For example, see Vital, *Etz ḥayyim*, Gate 43: 3; *Peri Etz ḥayyim, Derushai haLayla*, Derush 4; *Sha'ar haKavvanot, Derushai haLayla*, Derush 4; *Sha'ar Ma'amarai RaSHB"I, Perush Sifrah deTzni'utah* 1, this locution occurs over 7 times in Lurianic Kabbalah.

[86.] For example, see Vital, *Etz ḥayyim*, Gate 12: Ch. 2; ibid., Gate 20: Ch. 9; ibid., Gate 27: Ch. 2, etc. This locution occurs over 50 times in *Etz ḥayyim* alone.

[87.] For example, see Vital, *Etz ḥayyim*, Gate 3: Ch. 3; ibid., Gate 6: Ch. 8; ibid., Gate 11: Ch. 6, etc. This locution occurs over 80 times in *Etz ḥayyim* alone.

[88.] It is curious that, despite a focused interest in birthing, this developmental stage and its articulation appears nowhere in Lurianic Kabbalah.

[89.] Vital, *Etz ḥayyim*, Gate 11: Ch. 7; ibid., Gate 13: Ch. 9; ibid., Gate 17:1, etc. This locution occurs over 30 times in *Etz ḥayyim* alone.

[90.] Vital, *Etz ḥayyim*, Gate 34: Ch. 1; ibid., Gate 34: Ch. 3; ibid., Gate 40: Ch. 8, etc. This locution occurs over 370 times in *Etz ḥayyim* alone.

[91.] Vital, *Etz ḥayyim*, Gate 12: Ch. 4; ibid., Gate 15: Ch. 1; ibid., Gate 20:1, etc. This locution occurs over 40 times in *Etz ḥayyim* alone.

that sometimes sets in, even within mystical texts. The clarion call of the poet is clear—the quest must remain forever in motion. Such dynamism allows for oscillation. And it is precisely such an oscillation that supports this doubling of secrecy whereby transmigration is an embodied secret and impregnation is an ensouled secret. Only when existence oscillates between embodiment and ensoulment can the opening of secrecy reveal redemption through mystical vertigo.

CHAPTER VI

CAUGHT IN THE INFINITY CATCHERS: *DEVEKUT* AS THE WEB OF DISCOURSE
SHAI TUBALI'S "COME HERE," "I CAME TO GOD," AND "INFINITY CATCHERS"

Words breathe in unique textures. Once words are conjoined into phrases and sentences, the attuned will then hear the engendering of language within discourse. The discourse of the unique is primarily male, what multi-disciplinary cultural theorist Michel de Certeau calls *henology*, while an altered feminine discourse is *heterology*.[1] The shimmering between *henology* and *heterology* opens both the mystic and the poet to that fine web between the infinite and the finite, getting caught in infinity catchers. That very rhythm of mystical vertigo between and betwixt is a form of *devekut*—the web that is discourse itself. As the human poet seeks beyond self, there is an entanglement with the divine, leaving its residue in the web. But what does the poet discover as the self is reconstituted, resurfacing from these webs of discourse? And once ensnared in these unique and altered webs of *henology* and *heterology*, how does the texture of experience and its language continue to transform the hybridity of the seeking subject?

As a poet navigating these webs of discourse, Shai Tubali's poetry is uniquely poised to address that cascading of non-dual consciousness in and out of language and experience. Born into an Israel scarred by the Yom Kippur War, Tubali's story begins in Ramle, 1976. While too young to serve in the Israel Defense Force during the war, Tubali is exposed to the diverse cultural matrices of Israel through his experiences as a documentary editor and producer for I.D.F. Radio, culminating in his receipt of the Israeli Ministry of Arts and Science Literary Award in 1995 at age nineteen. Tubali's poetry imagines journeys immersed in

---

[1]. Michel de Certeau, "The Arts of Dying," *Heterologies: Discourse on the Other*, trans. B. Massumi (Minneapolis: University of Minnesota, 1986), 165.

non-dual mystical apperception that betray an unquenchable yearning to share that very same *in*volution of spiritual consciousness already explored in our second chapter. For the poet, *devekut* takes place through a concretion of the spiritual by engendering non-dual discourse. Tubali is not content in remaining delimited by a dualistic discourse where *devekut* is either theologically unique (*henology*) or mystically altered as other (*heterology*). Rather, the poet dares to ensnare lost recollections of non-dual consciousness as recorded in the poetic record of experiences.

Rather than sketch out the theological datum of the poetry at hand, this next chapter explores the devotional reality of mystical experience behind the poetry of Tubali's written word and its correlations to the textures of discourse through the lens of French thinkers, cultural theorist, Michel de Certeau (1925-1986) and linguist, Henri Meschonnic (1932-2009).

In carving out his own mystical lexicon drawn from the palette of mundane experience, Tubali's contemporary poems offer a window into the variety of unitive mystical experiences of the One. This One is dynamic, constantly revealing its concealed origins by bringing the immediacy of the touch back into lived mystical experience. The written record of such non-dual mystical experience is what the poem ensnares in the naked nets of infinity catchers, otherwise known as poems. *Devekut*, that web of entangling discourse, will now be explored in three poems by Tubali, the first baring the same title as his collection, *Infinity Catchers*:

לוכדי נצחים

.1

לוֹכְדֵי נְצָחִים בְּרִשְׁתוֹת דַּיָּגִים הֵמָּה הַשִּׁירִים
מְפַרְפְּרִים בָּן קוֹרְאִים וְהוֹמִים נִתְפַּסְנוּ בְּאֵין יְכֹלֶת
לָצֵאת עוֹד
תְּפֹס לְךָ נֶצַח, הוֹ דַּיָּג-מְשׁוֹרֵר וְהָבֵא לְאִשְׁתְּךָ
שֶׁתָּכִין מַעֲדַן מְלָכִים לַאֲרוּחַת הָעֶרֶב
לוֹכְדֵי נְצָחִים בְּרִשְׁתוֹת דַּיָּגִים הֵמָּה הַשִּׁירִים
מְעַרְבְּלִים וּמְהַפְּכִים בְּתוֹכָן זְמַנִּים לִשְׁגָעוֹן
וּבְדַל הָאֵל-זְמַן שֶׁמֵּצִית בָּהֶם נְגוֹהוֹת אוֹר
כְּמוֹ נָשְׁלוּ מִמַּעֲמַקִּים דְּגִיגֵי-זֹהַר
מְעַרְבְּלִים וּמְהַפְּכִים בָּן צוּרוֹת שֶׁל זְמַנִּים מְשֻׁנִּים

שֶׁרֻבָּם לֹא יִקָּרְאוּ לְעוֹלָם וּבְטֶרֶם קָרוּ

לָכַדְתָּ אוֹתָם כִּשְׁלַל יוֹם. הוֹ דַּיָּג-מְשׁוֹרֵר, הִנֵּה הֵמָּה, הַשִּׁירִים,

מְגַלִּים אֶת עַצְמָם כְּזֹהֲרוּרֵי אוֹר שֶׁל מַה שֶׁפָּסַק לִהְיוֹת גַּשְׁמִי

וְאַתָּה, הַלּוֹכֵד, אַף לֹא יָדַעְתָּ שֶׁמָּצָאתָ, וְרַק מִשֶּׁהִבַּטְתָּ עֲמֻקּוֹת בָּרֶשֶׁת,

גִּלִּיתָ. רְאֵה, אֵיךְ נְצָחִים מִשְׁתַּגְּעִים שָׁם, לֹא בְּרוּרִים לְעַצְמָם,

מְלוֹתֵיהֶם כִּשְׁבִיס מְרַקֵּד לְעֵינֵי-כֹל, יוֹקְדוֹת אֶת סוֹדָם הָאָבוּד.

.2

לוֹכְדֵי-נְצָחִים בְּרִשְׁתוֹת דַּיָּגִים הֵמָּה הַשִּׁירִים,

מְגַלִּים אֶת נִסְתְּרֵי הַנִּגְלוֹת

כְּמוֹ הָיוּ צִדָּם הַמּוּאָר וְהַבִּלְתִּי-מֻכְחָשׁ,

מָקוֹם שָׁם פָּסַק כָּל-בָּשָׂר וְיָד אֵינָהּ מְמַשֶּׁשֶׁת.

צָרִיךְ לְהוֹרִיד רֶשֶׁת-מַעֲמַקִּים, הוֹ דַּיָּג-מְשׁוֹרֵר,

לֹא בַחַכָּה תִּתְפְּסֵם, כִּי בַּמַּיִם הָרְדוּדִים

תִּמְצְאוּ רַק צוּרוֹת, בְּעוֹד שֶׁבִּשְׁבִילֵי נְצָחִים

זֹהַר שֶׁל רְשָׁתוֹת עֲיָרְמוֹת וְיָדְכֶם הַמּוּשֶׁטֶת

שֶׁלּוֹכֶדֶת כָּל מַה שֶׁהָעַיִן אֵינָהּ יְכוֹלָה לִרְאוֹת.

Infinity Catchers

1.
Poems are infinity catchers in fishnets
quivering between reading and yearning they become listless when caught
unable to escape any longer
catch yourself infinity, O fisherman-poet and bring some home to your wife
so she can prepare a dinner fit for kings
Poems are infinity catchers in fishnets
blending and inverting time within themselves for insanity
and in the paucity of non-time in which splendors come to light
as if they fell from the depths of fishing-splendor
blending and inverting time between forms of different times
most of which will never take place even if they have already happened
catching them like plunder of the day. O poet-fisherman, behold they, the
poems reveal themselves as radiant light of the no longer embodied
and you, the trapper, even though you did not know you found, while staring
at the depths of the netting,
you discovered it. See how eternities take, go crazy there, unclear to
themselves, like a fillet dancing for all to see with their lost secrets glowing.

2.

Poems are infinity catchers in fishnets
Revealing concealed revelations
As in all their illumined and undeniable senses,
The place that stopped all flesh, where no hand can touch.
One must lower a deep net, O poet-fisherman,
You won't catch them with a fishing rod, for in shallow waters
You'll only find forms, still in eternal pathways
Splendor of naked nettings and your extended hands
That trap all that the eye cannot see.

With a unique ability to navigate webs of poetic discourse from the popular to the pensive, Shai Tubali is equally at home in the web of spiritual-philosophical discourse. Given this predilection for the philosophical, Tubali's poetry seeks to bridge the finite to the infinite through experiences familiar to the collective and words that reflect it. So taking leave of the shores of rational inquiry and wading into the waters of supra-rational discourse is a daring but necessary shift for the poet. This is less a leave-taking than a return to origins—the origin of non-dual consciousness symbolized by the sea. Whether that rational inquiry is embodied in the form of philosophy, religion, or *halakhah*, what such inquiry seeks is to catch its apparent opposition–namely, the supra-rational, often cordoned off as the mystical, the realm of the spirit or *kabbalah*. Yet as we have already seen regarding Morgenstern's hybridity of non-dual mystical consciousness in the opening chapter, what truly nourishes the rational and the supra-rational is their unitive oscillation through the experience of *devekut*. As *devekut* itself undergoes transformation in the contemporary twenty-first century cultural matrices of Israel, the more hybridized the subjectivity that emerges, the more it challenges the very boundaries of mystical experience. That merging of interior and exterior boundaries, here symbolized by the fisherman, the nets and the sea, moves beyond vulnerability into a deeper, non-dual experience of reality were all elements create a complete landscape of the soul.

What Tubali does so deftly in this poem is to use a most mundane metaphor to capture a reality far beyond it. Rather than imagine the poet-as-alchemist as Halevy did in the previous chapter, here Tubali envisions the poet-as-fisherman at sea catching words for poetry in nets. More than merely co-opting the multi-perspectival mystical marine credos of a *Moby Dick*,[2] the Hebrew poet, like Jonah, evokes the redemptive power of the word—no matter how errant—by daring to speak it to life.[3] The oral quality of poetry is what links that yearning—of every fisherman at sea searching for a catch, of every poet grappling with words for the poem—to recover its link to an ancient past imbued with aromas of futurity. While some post-modern theorists argue the oral form is of minor concern, nothing more than *anamnesis*[4]—a way of recalling to mind what has already been forgotten—the task of the poet is to continue to be vigilant in calling out to the collective so that what truly matters is never forgotten.

If poems fulfill their roles within language to serve as "infinity catchers in fishnets," then what matters is never forgotten. What remains is a "quivering between reading and yearning." This quivering is not a solitary experience; rather, that quivering desire of the fish to escape, of the word to take leave, that the fisherman is able to net becomes material for meaning.[5] It is a meaning that must be shared, so even if you can "catch yourself infinity, O fisherman-poet and bring some home to your wife"—all in the service of sharing desire, "so you can prepare a dinner fit for kings." While it is true that the subject may prevail where the oral resides, but as Meschonnic warns, the subject is more than the individual, more than *Dasein* as the locus of being. The subject is forever intertwined in relations of reciprocity with the *other*, a continuous matter of intersubjectivity.[6] The poem challenges the very boundaries of inside-out, to the point where the *other* invades the self.[7] This process of "spilling over" causes transformation; as seen in the *heterology* of de Certeau, the subject becomes mystically altered as *other*.

---

2. Dowling suggests that the fisherman's tale of *Moby Dick* should be read as an epic prose poem, in *Chasing the White Whale: The Moby-Dick Marathon; Or, What Melville Means Today* (Iowa City: University of Iowa Press, 2010), 189-214, esp. 190.

3. Henri Meschonnic, *Jona et le signifiant errant* (Paris: Gallimard, 1981), 77-134; for more on Meschonnic and why his work remains at best fragmentary in English, see Boulanger's comments in his preface to Henri Meschonnic, *Ethics and Politics of Translating*, trans. & ed. Pier-Pascale Boulanger (Philadelphia: John Benjamins Publishing Co., 2011), esp. 15-20.

4. Donald Wesling and Tadeusz Sławek, *Literary Voice: the calling of Jonah* (New York: SUNY Press, 1995), 168-169.

5. Henri Meschonnic, *Critique du rythme* (Paris: Verdier, 1982), 377.

6. Wesling and Sławek, *Literary Voice*, 169.

7. Ibid., 169-170.

This transformation is precisely what allows the poet to see reality otherwise, "blending and inverting time between forms of different times"—through the rhythm of the poem itself. For rhythm takes place in time. Just as the rhythm of the waves intoxicates the fisherman, it is the rhythm of the words in the poem that imbues the Hebrew poet—as the *'ivri*—with the power of boundary-crossing.[8] In this sense then, for Tubali, the fisherman embodies the boundary-crosser—taking leave of the shore of conventional language, wading through waves of the oceanic feeling and netting hidden catches within its depths of pre-understanding,[9] returning them to the shore of language, spoken once again through the poem. It is the rhythm of the words, then, that makes material for meaning,[10] so the catch that the fisherman-poet brings back is "radiant light of the no longer embodied" to be shared. Through the sharing of intersubjectivity, the poet as trapper of material for meaning reveals the light that has been concealed within words, "glowing with their lost secrets" in returning to shore.

How can the fisherman-poet reveal that which has been concealed all along? In returning to the shore to share the material for meaning, is the poet revealing those lost (sometimes duplicitous) secrets? Is there really any longer a need for secrecy here, in contrast to the coercion of secrecy unveiled in the last chapter?

Words that hover in the oceanic depths of pre-understanding await disclosure, even "take pleasure there" as the fisherman-poet unpacks the catch of the day's last journey. Each journey, whether wading in deep or shallow waters, requires an awareness, an openness to see the glowing secret of language. The secret is that words are not divorced from experience. Even in seemingly shallow waters, those "eternal pathways" still stick to the words. To merely live life as a fisherman, fishing for the forms of words alone is necessary but not sufficient. To live life as a fisherman-poet requires something more—the courage to "trap all that the eye cannot see." How? By allowing word and experience to intertwine. Even after the moment of mystical union has expired, still the "Splendor of naked nettings and your extended hands" reach out in mystical vertigo, touching God.

---

8.   Ibid., *Literary Voice*, 170.
9.   Henri Meschonnic, *Critique du rythme*, 377.
10.   Ibid.

But to touch God, first one must walk towards those "eternal pathways" that the poet vigilantly calls to the collective. Tubali dares to traverse this path in his next poem, "I Came to God":

הלכתי לאלוהים

כְּמוֹ חַוָּה בְּגַן עֵדֶן הִתְהַלַּכְתִּי מַעֲדַנּוֹת
עַד שֶׁהִגַּעְתִּי אֵלָיו
טִפַּסְתִּי וְהִתְיַשַּׁבְתִּי עַל יְרֵכָיו הָאַדִּירוֹת.
שָׁאַלְתִּי אוֹתוֹ: מַה לִי וְלַתַּפּוּחַ, הֲרֵי נָתַתָּ אוֹתוֹ בְּיָדִי,
וְלָמָּה נִבְרֵאתִי בְּצֶלֶם הָאָדָם הֲלֹא אֲנִי יֵשׁוּת נִפְרָדֶת
וְכָל תְּחוּשׁוֹתַי אֲחֵרוֹת?
וֵאלֹהִים לֹא אָמַר דָּבָר, רַק הִכְנִיס אֶת רֹאשׁוֹ בְּרַחְמִי
וְהִרְהֵר.
מַחְשָׁבוֹת שֶׁל מַמָּשׁ לֹא חָלְפוּ בְּרֹאשׁוֹ אָז,
אֲבָל לְבַסּוֹף הִגְלָה אֶת עַצְמוֹ
מִגַּן הָעֵדֶן.[11]

I Came to God

Like Eve in the Garden of Eden I strolled myself through tenderness
until I reached Him
I grasped His thighs and sat myself down in that grand place.
I asked Him: What is this apple to me, seeing that You put it into my hand,
And why have I been created in the divine imprint if I am a distinct existent
with all my senses separate?
And *Elohim* said nothing, merely tucked His head in my lap
and pondered.
Real thoughts did not flutter through His head then,
but in the end He exiled himself
from the Garden of Eden.

To be ready to walk towards those "eternal pathways" and vigilantly call to the collective, the Hebrew poet, Tubali, needs to shift persona. Shifting from the moment of oceanic merging with the fisherman-poet, now there is a return to the source of creativity itself—Creation. But the poet's return is strange, choosing to return "like Eve," approaching through an

---

[11.] Tubali, *Infinity Catchers*, 11.

altered feminine discourse of *heterology*. Immediately, from the first words of the poem, the experience of *devekut* is no longer something that is theologically unique (*henology*); it inclines towards a mystical alteration as other (*heterology*). This shift allows for a complete rediscovery of the Garden of Eden narrative in relation to the self.

The journey is a reflexive one, indicated by reflexive verbs of strolling oneself and sitting oneself into the merging moment of *devekut*. This turning inwards allows for a questioning of the very premise of Eden and the falling after having eaten the fruit. So the inner questioning resounds: "And why have I been created in the divine imprint if I am a distinct existent/with all my senses separate?" How could any duality really exist between the human and divine if creation is nothing more than a manifestation of non-dual consciousness? That *Elohim*, the divine collective powers, has no response is troubling indeed. Just as the first set of Tablets are broken, requiring a second set for the human-divine journey to continue, so too this first take on creation is broken. Realizing the brokenness of this version of creation, the poet sets out to turn inwards and reveal creation anew—to salvage non-dual consciousness through the poem itself. For if "...in the end He exiled himself/from the Garden of Eden," then the human still has the capacity to recover that lost non-dual consciousness. Such a pre-understanding is necessary if the material for meaning is to create poetry that is transformative.

Such transformation takes place through touching that requires a stretching beyond the immediate to that very God in exile. Such touching then becomes a ~~touching~~ that quivers for intimacy amidst exile, as evinced in the next poem, "Come Here":

בוא הנה

אֱלֹהֵי הַדְּמָעוֹת הָעֲצוּבוֹת
בּוֹא נָא אֶל אֱלֹהֵי הַדְּמָעוֹת הַשְּׂמֵחוֹת
הִסְתּוֹפֵף בְּצִלּוֹ, בְּכֵה אֶצְלוֹ הוּא יַגִּיד לְךָ
מַה לַעֲשׂוֹת וְאֵיךְ לַעֲצֹר
כְּשֶׁאֵין עוֹד צֹרֶךְ.[12]

_____

12. Tubali, *Infinity Catchers*, 37.

Come Here

gods of sad tears
O come to the gods of joyful tears
take shelter in the shade of the One, cry by the One who will tell you
what to do and how to stop
when there is no need

Does this poem mark the return of the very God gone into self-imposed exile? *Elohim*, the collective divine powers, is now seemingly divided into distinct aspects—of sad tears versus joyful tears. Why the tears? Why this division in the godhead? The poet assuages each facet of divine weeping to realize that soon there will no longer be a need for tears. Such stark anthropomorphisms or human projections of the divine will once again be cast away as the poet guides such words back to their non-dual origin. Just as Adam-Eve self-reflects to ask: "And why have I been created in the divine imprint if I am a distinct existent/with all my senses separate?" now God must confront the self-reflective over duality: namely, how could any duality really exist between one facet of the divine and another if creation is nothing more than a manifestation of non-dual consciousness? If tears bare the divine imprint, then there is no distinction between tears of joy and tears of sadness—there are no gods but the god of one tear.

The poem itself trails off into the time-space of that day "when there is no need"—only unified desire. Much of the balm comes from the experience of *devekut* that is no longer something that is theologically unique (*henology*) but inclines towards a mystical alteration as *other* (*heterology*). And then the very unified rhythm that has been ruptured into the duality of sad and joyful tears, of the masculine and feminine can be re-unified. What the rhythm of these poems by Tubali has shown is how to stretch beyond the exilic God to reach back into the touching of the immediate. The immediacy of touching that is ~~touching~~ still quivers for intimacy. Whether a fisherman-poet wading through the edenic waves of the sea or Adam-Eve strolling in the tenderness of the Garden, the task of every age and the calling of every poet is to reveal such concealed intimacy through the touch. It is through such ~~touching~~ that the God quivering for intimacy can once again be redeemed through mystical vertigo.

CHAPTER VII

AUTO-EROTIC COSMOGENY AS *DEVEKUT*:
REBIRTHING GOD AS SELF
IN HAYA ESTHER'S *MY FLESH SPEAKS G!D*

אֶת הַחִבּוּר הַקּוֹסְמִי שֶׁאֲנִי

אִשָּׁה בְּתוֹךְ הַגּוּף שֶׁלִי

וְהַגּוּף שֶׁלִי יוֹשֵב בְּתוֹךְ הַנְּשָׁמָה שֶׁלִי

זֶה רַק אַתָּה יוֹדֵעַ, אֲנִי מַאֲמִינָה בְּךָ

שִׂישׂוּ בְּנֵי מֵעַי

וְזוֹ רַק הַהַתְחָלָה[1]

> *this cosmic composition of me as*
> *an embodied woman,*
> *my body sitting in my soul*
> *only you know this, I believe in you*
> *rejoice children of my innards*
> *and this is only the beginning*

One who has never experienced the delight of a song of self, has never truly delighted in the mystery of the real Me. This next chapter considers "the possibility of a mystical embodiment in nontraditional forms"[2] that stems largely from Gershom Scholem's speculations about such possibilities being embodied as an *Intuitive Kabbalah*.[3] Such mystery experienced in the linguistic motion of great poetry—most recently in the Hebrew poetry of Haya Esther—is a motion that is often auto-erotic and cosmogonic.

---

[1]. Haya Esther, *My Flesh Speaks G!d* [Hebrew] (Jerusalem: Carmel, 2001), 183.

[2]. Gershom Scholem, "Reflections on the Possibility of Jewish Mysticism in Our Time (1963)," *On the Possibility of Jewish Mysticism in Our Time & Other Essays*, trans. J. Chipman (Philadelphia: JPS, 1997), 19.

[3]. I am indebted to Harold Bloom, who informed me of how he and his longtime friend, Scholem, would refer to the poetry of Walt Whitman as *Intuitive Kabbalah*. Aside from the reference to Bucke, the intuitive approach to kabbalah in this context means that such poets are not constricted by the theosophic or cosmic terms, rather intuitive kabbalists are at the height of their creative powers, seeing that they are ultimately not bound by the limits of a given system. Their usage of these technical terms is much more free than has been evident in the history of Jewish mystical thinking.

This *jouissance*—as embodied and experienced in these opening fragments of poetry—I argue, is a process that is intrinsically auto-erotic within the self-generating process of creating the cosmos called cosmogenesis. What is unique about the writing of such contemporary Hebrew poetry is how it exceeds the bounds of any kind of precedent in "automatic writing"[4] that came closest to evoking traces of auto-erotism and cosmogeny. That *sui generis* erotic pleasure experienced within the process of reading and writing itself—what Barthes once called *"le plaisir du texte"*[5]—is finding its embodiment within a number of burgeoning Hebrew poets writing some of the most compelling poetry today. Haya Esther exemplifies one such Hebrew poet, whose songs of be/coming self will serve as the focus of this chapter with her epic poem, *My Flesh Speaks G!d*. The deeply personal texture of this poetic self-exploration takes leave where everyman, Job, left off—"From my flesh do I see God," [וּמִבְּשָׂרִי אֶחֱזֶה אֱלוֹהַּ] transforming into *My Flesh Speaks G!d* [אֱלוֹהַּ מְדַבֵּר בִּשׂרִי],[6] from *seeing* to *saying* the truth. That truth is experienced through a unique form of non-dual mystical apperception known as *devekut*.

Prior to the birth pangs of the State of Israel and the ashen endings of the *Shoah*, Haya Esther (Godlevsky) was born in 1941 and raised in an Orthodox family in Jerusalem. She eventually left that religious culture

---

4. Decades after Whitman burst onto the American poetry scene, the burgeoning of Surrealism began to incorporate some of this approach into what became known as "automatic writing." It is worth noting how one of Surrealism's proponents, André Breton envisioned this approach to writing as reiterated in Balakian's mapping:

    ...Breton's automatic writing assumed a triple convergence: the psychological concept of the liberation of psychic inhibitions, the mathematical one of the coincidences of chance verbal encounters, and the hermetic one of the oracular function of the medium-poet.

    A. Balakian, *André Breton, Magus of Surrealism* (New York: Oxford UniversityPress, 1971), 61.

    This triple convergence of the psychological, the mathematical, and the hermetic is already evident inWhitman's poetry, but articulated perhaps most lucidly as a theory of writing by Breton.

5. Roland Barthes, *Le Plaisir du Texte* (Paris: Éditions de Seuil, 1982).

6. The poem is at play with Job 19:26. For a nuanced reading of the personal experience as a way of knowing, see Ed Greenstein, "'On My Skin And in My Flesh': Personal Experience As a Source of Knowledge in the Book of Job," *Bringing the Hidden To Light: Studies in Honor of Stephen A. Geller* (Winona Lake: The Jewish Theological Seminary & Eisenbrauns, 2007), 63-77.

to explore the secular culture of Israel. This led to her pursuit of higher education in the primarily secular settings of the Hebrew University in Jerusalem, studying Jewish History and education. Still Esther managed to straddle both worlds by teaching and writing Bible study programs for secondary schools. The deepest impression and influence upon entering this other cultural sphere, much like Admiel Kosman's experience at the Bezalel Institute,[7] came from Esther's experiences of studying art at the Israel Museum. Esther's poetry is part of a larger aesthetic conversation with her painting that lead to solo as well as group exhibits in Israel and beyond.[8] Her eclectic *oeuvre* has garnered critical attention in Israel, being awarded numerous prizes, especially the coveted *Prime Minister's Prize* (2002). Throughout her eclectic *oeuvre*, questions of artistic inspiration and mystical apperception pervade to inspire an evolution of spiritual lexicon within an aesthetic setting.

But the central question returns for the Hebrew poet—why does the yearning for these mystical moments of union within the self remain so strong? "[M]ystical experiences may continue to flourish among human beings so long as the human race exists because mysticism is a basic human experience, connected to the very nature of man [*sic*]."[9] As one of the defining features of humanity, it is this "Cosmic Consciousness" that continues to differentiate humans from other forms of life. The shift from what Bucke categorizes as "Simple Consciousness" to "Self Consciousness" and then to "Cosmic Consciousness" is an important realization of mystical experiences and their role in the evolutionary trajectory of human consciousness.[10] To have a consciousness of the cosmos implies an understanding "...of the life and order of the universe."[11] Such a consciousness is exemplified by a "...state of moral exaltation, an indescribable feeling of elevation, elation and joyousness, and a quickening of the moral sense... [w]ith these come,

---

7. See above, chapter 2.

8. Her poetry and prose have also been translated into French: see Haya Esther, *Selected Poems* (Paris: Caracteres, 2002); idem., *Soft Stones* (Stories) (Paris: Caracteres, 2008).

9. Scholem, "Reflections on Jewish Mysticism," trans. J. Chipman (Philadelphia: JPS, 1997), 18.

10. Richard M. Bucke, *Cosmic Consciousness: A Classic Investigation of the Development of Man's Mystic Relation to the Infinite* (New York: E. P. Dutton, 1969), 1.

11. Bucke, *Cosmic Consciousness*, 3.

what may be called a sense of immortality, a consciousness of eternal life, not a conviction that he shall have this, but the consciousness that he has it already."[12] It is this "direct unmistakable intercourse" between God and human beings that makes this experience cosmic.[13]

This consciousness of conjoining mundane living with eternal life, otherwise known as *devekut*, was considered as a very limited part of the possibility of a contemporary Jewish mysticism as defined by Gershom Scholem, founder of the academic study of kabbalah at the Hebrew University. In reflecting on this narrow possibility, Scholem turned to contemporary nineteenth century exemplars of *Intuitive Kabbalah* in the poetry of William Blake (1757-1827), Walt Whitman (1819-1892) and Arthur Rimbaud (1854-1891).[14] As poetic exemplars of this *Intuitive Kabbalah*, Scholem goes on to correlate this form of intuitive mysticism as nascent in the record of mystical experiences within contemporary twentieth century mystics like Richard Maurice Bucke (1837-1902) and Edward Carpenter (1844-1929).

From Scholem's correlations of the poets and mystics, it appears that such an *Intuitive Kabbalah* stems from what the latter refer to as the "intuitions" of cosmic consciousness. But Scholem would often remark[15] how "...Whitman is a striking example of this phenomenon, which has had many advocates and representatives over the past three generations..."[16] In his important essay of 1963, Scholem attempts to locate the possibility of

---

[12.] Bucke, *Cosmic Consciousness*, 3.

[13.] Ibid., 3.

[14.] Harold Bloom suggested this notion to me of *Intuitive Kabbalah* as drawn from his conversations with Scholem, and it is evident from Scholem's correlations of Whitman and Bucke that *Intuitive Kabbalah* stems from what Bucke referred to as the "intuitions" of cosmic consciousness, see A. Lozynsky, *Richard Maurice Bucke, medical mystic: Letters of Dr. Bucke to Walt Whitman and His Friends* (Detroit: Wayne State University Press, 1977), 170. See also R. M. Bucke, *Cosmic consciousness: a study in the evolution of the human mind* (New Jersey: Citadel Press, 1989).

[15.] Aside from remarks made in the aforecited essay, see Scholem, "On the possibility of Jewish Mysticism," compare with Scholem's comments on Whitman's friend and executor, Richard Maurice Bucke, see above no's 11-14 as well as Scholem, "Religious Authority and Mysticism," *On the Kabbalah and its Symbolism*, trans. R. Manheim (New York: Schocken Books, 1965), 16-17.

[16.] Scholem, "On the possibility of Jewish Mysticism," 18.

a contemporary expression of mysticism that is much more "amorphous"[17] than it has ever been, not bound by religious authority as its single interpreter any longer. Its inspiration or source of holiness, according to Scholem, "...will be revealed within the innermost sanctums of this secularity, and the traditional concept fails to recognize mysticism in its new form."[18] He foresees a tension whereby these new forms of mysticism, specifically in poetry, will not fit the mold of the generally "...conservative traditional conceptions of the mystics, but will have a secular significance."[19]

The site of secular significance to which Scholem speaks apparently regarding Anglophone poets, ironically has become his own culture of Israel. Yet perhaps due to his suspicion and need for critical distance as a scholar, Scholem was wont to see the contemporary mysticism continuing to sprout up right in his own back yard within the richness of Israeli poetry. To appreciate the correlations of the auto-erotic and cosmogonic in these songs of be/coming, it is important to recall how Israeli poetry continues to serve "... as a realm ... to record and debate the relation between public trauma and private experience."[20] Although war epitomizes *thanatos* or the death-instinct, the conviction to continue writing from the place of impassioned "nature-poetry-during-wartime" is what brings out poetry's perennial *eros*.[21] It took a pioneering female Hebrew poet like Leah Goldberg to argue that "...there is not only permission for the poet

---

17. Scholem, "Religious Authority and Mysticism," *On the Kabbalah and its Symbolism*, trans. R. Manheim (New York: Schocken Books, 1965), 17.

18. Scholem, "On the possibility of Jewish Mysticism," 18.

19. Ibid.

20. Barbara Mann, "Hovering at a Low Altitude: Dahlia Ravikovitch," *Reading Hebrew literature: Critical Discussions of Six Modern Texts*, A. L. Mintz, ed. (Hanover: University Press of New England, 2003), 216.

21. A. B. Yoffe, *Leah Goldberg: A Memoir* [Hebrew] (Jerusalem: Ts'erikover, 1984), 98-109. This debate over the task of the poet spills over into what constitutes the canon of Hebrew into poetry. See Hannan Hever, *Producing the Modern Hebrew Canon: Nation Building and Minority Discourse* (New York: NYU Press, 2002), 1-10. A counter canon is also being explored by feminists, see for example Shirley Kaufman, Galit Hasan-Rokem, and Tamar Hess, ed's *The Defiant Muse: Hebrew Feminist Poems* (New York: Feminist Press at CUNY, 1999). Compare with the Hebrew works included in another important reflection on canon, Ruth Wisse, *The Modern Jewish Canon: A Journey through Language and Culture* (New York: Free Press, 2000). The autonomous authority of aesthetic power is proffered in another work on the canon of Western Civilization, see Harold Bloom, *How to Read and Why* (New York: Scribner, 2000).

to write love poetry during times of war," but it is incumbent upon the poet to recover *eros* in her poetry, "...for in times of war the value of love outweighs that of death."[22] This peculiar nexus—of public and private experience of trauma, of the value of love and death—is part of the warp of the "auto-erotic" interwoven into the woof of *eros* in Hebrew poetry.

Why then do the "auto-erotic" and "cosmogonic" share a correlation within this current direction in Hebrew poetry? Both the "auto-erotic" and the "cosmogonic" deal with some aspect of self-satisfaction. *Eros* is the passion of love. This passion becomes "auto-erotic" as the erotic pleasure embodied within the depths of one's inner self is experienced in the absence of an *other*, or when the yearning for that *other* is fully internalized. Standing in apparent contrast is the "cosmogenesis" or "cosmogony," that is, the story of the cosmos' creation of itself from itself. This creative act reveals the birthing or begetting process. How such seemingly unrelated terms come into correlation is through the convergence of the mystical and the poetical within the *eros* of Hebrew poetry.

Self-delight is part and parcel of creation, and by extension creativity—so much so that the very creative process takes place when the Creator bemuses Itself within and by Itself in order to unravel the created world. *Bemusement*[23]—concatenating after its mystical origins[24]—is utterly

---

22. Yoffe, *Leah Goldberg: A Memoir*, 102.

23. I am grateful to Elliot Wolfson for sharing this brilliant translation of משתעשע

24. קודם האצילות היה א"ס [אין סוף] לבד משתעשע בעצמותו ובאורו הסתום וכשעלה ברצונו הפשוט להמציא כי אין... עולמות נתפשט מאורו י' א' [יו"ד אחד] ...וולזה לא היה ניכר וזה הבירור היה ע"י בוצינא דקרדינותא גבול ומדה כי אם ע"י וכפי השתלשלות העולמות כן יתלבש להמצא לתת לו גבול...

Before the [consciousness] of Intimacy, the Limitless One was alone bemusing in its own essence, in its own sealed light. So when it arose in [this Limitless One's] primal desire to found universes from its own light [through the primal inscription of] one letter *Yod*, ...And this remains beyond recognition, which is clarifying by way of the hardening spark. ...For there is no bound or quality except through it. For through the process of unraveling of universes will [this light] become enshrouded to be embodied so as to receive its border...

For the full text and its context within Lurianic Kabbalah, see Ronit Meroz, "*Ḥiburim Luriani'im Qedumim,*" *Massu'ot: Studies in Kabbalistic Literature and Jewish Philosophy In memoriam of Professor Efrayim Gottlieb o.b.m.* [Hebrew] ed. M. Oron and A. Goldreich (Jerusalem: Mossad Bialik, 1994), 327. On the denotative nuance in this expression, ranging from "hardening" to "darkening spark," see Yehudah Liebes, *Chapters in a Dictionary of Zohar,* [Hebrew] Ph.D. dissertation (Jerusalem: Hebrew University, 1976), 146-151.

inverted and transformed in the epic poem of Ḥaya Esther, called, *My Flesh Speaks G!d*. This is a Hebrew touchstone in the songs of self-delight in rebirthing the embodied reality of the real Me by way of auto-erotic cosmogony as *devekut*.

There remains, however, a certain intransitivity within erotic poetry—a gap between poet and person.[25] Entry into strong poetry is through an evasive gateway, for it is through the allusiveness of intransitivity that this door is opened to explore one's self. The *self* can be seen as personality, *soul* as character, and the real Me as mystery.[26] Ḥaya Esther's satisfaction comes through the self-delight of embodiment in this epic poem, *My Flesh Speaks G!d*. The poem explores a mapping of self, soul, real Me within an epic form. Part of the challenge is to understand whether or not Esther follows or deviates from a more classic mystical mapping of *nefesh* or libidinal-soul, *ruah* or spirit-soul, *neshamah* or pneumatic-soul, *ḥayah* or vital-soul, *yeḥidah* or unified-soul into a new trajectory within a Hebrew imaginality from the poet's own flesh.

Through a coincidence of opposites in Esther's poetry a hierarchal fivefold system gives way to a more organic and intuitive path. This intuition is manifest through an enumeration of the embodied parts that compose a new whole. Rather than write preferentially using *nefesh* over *neshamah*, there is a much greater evocation and exploration of embodied regions that reveal their own *hylic* vitality in this poem. Rather than search for the limits of ensoulment within body, the poet inverts this search into an exploration of embodiment as the limits of the soul.

What is it about this epic poem that encourages the rending of the mask of my self—the persona of the poet—to reveal the real Me as her embodied self? The poet is in search of this real Me through her own unique explorations of embodiment. This embodied experience, like the poem, is only possible when read in relation to one another rather than in isolation from one another.[27] Esther's poem enters into a deeply ecstatic realm. Even while in this ecstatic mode, there is not the usual alterity

---

25. Harold Bloom, *Walt Whitman, Modern Critical Views* (New York: Chelsea House Publishers, 2007), 5.
26. Ibid., 2.
27. Ibid., 5.

directed towards the body. Rather Esther's poem is the experience of her spirit—a metalyptic rolling over of souls through embodiment. The poet does not ascend to unite with a divine psyche, but experiences her insight by deepening an embodied awareness that already dwells within.

Such a scandal of self-delight in this epic poem of Ḥaya Esther is most prominent in the paradoxical self-desire of her cosmic I. In the course of this epic poem, Esther will imagine her gushing forth "from the belly of history," in opposition to her third-person, embodied self, as evoked through "her womb... her flesh... her conjugal rights..." How does such a paradox of self overcome the typological dualism within the poem between the cosmological persona and the daemonic real Me[28] towards non-dual mystical apperception? Consider the paradox operative in the following passage from *My Flesh Speaks G!d*:

נוֹהֶמֶת בָּאוֹר הַבּוֹהֵק
צִפָּרְנַי נְעוּצוֹת בַּשֶּׁמֶשׁ
וְאִישׁוֹנַי דּוֹקְרִים
שָׁאַפְתִּי הִזְרַעְתִּי
נָשַׁפְתִּי יָלַדְתִּי
נוֹצָה עָפָה בִּנְשִׁימָתוֹ שֶׁל הָאֵל
וְנִשְׁמַת אֲדֹנָי פָּרְצָה הַחוּצָה
עִם הַדָּם וְהַנּוֹצוֹת
צָמְחוּ לִי נוֹצוֹת נְבוּאָה אֲדֻמּוֹת
עַפְתִּי לְמַעְלָה מִן הַשֶּׁמֶשׁ
מָשַׁק כַּנְפֵי הַהִיסְטוֹרְיָה
רָעַף כְּמַלְאָךְ
עַצְמִי גָּח אָפֵל בְּתוּלֵי הַיּוּלִי[29]

bellowing in light whitening
my nails penetrating the sun
and my pupils wincing
I yearned, I came
I sighed, I birthed
I wandered, flew into the breath of the deity
so the soul of *Adonai* burst open
with blood and feathers

---

28. Ibid., 7.
29. Esther, *My Flesh Speaks G!d*, 8.

I'm sprouting red feathers of prophecy
I flew beyond the sun
the wings of history rustled,
trickled like an angel
My self gushed my dark, hylic virginity

Recalling that the opposition between the cosmological persona and the daemonic real Me is an aestheticization of the gnostic dualism so precious to Bloom that serves as a challenge to this hermetic final verse. From the deep dualism of a gnostic perspective, there is a privileging of the *pneumatic* self over the *hylic* self. Yet here the poet, Esther, challenges such gnostic dualism, going so far as to even rescind this oversight by re-embracing a non-dual embodied or *hylic* self, rather than conforming to the default of fleeing from it into the spiritual or *pneumatic* realm.

But what exactly is meant by such *hylic/pneumatic* dualism? Those ruled by instinct, urges, and bodily sensations are known as *hyletics*, whereas those who arrogantly follow law and doctrine are known as *psychics*.[30] The desire of the Hebrew poet here is to challenge the gnostic dualism, so as to elevate toward a non-dual embodied consciousness. Such consciousness is an entry into the liberating experience of *gnosis* by way of becoming a *pneumatic*. As a *pneumatic,* one renounces the illusion of duality to then embrace the real—namely, the non-duality of existence.[31] Paradoxically the

---

[30.] This division of the *hylic* from the *psychic* stems from the primordial division of masculine and feminine, see Krause, Robinson and Wisse, eds., "The Apocalypse of Adam," *Nag Hamadi Codices* (Brill: Leiden, 1979), V, 64: 20-22, 155: "Then god, the ruler of the aeons/and the powers, divided us in wrath. Then/we became two aeons." While beyond the scope of this investigation, consider Harry Fox's correlation of two *torot* (i.e. *Beit Hillel* and *Beit Shammai*) as *hylic* and *psychic,* see bSanhedrin 21b.

[31.] Stephan A. Hoeller, *Jung and the Lost Gospels: Insights into the Dead Sea Scrolls and the Nag Hammadi Library* (Wheaton: Theosophical Publishing House, 1989), 110-111; J. J. Poortman, *Vehicles of consciousness: the concept of hylic pluralism (Och⁻ema)* (Netherlands: Theosophical Publishing House, 1978), where Poortman explicates the terminological considerations of *hyle* as follows: "By hyle is meant matter in a very broad sense, thus embracing both ordinary matter and this possible finer, more subtle matter..."; ibid., *Vehicles of consciousness,* 8. Further on in his discussion of this term *hyle,* Poortman explains: "I shall, then, use the word 'hylic' as the generic term for all kinds of matter and, at the same time, the word *pneuma,* which, although it is rather unusual in English, is really quite suitable for the purpose, for the various finer forms of matter." Ibid., *Vehicles of consciousness,* 18.

virginity the poet seeks throughout the poem is part of a cycle to recover her procreative potency as fully embodied. Rather than escape her *hylic* self to flee to the *pneumatic* realm, the poet choses to draw forth the spirit from within the womb of her own embodied self. It is from this embodied positioning that she then experiences and embraces her cosmological self:

אֶת הַחִבּוּר הַקּוֹסְמִי שֶׁאֲנִי

אִשָּׁה בְּתוֹךְ הַגּוּף שֶׁלִי

וְהַגּוּף שֶׁלִי יוֹשֵׁב בְּתוֹךְ הַנְּשָׁמָה שֶׁלִי

זֶה רַק אַתָּה יוֹדֵעַ, אֲנִי מַאֲמִינָה בְּךָ

וְזֹו רַק הַהַתְחָלָה

שִׂישׂוּ בְּנֵי מֵעַי[32]

this cosmic composition of myself as
an embodied woman,
my body sitting in my soul
only you know this, I believe in you
and this is only the beginning
rejoice children of my innards

From this profoundly cosmological self, the poet then connects to her somatic self. This is the arc which her poem travels in the course of a few verses, from "this cosmic composition of myself as an embodied woman" to the "children of my innards." Such rapid shifting— a fluttering between the cosmological and somatic self—is a recurrent trope within Esther's epic poem. It is with such rapid strokes that the poet is enabled to open her embodied birthing of the cosmological self into the whole universe:

גַּחְתִּי מִמְּעֵי הַהִסְטוֹרְיָה

חֲבְיוֹנֵי עִתִּים

רָשְׁיוֹת הָאֹפֶל הַנּוֹרָא

הַגֻּלְגֹּלֶת הִתְבַּקְּעָה

מֵאֵיפֹה לָצֵאת?

תַּגִּידִי הֵם לֹא נְעוּלִים? הַפֶּה?

רַגְלַיִם? יָדַיִם ? מְעָרָה? מֵהַלֵּב

מֵהַנְּשִׁימָה?

מֵהַפְּטָמוֹת? כְּלָיוֹת? בַּלּוּטוֹת הַלִּימְפָה?

---

32.   Esther, *My Flesh Speaks G!d*, 7.

מֵאֵיפֹה הַיְצִיאָה
תְּאוֹמִים? נְקִיק שֶׁבֵּין רַגְלֵי? נַרְתִּיק?
הָרַת עוֹלָם פִּשַּׂקְתִּי אֶת רַגְלֵי
פְּעָרֵי פְּעָרֵי
בְּשַׂר הַדָּם נִפְלַח
שֹׁרֶשׁ הַהִתְרַחֲשׁוּת בַּמְּעָרָה
לִבָּתִי
שֶׁבֵּין רַגְלֵי
מִתְקָךְ נַרְתִּיק נִלְפָּת
הִתְעוֹפַפְתִּי הַחוּצָה
צֹורַחַת[33]

I gushed forth from the belly of history
secret moments
permits of terrible *tenebrae*
the skull has split open
from where?
say aren't they locked? mouth?
legs? hands? cave? from the heart?
through breathe?
nipples? kidneys? lymph nodes?
womb? vulva? navel?
where's the exit
that fits the split between my legs? casing?
birthing the world I spread my legs
my orifices, orifices
the flesh of blood split open
root of happening in the cave/ity
between my legs
my heart
your pleasure a casing twisting and turning
I flew outside
screaming

To gush beyond boundaries leads to the overturning of many waves of
Zionist poetry that never truly opened to the space of the embodied
feminine.[34] Nevermind writing from a womb of her own, Esther gushes

---

33. Esther, *My Flesh Speaks G!d*, 183.
34. Miryam Segal, *A New Sound in Hebrew Poetry: Poetics, Politics, Accent* (Bloomington:

forth even further to begin the poetic process of enumerating her own embodiment. Such an enumeration—a contemporary *Shiur Qomah* that contemplates the divine stature in phantasmagoric proportions[35]—reveals a unique moment of pleasure for the poet. The pleasure that comes from this birthing of her cosmological self brings forth a different kind of *jouissance*. The divinity she inscribes through her writing comes from the embodied experience of her cosmological self. This birthing moment is a subtle point, oscillating between pleasure and pain. Her yearning to realize some equanimity between the pushing and pulling of embodied desires is a veritable mystical vertigo as evinced in this passage:

לִמְצֹא אֶת נְקֻדַּת הַחִבּוּר בֵּין הַכְּאֵב לַתַּעֲנוּג

לְהַנְצִיחַ מַרְאֶה פָּנַי כְּשֶׁאֲנִי

יוֹלֶדֶת וּכְשֶׁאֲנִי מִשְׁתַּגַּעַת מִתַּעֲנוּג

יָדַעְתִּי אוֹתָם אֶת הַהֵינוּ הָךְ:

פְּנֵי אִשָּׁה קַמְאִית נוֹהֶמֶת תַּעֲנוּג

– פְּנֵי חַיָּה

פְּנֵי חַיָּה יוֹלֶדֶת יְפִי נוֹרָא

– פְּנֵי אִשָּׁה

פִּי הַטַּבַּעַת מוֹצִיא רֹךְ בְּלִבּוּבָיו

בִּכְנִיסוֹתָיו בִּיצִיאוֹתָיו

פְּנִינִים שֶׁגִּדַּלְתִּי בְּקוֹנְכִיּוֹת בָּשָׂר

נֹגַהּ הִלּוּלֵי זֶרַע

נָתַתִּי לָהֶם לְהִכָּנֵס שׂוֹחִים

בְּמִפְלֵי הַקֶּצֶף הַשּׁוֹצֵף

לְהִתְאַהֵב לְהִתְרַגֵּשׁ לְהִתְפַּעֵם

בְּאֵשׁ הָרֶחֶם הַבּוֹעֵר

זָרַעְתִּי אוֹתָם הֵיּוּלֵי זֶרַע

זוֹלְלִים אֶת הָאֵינְסְטִינְקְט

אֲנִי לֹא יוֹדַעַת שֹׂבַע[36]

to find the point between pain and pleasure
to keep the look on my face and when I'm
birthing when I'm in the throes of pleasure

Indiana University Press, 2010), esp. 49-100.

35. Gershom Scholem, *On the Mystical Shape of the Godhead: Basic Concepts in the Kabbalah*, trans. J. Chipman (New York: Schocken Books, 1991), 15-55.

36. Esther, *My Flesh Speaks G!d*, 11.

I let them know why:
primal woman's face screaming pleasure
—animal's face
animal's face giving birth awesome beauty
—face of a woman
anus oozes in its contractions
while penetrating and leaving
pearls I grew in the flesh conch shell
shone ecstasy of seed
I let them penetrate swimming
in the foamy waterfalls
to fall in love, to emote and arouse one's self
in burning fire of the womb
I inseminated them with hylic seed
berating the instinct
I know no satiety

Empowering her cosmological self through the somatic self, the poet is again evoking the inseminating power of her *hylic* seed rather than reverting to the *pneumatic* self that would disembody her experience. It is precisely Esther's embodied experience that sets her epic poem apart as a uniquely feminine voice. Esther goes deeper into her cosmological self by penetrating her libidinal center, those "pearls I grew in the flesh conch shell." She is unflinching in her journey into embodied self so as to reveal another inner layer of the concealed, cosmological self. The constellations of the cosmos shine from within her embodied self. The texture of this discovery, marked by the shift from third person to second person, is all the more unusual in this next passage as it reveals the unexplored territory of embodiment:

רַחְמָהּ שָׁחֹר
שְׁאֵרֵי בְּשָׂרָהּ שְׁפָטִים
שְׁאֵרָהּ לְהָבִים
עוֹנָתָהּ עֲוִיתוֹת
כְּסוּתָהּ כְּסוּחִים
קְרוֹבָהּ קִרְבַת שֵׁד וְלִילִית
טְרוּפָהּ קָרוֹב
עֲנָבְלֶיהָ עוֹנוֹת
שָׁדֶיהָ יוֹקְדִים
שָׁדֶיהָ חֲנִיתוֹת

פִּטְמוֹתֶיהָ פְּרָעוֹת
טַבּוּרָה עִוְעִים
תִּדְקֹר
רָצֹח
סַכִּינִים
כּוּסָה שִׁגְעוֹנוֹת
כַּמַּיִם קִיטוֹר מְכַסִּים
וְהָרֶחָם יִשְׁמָרְךָ אֱלֹהִים[37]

her womb, black
her flesh's meals, judgments
her food, flames
her conjugal rights, convulsions
her enshrouding, slashes
her intimate relations, demon & Lillith
her insanity, close
her uvula, seasons
her breasts, aflame
her breasts, speak
her nipples, exposing
her navel, confounding
she'll penetrate
murder
knives
her vagina, insanities
like the enshrouding moistness of mist
but the womb shall protect you *Elohim*

For the poet as "the womb" to offer protection to the divine "you *Elohim*," especially from the second person, crosses a boundary of intimacy with the transcendent. Almost unheard of in Hebrew poetry, yet Esther's approach is most radical as she is challenging the obligation to transgress the transcendent trajectory by instead drawing the reader back to her own *hylic* embodiment. The vertical metaphor of the divine as exterior begins to dissolve in this poem. It is a more nuanced approach to the multiplicity of nominations that comprise the experience of the divine—beyond the traditionally transcendental address of God as the supernatural beyond

---

[37.] Esther, *My Flesh Speaks G!d*, 160-161.

human sensation and perception. Not only does this nuance allow for greater intimacy, but the poet is also admitted (back) into the divine family, so as to re-present her angelic status:

אֲדֹנָי נוֹתֵן לִי אֶת שֵׁם מִשְׁפַּחְתּוֹ,
מַכְנִיס בִּי לַוְּרִידִים
אֲנִי מַאֲמִינָה בְּךָ
אֲנִי חוֹתֶמֶת עַל כָּל מַה שֶׁנּוֹלָד מִמֶּנִּי
בִּשְׁנֵי שְׁמוֹתַי הַפְּרָטִיִּים
אֲנִי עוֹמֶדֶת לִרְצֹחַ אוֹתְךָ כְּמוֹ מְאַהֵב
לִמְחֹק אוֹתְךָ בְּזִיּוּנִים אַדִּירִים
רוֹקֶמֶת מַחְשָׁבוֹת לְמַחְשָׁבוֹת
תּוֹפֶרֶת פּוֹרֶמֶת אֲנִי אֶתְעַלֵּס אִתְּךָ
אֶחֱוֶה אוֹתְךָ אֶגְמֹר אִתְּךָ
הַזְּרִיחָה שֶׁתָּבוֹא
תִּהְיֶה נֶהְדֶּרֶת כְּשֶׁאַתְּ
כְּבָר לֹא תִּהְיִי אֶלֶף שְׁמָשׁוֹת
שֶׁאֲנִי אֶהְיֶה רִבּוֹן עוֹלָמִי
קָרוּעַ קָרוּעַ
קוֹרַעַת נְיָרוֹת גְּדוֹלִים וְצוֹבַעַת
אוֹתָם בִּצְבָעִים עַזֵּי מַבָּע
וְיֵשׁ לִי רַגְלַיִם נֶהְדָּרוֹת יָפוֹת
מְחֻטָּבוֹת מוֹרוֹת עַל
כִּשּׁוּרֵי הָרוּחָנִיִּים
הָאֶצְבָּעוֹת אֲרֻכּוֹת מְעֻדָּנוֹת מוֹרוֹת
עַל הַכְּנָפַיִם הָאֲצוּרוֹת בְּבִטְנִי
קָרוּעַ
קוֹרַעַת עֵינֵי לְרַוְחָה
קוֹרַעַת שָׁדַי לְרַוְחָה
קוֹרַעַת רַגְלַי לְרַוְחָה
קוֹרַעַת לִבִּי לְרַוְחָה[38]

Adonai gives me his family name,
penetrating into my veins
I believe in you
I'm signing off on all born from me
in my two personal names
I'm about to kill you like a lover,

---

38. Esther, *My Flesh Speaks G!d*, 184.

to erase you with magnificent sex
weaving thought to thought,
stitching, rending I take pleasure in you
I'll speak of you, I'll consummate you,
the sunrise that'll come
will be stunning when you
already won't be a thousand lights,
then shall I be the Lord of my Universe
torn, torn,
tearing huge papers
and coloring them in bold colors
I have beautiful, stunning legs,
their shapeliness displaying
my spiritual prowess
long, delightful finger pointing to
the trapped wings in my belly
Torn
tearing my eyes free
tearing my breasts free
tearing my legs free
tearing my heart free

Any preconceived notions of language about the divine are by now utterly torn apart by the poet. Through this breached birthing the poet tears into new embodiments of ancient names. This tearing through names, (קוֹרַעַת *kora'at* being a *triple entendre* in Hebrew that is simultaneously tearing, happening as well as reading), exemplifies how great poetry serves as both a sign of mourning her subjugated past, while embracing the liberation these names reveal for the future. This is a futurity that opens the possibility of seeing, nourishing, moving, and feeling differently. Such a fourfold tearing is what opens the poet to a fourfold betrothal, bringing her one step closer to redemption through the *hylic* self into the *pneumatic* self. It is in this prophetic vein that her fourfold betrothal unfolds to the beloved through her daring language:

הֲרֵי אַתְּ מְקֻדָּשָׁת לִי
הֲרֵי אַתְּ בּוֹעֶרֶת
הֲרֵי אַתְּ מָתְרֶת
הֲרֵי אַתְּ מָתְּכַת[39]

---

39. Esther, *My Flesh Speaks G!d*, 186.

Behold you are betrothed to me
Behold you are burning
Behold you are permitted
Behold you are liquefied

Such breathtaking language spans antiquity to the contemporary moment in a fourfold fellswoop of verses all beginning with the formulaic הֲרֵי אַתְּ *harei 'at* [Behold you]. Resonating with the density of an alchemical betrothal formulae,[40] once symbolized by the prophetic re-reading of biblical poetics, it is now beginning to ring with a new immediacy. Rather than move in the direction of symbolic divorce, like Hosea, the poet Esther choses to deepen her connection by tearing at its seams without casting off the tradition entirely.

As the poet burns through the dualism of what is permitted/forbidden, betrothal is liquefied. The same language that once bound a female partner into a subjugated expression of betrothal to her male partner is now the very language that frees her. As envisioned anew by the poet, to become fully betrothed or *mequdeshet* [מְקֻדֶּשֶׁת] is to be set free by way of melting into a molten condition or *mutekhet* [מֻתֶּכֶת]. This is a hermeneutics even

---

40. See Mordechai A. Friedman, "Israel's Response to Hosea 2:17b: 'You are my husband'," *JBL* 99/2 (1980), 199-204. Negating tradition could be said to begin with the act of divorce. Friedman attempts to reconstruct the betrothal formula from the residue of an apparent divorce formula, ibid., "Israel's Response to Hosea," 202:

> The divorce formula in Hos 2:4 does not negate the marriage declaration, but the covenant of marriage was entered mutually. Accordingly, husband and wife each recited a separate formula—"You are my wife" and "You are my husband." Divorce, contrariwise, was unilateral; and, accordingly, the husband alone pronounced the double formula: "You are not my wife, and I am not your husband." Compare the symbolic divorce of the people in Hos. 1:9: "You are not My people, and I will not be your (God)."

This active linguistic volition to enter into partnership contrasts strongly with the passivity of the bride in the familiar Babylonian-style *ketubah* wherein she accepts the terms of the partnership silently: "...she accepted the proposal and became his wife." Ibid., "Israel's Response to Hosea," 204. What Friedman's research points out is how radically different the Palestinian custom was in that "...the obligations which the husband undertakes as part of his proposal—"I will nourish, provide for, honor, and esteem"—are paralleled by obligations to which the wife commits herself in response: "to serve, attend, honor and esteem him." Ibid., "Israel's Response to Hosea," 204. See also idem., *Jewish Marriage in Palestine—A Cairo Geniza Study: Marriage Contracts according to the Custom of Eretz Israel*, Vol. I; idem., *The Ketubba Traditions of Erez Israel*; Vol. II. (Tel Aviv: Tel Aviv University, 1984).

more radical than the collocation or *tzeruf 'otiyot* [צֵירוּף אוֹתִיוֹת] of Bialik,[41] for Esther's poetry deepens her *mis*reading the poetics of tradition through the feminine self. This radical poetic path of collocation is one in which she is "betrothed" [מְקֻדָּשָׁת] as a poet to her language by being "liquefied" [מְתֶּכֶת]. This process takes place here as each word in the fourfold formula of the opening and closing letters [מְתֶּכֶת-מְקֻדָּשָׁת] remains intact, while the inner essence of the words transvaluates completely [מְתֶּכֶת-מְקֻדָּשָׁת]. Here, the Hebrew poet tears into new ways of embodying ancient names—the form remains while its inner essence has been transformed.

Her final poetic gesture is to begin the process of writing the poetry that is already ovulating within her embodied self. Now that her embodiment has opened on its own terms and linked to language, the poet gives birth to the poem that is written in blood—"into this beautiful red" ink of existence. This is the vital inspiration that courses through her very veins. Through the mystical shape of her own limbs she writes the poem of her existence, the song of her embodied self. Hers is the song that no longer succumbs to the language of acquisition. This is a recovery arching back to its prophetic source. It takes place, however, the moment before such words were extrapolated into the matrimonial formula. That rabbinical formula of matrimony *par excellence*, "Behold you are betrothed to me" or *harei 'at mekudeshet li* [הֲרֵי אַתְּ מְקֻדֶּשֶׁת לִי] is what denotes the ritual acquisition or transfer of the female body from the house of the father to that of the husband. While the words of the poet here resonate with the same radical *poesis* as the prophet Hosea, in declaring "And it shall be, on that day, says YHVH, you shall call me 'my man' or *'ishi* [אִישִׁי], and you shall no longer call me 'my master' or *ba'ali* [בְּעֲלִי]," there is still something new taking place. Beyond merely traversing the prophetic path, this song burns through that patriarchal *nomos* that has repressed subjectivity by way of language. The poet opens into a new language for cosmological feminine self that is now free to flow on her own terms rather than those proscribed

---

41. *Tzeruf* or collocation being referred to here is *tzerufai shirah min ha'aggadah vehaqabbalah*, "collocation of poetry from lore and mysticism" that echoes Bialik's usage in his treatise on the philosophy of language, see Haim N. Bialik, "Un/veiled in Language" [Hebrew], ed. H. N. Bialik (Tel Aviv: *Knesset*, 1915). See Aubrey L. Glazer, *Contemporary Hebrew Mystical Poetry: How It Redeems Jewish Thinking* (New York: Edwin Mellen Press, 2009), 31-59, esp. 37-39, 54.

by the language of patriarchy. This is the song Esther has been praying to give birth to all along. To realize such a song that her womb opens from this poem, truly a song of songs, she needs to be immersed in the *devekut* of her auto-erotic cosmogony, bridging the *hylic* and the *pneumatic*, as witnessed in these verses:

שִׂימִי תְּ'שָׁמַיִם בְּעֹמֶק הָרֶחָם שֶׁלָּךְ

תְּנִי לִי חֲלֵב דָּם

תִּהְיוּ לִי מַלְאָכִים

תְּנִי לִי לָשִׂים אֶת הָאֶצְבָּעוֹת

בְּתוֹךְ הַיֹּפִי הָאָדֹם הַזֶּה. [42]

put th' heavens in your womb's depth
give me blood's fat
let me have angels
let me put my fingers
into this beautiful red.

All strong poets write with the hope that the poem will once again be released back into its source as song. Sometimes this song may even become an embodied prayer. This revelation for Esther is a movement from within her own embodiment into a radically *pneumatic* language. The task of the Hebrew poet is no longer one of reframing but of articulating and envisioning anew a prayerful poetry that addresses the "unprecedented concerns that women bring to prayer."[43]

Yet it is precisely where matters end for the theologian that the task of the poet commences—to envision anew a liberating language of embodiment for the soul. The history of repression that stems from instantiating *psychic* truths leads the poet to return to her own *hylic* truths. Yet to fully realize the redemptive power of this language of embodiment, it must be reborn from its *hylic* into its *pneumatic* expression. This embodied, prayerful poem of Ḥaya Esther appears heretical in its return to the *pneumatic* from the *hylic*. This need to return to non-dual mystical apperception cannot ignore its embodied source, thus the poet is traversing

---

42. Esther, *My Flesh Speaks G!d*, 188.
43. Rachel Adler, "And Not To Be Silent: Toward Inclusive Worship," *Engendering Judaism: An Inclusive Theology and Ethics* (Philadelphia: JPS, 1998), 65.

the way of a Hasidic bypath. In re-reading of the liturgical phrase "as for me and my prayer" or *va'ani tefilati* [וַאֲנִי תְפִלָּתִי], the poet collocates in writing her *pneumatic* self from the *hylic* embodiment to read "so I am my prayer." These words are then what open the possibility of a rebirthing the real Me, a true redemption of self as embodied in the deepest, prayerful poetry:

הֲיָדַעְתָּ שֶׁאֲנִי אִשָּׁה צְרוּפָה?
הֲיָדַעְתָּ שֶׁאֲנִי הִמְנוֹן תְּפִלָּה?[44]

Didn't you know—I'm a collocated woman?
Didn't you know—I'm a prayer anthem?

What is the nature of this collocation of *hylic* to *pneumatic* self–a kind of auto-betrothal—taking place? What is the fourfold experience of "betrothed-burning-permitted-liquefied" that correlates and collocates the cosmological and somatic self, prayer and anthem? Such a collocation of being "betrothed-burning-permitted-liquefied" evokes an alchemical liberation. The alchemy of collocation necessary in smelting through these divine names to redeem their core from the accumulated dross of patriarchy is the task of the poet. Esther as poet must betroth the cosmological and somatic self, prayer and anthem all through this collocation that allows for a dissolution of their false, patriarchal categories. This smelting—a process of clarifying the roots of language's nominative power—is at times phantasmagoric, inducing disorientation. It is a process of clarification through what Kronfeld calls "defamiliarization."[45] By defamiliarizing those once familiar limbs through their inscription, the very way in which this epic poem is being written allows for the embodied soul of the poet to then reveal how—

---

44. Esther, *My Flesh Speaks G!d,* 145.

45. See Hannah Kronfeld, *On the Margins of Modernism* (Berkeley: University of California Press, 1996). In a recent rejoinder to her landmark study, Kronfeld remarked about the process of "defamiliarization" as a facet of the de-territorialization inherent to what is erroneously called, "minor literature" ("Jewish Literatures Beyond Deluze and Guttari, Take II," AJS: Chicago, Dec. 20, 2004). Compare with Gilles Deluze and Félix Guattari, *Kafka: Toward a Minor Literature trans. D. Polan Theory of History and Literature,* Vol. 30 (Minneapolis: University of Minnesota Press, 1986), 16-28.

הַשִּׁיר הַזֶּה שׂוֹרֵף אוֹתִי בַּשְׂפָיוֹת הוֹ

שְׂפָתַיִם בַּשְׂרָנִיּוֹת שֶׁלִּי

אַחַת אֲרֻכָּה קְצָת יוֹתֵר מֵהַשְּׁנִיָּה

זֶה מֵהַלֵּדוֹת אַרְבַּע לֵדוֹת יַקִּירִי

וְיֵשׁ לִי מָקוֹם לָשִׂים אוֹתְךָ

לְעוֹרֵר אוֹתְךָ כָּל כָּךְ עַד

שֶׁתִּשְׁתַּגֵּעַ

אֲנִי מַמְשִׁיכָה לָשִׁיר

חִצִּים בְּרָקִים נְקֻדּוֹת

פְּסִיקִים רְקוּדִים

חַבֵּק אוֹתִי יֵשׁ לִי זְכוּת

הַשִּׁירִים שֶׁלִּי בֵּינְתַיִם

מוֹרִים לִי אֶת הַדֶּרֶךְ קָדִימָה

שִׁירֵי בִּיאָה שִׁירֵי נְבוּאָה

חַבֵּק אוֹתִי יֵשׁ לִי זְכוּת[46]

this poem burns my labia,
O my fleshy labia
One lip a bit longer than the other,
from birthing, four births my dear
& I have space for you,
to awaken you, so much so
'till you lose it
I continue to sing
arrows, lightning, periods,
commas, dances
embrace me I deserve it
in the meantime my poems
show me the path forward
songs of coming, songs of be/coming
embrace me I've got it coming to me

Amidst the collocations of these "songs of coming, songs of be/coming,"[47] the magical moment is captured in language as poetry returns into its origin as song. All that separates "songs of coming" [שִׁירֵי בִּיאָה] from redemptive

---

46.   Esther, *My Flesh Speaks G!d*, 174-175.
47.   While this brilliant poetic rendering proffered by Harry Fox is a feat of poetry all its own, the heretical undertone of Esther's verse, שִׁירֵי בִּיאָה שִׁירֵי נְבוּאָה is more literally rendered as "songs of intercourse, songs of prophecy." What Fox captures in his translation is the transformative capacity of embodied pleasure of a collocated spiritual insight.

"songs of be/coming" [שִׁירֵי נְבוּאָה] is a messianic tittle.[48] This awakening then takes place through an astounding cosmological embodiment. It is that paradoxical self-desire that alludes to non-dual mystical apperception operating at once in Esther's cosmic I that is also gushing forth "from the belly of history." Such an account of rebirthing in the first person seems to stand in direct opposition with her account in the third person, embodied *self* as evoked through "her womb... her flesh... her conjugal rights ..." Does this seeming paradox of representing the *self* then challenge Bloom's gnostic dualism? Namely, is it possible for any opposition within the poem to co-exist between the cosmological persona and the daemonic real Me?[49]

It is precisely the power of this paradox that presents the poet with the possibility of a return to non-dual apperception. In demanding to "put the heavens in your womb's depth," her return is intentionally through the *hylic* self as a path to non-dual *devekut* with the *pneumatic* self. No longer is there that yearning for a vertical ascent toward some divine stratosphere only from without. Rather, cosmic consciousness for the poet can only be encountered through her fully embodied engagement. In deftly recasting the radical Deuteronomistic phrasing, the poet decries how the heavens are not *above* but *within*, what she, and her Hasidic precursors,[50] aptly call the "the inner god point within me" [נְקוּדַת הָאֵל שָׁבִּי]. Recovering that inner point is an embodied revelation of non-dual apperception no longer hidden away. Just as at the very moment when language seems to have answered all desire, there is more. After having written enough to satisfy the desire of the *hylic self*, the writing of desire must continue. In this sense, the writerly desire of the *hylic* self by Ḥaya Esther is akin to Roland Barthes at the close of his autobiographic reflections:

"And afterwards what does one write? Can one write any more? One writes with one's desire and I have not yet finished desiring."[51] So too Esther, having just written to reveal her *hylic* layer within her *pneumatic*

---

48. הָאֵ[וּ]בִ(י)בָ[נ] that is, a *nun* and an elongated *yud*, both of which are letters pregnant with messianic symbolism.
49. Esther, *My Flesh Speaks G!d*, 7.
50. On the usages of inner divine point, see for example R. Shneur Zalman of Lyadi, *Sefer HaTanya, Igeret HaKodesh*, ch. 4.
51. "*Et après quoi écrire maintenant? Pourrez-vous encore écrire quelque chose? –On écrit avec son désir, et je n'en finis pas desirer.*" See Roland Barthes, *Roland Barthes par Roland Barthes* (Paris: Editions du Seuil, 1980), post script on back jacket.

self returns to this grounding question. It is the question that every strong poet confronts, namely, how does one continue to write after the initial desire to write has been satiated?

הַאִם אוּכַל לְהַמְשִׁיךְ לְהִתְקַדֵּם

לַשְּׁלֵימוּת שָׁלִּי אַחֲרֵי שִׁיר כָּזֶה?

לִנְקוּדַת הָאֵל שֶׁבִּי?

לָאַלְמָוֶת? לַנֶּצַח הַנִּכְסָף?

הַאִם אֲנִי עֲדַיִן אָדָם שָׁלֵם?

חוֹשֶׁבֶת שֶׁכֵּן

כִּי כָּל מַה שֶּׁכָּתַבְתִּי הֲרֵי כָּתַבְתִּי לְעַצְמִי

מָזוֹן לָרוּחַ מַרְפֵּא לַגּוּף

כִּי כָּל זֶה נָשַׁר מִמֶּנִּי אֵיךְ שֶׁהוּא[52]

> After a poem like this shall I continue
> to progress towards perfection?
> To the god within me?
> To immortality? To yearned eternity?
> Am I still a whole human?
> Think so
> Because all I've written is for my self
> Sustenance for spirit, salve for flesh
> For all of this has fallen from me somehow

Remaining wholly human—undivided by dualism—is a process of uncovering the non-dual reality within the *self*. The poet reveals how the sustaining power of language is necessary for more than the *psychic*, but for the *hylic* self in *devekut* with the *pneumatic* self. This song of self-delight does more than problematize the relationship between the cosmological persona and the *daemonic* real Me. The Hebrew poet Ḥaya Esther realizes the redemptive need for bringing the *hylic* layer back into the forefront of an embodied *pneumatic* language. Through the soul's experience of embodiment, a new song of *hylic-pneumatic* self may be discovered in a *devekut* of auto-erotic cosmogony. This new song of collocative *devekut* is what allows cosmic consciousness to shine through the mystical vertigo of her embodied real Me.

---

52. Esther, *My Flesh Speaks G!d,* 147.

CHAPTER VIII

(HIT)DAVEKUTH AS DURÉE
OF THE GODLOVER:
DISENTANGLING INTUITIVE TIME IN BINYAMIN
SHEVILI'S "HOMOSEXU*E*LITY"

בָּרוּךְ אַתָּה עוֹזְבֵנוּ אֲדֹנָי אֱלֹהֵינוּ

לֹא מֶלֶךְ הָעוֹלָם בַּקָּשָׁתֵנוּ

בִּתְפִלָּתֵנוּ שֶׁתְּחַיֵּנוּ

וּתְקַיְּמֵנוּ

וּתְבִיאֵנוּ

לֹא

לַזְּמַן

הַזֶּה

Blessed are You, our Abandoner, Lord our God

Not Master of the Universe our petitions

within our prayers that you should enliven us

and that you should sustain us

and that you should bring us

not

to this

time.[1]

Time of the True Dissolving into the Real: Durée *of* Devekut

On the cusp of creative pleasure and horrible pain, why does the intuition
of time always remain? If this intuition of time—in pleasure and in pain—is
beyond the intellect, how does it remain? In poetry, experiences in time
remain through the word, as will be seen in the writing of Jerusalemite
poet, Binyamin Shevili (b. 1956). But in philosophy, experiences in time

---

[1.] Binyamin Shevili, *A New Dictionary of Afflictions,* [Hebrew] (Tel Aviv: Schocken Press,
2004), 62.

remain through *durée* or duration. Rather than being an objective unit, *durée*, for Hénri Bergson (1859-1941), is the closest one can approximate to the subjective perception of space-time. Experience is then a succession of separate, thing-like states, no less an abstraction from lived consciousness than time as measured by the hands of a clock. Whether separate frames of an experience or the hands of a clock, both ways of measuring time appear to be highly spatial. By contrast, lived consciousness takes place in a spatio-temporal continuum of intimate elements. Such elements are representative of others and neither is distinguished from nor isolated by abstract thought. Despite Einstein's objections to *durée* regarding its limits of relativity in time,[2] Bergson eventually came to terms with the reality that time is non-linear. This non-linearity of *durée* thus escapes objective measurement. What Bergson's *durée* allows for is the experience of time and its contemplation to open into a deeper awareness. Such awareness begins from lived consciousness.

The conditions for the awareness of lived consciousness has radically changed since Bergson—namely, since the birth pangs of the State of Israel and the ashen ends of the *Shoah*. Even if symmetrical causality (linking cause to effect and effect to cause) could be ascertained, relativity shatters such seeming consistency—why? Relativity still consists "in the multiplicity of causal decompositions of becoming."[3] While that intuitive sense of time–of *before, during* and *after*—still remains, the argument lingers for a causal interconnection of phenomena. For example, the catastrophe of the *Shoah* is causally linked to the effect of the State of Israel being born. So while intuitive time may be restricted to "fragments of psychic becoming"[4] its non-linear nature makes it difficult, if not impossible, to neatly disentangle it from universal time.

Where does such entanglement in time leave language and its relations? In the margins of this correlation in time, some unexpected problems facing twenty-first century Jewish philosophy arise, affecting language used by mystic and poet. With the threefold challenge of a diminishing

---

[2.]   Hénri Bergson, *Durée et simultanéité a propos de la théorie d'Einstein* [1921] (Paris: P.U.F., 1992); Hénri Bergson, *Duration and Simultaneity*, trans. Leon Jacobson (Indianapolis: Bobbs-Merrill, 1965); compare with Robin Durie, *Duration and Simultaneity: Bergson and the Einsteinian Universe* (Manchester: Clinamen Press, 1999).

[3.]   Henry Mehlberg, *Time, Causality, and the Quantum Theory: Studies in the Philosophy of Science*, ed. Robert S. Cohen, *Volume 1: Essay on the Causal Theory of Time* (Boston: Kluwer, 1980), 260.

[4.]   Mehlberg, *Time, Causality, and the Quantum Theory*, 260.

Diaspora, an Israel striving to be egalitarian and democratic, and the need to relearn one's relation to time and otherness through language, the task of redemption becomes most urgent.[5] Who then is best poised to catalyze this reorientation towards language—the poet or the philosopher?

This seismic shift for twenty-first century Jewish thinking and its language finds illumination from the darkness in returning to Bergsonian *durée* in Israel.[6] Carrying forward an obscure, self-reflexive rendering of *devekut* as *hitdabbekut* in the definition of time by Hasdai Crescas (1340-1410, Spain) allows for Harvey to point to the relation between time and the *other* as a lost bypath of Jewish thinking. That intrinsic relation between time and the *other* is how Bergson's thought is carried forward by Emmanuel Lévinas (1906-1995),[7] who fleshes out the lived consciousness and responsibility implied by *durée*. While some redressing of the inequality of the feminine as mysterious *other*[8] has been made recently by way of a phenomenology of maternity,[9] a repositioning the role of eros within sexual ethics remains a further redemptive responsibility of liberation.[10]

The liberation yet to be fully redressed, however, is an ethics of time and the *other* in the realm of homo-erotic imaginality[11] and homosexual relations. How the non-dual mystical experience is perceived within the realm where the *other* appears neutralized as the *same* is of critical importance for the *in*volution of *devekut*. Does it differ from such apperception in hetero-

---

5. Warren Zev Harvey, "New and unexpected problems facing 21st-century Jewish philosophy," *Studia Judaica* 11-12 (2004): 187.

6. Warren Zev Harvey, "The Term '*hitdabbekut*' in Crescas' Definition of Time," *JQR* 71, 1 (1980): 46-47.

7. Emmanuel Lévinas, *Temps et L'Autre* (Paris: PUF, 1948).

8. Simone de Beauvoir, *Le deuxième sexe* [1949], vol. 1 (Paris: Gallimard, 1976), 15-16n1.

9. Hanoch Ben Pazi, "Rebuilding the Feminine in Lévinas' Talmudic Readings," *Journal of Jewish Thought and Philosophy* 12, 3 (2003): 1-32. See also Lisa Guenther, *The Gift of the Other: Levinas and the Politics of Reproduction* (Albany: State University of New York Press, 2006), esp. 19-29, 95-107, 161-165.

10. Alain Mayama, *Emmanuel Levinas' Conceptual Affinities with Liberation Theology*, American University Studies 7 (New York: Lang, 2010), 100-112.

11. Wolfson remains a pioneer in regards to making this distinction, specifically as it relates to homo-erotic imaginal mystical companionship, for some examples, see Elliot R. Wolfson, *Language, Eros, Being: Kabbalistic Hermeneutics and Poetic Imagination* (New York: Fordham University Press, 2004), 296-332; Wolfson, *Circle in the Square* (New York: SUNY Press, 1995), esp. 107-110; Wolfson, *Through a Speculum That Shines* (Princeton: Princeton University Press, 1994), esp. 368-392, etc.

erotic imaginalities and heterosexual relations? To what degree does the love of friends inspire or facilitate non-dual mystical apperception in such imaginalities and relations?[12] It is the poet, as unflinching iconoclast, who breaks through the dualism of homosexual/heterosexual through a vigilant non-dual mystical apperception. Such apperception takes place frequently through intimate moments of love in friendship.[13] This chapter will be concerned with the poetry of homo-erotic imaginalities and homosexual relations between godlovers and its relation to the entanglement of time.

With the entanglement of intuitive time and universal time, an indelible mark is made upon poetry and poetic existence. Existence, however, is marked by its fluttering between the True and the Real. If what is True is eternal, then what is Real is ephemeral. Time is then the measure of the passage from the True to the Real and back again. What allows the human to taste both worlds—oftentimes fluttering between the True and the Real—is a deeper connectivity beyond entanglement. That form of connectivity is called *devekut*.

Despite that human need for connectivity with the *other*, most systems for measuring time are less concerned with the True and more molded by the Real, less connected to the eternal and more connected to the ephemeral. Consider the difficulty in letting go of the hourglass as an image that describes universal time. The grains of sand may symbolize each individual moment, but the unstoppable nature of universal time is flowing

---

12. Compare with Lawrence Fine, "Spiritiual Friendship: Go Among People Who Are Awake and Where a Light Shines Brightly," *Jewish Mysticism and the Spiritual Life: Classical Texts, Contemporary Reflections,* ed. Eitan Fishbane and Or N. Rose (Vermont: Jewish Lights, 2010), 112-118.

13. The poet's love of friends and in friendship has inspired some of the most important contemporary mystical poetry of the last centuries. For this general trajectory from Walt Whitman to Hart Crane see, Robert K. Martin, *The Homosexual Tradition in American Poetry* (Austin: University of Texas Press, 1979), as well as *Gay & Lesbian Poetry in Our Time: An Anthology,* ed. Carl Morse (New York: St. Martin's Press, 1988). See also Piotr K. Gwiazda, *James Merrill and W.H. Auden: Homosexuality and Poetic Influence* (New York : Palgrave Macmillan, 2007). Specifically, consider the friendships that Allen Ginsburg fostered with Jack Kerouac and William S. Burroughs and its legacy of poetic record of mystical experiences as well as the creation of *School of Disembodied Poetics* at Naropa Institute, see Allen Ginsburg, *The Book of Martyrdom and Artifice: First Journals and Poems 1937-1952,* Juanita Lieberman-Plimpton, Bill Nagan, Bill Morgan eds. (Cambridge: Da Capo Press, 2006); consider also the mystical doctrine of universal brotherhood envisioned by Walt Whitman in his poetry and how the love of comrades constitutes a new sexual ethic, see Juan A. Herrero-Brasas, *Walt Whitman's Mystical Ethics of Comradeship: Homosexuality and the Marginality of Friendship at the Crossroads of Modernity* (Albany: SUNY Press, 2010), 33-56.

from one end of the hourglass to the other. The power intrinsic to "this time" or *la'zeman haze* as anything more than Real seems out of reach, and it is equally hard to grasp the "multiplicity of causal decompositions of becoming"[14] for Truth outside of this moment. Yet this opening poem by Binyamin Shevili challenges even "this moment" as being singular and outside of such multiplicity. By wandering into the realm of "not this time" [לֹא לַזְּמָן הַזֶּה], the poem beckons the reader to question: Can a time other than "this moment" ever really be noticed, recorded, unified with or even be blessed? How is this moment unique, if it is pregnant with the multiplicity of causal decompositions of that which is becoming?

Akin to the top half of a broken hourglass, one comes to realize by entering into the form of the opening poem that the texture of intuitive time through word forms is shattering open into universal time. Beyond the revealment of the Real dwells the concealment of the True. This opening poem by Hebrew poet, Binyamin Shevili is an intentional misreading of an ancient prayer about marking the blessing of intuitive time in the face universal time—the archetypal Hebrew hourglass. The blessing known as the *She'ekhaiyanu* has been read through the centuries as a marker of intuitive and new experiences formed in the following language:

בָּרוּךְ אַתָּה אֲד-נָי אֱלֹהֵ-ינוּ
מֶלֶךְ הָעוֹלָם
שֶׁהֶחֱיָינוּ
וְקִיְּמָנוּ
וְהִגִּיעָנוּ
לַזְּמַן הַזֶּה

Blessed are You,
Master of the Universe,
who has enlivened us,
sustained us,
and
brought us
to this
moment.

---

14. Mehlberg, *Time, Causality, and the Quantum Theory*, 260.

Daring to write against the hourglass view of time, Shevili's brilliant misreading seeks to unravel this temporal entanglement. By breaking out of the hourglass view of universal time and the apparent fullness of its measure, yet another view of intuitive time shatters the mold, expressed negatively as: "Not Master of the Universe our petitions.../not/to this/time."

With these few grains of sand about to escape the broken hourglass of universal time into the journey of the intuitive time that intimately marks existence, Jerusalemite poet, Binyamin Shevili dares to imagine the very emptiness of such time. The poet's misreading of the ancient Hebrew marker of time, the *She'hekhaiyanu*, is iconoclastic to the core of the human experience of intuitive time. If universal time cannot truly capture and record the intimacy "/not/to this/time," then what happens to this moment of intuitive time that is now escaping? How will it ever be known? In merely eight lines, the poet rends the veil of universal time revealing the intimate journey of intuitive time.

Amidst all the pain it can bring in its wake, the poet is committed to journeying through a different layer of existence, one that is open to the emptiness that hovers inside intuitive time. Through this pain of separation of lover from beloved, the poet yearns to return to the unity of primal experience—a residue within the multiplicity of causal decompositions of becoming. While the philosophical retrieval of neglected mystical pathways has been rehearsed elsewhere,[15] in what follows, the poetic path of Hebrew poetry re-imagines *devekut* as an authentic sign of contemporary mysticism. Through Binyamin Shevili's *devekut* as *durée* of the godlover, the poet reveals new ways of imagining homo-erotic imaginalities. This chapter seeks to articulate the possibility of a multiplicity of causal decompositions through "complete submersion" of identity[16] in the *durée* of intuitive time

---

15. See Aubrey L. Glazer, "*Durée, Devekuth, & Re-embracing the Godlover: Involution of unio mystica* via Collocative HomosexuELity," *Vixens Disturbing Vineyards: Embarrassment & Embracement of Scriptures, Festschrift in Honor of Harry Fox leBeit Yoreh* (Boston: Academic Studies Press, 2010), 515-531.

16. Such a claim of "complete submersion" within *devekut* is *contra* Gershom Scholem, *Major Trends in Jewish Mysticism* (New York: Schocken Books, 1947), 122-123: "...it is only in extremely rare cases that ecstasy signifies actual union with God, in which the human individuality abandons itself to the rapture of *complete submersion* in the divine stream. Even in this ecstatic frame of mind, the Jewish mystic almost invariably retains a sense of the distance between the Creator and His creature...he does not regard it as constituting

between godlovers.[17]

Beyond the Illusion of Real Time:
Sabbatical Union Erupting into True Time

While time may be a co-ordinate or even a dimension, the grand illusion persists that time still flows[18]—*why?* Elucidating this mysterious flux, after quantum physics, reveals yet another layer of the human self. Without a real understanding of the flow of time and its illusion, one will know neither where one is going nor what part one is playing in the unfolding cosmic drama.[19] As much as this myth of time's flux may be a residual cerebral process from the perspective of physics, for the journey of the soul this sense of flux persists through the image of seasons. How does this poetic journey through seasons of intuitive time, intoxicated with an eternality of heaven and hell, then shed light on that crucial divine element connected with the human self—the soul?

It is through this experiential dimension of time's flux in relation to an *other* that expands the profundity of existence. Such profundity

---

anything so extravagant as identity of Creator and creature."[my itals.] Scholem's doubt regarding the possibility of complete submersion of identity remained even in later years: "The Jewish mystics used the term *devekuth* to denote this ultimate aim. The term, meaning literally "cleaving" or "adhering" to God... the act itself, which may or may not include a state of mystical union." See Scholem, "Mysticism and Society," *Diogenes, Eranos Lectures,* vol. 58 (1967), 16. Compare with Moshe Idel, *Studies in Ecstatic Kabbalah* (New York: SUNY Press, 1988), 21n11, who challenges this ecstatic kabbalah there are "philosophical texts which openly speak about the possibility of total union with God."

17. For further reflections on *unio mystica* via love and intellection culled from Abulafia in *Sefer 'Or ha-Sekhel*, see Idel, *Kabbalah and Eros* (New Haven: Yale University Press, 2005), 79.

18. Paul Davies, *About Time: Einstein's Unfinished Revolution* (New York: Simon & Schuster, 1995), 255: "The flow of time has no significance in the logically fixed patterns demanded by deterministic theory, time being a mere coordinate. In a theory with indeterminacy, however, the passage of time transforms the statistical expectations into real events."

19. Davies, *About Time,* 278: "Attempts to explain the flow of time using physics, rather than trying to define it away using philosophy, are probably the most exciting contemporary developments in the study of time. Elucidating the mysterious flux would, more than anything else, help unravel the deepest of all scientific enigmas—the nature of the human self. Until we have a firm understanding of the flow of time, or incontrovertible evidence that it is indeed an illusion, then we will not know who we are, or what part we are playing in the great cosmic drama."

lies in the ongoing entanglement of universal time with intuitive time that is *devekut*. The seeming passage of time then invites an awareness of the infinitude pregnant within each moment. Such an infinite sense in intuitive time then encompasses past and future within the fullness of the present. These seasons of love and loss open every human by entangling them into tasting the aroma of infinity within the finitude of existence. Such a quest for reunion and submersion in timeless love is the *telos* of the mystical experience. For mystic and poet alike, this quest often finds a home in the Sabbath, a moment where Shevili also sees the eros of time otherwise:

בְּ	in
קָרוֹב	time
יָבוֹא	Sabbath shall
שַׁבָּת	come
כְּמוֹ	like
מֶלֶךְ	a king
לֹא	not
כְּמוֹ	like
מַלְכָּה	a queen
לְבוּשׁ	garbed in
שְׁחֹ	bl
רִים	ack
בְּחֶרֶב	with a sword
פִּיפִ	dou-
יוֹת	ble-bladed
יְקַצֵּר	which shall shorten
אֶת	the
הַכְּאֵב	pain
וְגַם אֶת	and the
הַגַּעְגּוּעִים	longings. [20]

---

20.   Binyamin Shevili, *A New Dictionary of Afflictions*, 52.

Tearing into the holiness of time, the poet sees the coming of the Sabbath. Shevili exposes the longing at the core of this irruption of infinitude into the finite, of universal time into intuitive time. This narrowing of the universal into the intuitive is a painful moment, cutting like a double-edged sword.[21] This double-edged sword of the Psalmist is extrapolated by Shevili from the bed into life—there is no place devoid of desire.

If the erotic imaginal–that interworld between imagination and reality—is all-consuming, while embodied by both edges of the sword, then one side is hetero-erotic, while the other side of this double-edged sword for Shevili is homo-erotic. This perspective within eros allows for the true fluidity of the Sabbath to come to the fore. Just as Shevili's double-edged eros echoes in his precursor, R. Shlomo haLevi Alkabetz (1505-1576) and his liturgical poem, *Lecha Dodi*, that welcomes the reunion of the lover with the beloved where gender is constantly in motion,[22] so too Shevili invites a relationship with the other side of queen through king. The gendered oscillation between queen [מַלְכָּה] and king [מֶלֶךְ] all rests in the balance of a single letter [ה].

This more restrained alchemy serves as a taste of how Shevili's poetry allows an eruption of the True into the Real, of universal time into intuitive time. The belonging that comes from such intense longing is quenched through the unique experience of time as cleaving. To more fully understand the importance of Shevili's poetic contribution to the unspoken Jewish experience of *unio mystica*, a brief history of *devekut* has been presented elsewhere.[23] *Hitdavekuth,* however, is more accurately rendered as continuity, continuousness or the very continuum which yields *durée.*[24]

---

21. "Let the pious exult in glory: let them sing hymns even on their beds with the high praises of God in their throats and a double-edged sword in their hands..." (Psalm 149: 5-6).

22. While Kimmelman's reading of this *piyyut* acknowledges its erotic nature, Wolfson accentuates the nuance of eros. See Reuven Kimmelman, *The Mystical Meaning of Lekha Dodi and Kabbalat Shabbat,* [Hebrew] *Sources and Studies in the Literature of Jewish Mysticism* 9; (Los Angeles: Cherub Press, 2003) to compare with Elliot R. Wolfson, "Eunuchs Who Keep Sabbath: Erotic Asceticism/Ascetic Eroticism," *Language, Eros, Being: Kabbalistic Hermeneutics and Poetic Imagination* (New York: Fordham University Press, 2004), 296-332.

23. See Glazer, "*Durée, Devekuth,* & Re-embracing the Godlover," 515-531.

24. Warren Zev Harvey, "The Term '*hitdabbekut*' in Crescas' Definition of Time," *Jewish Quarterly Review* 71, 1 (1980), 46-47. See also Glazer, "*Durée, Devekuth,* & Re-embracing the Godlover," 529-531.

Unsaid Hitdavekuth: *Involution of Homosexuality*

The tension between truly loving another soul of the same sex and its apparent prohibition in the exoteric reading of Scripture confounds many readers, seekers, and lovers. Yet one does not even have to venture into the orchards of the esoteric to experience the eros between godlovers in the Song of Songs, between the intertwining of souls between Jonathan and David,[25] between oneself and a companion, to realize that such eros permeates existence. Yet with a narrative as strong as the homo-erotic covenant between Jonathan and David barely used by mystics in their exegesis, the power of such *unio mystica* appears to be marginalized.

While mystics through the ages have been nourished by the homo-eroticism at the esoteric root of the exoteric text, it is poetry that allows for unbound expression of the homo-erotic imaginal as non-dual mystical experience. The highly eroticized metaphysical system of the Kabbalists lent itself to supererogatory and hypernomian behavior on the inside while carrying a minimally traditional, if not entirely nomian life, on the outside.[26]

Part of the problem surrounding the integration of homoerotic imaginality comes back to dualistic thinking. Thinking about gender and sexuality tends to be dualistic—either essentialist or constructivist. The essentialist sees sexuality as an intrinsic reflection of gender that can be anchored relative to the essence of one's being. Thus the essentialist argues that homosexuality is a malady that can be cured—namely, one's essential nature as a male is heterosexual. The constructivist sees gender as a fluid construct played out in various cultural scenarios. Thus the constructivist argues for homosexuality as fluid expression where there is no fixed signifier, or that the phallus[27] is always shifting from its site of origin in the process of meaning-making. While immobility or motion typify such dualism, what

---

25.   1Samuel 18:1.
26.   Shaul Magid, "Leviticus: The Sin of Becoming a Woman: Male Homosexuality and the Castration Complex," *From Metaphysics to Midrash: Myth, History and the Interpretation of Scripture in Lurianic Kabbalah* (Bloomington: Indiana University Press, 2008), 111-142.
27.   Jacques Lacan, *The Seminar of Jacques Lacan*, vol. 20, trans. Jacques-Alain Miller (New York: Norton, 1988), esp. 16, 18; compare with Judith Butler, "The Lesbian Phallus and the Morphological Imaginary," *Bodies That Matter: On the Discursive Limits of "Sex"* (New York: Routledge, 1993), 57-92.

seems lacking is a re-embracing the *ars erotica*[28] of Judaism.[29] However, a third path of non-dual mystical apperception has yet to be fully articulated.[30]

True Homo-eroticism within Real HomosexuELity: Revealing the Journey of the Godlover

Desire is not *about* union, desire *is* union. This intense desire for *unio mystica*—towards original and final unity—finds the strongest reading in the poetry of Jerusalemite, Binyamin Shevili. While the ecstatic mystical journeys of pioneering poet, Pinhas Sadeh (1929-1994) have much to contribute to the inner evolution or *in*volution of a contemporary mystical lexicon in Hebrew, it is Shevili whose erotic poetry is of another experiential register of mysticism. Such mystical experience knows no bounds, and in a singular voice Shevili is able to break down all barriers between self and other in the face of universal desire.[31] I argue that Shevili's desire for ecstatic mystical union through homo-eroticism is reflected powerfully through his collocations in language. What is so unique about these homo-erotic collocative poems is that there has not been such a powerful expression since some lost moments in the margins of royal biblical friendships in Israel,[32] of Talmudic romances between sages in Persia,[33] and medieval wine poems of erotic encounters between courtiers and servant boys from the Golden Age in Spain.[34] Unabashedly rending the veil of euphemism, Shevili's poems reveal remarkable journeys. The poetic record serves as a search for authentic erotic union that traverses all boundaries between heterosexual and homosexual. This is a search for non-dual mystical consciousness. The power of this poetic vision articulated

---

28.   Michel Foucault, *Histoire de la Sexualité* (1976), 3 tomes (Paris: Gallimard, 1994); Michel Foucault, *The History of Sexuality*, 3 vols (New York Vintage Books, 1990).

29.   Glazer, "*Durée, Devekuth,* & Re-embracing the Godlover," 531-535.

30.   See above no. 12.

31.   Jill Amuel, "There Also Is a Different Love,"[Hebrew] *Dimui Journal* 10 (Jerusalem 1995): 26-29, 81.

32.   For examples, see Thomas M. Horner, *Jonathan Loved David: Homosexuality in Biblical Times* (Philadelphia: Westminster Press, 1978), 26-39, esp. 59-85.

33.   For examples, see Daniel Boyarin, *Carnal Israel: Reading Sex in Talmudic Culture* (Berkeley: University Of California Press, 1993), 215-219.

34.   For examples, see Raymond Scheindlin, *Wine, Women, and Death*: Medieval Hebrew Poems on the Good Life (New York: Oxford University Press, 1999), esp. 29, 82, 86, 88.

in Hebrew takes leave where earlier aforementioned sources and even contemporary sources—whether in Israel or America—remain incomplete.[35] What begins with alchemical fascination leads to deeper liberation in the poetic experience of collocative homo-eroticism.

This collocative homo-erotic poetry is strongest in Shevili's cycle, "homosexuEL" [הוֹמוֹסָקסוּאֶל]. By collocative language or *zeruf 'otiyot*, Shevili is riding the wave of mystical praxis beginning with the first biblical artist, Bezalel, continuing through to the pioneering Hebrew poet, Bialik. Rather than a transmutation, this is a collocation of letters—an intimate conjoining that approaches *devekut*. In experimenting with the linguistic form of the journey towards non-dual consciousness, Shevili's poetic form deftly conveys the rocking motion of a boat. By setting off on this journey into the unknown depths, the poet and the reader both experience the *to and fro* motion of being at sea journeying by boat. Shevili embarks on this journey towards non-dual mystical consciousness through his Hebrew poetry. It is this beloved traveler who reveals through homosexuality how the nature of Jewish mysticism can never be the same, for it never was quite as it had been imagined.

*

אֲנִי הַנּוֹסֵעַ הַמְאֹהָב
וְהַמִּתְקַדֵּם אֵין
לִי צֹרֶךְ בִּשְׁלָשׁלָאוֹת
מַשָּׂאִי בְּשָׂרִי הַדָּל
וְהָעֲצָמוֹת כִּי אֲנִי הָאֱמָת
שֶׁל כָּל הַהַתְחָלוֹת
לִי הַכֹּל רְאִי לְיָפִי שֶׁל
הָאֶחָד לְהַגִּיעַ לַזֶּרַע
שֶׁל הַטִּפָּה בְּיַמּוֹ חָפַצְתִּי
אֲנִי הַנּוֹסֵעַ הַמְאֹהָב
וְהַמִּתְקַדֵּם גַּרְעִין אֲנִי בַּחַמָּה
הַבּוֹעֶרֶת בְּיָפִי רְקוּדָה
אֶל תּוֹךְ הָרֶחָם שֶׁל
הָאֶחָד[36]

---

35. For recent reflections on LGBT spirituality in the American Jewish world (and in the Israeli Jewish world), see Glazer, *"Durée, devekuth, & re-embracing the godlover,"* 542n107.

36. Benjamin Shevili, *Poems of the Grand Tourist* [Hebrew] (Tel Aviv: Schocken Books, 1999), 61.

I am the beloved traveler
    and advancing no
need for chains
    my journey my meager flesh
and my bones for I the truth
    of all beginnings
to me all is a mirror to the beauty of
    the One to reach the flow
of the drop in its ocean is all I desired
    I am the beloved traveler
and advancing I am a solar nucleus
    that is burning in her dance's beauty
into the womb of
    the One.

This journey toward unification "into the womb of/the One"—toward the ensouled body—arouses the apparently residual dualism. Just as there is a distancing and tearing away of each strophe, so too the body gets away from the soul. A more robust sexuality is missing here as there are no letters available to map out any union with god or lover. This leg of the journey allows for a rediscovery of embodied desire necessary for the non-dual mystical apperception through the soul:

הוֹמוֹסָקְסִי

הַגּוּף שֶׁלִּי רוֹצֶה

לִזְלֹל וְלִסְבֹּא

אַחַר כָּךְ הוּא רוֹצֶה לִישֹׁון

גּוּף שֶׁלִּי רוֹצֶה

לְכְלוֹן וְזֶהֲמָה

אַחַר כָּךְ הוּא רוֹצֶה לְעַנּוֹת אֶת הַנְּשָׁמָה

אֲנִי אוֹמֵר לוֹ

גּוּף סוֹפְךָ לָמוּת

אֲנִי אוֹמֵר לוֹ

גּוּף אַתָּה בַּקֶּבֶר תֵּרָקֵב

אֲבָל הַגּוּף

עוֹנֶה לִי

בְּכָל זֹאת

אֲנִי רוֹצֶה [37]

---

[37]. Shevili, *Poems of the Grand Tourist*, 69.

Homosexy

My body desires
>> crawling and suffering
>>> afterwards it desires sleep
>> My body desires
> filth and sludge
afterwards it desires answering the soul

I tell it
> body your end is to die
>> I tell it
>>> body you shall rot in a grave
But my body
> answers me
>> you'll rot in the grave
>>> even so
>>>> I desire

It is no coincidence that opening the fourth section of the poetry cycle, *Poems of the Grand Tourist* is this series entitled, "HomosexuEL." The form of this poem reflects the oceanic oscillation. Following this beloved traveler, the reader enters into the undulating ocean of love, so nearing the poem's end this traveler has shifted position. The movement is inclined towards *devekut* with the One—an embodied non-dual consciousness. The opening journey of the beloved within this series is a search for the divine visage of *EL* hovering within the mysterious collocation of homosexu*EL*ity. Shevili deploys such poetics frequently in this series, beginning the journey with the subtlest of vowel collocations. To the casual reader, homosexuEL is basically the same as homosexual, but to the attuned reader, homosexu*EL* [הומוסקס וְאֵל] is not at all homosexu*AL* [הומוסקסוֹאָל]. This concealed revelation rests in the difference of one vowel ([אֶ] as opposed to [אָ]) shifting the meaning profoundly. While the form of the word undergoes a most minute shift, its content undergoes a radical one. This is the search for God as the primordial and universal facet of the pre-Israelite pantheon known as *El* [אֵל] that invites the traveler to continue wandering through identity into unchartered territory of homo-erotic imaginalities and homosexual relations:

בְּגֶשֶׁם הָרַב הַיּוֹרֵד עַכְשָׁו הוֹ יְדִידִי הַמְאֹהָב
עַל מִטָּתִי אֶשְׁכַּב אֶשְׁאַל עַל אֱלֹהַי וַאלֹהָיו
הַמַּסְתִּיר פָּנָיו אֶכְאַב אֶדְאַב אֶת שְׂמִיכָתִי אֶסְחַב
וּבְמִטָּתִי בְּדִמְיוֹנִי עַל אֱלֹהַי אֶשְׁכַּב[38]

O beloved friend in the great rain that now falls
I'll lay upon my bed I'll seek his god and mine
that hides his face I'll suffer I'll undergo I'll drag my blanket
I'll lay in my bed in my imagining my god

The journey begins in separation. Each lover's god is alone, separate as these lovers reunite. Their conjoining allows each one to discover the spirit of their ensouled bodies even while their spiritual connections remain as "my god and his god" [אֱלֹהַי וַאלֹהָיו]. But as the journey into union unfolds, any final separation between gods and lovers must dissolve. It is in bed that the lover interrogates after his own god as well as seeking his lover's god. No dualism between the lovers can remain—especially in the divine pantheon—that would separate one from the other in this quest for intimate reunion. One god appears hidden while the other is revealed. If the beloved's god is revealed while his lover's god is concealed, then an oscillation is experienced in such a union—ecstasy in the sight of the other's god. Such an encounter melds one ensouled body into the other. This collocates lovers and gods, in body and in word.

A most brilliant example of this collocative homosexuality is found in the following poem that continues the journey of this cycle:

סַע לְאָן שֶׁתִּסַּע אֱלֹהֲבִי
אַחֲרֶיךָ אֶרְדֹּף
כְּמוֹ כּוֹכָב נוֹדֵד בְּבִטְנְךָ
סַע לְאָן שֶׁתִּסַּע אֱלֹהֲבִי
אֲנִי בְּךָ וְאַתָּה בִּי[39]

Journey to where you shall journey mygodlover
I'll chase after you
as a lone star in your belly

---

38. Shevili, *Poems of the Grand Tourist*, 47.
39. Ibid., 51.

Journey to where you shall journey mygodlover
I'm within you and you're within me

This poem conveys the depth of the journey for the ensouled body. The lover continually seeks reunion with the beloved. But the nature of the reunion is already collocative. Here two separate and distinct words "my god" [אֱלֹהַי] and "my lover" [אֲהָבִי] melt away their differences, merging into a new word, "mygodlover" [אֱלֹהֲבִי]. This act of collocation merges the divine and human experience of language into a strong non-dual mystical apperception.

As a mode of revelation and liberation, these collocations continue in another poem from this cycle. Here a liberated "homosexbird" is revealed by Shevili's collocating the word "homosexual" [הוֹמוֹסֶק] with "bird" [צִפּוֹר]. By collocating this transmigrating symbol of the soul through the migratory pattern of birds, an even deeper evocation of the flight into erotic freedom becomes possible.[40]

הוֹמוֹסֶקְצְפּוֹר

לְאָן אֲנִי שַׁיָּךְ הַאִם אֲנִי תַּיָּר אוֹ שֶׁאֲנִי שָׁבוּי תְּנוּ
לִי לָשׁוּב אֶל הָרֵאשִׁית וּלְהַסְבִּיר אֶת הָעַצְבוּת
שֶׁמְּצִיאוּת הִיא הַתְּפִילָה שֶׁל צַיָּדִים שֶׁנִּכְנְסָה אֶל הַשָּׂדֶה
פִּתּוּי וּמַלְכּוֹדוֹת וְדַחְלִילִים הִסְתִּירוּ אֶת עַצְמָם
בַּעֲרֵמוֹת שֶׁל שִׂמְחָתִי
אֲנִי הָיִיתִי פַּעַם לַהֲקָה שֶׁל צִפּוֹרִים הַצַּיָּדִים רָאוּ
אוֹתִי וְהֵם קָרְאוּ
לִי
בְּקוֹלוֹת כָּל כָּךְ מוֹשְׁכִים שֶׁבָּאתִי אֲלֵיהֶם וְאָז
רָאִיתִי אֶת עַצְמִי
בְּלוּלָאוֹת
עַל צַוָּארִי לְזוּז נִסִּיתִי אַךְ כְּכָל שֶׁנֶּאֱבַקְתִּי
נִתְהַדְּקוּ הַחֲבָלִים
וְלָחֲצוּ
אוֹתִי
הֵכַנְתִּי אֶת עַצְמִי לָמוּת טָבַעְתִּי בְּיִסּוּרִים

---

40. Compare with Magid, "Leviticus: The Sin of Becoming a Woman," in light of contemporary appropriations by Shevili of a Muslim homo-eroticism into his Hebrew poetry that normalizes homosexual desire.

שָׁכְחַתִּי מָה הָיִיתִי לְפָנִים
אֲנִי הָיִיתִי פַּעַם לַהֲקָה שֶׁל צִפּוֹרִים[41].

Homosexbird

To where am I bound, am I a tourist or hostage let
me return to the beginning and explain my sorrow
that reality is the prayer of hunters who have entered
        into the field bait and traps and scarecrows hid themselves
        in the heaps of my happiness
    I was once a flock of birds, the hunters saw
me and cried out to
    me
with such seductive voices that I came out to them
    and then I saw myself
    in the loops
around my neck I tried to move even as I was strangled
    the ropes tightened
    and they beat
    me
I prepared myself to die, I drowned in afflictions
    I've forgotten what I was before
        I was once a flock of birds.

Like many of the Golden Age courtier poets—whether Sufi Jewish or Muslim—contemplation of the male wine servant at shared symposiums was common practice. Here the birds are the object of contemplation and transformation. Are the male birds in spiritual conversation with female birds or with other effeminate male birds? Likely the latter, as contemplation and conversation were again the case with wine servants described as effeminate.

The poet envisions himself returning to his origin, flying within a school of birds. Much of his poetics plays with the migratory notion of birds as the symbol of desirous soul. Considering the self-professed Sufi and Sabbetean influence of Shevili, these collocative exercises chart a new path back into Jewish mystical praxis within Hebrew poetry. In the course of flying through ancient

---

41.   Shevili, *Poems of the Grand Tourist*, 68.

memories, the poet recalls his true freedom embodied so splendidly in the symbol of the bird. The transmigration of souls, so often symbolically associated with the bird,[42] suits the poet upon this journey from affliction to love.

It is the erotic experience encountered by being bound to a flock or a group—often referred to as *dibbuk haverim* or a mystical camaraderie[43]—that arouses the poet into non-dual mystical apperception. What binds each bird together is their desire to fly and be free. Their flight is stronger when it takes place together, especially with the dissolution of an individual's identity. This unification of the group evokes a larger organism at work whereby the macrocosm is revitalized by the microcosm. Such a shifting between worlds and perspectives is once again embodied by the two separate and distinct words "homosexual" [הוֹמוֹסָקצָאָל] and "bird" [צִפּוֹר] as they each merge through collocation into "homosexbird" [הוֹמוֹסָקצִפּוֹר]. This collocation is a mystical marker for the soul's journey, as it returns from its exile into the secret circle of self:

שִׁירֵי גָּלוּת אִדְרָא

אַתְּ צִפּוֹר הָעוֹמָדָת עַל גָּדֵר תַּיִל
בֵּין אֶרֶץ מַיִם וְשָׁמַיִם
אֲנִי אָבוּד יוֹתֵר מִמֵּךְ

טוּרֵי הַמַּיִם שֶׁבַּיָּם זוֹרְמִים
אֶל מוֹלַדְתִּי
בָּאִים לְבַשֵּׂר לָךְ אֲהוּבָתִי
אֶת
גָּלוּתִי

חוֹמוֹת הַשִּׂמְחָה
מַקִּיפוֹת אוֹתִי בְּאִדְרָא
שֶׁל
עַצְבוּת

מֵחַלּוֹן חַדְרִי רַק חֶלְקַת יָם קְטָנָה

---

42. Especially in Sufi poetry, for example, see the twelfth century *locus classicus*, Farid al-Din Attar, *The Conference of the Birds*, trans. A. Darbandi and D. Davis (New York: Penguin Classics, 1984).

43. On *dibbuk haverim* in Galilean spirituality of 18th-century Israel, see Aubrey, L. Glazer, ed. tr. *Three Lost Tiberian Masters in Search of the Alchemy of Love* (Louisville: Fons Vitae, *forthcoming*)

נוֹשֶׁבֶת בֵּין עַרְבַּיִם בְּצִלְלֵי
שֶׁמֶשׁ אֲדֻמִּים
וּמִלִּבִּי נִשְׁקֶפֶת הוֹי חֶמְדַּת יָמִים
אַתְּ יְרוּשָׁלַיִם.[44]

Exile poems of the secret circle

You are a bird perched on barbed-wire fence
between earth water and heavens
I am more lost than you

Pillars of water in the sea flow
towards my nativity
they bring you news of my love
of
my exile

Walls of happiness
encircle me in the secret circle
of
sadness

Only a fragment of sea from my room's window
blowing at eventide through shadowed
crimson sun
O delight of days revealing from my heart
you are Jerusalem

Perched between heaven and earth as a bird, the soul knows the journey before it. Flying with the school again symbolizes the unified group or *dibbuk haverim*, but here the formation itself is a mystery. Such a mysterious path for the mystic happens in the formation of the secret circle or *'idra*. It is only within this sacred formation, that the poet is aroused from the sadness of singularity by circumcising the heart—that is, the navel of the spiritual universe, Jerusalem.[45]

Moving from the fragmentary vision of the window to the heart of Jerusalem, the poet soars from depression to ecstasy, merging in flight

---

44. Shevili, "Exile poems of the secret circle," unpublished.
45. Compare with Morgenstern's spiritualization of Jerusalem in chapter 1, esp. n.139.

heaven and earth. This journey into the primordial sea, undergirding the very Foundation Stone of Jerusalem, leads to a dissolution of self into the "pillars of water in the sea flow/into my nativity." Such a flight from the confines of a uni-dimensional perspective gives the imagination its needed freedom to soar.

In this next flight, the poem is still guided by the bird, however this time traversing from *eros* to *thanatos*, from love into the realm of death:

הוֹמוֹסָקְסוּמֶת

כָּךְ כִּמְעַט בְּסוֹף הַסּוֹף לְיַד הַחוֹף כְּשֶׁהַשְּׁחָפִים
בִּמְעוּפָם דּוֹאִים
טוֹבֵעַ בְּעַצְבוּת הִבַּטְתִּי מֵחַלּוֹן חַדְרִי וּרְאִיתִים
פּוֹשְׁטִים יָדַיִם הָאֶחָד אֶל הַשֵּׁנִי
נָחֲתוּ לָהֶם שְׁנֵי צִפּוֹרִים זָכָר וּנְקֵבָה הַזָּכָר
שָׁקֵט עָמַד עַל הֶעָפָר וְהַנְּקֵבָה
קָפְצָה וְצִפְצְפָה וּבִשְׂפַת הַצִּפּוֹרִים שָׁמַעְתִּי
הַצִּפּוֹר אוֹמֵר לַצִּפּוֹרָה כַּמָּה מִלִּים עַל מָוֶת

"וּפוֹלוּס לֹא קָם הוּא רַק נָשַׁף בְּקֹצֶר נְשִׁימָה לְיָדוֹ
עָמַד תִּימוֹטְיוּס מַנִּיחַ עַל מֵצַח פּוֹלוּס שְׁתֵּי יָדָיו
עָמַד שָׁם בֵּין כֻּלָּם גַּם טִיטוּס וְנִזְכַּר אֵיךְ
בְּאִגֶּרֶת שֶׁשָּׁלַח אֵלָיו צִוָּה
לִכְרֵיתִי לַךְ אֶל אִי הָעַקְשָׁנִים חוֹשֵׁב לוֹ טִיטוּס אָכֵן
לֹא כָּל דָּבָר יָדַעְתִּי הַמּוֹרֶה עַל כֵּן אָנוּ מֵתִים
וּפָלִימוֹן מָלֵא הַבָּשָׂר וְהַפָּנִים הַדְּשֵׁנוֹת מִתְפַּלֵּל
לוֹ כָּל אוֹתָהּ שָׁעָה שֶׁפּוֹלוּס
גָּסַס לוֹ יְהִי לוֹ לַצַּדִּיק הַזֶּה שֶׁכָּל חַיָּיו
נִטְרַד בַּהֲפָצַת דְּבָרָיו שֶׁל הַנִּרְדָּם
לוּ יְהִי לוֹ בֵּית מָלוֹן זְמַנִּי לַנִּרְדָּמִים
וְכָךְ עִם עֶרֶב רַד נְשָׂאַרְנוּ עֵירֻמִּים לְעוֹלָמוֹ
הָלַךְ לוֹ הַמּוֹרֶה כַּאֲדוֹנוֹ
עַכְשָׁו הוּא מְצַיֵּץ וְשָׁר חָפְשִׁי שִׁירָה
לְלֹא מִקְצָב לְלֹא כְּלָלִים לֹא
מְגֻיֶּסֶת בְּלִי שִׁרְיוֹן וּבְלִי מַדִּים".

עָף לוֹ הַצִּפּוֹר לְקָאן וְאַחֲרָיו הַצִּפּוֹרָה

בְּקַפְּסָלִי לְיַד חוֹרָה עִיר בֵּירָה שֶׁל קִיתָרָה
הִקְשַׁבְתִּי לַסִּפּוּר שֶׁל הַצִּפּוֹר לַצִּפּוֹרָה[46]

---

46. Shevili, *Poems of the Grand Tourist*, 66.

Homosexudeath

So it was, almost at the end's end, along the coast with
the seagulls soaring in their flight
Sinking in depression I glanced out of my window &
I saw them extending hands one to the other
Two birds, male and female, descended to them,
The quiet male stood upon the earth, & the female
Hopped and chirped in bird language,
I heard a few words about death

"And Paul did not arise, he only exhaled a short breath,
at his side, Timothy laid his hands on Paul's brow
There in their midst Titus stood and recalled how
in the epistle he sent instructing him to
walk to Crete where there were no stiff-necks, thinks
Titus, since I did not know that everything teaches
why we die, & Philaimon full of flesh, with his grassy
face praying all the while as Paul
gasped if only he would be his saint all his life
preoccupied with disseminating this sleeper's words
if only he had a temporary hotel for sleepers
& so with eventide falling we remained naked, off he
went to his world, the teacher as his master

now he chirps & freely sings a song
without rhythm without rules
conscripted neither by armor nor garbs."

The bird flew to him at Kaff & after him the female bird
in my capsule beside Hora, the capital of Kiterah
I listened to the story of the bird told to the female bird

Although the scriptural allusions here are by and large Greek rather than
Hebrew, Shevili dares, much like his mystical poetic precursor, Pinhas
Sadeh, to deploy the poem as a gesture of re-scripturalizing. That process
is a search for authentic, albeit forgotten, Jewish mystical experiences
and return them to their origin in Hebrew poetry. By contextualizing a
communal *unio mystica*, albeit within this New Testament setting, Shevili,
the poet is open to listening with newly attuned ears of the heart.

This recovery of a lost non-dual mystical apperception—torn asunder by the birth of Christianity in relationship to Judaism—takes place once again through collocation. Here what began its earlier flight into the collocation of two distinct words above of "homosexual" [הוֹמוֹסָקְצָאֵל] and "bird" [צִפּוּר] that merged into the union of the "homosexubird" [הוֹמוֹ סָקְצפּוּר] now shifts its migratory pattern, finding its rest and reincarnation through death [הוֹמוֹסָקְסוּמֶת]. Already lucid in some of Bialik's bird poems,[47] the *eros* soaring so free is shadowed by *thanatos*—that impending death on the underside of every flight to freedom.

But why does the poet bring a biblically prohibited bird, like the seagull,[48] as his guide for the flight into freedom? This flight through the impure to recover the pure goes beyond reclaiming forgotten Christianity. It extends all the way into the non-dual depths of a Sabbetean journey.[49] Such a migratory pattern, nearing death, parallels a hypernomian[50] movement through the law. Only by way of dissolving this deadly dualism of Judaism/Christianity, permitted/forbidden can redemption take place.

Devekut *as the* Durée *of the Godlover: Disentangling Intuitive Time*

The iconoclastic path of the godlover, traversed so boldly in Binyamin Shevili's poetry cycle, "homosexuELity," reveals the depth of desire and the degree to which individuality can abandon itself to the rapture of immersion in the divine stream. This journey into non-dual consciousness challenges the accretion of dualisms that pervade many facets of Hebrew cultures in Israel.[51] Not bound by the conventions of Tel Aviv or Jerusalem, this Hebrew poet continues in search of the Isra*EL* in the offing. Rather than succumb

---

47. For example, see Bialik's bird poems ('*El haTzippor, Tavas Zehavi Perah Lo, Hachnisani Tahat Kenafeikh, Shirah Yetomah, Bein Nahar Perat uNahar Hidekel*) and compare with Pinhas Sadeh's reading of these transformational bird poems, see Pinhas Sadeh, *Tavas Zehavi: Mivhar Shirai Bialik* (Tel Aviv: Dvir-Schocken, 1985), 175-185.

48. The seagull figures as part of a list of biblically impure birds, see Leviticus 11:16.

49. For the Sabbetean cycle that figures prominently within the poet's *œuvre*, see Shevili, "A Boy Flies a Kite in the Seventeenth Century," [Hebrew] *Poems of the Grand Tourist*, 89-104.

50. On hypernomianism and its relation to non-dual mystical apperception, see above the delimitations of Morgenstern and Wolfson, chapter 1, esp. n.154.

51. See chapter 1.

to depression over the current dualism of the status quo of religious/secular existence so stultified in Israel because of its disconnection from that journey, the poet presses on. The journey to recover Israel as Isra*EL* is a struggle that must overcome the darkness and depression from constricted consciousness while inclining toward the integral wholeness of expanded consciousness. That journey of return into non-dual mystical apperception is a consciousness attuned to universal time nestled within the womb of intuitive time.

As the possibility of returning human consciousness into its original non-dual reunion within the divine stream once again becomes imaginable, the constellation of another authentic Jewish mystical experience is revealed. This necessary *involution* of time for *unio mystica* is revealed by way of this poetic journey of homosexuELity. *In*volution of non-dual consciousness is a poetic process of self-finding.[52] This unfolding of evolutionary relations leaves its mark upon the imaginal and *vice versa* as part of that rediscovery. This is a rediscovery that takes time—a subtle *durée* to bridge between the True and the Real. The *durée* of the godlover's grasp is sensed—touching God—in *devekut*. Yet only the true godlovers—the mystical poet and the poetical mystic—are daring enough to take leave upon this journey to rediscover that lost unity, to once again touch God in mystical vertigo. That unity is entangled within time—the True within the Real, intuitive time within universal time, "not this time" already "within this time"—all returning in this moment as One.

---

52. Sri Aurobindo, *The Human Cycle, Ideal of Human Unity, War and Self Determination* (Pondicherry: Lotus Press, 1970), 158.

CHAPTER IX

PARABLES AND PRAYERS OF LOVE AND RAPE:

DEVEKUT AS DEPTH AND FLOW OF SELF IN TAMAR ELAD-APPELBAUM'S "PSALMS FOR JERUSALEM"

Is there any difference between mystical apperception experienced by the individual as opposed to that experience within a communal structure? Is there any difference between the mystical textures that come to light in living out the distinctive materiality of bodies versus those engendered through social conventions? This very difference between experience and social structure correlates to the difference between "female" sex and "feminine" gender.

Accordingly, there is a shift amongst some contemporary feminists, like Battersby, to re-imagine "thinking female selves in terms of patterns emerging out of flow and movement" without "giving up a 'depth' model of self..."[1] The specificity of the female subject-position cannot be essentialized—it is neither solely biologically determined as "female" sex, nor the result of cultural construction as "feminine" gender. Rather, it is through what Battersby envisions as the self that is continually established through responses, repetitions and habitual movements—namely, different temporalities of experience over time.[2] It is through the fluidity of self-revelation that depth and flow of self merge in *devekut*. While such repositioning of the female subject, by and large, is a product of American feminism, there are many echoes emanating from Israel acknowledging the unique texture of women's dialogue.[3] This next chapter will explore how the Hebrew poet, Tamar Elad-Appelbaum, redresses these differences through her poetry.

---

[1]   Christine Battersby, *The Phenomenal Woman: Feminist Metaphysics and the Patterns of Identity* (New York: Routledge, 1998), 197.

[2]   Battersby, *The Phenomenal Woman*, 197, 207.

[3]   For example, see Galia Golan, "Reflections On Gender In Dialogue," *Nashim: A Journal of Jewish Women's Studies & Gender Issues* 6 (2003): 13-21.

Just as with the renaissance of Hebrew culture concomitant the rebirth of the State of Israel and its language through female poets,[4] cultural questions were already coming to the forefront of Zionism in 1982. At that point Israel Harel established *Nekuda*, the organ of *YESH"A* (the acronym for both the settlements of Judea, Samaria and Gaza, while also being the Hebrew word for redemption). Amidst the cultural questions, there emerged a group of writers, poets and critics including: Hava Pinhas-Cohen; Bambi Sheleg; Shmuel Lehrman; Mira Kedar; Yonadav Kaploun and Zippora Luria. They each wrote with an enthusiasm and curiosity for something new being born again in the Zionist atmosphere. The shift was from an ideological connection to the land of Israel moving towards a more individual experiential level. A new wave of poetry first crystallized from those interactions and experiences. As Hava Pinhas-Cohen founded the multidisciplinary journal, *Dimui*, a home was established for the post-Yom Kippur War artists and poets.

The shift taking place was from Zionism back to Judaism, as the blossoming of poetry began as an attempt by religious society to integrate into Israeli culture. Amidst these voices, another ebb is flowing within the next wave of Zionist poetry in Israel. These young voices are currently coming from a poetry project called, *Return the Spirit* [*Mashiv haRuah*]. The journal began through the gatherings of these self-proclaimed spiritualist poets from all backgrounds and affiliations, whether secular [*ḥiloni*] or national-religious [*da'ati le'umi*]. They would meet periodically to write around topical themes of the spirit and challenges of the soul. For example, a recent four-month project was dedicated to the writing and creating of new hymns and psalms. After their quarter year incubation, the poets returned to their poetic community of *Mashiv haRuah* to share their discoveries.

This spirit of a community of poets fostered by this journal, *Mashiv haRuah,* was established in 1994 by a rotating editorial board that originated with Shmuel Klein, Yoram Nissinovitch, Nahum Petchnik and Eliaz Cohen. From within this communal structure of new spiritualist poets most recently there has arisen a Jerusalemite poet of great spiritual depth and vision named Tamar

---

4. See Glazer, *What Are Hebrew Female Poets For? Engendering Authenticity From Silence to Scream in Hebrew Poetry,"* Review of Miryam Segal's *A New Sound in Hebrew Poetry: Poetics, Politics, Accent* (Indiana University Press, Bloomington 2010, 206 pps), *Nashim: A Journal of Jewish Women's Studies & Gender Issues (forthcoming).*

Elad-Appelbaum. Born to a modern-Orthodox Zionist family, growing up in Jerusalem with exposure to the arts and studying Jewish philosophy at Hebrew University has influenced Tamar's path to spiritual awakening, culminating in her ordination as a *Masorti* rabbi in 2005. Forever a poet, even as rabbi, Tamar prefers linguistically to engender this title in the feminine as *raba*. While her work has focused on training community professionals, much of her focus deals with spreading Jewish literacy—especially poetry and *piyyut* in all aspects of Jewish life. Her return to the Schecter Rabbinical Seminary as Associate Dean was a watershed moment that ended with a deluge surrounding her recent resignation. As visionary leader and teacher, Tamar continues to serve as co-editor of the poetry journal, *Mashiv haRuah*, as well as writing her own poetry, all the while living in Jerusalem with her husband Yossi and their three daughters. Her poetry reflects a contemporary spiritual quest to rediscover the hidden layers of Zion, currently concealed in the hegemonic religious culture of Israel, through a language imbued with Jewish sources, at once traditional and innovative. This chapter will explore the poetic power of her parables and prayers of love and rape through her *devekut* in Jerusalem.

—

מָשָׁל לְמָה אֲנִי דוֹמָה

לְמַלְכָּה שֶׁהָיוּ לָהּ מִלִּים הַרְבֵּה

וְהִנִּיחָה אוֹתָן מִבַּיִת לַחֶדָר הַחִיצוֹן.

אוֹתָן מִלִּים הָיָה לָהֶן הֵיכָל מִשֶּׁלָּהֶן

וְהָיוּ יוֹצְאוֹת מִתּוֹךְ עַצְמָן וּבָאוֹת בּוֹ

וּמַנִּיחוֹת רְטִיּוֹת שֶׁל סוֹד עַל פִּיהֶן.

וְהָיְתָה הַמַּלְכָּה יוֹדַעַת אֶת הַמִּלִּים

וְלֹא הָיְתָה יוֹדַעַת מְקוֹם הַהֵיכָל כְּלָל.[5]

*

A parable to what shall I be likened
To a queen who had many words
And who took them from the house and left them in the outer room.
Those same words had their own palace
And they would go out from themselves and come into it
And they would put patches of secrecy on their mouths.

---

5. Tamar Elad-Appelbaum, *Mashiv haRuah* 24 (Fall 2007): 9.

And the queen knew the words
But she did not know where the palace was at all.

Playful, the poet here is describing her craft. While poetry tends to reveal its mystery, the poem at hand conceals by wrapping the experience in a parable. Here the poet poses her first challenge to dualism. This parable plays with conventions of female/feminine dualism which represent the very boundaries between experience and social structure. The creative force here is a sovereign power that is a feminine (queen) rather than conventional masculine (king) sovereignty. This power is the divine fiat that creates reality through language. Yet it is precisely the power housed in these words that escapes the poet. She may yearn to reveal their secret inner potency but these words remain sealed. Moreover, words are animated with an almost independent power, regenerating through a life of their own.

The shift from house [בַּיִת] to outer room or courtyard [חֶדֶר הַחִיצוֹן] to the palace [הֵיכָל] marks a journey. This is a journey that the words embark upon independent of the poet. Here, the poet poses her second challenge to dualism. By revealing her struggle as a creative force in creating the poem, she is confronting the abyss that can often separate language from experience. As she yearns to realize non-dual mystical apperception, the poet already sees before her the need to journey beyond the walls of her nativity symbolized by the house. Yet in embarking upon this journey beyond the confines of the *same* toward the *other*, she encounters limitations. How can she bridge the abyss separating the ascent of pristine words amidst the descent of human experience? The task of the poet is to overcome this dualism, but through the parable she admits to the struggle ahead.

That sense of struggle is amplified a thousand-fold in the next poem, as it confronts the symbol of radical evil:

—

זְכֹרִי אֶת אֲשֶׁר עָשָׂה לָךְ עֲמָלֵק.

מְקֹרָה.
קָרִי.
קֹר.
רָקָב.

וְאַתְּ
עֲיֵפָה, יְגֵעָה וְצוֹעֶקֶת
וְכָל כָּךְ יְרֵאָה
אֱלֹהִים
יַלְדַּת אַהֲבָה הָפַכְתְּ בֶּן-חֹשֶׁךְ לְאִשָּׁה חִוֶּרֶת
קוֹלוֹ וּנְשִׁימוֹתָיו הוֹרְגִים עָלַיִךְ כָּל הַיּוֹם.

אָחוֹת, נָשִׁים עוֹלוֹת אֵלַיִךְ מִמִּדְבָּר
וְהֵן עֵדוֹת.
תּוֹמְכוֹת הֵן בְּיָדַיִךְ
תַּמְרוּרִים.
קוֹלֵךְ עוֹשֶׂה בַּמִּלְחָמָה.

שָׁנִים אַחֲרֵי מְסוֹף עוֹלָם וְעַד סוֹפוֹ
נִשְׁמַעַת בִּשְׂדוֹתַינוּ צְעָקָה
(שֶׁלֹּא יֹאמְרוּ שֶׁלֹּא צָעַקְתְּ שֶׁלֹּא צָעַקְנוּ)
זִכְרִי לְמַעֲנֵךְ.
זִכְרִי לְמַעֲנֵנוּ.
וּלְמַעַן בְּנוֹתַיִךְ שֶׁבְּדַרְכָּן אֶל כָּאן
חַמָּנִיּוֹת שֶׁל יַלְדוּתֵךְ
צוֹעֲקוֹת בְּכֹחַ:
עֲמָלֵק[6]

*

Remember what *Amalek* did to you.

Accident.
Seed-spill.
Bone-chill.
Rot.

& you
Tired, toiling & screaming
& so in awe
Elohim
Love child, you turned a son of darkness into a pale woman
His voice and soul killing you all day.

———————

6. Tamar Elad-Appelbaum, *Mashiv haRuah* 24 (Fall 2007): 11.

Sister, women ascending to you in the desert
& they are witnesses.
in your hand they support
sorrow.
Your voice makes in war.

Years after from one end of the world to the other
A scream is heard in our fields
(so they won't say you didn't scream, that we didn't scream)
Remember for your sake.
Remember for our sake.
& for the sake of your daughters on their way here
Sun-pillars of your childhood
Screaming strongly:
Amalek

From the outset of this daring poem that confronts the travesties committed in the name of radical evil—*Amalek*—the poet does not shy away from her connection to this pain. Her pain is unique. That is why the poem cries out to all females—even like this poet—with the feminine imperative, in contrast to the scriptural injunction addressed exclusively in male imperative language to "Never forget what *Amalek* did to you."[7] This injunction to utterly erase the memory of *Amalek* has a long and tortured history without redemption.

It begins with betrayal and ends with betrayal. Timna seeks a suitor with the tribe of Jacob, according to the scriptural account, but is refused. This rejection takes her to the warring tribe, where she marries Eliphaz, son of Esau. This is a union catalyzed by betrayal thus leading to the birth of *Amalek*.[8] The betrayal grows from the individual experience to the collective, so that eventually the tribe of *Amalek* attacks the entire tribe of Israel. But they attack from behind, killing only women, children and the infirmed.[9] So then the injunction to "utterly erase *Amalek* from under the heavens"[10] has a more spiritually compelling context which might rectify such disturbing behavior. Even many generations after the

---

7. Deuteronomy 25:17
8. Genesis 36:12-16.
9. Exodus 17:8-13.
10. Exodus 17:14, Deuteronomy 25:19.

trauma of this betrayal, the scars remain unhealed.[11] Yet memory of this pain remains more distant than the experience itself.

The female voice of the poem is foreboding, lest there be a lapse in the vigilance of memory. To remember precisely the suffering that was experienced, a sign is needed: "Years after from one end of the world to the other/A scream is heard in our fields/(so they won't say you didn't scream, that we didn't scream)." Her poem is that clarion call to remind, not once but twice, the individual female and its feminine collective to remember. It is by screaming the very name of evil itself, *Amalek*—rather than erasing it— that the memory can be embodied anew in the present. Amidst the trauma, her call to conscience is a yearning for non-dual mystical apperception.

Seeing how such trauma invades intimacy by destroying boundaries, the poet seeks restitution. But such restitution—whether by the scriptural erasure of the memory in general, or its rabbinic interpretation as a drowning out the name *Haman* while reading the Scroll of Esther, or for every scribe beginning the day's writing by erasing the written name of *Amalek*—can only provide so much solace for the feminine. Such dualistic expressions of restitution appear to hinder more than to heal. The pain of the past is redeemed only when it is allowed to re-enter the realm of experience through the embodied scream. In this scream, the dualism— individual/collective, body/soul, female/feminine—is broken down. What emerges through this sonorous community is both a restorative and redemptive non-dual consciousness.

But how far reaching is such redemption? Can evil be redeemed to once again bring forth the good? Can darkness be redeemed to once again bring light? This kind of interrogation underlies the next poem:

—

בַּלֵּילוֹת רַבָּה אֱמוּנָתֶךָ

גּוּף שׁוֹמֵט לְאַט מֵאֲחִיזַת הַיּוֹם, נֶפֶשׁ
פּוֹעֶרֶת אֶת פִּיהָ לַחֲלוֹת פְּנֵי מַלְכוּת.

---

11. For the residual presence of Amalek during the time of King Saul and David, see I Samuel 15: 2-15; for the residual presence of Amalek during the time of Queen Esther and Mordecai, see Esther 17:16.

כָּל הַצְּלָלִים נָסִים
מִפְּנֵי דּוֹדִים בָּאִים אָל אֲהוּבוֹתֵיהֶם
נָעִים בַּחֲשֵׁכוֹת וּמְבָרְכִים הַרְבֵּה

הַנֵּה אֱמוּנָתָךְ.[12]

At nights your faith is greater

Body loosens, falling from the day's hold, the soul
its mouth gaping to implore the face of sovereignty.
All the shades fleeting
As lovers unite with their beloveds
moving pleasantly in the darkness, blessing much

Here is your faith.

In a world where general cataclysms—natural or supernatural—are known by name (Auschwitz, Hiroshima, and others), every waking moment feels inundated with suffering. Yet this suffering is part and parcel of what it ultimately means to be human. To be embodied is to be vulnerable. But along with such vulnerability comes great fear. All of life's passions are as Greek philosopher-poet, Lucretius, already wrote centuries earlier, "...the wounds and plagues of life," and "are nourished for the most part by this dread of death."[13] In confronting the fear of that darkness encircling death's shady abode, the Hebrew poet and the Greek philosopher see eye to eye. However, each one responds differently to death's challenge.

To obliterate the afterlife in one fell-swoop, as was the ingenious way of Lucretius, is a strategy for living life more fully so that the dread of death might not hold sway over the human condition indefinitely. But the Hebrew poet embraces life by choosing to penetrate this darkness rather than obliterate it; she dares to look deeper into the love flowing between lovers. Can the poet overturn the inertia of darkness to light, of hopelessness to hopefulness?

12. Tamar Elad-Appelbaum, "At Nights Your Faith Is Greater," [Hebrew] *Mashiv haRuah* 24 (Fall 2007): 15.
13. Titus Lucretius Carus, Book III, *On The Nature of Things*, Bohn's Classical Library, trans. R. J. S. Watson (London: George Bells & Sons, 1893), Pitt Press Series, 102, 229.

The poet dares opening in the language of prayer, but cautiously in this prayerful poem. Drawing from a glorious tapestry that interweaves gratitude before a sovereign presence and the return of the soul into its embodied state, this morning liturgy already has its theology in place:

מוֹדֶה - מוֹדָה אֲנִי לְפָנֶיךָ
מֶלֶךְ חַי וְקַיָּם,
שֶׁהֶחֱזַרְתָּ בִּי נִשְׁמָתִי בְּחֶמְלָה,
רַבָּה אֱמוּנָתֶךָ

I am grateful before You
O Living King
That you returned my soul unto me
With lovingkindness
Great is Your faith.

But the poem at hand seeks to disrupt this theology by peeling back its layers. It begins by misreading a key verse from Lamentations, already sculpted into morning liturgy, "[They are new every morning]; Great is your faith."[14] When the poem opens, "At nights your faith is greater" it is challenging this verse's linkage of an expansive faith to its pathetic fallacy of expansive light that dawns with each new day. The poet seeks out a faith she can grasp, and reveals how such touching takes place, even and especially in the absence of light—a veritable mystical vertigo!

To make the liturgical declaration that "Great is Your faith" suggests that God as King has faith in His subjects to return worthy souls to worthy subjects. But these two words "great" [רַבָּה] and "faith" [אֱמוּנָתֶךָ] are more often separated by juxtaposition rather than bound together as a cluster. Consider for example the Psalmist's interweaving of parallelism with these words "great" [רַבָּה] and "faith" [אֱמוּנָתֶךָ]:

ו) יְהֹ-וָה בְּהַשָּׁמַיִם חַסְדֶּךָ **אֱמוּנָתְךָ** עַד שְׁחָקִים
ז) צִדְקָתְךָ כְּהַרְרֵי אֵל מִשְׁפָּטֶיךָ תְּהוֹם **רַבָּה** אָדָם וּבְהֵמָה תוֹשִׁיעַ יְהֹ-וָה[15]

---

14. Lamentations 3:23.
15. Psalm 36:6-7.

6 O YHVH, Your **faithfulness** reaches to heaven; Your steadfastness to the sky;
7 Your beneficence is like the high mountains; Your justice like the **great** abyss;
human and beast You deliver, O YHVH.

To map out the contours of the universe and how far divine power extends, the
Psalmist resorts to dualistic imagery of heavens/abyss coupled with the pathetic
fallacy of faith/judgment. While these values may be unified, their analogues
in nature describe boundaries. Why then must prayer overcome this dualism?

For the sake of connectivity. To remain connected to the divine amidst
darkness is what redefines the contours of the apparent dualism of light/
darkness. For that inner light to emanate, it needs contrast, so darkness
serves as a context for opening as the: "Body loosens, falling from the
day's hold, the soul/its mouth gaping to implore the face of sovereignty."
Embodiment serves to protect the soul through the course of the quotidian,
all the while the inner light glimmers within. But the contrast is muted,
so with the setting of the sun and the arrival of evening, the body can let
go of its protective role to let the soul once again emerge. In this moment
of emergence of the soul with "its mouth gaping to implore the face of
sovereignty," there is a reunion of sorts taking place. At that moment
when the soul beckons, calling out to its source, this is also the moment
when "...lovers unite with their beloveds/moving pleasantly in the darkness,
blessing much." Under the cover of darkness, love is made and so blessing
abounds. In the absence of light, in the moment of greatest concealment
when "All the shades fleeting" the poet can then reveal that hidden spark,
as she declares before her godlover—"Here is your faith."

In the course of a few lines, the poet accomplishes a deep exploration
of faith, framed by *inclusio*. The dualism of faith is challenged through
its inversion. Faith is not only found in light, but also even more deeply
discovered in darkness. Faith is not merely an act of surrender; it demands
a deeper sharing of love that is made in partnership between lovers and
beloveds. It is through such different temporalities of experience over time[16]
shared between lover and beloved, between darkness and light that mystical
apperception is realized. It is only by way of such fluidity of self-revelation
that the depth and flow of female and feminine self return to self in *devekut*.

---

16. Battersby, *The Phenomenal Woman,* 197, 207.

CHAPTER X

SCENT OF DARKNESS:
A SYNESTHETIC DISSOLUTION
INTO *DEVEKUT*
YONADAV KAPLOUN'S CYCLES "SCENT OF DARKNESS" & "A WINDOW OF OPPORTUNITY"

How do the fruits of the mystical experience return to the reality of lived experience, especially when that world is ruptured? Is rupture and its apparent dissonance an end in itself or is it a means to a deeper unitive experience? To what degree are the senses altered through mystical apperception? Much of the challenge remains how to concretely express, even by approximation, *through* language what ultimately remains *beyond it*. The search for ways of expressing these revelatory moments of mystical vertigo influence much of the noble paradox so common to art as well as religion. What brings the diverse disciplines of art and religion into closer alignment is a faculty they both share—the imagination. To better understand the inner workings of revelation—whether in art or religion—it pays to sharpen language in its relation to the imagination.

It is precisely in the dynamic movement between touching and ~~touching~~ God, that the modalities of experience within the process of mystical apperception are revealed. The intertwining of the senses that commonly occurs during moments of mystical vertigo within revelation is called synesthesia. In the poetry cycles of Yonadav Kaploun about to be examined, the intertwining of the senses through synesthesia happens through moments of deep yearning capitulated by rupture. A closer look at what Hebrew literary critic, Dan Miron, astutely calls the "metaphysical dissonance" in Kaploun's poetry will serve as a pathway into the intertwining of *self* and *other* within unitive mystical experiences insofar as it affects the senses. [1]

[1.]   Dan Miron, "Yonadav Kaploun's Poetry: The Psalmody of Metaphysical Dissonance," [Hebrew]

Indeed, it can confuse the senses that it is possible for a poet as prolific and profound as Yonadav Kaploun (b. 1963), writing Hebrew poetry for three decades in Israel, to remain relatively unknown. Currently Kaploun is found traversing the map of Israel, teaching seekers and educators diverse Hebrew wisdom, from the Bible, Kabbalah, and Hasidism, to modern poetry and creative writing. Renowned in Israel beyond his books of poetry, Kaploun regularly contributes essays and criticism for the Israeli daily newspapers and literary journals.[2] But the poet's journey to Israel in 1970 exemplifies many ruptures, beginning with his emigration from Melbourne, Australia to his spiritual homeland of Jerusalem, Israel. While shifting from one arid landscape to another often reveals some sharp edges for acclimatization, a uniting thread amidst such transplantation was his education. Kaploun's intensive schooling in HaBa"D-Lubavitch Hasidism, and his continued studies at the Mercaz haRav Kook Central Yeshiva left an indelible mark upon his unique poetic lexicon.

In the process of deepening his mystical sensibilities through the dual lens of HaBa"D and Kookian mysticism, Kaploun became immersed in National-Religious Zionism as embodied in *Gush Emunim* and *Gal Einai Institute*. The *Gush's* messianic quest for an ever-expanding post-1967 Greater Israel by Rabbi Avraham Yitzhak Kook's grandson, Tzvi Yehudah, found a greater resonance within mainstream Zionism, even garnering Israeli government-sponsored settlements. By contrast, *Gal Einai* figurehead Rabbi Yitzhak Ginsburgh, Rosh Yeshiva of *Od Yosef Hai* in the settlement of Yitzhar (before its disengagement in 2001), alleged messianic incitement and justification of Baruch Goldstein's massacre of twenty nine Palestinian Muslims during prayer at the Cave of the Patriarchs in Hebron, understandably found a lesser resonance within mainstream Zionism.[3] Such a messianic impulse—amidst its ruptures—is interwoven into the daily discourse and experience of Zionism in Israel.

Given his deep grounding in Jewish mysticism, it is no coincidence that Kaploun, a gifted student, was chosen to become an early editor of Ginsburgh's mystical writings published through *Gal Einai*. All the while this burgeoning poet also was living in Yamit—a settlement in the Rafah

---

Yonadav Kaploun: Collected Poems as of Now (Bialik Institute: Jerusalem 2011), 291-348.

2. http://israel.poetryinternationalweb.org
3. Rabbi Yitzchak Ginsburgh, *Kuntres Baruch Hagever* (1995) in *Brother Against Brother: Violence and Extremism in Israeli Politics to the Rabin Assassination*, ed. Ehud Sprinzak (Free Press: New York, 1999), p. 259.

Plain region south of the Gaza Strip in the Sinai Peninsula, that emerged from the Six Day War in 1967 until 1982, when it was handed over to Egypt as part of the Israel-Egypt Peace treaty—and then he becomes one of the settlement's "defenders."[4] The disengagement from this messianic hope for Greater Israel left lingering scars of: settlers barricaded on rooftops before being dragged away by I.D.F. soldiers; Prime Minister Menahem Begin's last minute decision to raze Yamit's infrastructure lest evacuated settlers return for a final clash with the Egyptians; resistance by disciples of Rabbi Meir Kahane vowing to take their lives rather than surrender. For Kaploun as poet, taking leave of his teacher, Ginsburgh, as well as defending before being disengaged from Yamit, all stand as pathmarks in his ongoing search for redemption amidst the ruptures. It is to this poetry of rupturing *devekut* that we now turn in two of Kaploun's epic poetry cycles, both dated the Seventeenth of Tammuz.

Rupture in Jerusalem: Holy Writing with a Torn Heart

The date of the Seventeenth of Tammuz embodies a perennial tear within the spatio-temporal fabric of Jerusalem. Such a devastating tear demands a deeper *devekut* within and flowing forth from the very rupture. How such a rupture is experienced through cracks and crossing-over in the sensorial realm, or what is known as synesthesia, will be apparent in the two poetry cycles Kaploun composed over the course of numerous fasts through the years experienced on the Seventeenth of Tammuz. This temporal marker annually catalyzes the unraveling of a three week mourning period over the destruction of Jerusalem and her two Holy Temples. One immediately senses the degree to which this spatio-temporal rupture is embodied in signs of deepening prayer, accompanied by fasting during the intensity of the summer months. This fast bridges one rupture to the next, from Moses smashing the tablets upon descending Mount Sinai to find the Israelites dancing round the Golden Calf, to the breaching of the walls of Jerusalem by the Romans in 69 CE. Three weeks after that siege of valiant Jewish resistance, the Romans destroyed the second Holy Temple on the Ninth of Av. This bridging of one rupture to the next is sensed so strongly

---

4.   Miron, "Yonadav Kaploun's Poetry: The Psalmody of Metaphysical Dissonance," 292-293.

that this temporal template is also echoed in how the breach of the first Temple walls of Jerusalem by the Babylonians is remembered.

Given both Jerusalem Temples were experienced as the *axis mundi*, the umbilical cord of the cosmos, something changes in the fabric of existence with their destruction. The spatio-temporal center of the terrestrial and cosmic Jerusalem is destroyed twice over on a singular moment in time, so something of that rupture bleeds through the current spatio-temporal reality in Israel. Thus when Kaploun choses to compose and date two extended poetry cycles on the Seventeenth of Tammuz, the poet is writing with a torn heart.

Rediscovering Reciprocal Presence of the Sentient in the Sensible

How the realm of the senses affects one's perception of the world is critically important to reconsider the subtle play of rupture and its *devekut*. Already seeking a way to express an elemental power that connects human flesh with the flesh of the world, one encounters a phenomenologist like Maurice Merleau-Ponty (1908-1961). His vision of the chiasmic, intertwining tissue of Flesh[5] signifies the mysterious matrix of reciprocal presence of the *sentient in the sensible* and of the *sensible in the sentient*.[6] What is being rediscovered here by Merleau-Ponty is the sensed experience through the eyes of the seer. No longer is the world perceived through a transcendental ego alone: rather, perception through the senses takes place within a being itself *of* the sensible, a being which "knows it before knowing it."[7] This kind of embodied knowing through the senses is intuitive, almost supra-rational, in its ability to empower the sensate body with "an art of interrogating the sensible according to its own wishes, an inspired exegesis."[8]

Yet humans remain resistant to truly cultivating those intuitive powers of imagining a *sensible* landscape not simultaneously *sensed*. Similarly, humans appear unable to imagine a *sensing self* or *sentience* not somehow situated in a

---

5. Maurice Merleau-Ponty, *Le Visible et L'Invisible* (Paris: Gallimard, 1964), 170-201.
6. Merleau-Ponty speaks of the perception of colors for example, as an encounter "drawn up from the depths of imaginary worlds." See Merleau-Ponty, *Le Visible et L'Invisible*, 132.
7. Merleau-Ponty, *Le Visible et L'Invisible*, 133.
8. Ibid., 135.

field of sensed phenomena. In perpetuating the distinction between human "subjects" and natural "objects" that primordial reciprocal relationship is lost.[9]

By bouncing back and forth between scientific determinism and spiritual idealism, contemporary discourse avoids the possibility that both the *perceiver* and the *perceived* are truly interdependent Flesh. This is a Flesh that is at once intertwining the *sensible* and *sensitive*.[10] Even so, while seeing the fuller spectrum of interdependence as a necessary corrective, there remains a yearning to realize a deeper sense of how this chiasmic, intertwined awareness leads to greater equanimity through such *devekut*. By refocusing the Western mind on sensuality of exteriority or descending consciousness, one may still miss what lies beyond it—namely the eros of interiority or ascending consciousness. While the Western mind needs to see anew how the earth is filled with true glory, there is an equally urgent need to see how a deeper presence envelops that very same world.

The desire for a deeper sense of this chiasmic, intertwined awareness hovers in *synesthesia*.[11] Perception is not limited to merely its visual aspect of seeing, but a fuller intertwining of the *sensible* and *sensitive* which includes touching, tasting, hearing and smelling. While considered pathological by contemporary neuroscientists, such a sense of this chiasmic intertwining of the senses through synesthesia embodies the immediacy of a pre-conceptual experience of existence. That immediacy of experience from the perspective of the life-world does not deny divergent modalities of the senses, rather it reveals the degree to which the intertwining senses "are complementary powers evolved in a complex interdependence with one another."[12] It is this primordial vibrancy coursing through the senses that allows for the opening of a new language and experience of *devekut*.

It is such an inspired exegesis—the chiasmic intertwining of the senses through synesthesia—that is so vibrant in the Seventeenth of Tammuz poetic cycles by Kaploun. It is at moments of rupture, between the *sensible* and *sensitive,* that such a cross-over point can open the site of revelation. This experience of synesthesia taking place in the ruptures

---

9. David Abram, *The Spell of the Sensuous: Perception and Language in a More-Than-Human-World* (New York: Vintage Books, 1996), 52-53.
10. Ibid., 53-59.
11. Ibid., 59-62.
12. Ibid., 61.

of these next two poetry cycles—"Scent of Darkness" and "A Window of Opportunity"—expands the intertwined awareness leading to greater equanimity through such *devekut*.

רֵיחַ הַחֹשֶׁךְ

א

רֵיחַ הַחֹשֶׁךְ, רֵיחַ רַגְלַיִם
יָצָא וּבָא
בֵּין כּוֹכָבִים וּבֵין הַמִּסְדְּרוֹן הַמְּנֻהָרָה.
מְזֻרְזָנִים, שַׂקֵּי שֵׁנָה, סְבִיבָם הֵלוֹת-
אֲנָחָה דַקָּה - -

שֶׁקֶט. מִישֶׁהוּ בּוֹכֶה.
בֶּחָלָל - נְסִירָה.
רוֹעֶדֶת שְׁלוּלִית הַשֶּׁמֶן וּמִתְמַצָּה:
עַל נֵר הַזְּמַן מִתְלַחֲשִׁים קִירוֹת הַלֵּב
עַד כִּי עֲלָטָה - חֶדְלַת רָצוֹן אוֹ זִכָּרוֹן -
תִּזְרַח.

אוֹ אוּלַי הָיָה זֶה צְחוֹק?
עַרְבֵי הַקַּיִץ הָאָרוֹךְ, שֶׁהָיָה!
צִלְלֵי הַבְּרוֹשִׁים הַנְּסִיכִים; הַגּוּף
הַשּׂוֹחֶה מְפֹאָר בַּשָּׂדֶה, בְּפַאֲתֵי הָעִיר, שֶׁהָיְתָה!
אֶלֶף כֶּסֶף לָאַבִּיר שֶׁיַּחֲזִיר אֶת הַזְּמַן
וְלוּ שָׁנָה אֶחָת!

אֶחָד מִתְיַשֵּׁב.
רָצָה לְעַשֵּׁן אוֹ מַשֶּׁהוּ.

יָשֵׁן גַּם אֱלֹהָיו שֶׁל הַדָּתִי.

מִישֶׁהוּ נֶעֱמָד:
נֶעֱמָד לוֹ
לְתוֹךְ חוֹר שָׁחוֹר וְקַר...

וּדְמוּת שְׁקוּפָה כְּמַרְאֵה אָדָם
קָפְצָה מִכְּבְשָׁן
וְהֵקִימָה מְדִינָה.

וְשִׂרְבְּטָה אֶת הַפֶּתֶק
וְתוֹחֶבֶת לַכֹּתֶל

כִּי עַכְשָׁיו תֵּבֵל נִרְדְּמָה
וְחוֹלֶמֶת חֲלוֹם.

ב
הָיִינוּ וְרָאִינוּ אֶת הַמּוּסִיקָה
גּוֹוַעַת אֶל עַצְמָהּ
וְאֶת הַזְּמַן כַּעֲרָבָה אוֹסְטְרָלִית
סוּפַת סוּסִים מִתְרוֹמֶמֶת
לְרֵיחַ הַמַּיִם

קֶצֶף חַם וְאָבָק
כְּמוֹ עֲרָפֶל מָלֵא אֶת הַמַּכְתֵּשׁ הַתְּהוֹם –
יָצָאנוּ לִבְדּוֹק תַּ'שֶּׁטַח אוּלַי
שָׁבִיט חָדָשׁ יַחֲלוֹף נָגַע בּוֹ

דְּמָמָה רַבָּה לִטְפָה אֶת שִׁלְדֵי אֶצְבְּעוֹתֵינוּ
הַמְבַצְבְּצוֹת מִבַּעַד לַשַּׁרְווּלִים
דְּהוּיֵי-גָּוֶן

וְאִם שַׁעַר יִפָּתַח בַּחֲרִיקָה עַתִּיקָה
הֵיכָן יִהְיֶה אָז לְבֵי הַהוֹלֵם

ג
נְבוֹכִים הֶאֱפִירוּ כּוֹכָבִים;
נִצְמְדוּ אֵלַיִךְ
וְכָבוּ מִיָּד.

נֶאֱסְפָה אֶל הַשֶּׁקֶט פְּעִימָה
שֶׁאָבַד הַלַּיְלָה,
מְעוּפַת בְּגָדִים גְּדוֹלִים נִשְׁמְעָהּ:
הַר, הַר כָּל הַשָּׁנִים הַחֵל מִתְפַּשֵּׁט
לִצְחוֹקָן הֶעָלוּב שֶׁל גִּבְעוֹת הַחוֹל.

טוּרִים טוּרִים שְׁנַיִם קָרוֹת
נָקְשׁוּ עַכְשָׁיו מַה יִּהְיֶה.

כּוֹסִיּוֹת קָפְאוּ מוּרְמוֹת,

גְּבָרִים בְּגֵהִירָתָם,
וּבַיְּצִיעִים הַהוֹמִים עַם וּנְבִיאָיו -
חַלְיוֹת-צַוָּאר,
צְלָעוֹת -
כְּנְבָלִים לְבָנִים
מְנֻגָּנִים בַּעֲלָטָה.

נִרְדַּמְנוּ.
חוּטִים סְמוּיִים הִרְקִידוּנוּ מָחוֹל
בִּשְׁנַת לְלֹא-חָלוֹם.

רָאִיתִי שְׁרִיקַת חָלָל טוֹרֶפֶת
חוּט אַחַר חוּט,

וְטַל

רְסִיסִים נְשִׁיקָה עַל שְׂפָתַי

ד
דְּמָמָה קָמָה וְעָמְדָה.
לַבַּסּוֹף יֵדַע הַדָּבָר.

לְשׁוֹנָהּ כְּכוֹכָב מִתְקָרֵר,
אֶת הַשִּׁיר תְּלַקֵּק עַד מָוֶת.
צָחוֹר צַוָּארָהּ כְּקַרְחוֹן
שָׁט וְנִשְׁפָּט
אֶת סִירוֹת הַצוֹלְלִים
סְפִינַת הַמּוּסִיקָה.

גּוֹעָה שַׁאֲגַת הַיָּם.
גַּם שְׁרִיקַת הָרוּחַ בַּיְּעָרוֹת
אָבְדָה בָּחָלָל
וְהֵד אַחֲרוֹן
הֵד בְּכִי אָדָם
נֶאֱסַף אֶל חֵיק מְצוּקִים
וְהָפַךְ לְחוֹל.

עָמְדִי בַּצַּד לְרֶגַע, דִּמְמַת הָאַחֲרִית
הָעַתִּיקָה.
מִדַּי מֻקְדָּם דָּפַקְתְּ אֶצְלִי.

הַשְׁפִּילִי מַבָּטֵךְ
אֶל רַגְלַיִם שְׁתַּיִם
חֲלוּמוֹת עַל הַדֶּשֶׁא;
אוֹ אֶל עֹמֶק
רַךְ צַוָּאר - -

וְהַבִּיטִי בְּעֵינַי,
בְּעוֹד אֲנִי נוֹאָשׁ בּוֹרֵא בָּךְ
קוֹל חָדָשׁ
מִלָּה רִאשׁוֹנָה

בְּטֶרֶם תְּנַשְּׁקִי
אֶת שְׂעָרִי

ה
שְׁרִיר לֹא זָע בְּפָנָיו הַמְּחוּקִים
כַּאֲשֶׁר הִנִּיחַ לִי לְהִתְפַּתֵּל
מוּלוֹ אוֹ בְּקִרְבּוֹ.

אַתָּה וֶרֶד - הוֹאִיל לַלְחוֹשׁ לְעֵבֶר
גּוּפִי הַמִּשְׁתָּאֶה הַמְּיַצֵּג
אוֹתִי כָּרֶגַע.

אִם בֵּין קִירוֹת בֵּיתִי הַצּוֹחֵק,
אֵצֶל אִשְׁתִּי וִילָדַי,
וְאִם בְּיַעַר-בְּרֵאשִׁית הַמַּחְשִׁיךְ,
לְפָתָה אֶת גְּרוֹנִי אֵינוּתוֹ
וּכְמִיהָתוֹ הַנּוֹרָאָה לְנִיחוֹחַ וְרָדִים.

כָּל הָאָבִיב טִפַּסְתִּי
יָרוֹק כְּטִירוֹן
קוֹצֵנִי וּמְאֹהָב
וְהִגַּעְתִּי הֲלוֹם, אֶל גַּג
הַמַּחְסָן הָאָפֵל.

כָּאן - אִם אַךְ לֹא אֵרָדֵם -
הַנַּח לִי לַחֲלוֹם אֶת שְׁאֵרִית הַלַּיְלָה:
מִקְצוֹת מוּסִיקָה עַתִּיקָה,
חַד-קוֹלִית וְגַלְמוּדָה,
קָמִים לְאִטָּם הַשַּׁעַר וְהַמַּעֲלוֹת.

יִהְיֶה לִי בַּיִת.

י"ז בתמוז תשנ"ד - טבת תשנ"ה

Scent of Darkness

I.
scent of darkness, the odor of feet
went out and came in
between stars and the corridor the tunnel.
floor-mats, sleeping-bags, surrounding them subtle
halo-sighs — — —

quiet. someone's crying.
in the empty space—splitting apart.
the oil puddle quivers and is exhausted:
together the heart's walls are whispering about time's candle
until darkness—cessation of will or memory—
will shine.

or perchance was it laughter?

a long summer's night, so it was!
the sound of princely cypress; the body
swimming grandly in the field, in the outskirts of the city, so it was!
a thousand silver pieces to the knight that'll bring back time
and if only one year!

someone is taking a seat.
wanted to smoke
or something.

the religious guy's God is also asleep.
someone stood up:
standing there
inside a cold black hole.

and a see-through figure with human guise
jumped out of a crematorium
and founded a state.

and scribbled the note
shoving it in the wall

for the universe now has fallen asleep
dreaming a dream.

II.
we'd been & seen the music
expiring into itself
& time like an Australian willow
a gale of horses rearing up
to the scent of water

hot froth & dust
like darkness filling the abysmal crater—
we went out *ta' check the terrain*
perchance a fresh comet'll pass by we'll touch it

a deep silence stroked our fingers' skeletal frame
emerging from sleeves
shade-faded

& if a gate will open with an ancient creeking
then O where will my pounding heart be

III.
perplexed ones turned gray; stars
approaching you close
they were snuffed out at once.

gathered towards the silence was a throbbing that
the night had lost.
the flight of baggy clothes
was heard:
a mount, mountain of hoary years
began to extend
greeted by the pathetic laughter
of sand dunes.

set after set of cold teeth

chattered: now what'll be.

wineglasses held high froze.
stooping men.
& in balconies bustling with a people & its prophets—
neck vertebrae,
ribs—
like white harps
plucked in deep darkness.

we fell asleep.
unseen strings made us dance in a circle
in dreamless slumber.

i saw the whistling of empty space
preying string after string

& dew

its droplets a kiss
upon my lips

IV.
Silence arose and stood.
in the end the matter will be known.

the tongue of silence like a cooling star
consumes the song until it dies.
glacieresque, the neck of sielnce
set sail and sentenced
the divers' life-boats
the music's ship.

the roaring of the sea has died down.
so has the whistling of wind in the woods
lost in the empty space
and the last echo
echo of someone weeping
is gathered in to the cliff's bosom
and turned into sand.

stand aside for a moment, O ancient silence
of the End of Days.
you knocked much too early at my place.

lower your gaze
feetwards
that dream they're on the grass;
or towards the deep tenderness
of a neck --

and gaze into my eyes
while i'm still in despair creating within you
a new voice
a first word

before it kisses
my hair

V.
Not a muscle moving
in His featureless face
as He let me writhe
in His presence, or within Him.

He addressed a whispered "you're a rose"
to my wondering body that represents
me for the moment.

whether between the laughing walls of my house,
alongside woman-of-mine and the children,
or in a darkening primeval forest,
my throat grasped by His nothingness
and His awesome yearning for the scent of roses.

all spring long I climbed
green as a neophyte
prickly and in love
and i reached hither, the roof
of the dark storehouse.

here—if only i won't fall asleep—
let me dream the rest of the night:
from vestigial echoes of ancient music,
uni-vocal and solitary,
there slowly rise the gate and the steps, the Song of Ascents.

a House for me shall there be.[13]

17th of *Tammuz* 5754-*Tevet* 5755

In this fourfold poetry cycle, entitled, "Scent of Darkness" (1994-1995) a spiritual search is underway, at once magical and mundane. How strange for such erotic embodiment to be touching a metaphysical void. This strange polarity, as Miron has astutely noted,[14] is encountered through the aroma of eventide and the yearning to carry forward that aroma into an otherwise parched daytime. Such an encounter between the *sensible* and *sensitive* exemplifies "metaphysical dissonance" that Miron claims as emblematic of Kaploun's entire poetic *oeuvre*. In the close reading of the fourfold poetic cycle that follows, however I will challenge this reading of "metaphysical dissonance" to be incomplete. Given the chasm that often separates the literary critic from the philosopher, as a counterpoint to the former one must turn to the latter to see that intertwining of the *sensible* and *sensitive* reveals a unified Flesh of *devekut* amidst the ruptures.[15]

I. The vacuum that builds between an awakening and sleeping existence is found "in the empty space—splitting apart." That chiasmic, intertwining of the *sensible* and the *sensed* begins already in this first stanza. This is the intertwining of a synesthesia that begins to unravel as sleep moves into darkness, opening up a possibility for sensing the world otherwise. The question of which sensible realm is linked to which sense is also opening up with the uncertainty of laughter or crying. Darkness emerges from the

---

13.   My translation was first published in *Ariel: The Israel Review of Arts and Letters*, ed. A. Weil, no. 115 (Jerusalem 2003), 60-61. See also http://israel.poetryinternationalweb.org/, with special thanks to Yonadav and Uri Kaploun.

14.   Miron, "Yonadav Kaploun's Poetry: The Psalmody of Metaphysical Dissonance," 292-293.

15.   See above no's 521-528.

darkest of visual signs where "the oil puddle quivers and is exhausted:" reaching the point of something beyond what is any longer visible. In this darkness "... empty space—splitting apart" there is a splitting apart of the *senses* from the *sensible*, wherein "together the heart's walls are whispering about time's candle/until darkness—cessation of will or memory—/ will shine." The shining within the deepening darkness is the light that emerges from what poet and survivor, Paul Celan (1920-1970), once called the "congenital darkness of the poem." [16] After the *Shoah,* such congenital darkness abounds, to the point where "the god of the poem is indisputably a *deus absconditus*"[17]—and thereafter god-consciousness has inexorably shifted. That shift is already taking place from the onset of the journey into the Seventeenth of Tammuz in this cycle, seeing how "the religious guy's God is also asleep." The shift in the tribal god-consciousness of the religious guy's "Our God" especially under its hegemonic representation through the State of Israel and its rabbinate, already discussed,[18] is giving way to a more diaphanous divinity.[19] Such diaphanous divinity intertwines the *perceiver* and the *perceived* into a truly interdependent Flesh of the poem. This is a Flesh that is at once intertwining the *sensible* and *sensitive*[20] as becomes more strongly expressed and sensed through this rupture of the Seventeenth of Tammuz.

Time dissolves away in its temporal distinctions between moments where even the divine moves from dynamism into stasis. That is what is experienced in the act of fasting and praying, crossing over the threshold into the Seventeenth of Tammuz: "someone stood up:/standing there/inside a cold black hole." Yet it is from this black hole of deep sleep–the deepest darkness of catastrophe's rupture—that new light shines forth. From the inferno of the *Shoah,* the State of Israel is born: "and a see-through figure with human guise/jumped out of a crematorium/and founded a state." Notwithstanding the horrors of the historic moment, and the emergence of a people from this state of deepest darkness, what surrounds

---

16. Paul Celan, *The Meridian: Final Version-Drafts-Materials,* trans. P. Jorris (Stanford: Stanford University Press, 2001), s.v. Darkness, 87.

17. Celan, *The Meridian,* s.v. Darkness, 87.

18. See above, chapter 1, section 1.1.

19. See above, chapter 2.

20. Abram, *The Spell of the Sensuous,* 53-59.

this rebirthing is another impasse before entry, "for the universe now has fallen asleep/dreaming a dream." If Theodor Herzl (1860-1904) was such "a see-through figure with human guise" then his Zionist prophecy has been all but forgotten. While Herzl's clarion call to seed the state has too often been mistranslated as "if you desire it, it is no dream" rather "it is no fable" here the poet invokes something more than that project of secular, political Zionism. That something more is seen through a deeper look through the speculum of this "figure with human guise" that "jumped out of a crematorium/and founded a state." From the ashes of Auschwitz, Israel is born; yet in the process the prophetic nature of that rebirthing dream seems all but lost to the poet. Escape from the deep darkness of catastrophic rupture back into the light of redemptive nation-state building is followed by a more palpable darkness, leaving the poet and his prophetic impulse alone to continue dreaming about the flourishing of a future site of redemption that is the Zion of Israel.

II. Time begins unraveling, as past and present elide and intertwine. Yet precisely in their dissolution, there arises a temporal elision into an intertwined Flesh of vision and sound. There is a moment of seeing the sounds, "we'd been & seen the music" that leads to a deeper aroma of darkness, "expiring into itself/& time like an Australian willow/a gale of horses rearing up/to the scent of water." The journey begins while camping in the outskirts of Jerusalem, with the descent of darkness, until its aroma rapidly enables a shift to past time fluttering through the measure of the Australian willow" and "a gale of horses rearing up/to the scent of water." Those moments that raced through their temporal markers of the past now return, ebbing and flowing in a most mellow and languid motion, stilling the very flow of time.

Yet amidst the rupture within this temporal tissue, there is a looming light within the aroma of darkness, seeping forth from another site. This other site, normally concealed within the ground of existence, now is being revealed in the rupture to the poet as he is standing, praying and fasting. It is again that chiasmic intertwining of the *sensible* and the *sensed* earlier wherein synesthesia enters to open into a sensing of the world otherwise. That opening to light in the "congenital darkness of the poem" is the growing from the opening stanza's sound of being intertwined "together the heart's walls are whispering about time's candle/until darkness — cessation of will or memory — /will shine." It grows from a "whispering about time's candle" to the point where something more is shining through from the empty space of rupture. Bridging that abyss that separates the intertwining of the *sensible* and the *sensed*, here the poet again *sees* the sounds before him: "& if a gate will open with an ancient creeking/then O where will my pounding heart be." Such an abode that is expansive enough to intertwine the *sensible* and the *sensed* is a holy grounding of existence. It is this time-space the poet's heart races for in anticipation of the final stanza, where a further rebirthing takes place.

III. From the terrestrial *sensations* to the cosmic *sensibles*, the poet's vision is now expanding to bridge realms often ruptured. In the stilling of the night, the poet's attunement recovers what was "gathered towards the silence was a throbbing that/the night had lost." In this deepening silence, the terrestrial landscape merges with the celestial landscape, so the dreaming that was lost immediately upon the founding of the nation-state begins again. The illusory stasis of founding such a dream nation-state begins to dissolve as: "a mount, mountain of hoary years/began to extend/greeted by the pathetic laughter/ of sand dunes." The return of primordial time as this "mountain of hoary years" mythically resurfaces to battle with "the pathetic laughter/of sand dunes,"that momentary grounding of existence through the nation-state. Something more beckons the poet to be attuned to the prophetic impulse, yet this collision of primordial time with mundane time leads to another "dreamless slumber" where every celebratory gest is frozen, even "in balconies bustling with a people & its prophets—/ neck vertebrae,/ribs—/like white harps/plucked in deep darkness." In this moment of suspended animation, a different sort of music is heard. This is a primordial music of the soul played on "unseen strings" that brings the prophets into a circle of dance. Only in re-attuning to this primordial music will the prophecy, held in suspended animation since the post-*Shoah* birthing of the nation-state, reawaken inside the poet. Such a moment is more than merely reawakening, rather it is likened to a rebirthing through a resurrecting "dew/ its droplets a kiss/upon my lips." From the terrestrial *sensations* to the cosmic *sensibles*, the poet's vision now bridges upper and lower Jerusalem, realms often ruptured, once again returning to their primordial *devekut*.

IV. By entering into that state of synesthesia, intertwining the terrestrial *sensations* to the cosmic *sensibles*, the poet's vision is expanded and the prophetic impulse of dreaming is re-awakened. Full awakening is embodied in apotheosis, where the poet now merges within the "featureless face" of the Infinite One, the primordial time-space of poetic inspiration. The poet is the rose returning to its infinite garden, as the body is exfoliated so the soul returns into its primordial state of unity with its source. The yearning of the Ancient One "for the scent of roses" is an eternal desire to replenish the garden inside the forest with luscious souls. Such a soul is found in and embodied by the poet in his most mundane existence, domestic life: "whether between the laughing walls of my house,/alongside woman-of-mine and the children,/ or in a darkening primeval forest,/my throat grasped by His nothingness/and His awesome yearning for the scent of roses." The desire drawing the rose to the garden and the gardener to the roses continues to intensify, from its spring awakening to darker shades of love. Here in the prophetic throes of deep desire, an awakened dreaming intensifies "from vestigial echoes of ancient music,/uni-vocal and solitary."

In this state of imaginal visioning, the poet is most keenly attuned to see the sounds of what has remained ruptured for the entire poetic cycle. These sounds are echoing through the music of the Psalms, known as the Song of Ascents—the site of the ultimate experience of synesthesia. The dream of a rebuilt temple becomes a poetic reality—the reality of an *imago templi*.[21] So vivid is the reality of this imaginal *imago templi*, that the vision emerges through sound. That sound "from vestigial echoes of ancient music" is the sound of collective yearning to return from exile precisely as expressed through the Song of Ascents. Chanted across the lands of their dispersion, these echoes of a rupture in the primordial time-space

---

[21]. Henri Corbin, "*L'Imago Templi* face aux norms profanes," *Temple et Contemplation* (Paris: Flammarion, 1980), 285-292. See also Elliot R. Wolfson, "*Imago Templi* and the Meeting of the Two Seas: Liturgical Time-Space and the Feminine Imaginary in Zoharic Kabbalah," *RES* 51, Spring 2007, 121-135.

continuum—that is Jerusalem—here find their point of reunification. That reunification is "uni-vocal and solitary" as the rose and the gardener, as the neophyte and the featureless one, as the mountain and sand dunes, as the yearning and its source of desire intertwine back into their ruptured Flesh. The sound of redemption—a highly spiritualized Zionism—is now more sensible, sensed and thus embodied into a fuller living.[22]

The paradoxical nature of encountering the *sensible* and *sensitive* takes place again in another of Kaploun's poetic cycles, entitled, "A Window of Opportunity." In the close reading of the fourfold poetic cycle that follows, I will again challenge Miron's reading of "metaphysical dissonance" as insightful but ultimately remaining incomplete. Turning to see how intertwining of the *sensible* and *sensitive* reveals a unified Flesh of *devekut* in the ruptures opens "A Window of Opportunity" amidst its seeming closure:

חַלּוֹן אֶפְשָׁרִי

חַלּוֹן אֶפְשָׁרִי,
כְּמִין חָרִיץ בְּגַג הַבַּיִת הֶחָדָשׁ;

כָּאן הַזְּרוֹעַ נִשְׁעֲנָה
עַל זִכָּרוֹן נוֹאָשׁ:
נַעַר אָבֵל מִתְפַּלֵּל,
כְּכוֹכָב נִצַּת וְחָדֵל;
חוֹשֵׂף זְרוֹעַ הַחֻלְטָה נְחוּשָׁה.
עֵינָיו גַּחְלִילִים, וּלְרֹאשׁוֹ זֵר הַקּוֹצִים סָבִיב.

וּבַיִת אַחֵר - קִירוֹת אֲפֵלִים וְגַת סְדוּקָה -
מִתַּחַת לַבַּיִת.
וְעָמוֹק יוֹתֵר בַּצִּנָּה, בְּקַרְקָעִיּוֹת - בְּתַדְהֵמוֹת הָהָר -
קֶשֶׁת נְטוּיָה, עַמּוּדֵי עוֹלָם,
כְּתוֹבוֹת-זִמָּה וּפֶרַח וְחָתוּל,
מְרַרַת-נְבִיאִים שְׁפוּכָה - -

לַיְלָה גַּלִּים לְאֵין-חֹק
מֵאֲחוֹרֵי הַלַּיְלָה הַזֶּה,

---

22. On spiritualized Zionism, see chapter 1, n135.

וּבַדְּמָמָה הָרַבָּה -
גַּם לֵילוֹת-הָאוּלַי הָעִוְרִים שֶׁל בָּנַי אַחֲרַי.

כִּי לַע עָצוּם נִפְעָר כָּעֵת חָרֵשׁ.
סְבִיב הֶהָרִים הָרָמִים
מִתְעַנֵּק לְאַטּוֹ אֲדַמְדַּם
לַע-הָאַדִּירִים שֶׁל הַזְּמַן.

וּמָה תַּעֲשֶׂה לְפִיכָךְ הַיָּד הַנִּזְכֶּרֶת, הַחוֹזֶרֶת מִבְּעָתָה?
לְטַף תְּלַטֵּף בַּחֲשַׁאי
אֶת בֹּהַק הַגּוּף שֶׁהָיָה,
אֶת הַזְּרוֹעַ הַהִיא וְחָלְקַת-הַצַּוָּאר.
אֵצֶל חָרִיץ שֶׁל חַלּוֹן תִּרְשֹׁם לְמִשְׁמֶרֶת:
סָתָת אָהוּב וְאִלֵּם,
שָׁבָה עָמְדִי עַל אֶבֶן אַחַת
שֶׁלֹּא נֵרָדַם.

עַל אֶבֶן אַחַת
מוּל הַזְּרִיחָה הַנִּמְשֶׁכֶת
שָׁם יָשַׁבְנוּ
לוֹקְקִים אֶת הָאַיֶּלֶת.

בַּבְּקָרִים נִתְקְעוּ קְצָת עַרְפִּלִּים בַּוָּאדִי.
פֶּתַח הַמְּעָרָה - מִדֶּרֶךְ הַטֶּבַע - נֶעְלַם לְשָׁעָה.
סֶפֶר, לֹא-מַשֶּׁהוּ, נִסְחַף
בַּשִּׁטָּפוֹן הַנֶּהְדָּר. גַּם מִלִּים אֲחָדוֹת תָּפְסוּ
מִן הַשֶּׁמֶשׁ מֵרָחָק,
וּמֵרָחָק מִן הַגּוּף הֶחָדָשׁ, הָאֱלֹהִי.

- וּמָתַי הִתְפַּלַּלְתָּ לָאַחֲרוֹנָה?
- טוֹב, אָז מַהִי, אִם כְּבָר, תְּפִלָּה?

אַךְ אָנוּ יָדַעְנוּ כִּי הַכֹּל רַק עִנְיָן שֶׁל זְמַן.

אֵיךְ נַגִּיעַ לָעִיר,
אֵיךְ נַעֲלֶה אֶת הַחֹמֶר,
אֵיךְ נִבְרַח מִלְּשׁוֹן-הַיָּם הָעֲקֻשָּׁה
שֶׁיָּצְאָה לִלְחֹךְ עִקְבוֹתֵינוּ -
לְהַרְהֵר אַחֲרֵינוּ בְּיוֹם הַסַּגְרִיר -

—— 229 ——

עַל מַה צָרִיךְ לִבְכּוֹת,
אֵיךְ לָשִׁיר.

כִּנּוֹרוֹת לְחוֹף יָמִים.
מְשֻׁחָמִים וַחֲלוּלִים.
תַּחַת שְׁמֵי הַכָּחוֹל
אַסְפְּסוּף הַנְּשָׁמוֹת
כִּנּוֹרוֹת בְּתַחְתּוֹנִים.

עָרֵב וְעָצֵב רֵיחַ הַבְּשָׂרִים
שֶׁנִּצַּח אֶת רֵיחַ הַיָּם.
וְתוֹדָה לָאֵל עַל כִּי סָמוּךְ
הַמָּלוֹן לַחוֹף; שָׁם יְלַטֵּף הָאֶקְדָּח
בַּחֲדַר הַמִּטּוֹת,
וְשָׁם תְּעָרֵב הַשֵּׁנָה אֲבוֹדַת-הַחֲלוֹם
עָמוֹק בְּקִרְבֵי הַשַּׁחֲרִית הַנִּמְשָׁכְת - -

וּבְעוֹד קֶשֶׁת הַכִּנּוֹר - קְצֵה הַקֶּשֶׁת שֶׁהִתְנַחֲשָׁה! -
בְּכַף יָדִי,
קָרָאתִי לַסַּתָּת הָאִלֵּם:
הָאֵזֶן לְהֶמְיַת הַנֵּבֶל,
נֵבֶל הַצְּלָעוֹת הַקָּשׁוֹת שֶׁל דָּוִד.
הָאֵזֶן וְנַחֵם אֶת צִיּוֹן.

יָרַד לְסִינַי
וְהַר אֲבָנָיו בְּחֶזְהוּ.
כָּאן לוֹהֵט הַבַּרְזֶל בַּיָּדַיִם
אַךְ יֵשׁ בֵּית-מָנוֹס
לִנְקִישׁוֹת הַמַּקֶּבֶת וּלְתִקְתּוּק הַזְּמַנִּים.

צוּקִים נֶאֱנָחִים לְהִמּוֹג בַּמַּיִם
וְהַחוֹל עָנָו הוֹמֶה אֲלֵיהֶם
שְׁרִיקַת רוּחוֹתָיו וּלְחִישַׁת עַקְרַבִּים.

בֵּין רִבּוֹא אֲבָנָיו - כְּכוֹכָבִים מִתְחַנְּנִים עַל נַפְשָׁם, אֲבָנָיו -
עָמַד הָאַמִּיץ לְחַבֵּק
אֶת סֵפֶל הַקָּפֶה הַמָּתוֹק;
לְחַבֵּק אֶת דָּן בְּמַאֲהַל הָעֵירֹם
וְאֶת הַיֹּפִי רְוֵה הַשִּׁכְחָה.

מַקְשִׁיב בִּגְבוּרָה יַעֲמוֹד אַמִּיץ,

כִּי אִלֵּם הַסַּתָּת

וְעִוֵּר.

לֹא לְפָרֵשׁ בְּשֵׁם הָעִיר

לֹא לְהִתְעָרֵב לַיְלָדִים;

לֹא לִגְמוֹר דָּבָר וּלְנַסּוֹת לְהַגְדִּיר,

לֹא לְקַנֵּא בַּזְּקֵנִים.

כְּתֹב עַל אַף אֹרֶךְ הַזָּקָן,

בְּכֵה עַל אַף חֲנֻכַּת הַבִּנְיָן,

צְחַק עַד כְּלוֹת הַבָּבוֹת מִן הָאָרֶץ;

שֶׁלֹּא לְמַעַן נִשְׁמָתְךָ אַתָּה מִסְתַּתֵּת בָּאֲוִיר הַזֶּה

וְלֹא לְמַעַן רַעְיָתְךָ אֲשֶׁר אָהַבְתָּ.

לֹא לִקְנוֹת אֶת הַפֶּרַח.

לֹא לְשַׁיֵּף אֶת קוֹצָיו.

לֹא לַחֲנוֹת בַּיַּעַר שֶׁלְּפָנַי

הַנִּגְיָעָה בְּלֶב-לַיְלָה

וְלֹא בַּמִּדְבָּר שֶׁל אַחֲרַי.

כְּתֹב עַד כְּלוֹת הַזֶּרַע הַשָּׁחוֹר

שֶׁבְּקִסְתָּ דָּמְךָ,

עַד כְּלוֹת הָאוֹר הַמְסַמֵּא

הַדָּבֵק בַּלַּיְלָה הַגּוֹאָה –

לֵיל הַמִּטַּהֲרִים בְּמִקְוֵה הַבְּכִי.

נָח סַתָּת מִן הַנֶּצַח פִּתְאוֹם;

לְהַבִּיט בְּיָדָיו, לִשְׁמֹעַ קְצֵה סוֹד-מְלַאכְתּוֹ.

שֶׁמֶשׁ-הַהוֹזִים כְּבוּיָה בַּעֲצָמָיו

וְהָאָבָק שֶׁאַטָם אֶת עוֹרוֹ.

הִנֵּה יָדַי הַלּוֹטְפָה אֶת הַגֵּו בַּחֲשַׁאי

וְיָדִי הַמֻּכְרַכְתָּ תְּפִלִּין;

אֶצְבַּע לְהוֹרוֹת הַשָּׁמַיִם – וְעַד לְחָלָל הָרָחוֹק –

וְאֶצְבַּע לְנַחֵם אֶת הָעַיִן

הַנִּבְגָּדָה.

וְהִנֵּה חָרִיץ בֵּין הָרְעָפִים,

וְעַל הַגַּג יוֹנָה.

תּוֹדָה, אֲנִי אוֹמֵר,

אֶל תּוֹךְ הַמִּלְחָמָה.

י"ז בתמוז - כ"ד בתמוז תשנ"ח

A Window of Opportunity

A window of opportunity,
like a crack on the roof of a new building;

here the arm leaned
upon a depressing memory:
a mourning lad praying,
like a flickering, extinguished star;
exposes an arm tenaciously.
his eyes fireflies, and upon his head a crown of thorns.

And another house—dark walls and cracked winepress—
beneath the house.
And deeper still in the chilling cold, in the depths of the earth—in the
wonder of the mountain—
extended rainbow, pillars of the universe,
lustful writings, a flower, and a cat,
embittered-prophesy spilt — —

a wavy night to lawlessness
from beneath this night,
and in the multitudes of silence—
even the blind-maybe-nights of my children after me.

For a gaping jaw is now muted.
round the tall mounts
slowly giganting red
the mighty-jaw of Time.

What should a remembering hand therefore do, pale from alarm?
Secretly caressing
the glow of the body that was,
that arm and that plot of neck.
At the crack of a window the remembering hand shall chronicle:

Beloved and mute stonemason,
sit with me on one stone
lest we fall asleep.

On one stone
facing the prolonged sunrise
There we sat
licking the gazelle.

Slight morning fogs stuck in the wadi.
The cave's opening—naturally—vanished for the moment.
A book, not that great, swept
in the formidable flood. Even several words stayed away
from the sun,
and stayed away from the new body, the divine.

—So when was the last time you prayed?
—Well, what is prayer, now that you mention it?

Yet we knew that everything is just a matter of Time.

How will we get to the city,
how will we elevate the material world,
how shall we flee from the stubborn-tongue of the sea
that has gone out to lick up our footprints—
to reflect after us on a day heavy with rain—

About what should we lament,
how shall we sing.

Harps upon the shore of days.
Brown and hollow.
Neath the blue skies
a rabble of souls
harps below.

Delectable and melancholic the scent of flesh
that overcame the scent of the sea.
And thank god for the dwelling place
close to the shore; there the revolver
will be caressed in the bedroom,
and there a dreamless sleep shall be delectable
deep inside the continuous dawn — —

And still the bow of the harp resonates— the edge of the bow becomes a
snake!—

in the palm of my hand,
I cried out to the mute stonemason:
Listen to the yearning of the lyre,
lyre of the hard ribs of David.
Listen and console Zion.

Descended to Sinai
and the mountain of His tablets clutched at his chest.
Here the iron blazes in the hands
yet there is a house of refuge
to the knockings of the hammer and the ticking of Times.

Moaning cliffs fading in water
and the sand humbly yearns for them
the whistling of its winds and the whispering of scorpions.

Between the myriad of His stones—like stars pleading for the souls, His
stones—
the courageous one was about to embrace
the sweet cup of coffee;
to embrace Dan in the naked tent
and the beauty that is slaked with forgetfulness.

The one who hears in heroism will stand with courage,
for the stonemason is mute
and blind.

Don't expound in the name of the city
Don't intervene for the children;
Don't conclude and conceptualize,
Don't envy the elders.

Write despite the length of the beard,
Weep despite the inauguration of the building,
Laugh until the dolls are no longer in the land;
Not for the sake of your own soul are you being stone-masoned in this air
And not for the sake of your wife who you loved.

Don't buy the flower.
Don't polish its thorns.
Don't encamp facing the forest

the touch at the heart of night
and not in the desert of afterwords.

Write until the cessation of the black seed
in the inkstand of your blood
until the cessation of the blinding light
which cleaves in the mounting night—
the night for those purifying by immersion in tears.

A stonemason suddenly in repose from eternity;
to look at his hands, to hear the edge of his craft's secret.
The sun-of-hallucinators extinguished in His strength
and the dust which sealed His skin.

Behold my hand secretly caresses the back
and my hand which binds the phylacteries;
a finger to point to the heavens—and up until the distant void—
and a finger to console the betrayed
eye.

Behold a crack between the roofing tiles,
and upon the roof a dove.

Thank you, I say,
into the midst of war.[23]

17th-24th of *Tammuz,* 5758

Opening a Closing Window of Opportunity: Sentient *in the* Sensible

Continuing to write through the moment of deepest darkness—the
Seventeenth of *Tammuz*—Yonadav Kaploun's poetry cycle of *devekut*
in "A Window of Opportunity" (1998) remains resiliently rich in the
rupture. This cycle aroused through the senses, as the poet witnesses
"A window of opportunity,/like a crack on the roof of a new building;"
moving through the tropes of standing, praying and fasting as already

---

23.   Yonadav Kaploun, "A Window of Opportunity," *You Are Still Writing* [Hebrew] (Jerusalem:
      Keter Publications), 2004, 49-53 [my translation].

— 235 —

intimated throughout the last cycle, "Scent of Darkness."[24] The title of this cycle elicits multiple resonances within the Hebrew imagination, reflecting both a "A Window of Opportunity" within a narrow space transitioning to the more expansive space, or "a window of opportunity" as the end of its time draws near. Amidst the ongoing war in Israel-Palestine, every cease-fire is considered to be "a window of opportunity" or a "A Window of Opportunity"—a last ditch effort to approach that light of a different way of living at the end of a darkened tunnel. But that resolution, beyond laying down arms towards embracing the other in one's midst, appears forever in the offing as the poet will return to throw readers back "into the midst of war" by the final verse. And what kind of war is this exactly? A civil war? An international war? A cosmic war? Or a more personal spiritual war to recover a lost sense of authenticity? [25] The intertwining nature of the struggle allows each layer to cross-over, carrying forward the sense of synesthesia seen earlier.

But the direction of the "A Window of Opportunity " here for Kaploun moves beyond the political back to the spiritual, specifically the messianic. The opening is taking place in a moment of messianic supplication where: "here the arm leaned/upon a depressing memory:/a mourning lad praying,/like a flickering, extinguished star;/exposes an arm tenaciously./his eyes fireflies, and upon his head a crown of thorns." The mournful state of the unrealized messianic soul is a living memory that re-opens this watershed moment of awakening through praying and fasting. Supplications deepen into the darkness of the rupture through the embodied site of phylacteries. At this embodied site of memories encapsulated upon arm and head, through action and thought, this light flickers forth from the darkness. This shining forth from the "congenital darkness" of the poem is another way into "A Window of Opportunity" beyond crucifixion back to the devotional moment of messianism. Such a devotional moment is less about sacrifice through crucifixion, than it is a self-sacrifice. In sacrificing the self, a devotional self then emerges, re-emerging back into the stream of divine consciousness. That higher consciousness is struggling to re-unite with human consciousness through messianic yearnings.

---

24. Miron, "Yonadav Kaploun's Poetry: The Psalmody of Metaphysical Dissonance," 322-323.
25. Ibid., 323.

There is an emerging division in the messianism of "A Window of Opportunity " as symbolized in juxtaposing the images of two houses. More than mere juxtaposition, there is a *mise-en-abîme* operating here: "And another house—dark walls and cracked winepress—/beneath the house." The blueprint of the second house is already imprinted beneath the catastrophic ruins of the first house. This imprint upon the foundation stone of the first house bridges the terrestrial form to its celestial counterpart through an: "extended rainbow, pillars of the universe,/lustful writings, a flower, and a cat,/embittered-prophesy spilt — —" It is in the realm of this splitting that the facades of existence give way to a rustling of messianic consciousness. It is in these moments of rupture that convergence emerges wherein this redemptive impulse shines as a unitive wave of consciousness.

For this oscillation of such impulses to take place, there is necessity for rupture. Even within messianism itself, this movement is a subtle shifting from its destructive aspect to its constructive or redemptive aspect. Rather than follow a completely linear path, the messianic impulse straddles domains, its ebb and flow overlapping like a spiral. Each moment of this spiraling deeper brings into perspective the foundation stone that attempts to stay the abyss. That foundation stone of existence that is being straddled is the law. Sparks of illumination glimmer between annulment as fulfillment and rebuilding as redemption. This leads to moments fleeting in and out of antinomianism, into "a wavy night to lawlessness/from beneath this night," framed by silence. In the redemptive process, the laws of language itself are transformed through its embodiment.

Embodiment through the caress returns as the body begins to fall away. The question of embodiment returns the messianic soul back into awareness through the secret of a deeper caress. The poet seeking to reawaken such a sleeping consciousness thus embodied then wonders: "What should a remembering hand therefore do, pale from alarm?/Secretly caressing/the glow of the body that was,/that arm and that plot of neck./ At the crack of a window the remembering hand shall chronicle:" Here lies the magic of Kaploun's poetics in that the remembering hand is at once human and divine.

While "remembering" and "chronicling" is a language evoking the anthropomorphic vision of an accountant in the celestial spheres marshaling evidence against human subjects,[26] this same language ambiguously evokes the power of the aspirant engaged in the depth of prayer to instantiate self-transformation. After all, in the depth of any true prayer experience there is a convergence of human and divine consciousness. Such convergence opens a window into the evolution of such convergent consciousness upon its return. What is remarkable here is the degree to which this convergence amidst the rupture is opening a further chronicling of the road back to a future redemption.

That road of redemptive return needs some bridging between imagination and reality—an *imago templi* or an imaginal temple. Turning from the lone chronicling hand to the meeting of the "Beloved and mute stonemason" follows from the poet's beckoning the reader to "sit with me on one stone/lest we fall asleep." Losing awareness of the possibility of redemption is rendered through this recurring motif of falling asleep. Wakefulness, by contrast, comes in "facing the prolonged sunrise/There we sat/licking the gazelle." That fleeting presence of the divine beloved—often troped in Golden Age poetry as a gazelle—here becomes that convergence between the visionary poet and the adept stonemason. Together *imagination* (poet) and *reality* (stonemason) are transformed into the reality of redemption in merging with gazelle of the dawn. The very constitution of language itself has changed since their shared visionary experience at sunrise, seeing how: "Even several words stayed away/from the sun,/and stayed away from the new body, the divine."

Once language regains it redemptive capacity to convey human-divine yearnings, then prayer is also transformed. Prayer can no longer remain in rote, asphyxiating forms, so naturally the question arises: "About what should we lament,/how shall we sing?" Prayer is no longer *about* God; prayer *is* God. Such a transformation in prayer is not only in the realm of language, but also in the degree to which prayer now returns into its source so "... that everything is just a matter of Time"–that eternity within time, also known as God.

[26.] High Holiday liturgy, especially Reuven Kimmelman, "*Unetane Tokef* as a midrashic poem," *The Experience of Jewish Liturgu. Studies dedicated to Menahem Schmeltzer*, ed. D. Reed Blank (Leiden: Brill, 2011): 115-146

The journey to redemption of real temporality back into eternal time then turns to the "[h]arps upon the shore of days" and "a rabble of souls" in their yearning. This yearning is for a reunification of melody and word through the musicality of time. "Delectable and melancholic the scent of flesh/that overcame the scent of the sea" points to a surfacing and rebalancing of the non-manifest and the manifest by returning to the Flesh of the world. That Flesh bridges what earlier on for Merleau Ponty was the visible and the invisible. Awakening to this interworld of the Flesh through the sinews of the harp's strings is what allows for any seemingly delectable "dreamless sleep" to be transformed by the musicality of redemption.

The moment of gratitude that brings this poetic cycle to a close returns to the opening image of the broken down house. The vision is one to "behold a crack between the roofing tiles," only now the poet remarks upon a new level emerging from within the brokenness, so that there is "upon the roof a dove." To now be able to utter "Thank you" amidst the rupture means that the transition back to reality, "into the midst of war," is no longer devoid of hope. Rather, this transition back to the broken reality of war allows for a newfound resiliency amidst the rupture to re-orient the journey. So even though he is amidst the brokenness of war, when despair may reign supreme, the poet envisions reality otherwise–an unfolding redemptive reality. This reality is a tender moment of mystical vertigo in the redeeming embrace of eternal time within this fleeting temporal moment.

———————————— CHAPTER XI ————————————

I ALMOST VOWED TO TOUCH YOU: BREAKING THROUGH DOUBT TO DAILY *DEVEKUT*

ZELDA SCHNEERSON MISHKOVSKY'S "ON THAT NIGHT"

If only life, in all its complexity, could be summed up in six words or less![1] It would be too simplistic to see life as some philosophers would have it—"solitary, poore, nasty, brutish and short."[2] The challenge is to live with *simplicity* without being *simplistic*. Living simply *in the world* but *not of it*, the challenges do not disappear. Is it possible to navigate through the vagaries of life without the mooring of one's own soul anchored to God and the world? Touching God daily may indeed be a yearning of the poet and mystic alike, yet the sobering effect of reality is how much experience tends to be filled with an absence of the divine rather than a felt presence. Given this overwhelming sense of absence, does one give up in the seasons of spiritual draught or recommit to traversing onward?

No one has attempted so earnestly to bridge those moment of *devekut's* unraveling that underlies such seemingly barren moments as the poet Zelda.[3] A close reading of the poem by Zelda Schneersohn Mishkovsky

———

1. Not necessarily a new challenge, but considered novel in this age, see *It All Changed in an Instant: More Six Word Memoirs,* ed. Smith Magazine (New York: Harper Perennial, 2010); compare with the spiritual practice of few words containing much poetic depth, see Isshū Miura and Ruth Fuller Sasak, *The Zen Koan: Its history and use in Rinzai Zen* (New York: Harcourt, Brace & World, 1965).

2. Thomas Hobbes, "Of the Natural Condition of Mankind, as Concerning Their Felicity, and Misery," *Leviathan* (1651) (Cambridge: Cambridge University Press, 1904), Part I: Chapter XIII, 84.

3. For the major study of Zelda's biography and *oeuvre*, see Hamutal Bar-Yosef, *On Zelda's Poetry* [Hebrew] (Tel Aviv: *Hakibbutz Hameuchad*, 1988). See also Hillel Barzel, "Luminous Mirror of the Human Spirit," *Modern Hebrew Literature* 10 (1984): 35-37. More recently, for the first full length translation into English, see Marcia Falk, *The Spectacular Difference: Selected Poems of Zelda* (Cincinnati: Hebrew Union College Press, 2004); see also Varda Koch Ocker, "At the Turn of Childhood–A New Fruit by Zelda: An Annotated Translation," *Women in Judaism: A Multidisciplinary Journal*, Vol 4, No. 1 (2006); see also, Glazer, "A Butterfly Without Poise: Hermeneutics of Cordovero's *qefitzat ha-derekh* and *beḥina*—Path-Swerving through Zelda's Poetry," *Contemporary Hebrew*

(1914-1992) called "On That Night" will explore this very human predicament of disconnections and descents in *devekut*. That this poet became known simply by her first name is a testament to her accessibility in Israel as well as the intimacy she shared with Hebrew readers spanning a generation. Born in Russia in 1912, she passed away in Jerusalem in 1984. She was born in the city of Yekatrinoslav to Shelomoh Shalom and Rachel Schneersohn. Zelda's father was the great-great grandson of the third Lubavitcher Rebbe, known as the *Tzemach Tzedek* (Menachem Mendel Schneersohn). Her mother, Rachel Hen, descended from the Sephardic dynasty of Hen-Gracian, which traces its roots to eleventh-century Barcelona, Spain, while her paternal grandfather's grandfather, R. Elhanan ben Meir ben R. Elhanan, was a student of R. Shneur Zalman of Lyadi (1745-1812), the founder of HaBa"D Hasidism, solidifying this strong hasidic lineage. Thus Zelda grew up in a household imbued with deep spiritual roots.

Zelda's emigration to Israel with her mother in 1926 opened a new facet of her persona as a poet. While working as a teacher in Jerusalem she also painted and wrote poetry. On the surface, this somewhat bohemian lifestyle stood in stark contrast to her surroundings as well as her own personal observance. She remained in the ultra-orthodox milieu of *Ge'ula* in Jerusalem while soaring to artistic heights with the support of her husband. But it was only in 1967 that Zelda shepherded her first book of poems into full public view, for which she eventually won the acclaim of the Bialik Prize. Barren of her own biological children, Zelda's *Ge'ula* apartment was a sanctuary to all young artists in need. The most intriguing house guest that she eventually mentored early in her career as a poet was Yona Wallach (1944-1985). Wallach, a radical feminist, shocked her mentor, Zelda, when she published her controversial poem on *Tefillin* in *'Itton 77*, alongside one of Zelda's poems. This marked the end of their formal mentoring relationship, but that tension between a deep yearning for complete immolation in *devekut* and the need to remain responsibly grounded in this world continues to resonate in Zelda's poetry.

Oscillating between deep faith and doubt about the *Halacha* that regulated her life, so common among Hebrew poets spanning the past two

Mystical Poetry (New York: Edwin Mellen Press, 2009), 99-134.

centuries, nevertheless Zelda's poetry stands in a class all its own. Although Marcia Falk has contributed to the dissemination of Zelda's poetry into English, much work remains in appreciating the spiritual depths of *devekut* plummeted in the *œuvre* of this remarkable poet. Part of the challenge remains in how to read a poet so immersed in the hasidic tradition on her own terms, appreciating the nuances of a revolutionary spiritual lexicon that she is transmitting. There is little doubt that her poems are the record of mystical experience but there are indications of something more than "her intensely personal connection with the natural world" that Falk sees as central to Zelda's poetry.[4] As we now turn to one exemplary poem by Zelda, called "On That Night" let us consider again how it is possible to navigate through the vagaries of life without the mooring of one's own soul anchored in *devekut* to God and the world:

בַּלַּיְלָה הַהוּא

בַּלַּיְלָה הַהוּא
כַּאֲשֶׁר יָשַׁבְתִּי לְבַדִּי בֶּחָצֵר
הַדּוֹמֶמֶת
וְהִתְבּוֹנַנְתִּי אֶל הַכּוֹכָבִים –
הֶחְלַטְתִּי בְּלִבִּי,
כִּמְעַט נָדַרְתִּי נֶדֶר –
לְהַקְדִּישׁ עֶרֶב-עֶרֶב
רֶגַע אֶחָד,
רֶגַע קָט וְיָחִיד, לַיֹּפִי הַזֶּה הַזּוֹרֵחַ.

נִדְמָה
שֶׁאֵין לְךָ דָּבָר קַל מִזֶּה,
פָּשׁוּט מִזֶּה,
בְּכָל זֹאת לֹא קִיַּמְתִּי
אֶת שְׁבוּעָתִי
לִי.
מַדּוּעַ?
הֲלֹא גִּלִּיתִי כְּבָר
שֶׁמַּחֲשַׁבְתִּי נוֹשֵׂאת אֶל אַרְמוֹנֶיהָ
אֶת מַרְאֵה עֵינִי,
כְּאוֹתָהּ צִפּוֹר שֶׁנּוֹשֵׂאת בְּמַקּוֹרָהּ

4. See Falk, in "Nature and Spirituality in Zelda's Poetry," *The Spectacular Difference*, 12-23.

קַשׁ, נוֹצוֹת וּסְחִי לִבְדֹק הַקֵּן.
הֲלֹא גִּלִּיתִי כְּבָר שֶׁמַּחֲשַׁבְתִּי
נוֹטֶלֶת (אִם אֵין לָהּ דָּבָר אַחֵר)
אֲפִלוּ אֶת מְחוּשַׁי
לַעֲשׂוֹת מִזֶּה מִגְדָּלִים.
שֶׁהִיא נוֹטֶלֶת אֶת מְחוּשֶׁיהָ
שֶׁל שְׁכֶנְתִּי,
וְאֶת הַנָּזִיר שֶׁמִּתְגּוֹלֵל בֶּחָצֵר,
וְאֶת פְּסִיעוֹת הֶחָתוּל
וְאֶת מַבָּטוֹ הָרֵיק שֶׁל הַמּוֹכֵר,
וְאוֹתוֹ פָּסוּק שֶׁפִּרְפֵּר בֵּין דַּפֵּי הַסֵּפֶר -
וְעוֹשָׂה מִכָּל זֶה אוֹתִי,
כֵּן מִכָּל זֶה. מִכָּל זֶה.
מַדּוּעַ לֹא קִיַּמְתִּי אֶת שְׁבוּעָתִי
לִי?
הֵן הֶאֱמַנְתִּי
שֶׁאִם אַבִּיט רֶגַע קָט וְיָחִיד
אֶל גָּבְהֵי שָׁמַיִם מְכֻכָּבִים,
תִּשָּׂא מַחֲשַׁבְתִּי אֶל הָאַרְמוֹן
אֶת אוֹר הַמַּזָּלוֹת.
הֵן הֶאֱמַנְתִּי
שֶׁאִם אַבִּיט כָּךְ
לַיְלָה אַחַר לַיְלָה,
יֵהָפְכוּ הַכּוֹכָבִים
אַט-אַט
לִשְׁכֵנַי.
יֵהָפְכוּ הַכּוֹכָבִים
לִקְרוֹבַי.
יֵהָפְכוּ הַכּוֹכָבִים
לִילָדַי.
מַדּוּעַ לֹא קִיַּמְתִּי
אֶת שְׁבוּעָתִי לִי?
כְּלוּם שָׁכַחְתִּי
מַה מְּקַנְּאָה הָיִיתִי בְּיוֹרְדֵי-הַיָּם
וּבְאֵלֶּה שֶׁבֵּיתָם עַל חוֹף הָאוֹקְיָנוֹס.
כִּי אָמַרְתִּי בְּחָפְזִי
הָרוּחַ הָרַעֲנַנָּה שֶׁל הַיָּם
חוֹדֶרֶת לְחַיֵּיהֶם,
הָרוּחַ הָרַעֲנַנָּה שֶׁל הַיָּם
חוֹדֶרֶת לְמַחְשְׁבוֹתֵיהֶם, הָרוּחַ הָרַעֲנַנָּה
חוֹדֶרֶת לְיַחֲסֵיהֶם עִם שְׁכֵנֵיהֶם

וּלְיַחֲסֵיהֶם עִם בְּנֵי מִשְׁפְּחֹתָם.
הִיא מְנַצְנֶצֶת בְּעֵינֵיהֶם
וּמְשַׂחֶקֶת בִּתְנוּעוֹתֵיהֶם.
כִּי אָמַרְתִּי בְחָפְזִי
אֶמֶת-הַמִּדָּה לְמַעֲשֵׂיהֶם
הִיא אֶמֶת-הַמִּדָּה שֶׁל הַיָּם וְתִפְאַרְתּוֹ
וְלֹא זוֹ שֶׁל הָרְחוֹב הָאֱנוֹשִׁי
וְלֹא זוֹ שֶׁל הַסִּמְטָה הָאֱנוֹשִׁית.
כִּי אָמַרְתִּי בְחָפְזִי
רוֹאִים הֵם עַיִן בְּעַיִן
אֶת מַעֲשֵׂי אֱלֹהִים
וְחָשִׁים בִּמְצִיאוּתוֹ
בְּלִי הַמְּחִצּוֹת שֶׁלָּנוּ,
בְּלִי הֶסַּח-הַדַּעַת שֶׁלָּנוּ.
בָּכִיתִי תָּמִיד
שֶׁכְּלוּאָה הִנְנִי
בֵּין הַכְּתָלִים שֶׁל הַבַּיִת,
בֵּין כָּתְלֵי הָרְחוֹב
בֵּין הַכְּתָלִים שֶׁל הָעִיר,
בֵּין הַכְּתָלִים
שֶׁל הֶהָרִים.

בַּלַּיְלָה הַהוּא כְּשֶׁיָּשַׁבְתִּי לְבַדִּי
בֶּחָצֵר הַדּוֹמֶמֶת
גִּלִּיתִי פִּתְאֹם
שֶׁאַף בֵּיתִי בָּנוּי עַל הַחוֹף,
שֶׁחַיָּה אֲנִי עַל שְׂפַת הַיָּרֵחַ
וְהַמַּזָּלוֹת,
עַל שְׂפַת הַזְּרִיחוֹת וְהַשְּׁקִיעוֹת.[5]

On that night,
as I sat alone in the still
courtyard,
and contemplated the stars—
I almost took a vow—
to devote every evening
one moment,
a singly tiny moment,

---

5.   Zelda Schneerson Mishkovsky, "On that night" [Hebrew], *The Poetry of Zelda* (Tel Aviv: HaKibbutz Hameuchad, 1985), 13-15.

to this shining beauty.

It would seem
that there is nothing easier than this,
simpler than this,
still I haven't kept up
my oath
to myself.
Why?
Surely I've already discovered
that my mind carries to its palaces
the sights I see,
like that bird that carries in its beak
straw, feathers and dirt to repair its nest.
Surely I've already discovered that my imagination
uses (if it doesn't have anything else)
even my ailments
to build towers.
That is uses my neighbor's
ailments,
and the paper rolling in the courtyard,
and the cat's footsteps,
and the vacant look of the vendor,
and that verse quivering among the pages of
the book,
and out of all this, yes, out of all this,
out of all this, makes me.
Why haven't I kept my oath
to myself?
For yes, I did believe
that if I gazed one tiny moment
at the heights of the starry skies,
my mind would carry to the palace
the light of the constellations.
And yes, I did believe
that if I gazed so
night after night,
the stars would
slowly slowly
become my neighbors.
The stars would become

my kin.
The stars would become
my children.
Why haven't I kept my oath to myself?
Did I forget
how envious I was of the seafarers
and of those whose house was by the ocean
shore.
For I said in my haste
the fresh sea breeze
penetrates their lives,
the fresh sea breeze penetrates their thoughts;
the fresh breeze
penetrates their relationships with their
neighbors
and their relationships with their family
members.
It glitters in their eyes
and plays with their movement.
For I said in my haste
the yardstick of their deeds
is the yardstick of the sea and its glory
and not that of the human street,
not that of the human alley.
For I said in my haste,
they see eye to eye
God's works
and feel the divine presence
without our barriers,
without our distractions.
I wept constantly
imprisoned
among the walls of the house,
among the walls of the street,
among the walls of the city,
among the walls
of the mountains.

On that night, when I sat alone
in the silent courtyard,
I discovered suddenly

that my house too was built on the shore,
that I live on the bank of the moon
and the constellations,
on the bank of sunrises and sunsets.[6]

One night spent in deeper awareness of *devekut* changes everything for Zelda. Her ability to focus on the transformation of that night comes through the awareness gleaned by sitting alone. It is no coincidence that she enters into this state of awareness by focused concentration or *hitbonnenut*, a signature spiritual practice of her Hasidic lineage.[7] However, Zelda is specifically able to enter this spiritual state at the moment she steps outside in *hitbodedut* and has contemplated the stars. While a seemingly apt natural rather than supernatural point of contemplation, something is afoot here. And it is no accident that her revelation takes place in the setting of seclusion or *hitboddedut* as practiced by Jewish contemplatives and mystics through the ages.[8] Sitting in the deeper awareness brought on by seclusion is a necessary prerequisite for communing with God so that the prophetic touch may soon follow. The poet takes leave on a whirlwind quest from the cosmic realm into the bosom of mundane living and then back to the constellations anew. How does she manage to move in and out of these realms?

Her oscillations are realized by recording the mystical yearning, the flight to and fro. No matter how intense her intimacy in touching God, she must return to live *in the world*, even if she is no longer *merely of it*. This subtle balancing is already felt in the opening and closing verses by their usage of the demonstrative pronoun "that." It should strike the reader as curious that a devotional poet like Zelda chooses the language of "that night" rather than the traditional resonance of "this night" from the Passover *Haggadah*. In the language of refrain within the four questions, children and all other seekers at the *seder* are able to question the infrastructure of Jewish life this one night. Gaining an appreciation for the difference of this night, of this particular moment in one's life

---

6. Tranlsation by Varda Koch Ocker, with minor emendations.
7. On *hitbonnenut*, see for example, R. Shneur Zalman of Lyadi, *Tanya*, ch's 14, 43, 48, 50, etc.
8. Moshe Idel, "*Hitbodedut* as Concentration in Ecstatic Kabbalah," *Jewish Spirituality: From the Bible through the Middle Ages*, vol. I (New York: Crossroads, 1986), 405-438.

is essential in advancing the journey toward spiritual freedom. Although each year, the *Haggadah*'s return to the interrogation of why "this night" is different from all others is to be recited ritually, by contrast Zelda's "that night" is a moment in time she will not return to again. What she learned there at that moment is singular. The mystical experience came and went such that the distance is now detectable. Whereas philosophers of language like Ludwig Wittgenstein distinguish between demonstrative ("that") and indicative language ("this") as indices to a reality that sometimes escapes language and "goes on holiday,"[9] by contrast, mystical poets like Zelda need the distance to write about the unitive experience precisely where language fails. While language tends to escape the mystic in that singular moment of touching God, the poet recovers its fragments through the distance of her demonstrative language.

Another curious refrain is Zelda's quickness in judging herself. This critical self-examination really raises its head when she compares her earth-bound life with that of the sea-farer. The one who casts off to the great sea is singularly able to "... feel His presence/without barriers,/ without distractions." This leads Zelda to weep over her imprisoned human state, feeling more like a cast-away from the starry skies upon the earth, left to dwell within the city, within her house in the overpopulated streets of her *Ge'ula* neighborhood. Zelda willingly admits that she has been free before, but more than the walls of her apartment, the habits of the mind can be so imprisoning. She recalls how "It would seem/that there is nothing easier than this,/simpler than this," yet somehow she falls prey to the comfort of familiar thinking and spiritual sloth. Then she is ready to ask herself the most critical question—why has she abandoned this taste of freedom? She cannot fully comprehend why she would neglect this power she possesses as a spiritual being, as a poet, as a mystic: "Surely I've already discovered that my imagination/uses (if it doesn't have anything else)/even my ailments/to build towers." This same imagination [*makhshavti*] that inspires her deepest forays into the poetic realm is also the mind [*makhshava*] that imprisons in the familiar, in the mundane. Once she experiences her catharsis of tears,

---

9.   Ludwig Wittgenstein (1889-1951) and his philosophy of language as it affects Jewish Thinking is further explored elsewhere, most recently see Glazer, *A New Physiognomy of Jewish Thinking* (New York: Continuum, 2011), 123-130.

is she able to bridge her earthbound existence with the cosmic journey of the sea-farers. Only once she realizes "suddenly" that her ways of thinking through existence contain the possibility of a deeper imagination can she be liberated.

The danger of dualism, of floating in the sea of separation that composes so much of reality, is that it leads to indifference, apathy and eventually misanthropy. If the mind cannot make room for the deeper imaginal possibilities that experience the interconnectivity of the heavens and the earth then it leads to hasty judgments of disconnection. The effect of such self-destructive feelings that manifest through disconnections are felt in Zelda's repetitive echo of the first half of the verse in "I said in my haste, [all humans are deplorable]."[10] Much of this poem is Zelda's misprision[11] or crucial misreading of hasty judgment of the burning need for unitive *devekut* that leads to disconnection from humanity. Earlier in Psalm 116:7, the stormy soul is assuaged by the Psalmist in saying: "Be at rest, once again, O my soul,/for the Lord has been good to you." Such lost faith is restored as the next verse recalls how "You have delivered me from death,/my eyes from tears,/my feet from stumbling." Moving through the misanthropy at the abyss of death leads to a release in weeping that opens this wandering soul to her home in a more expansive cosmos that is her god. That trust in having a home of the spirit is restored in a self-recognition that she spoke rashly in a moment of great suffering. It is suffering, catastrophe and loss that will often rupture that abiding connective tissues between the soul and God. But even in death's embrace, the image of being bound up in the bonds of life, that spiritual connective tissue between the soul and its source, cannot ultimately be severed. Breaking through the daily doubt into a deeper *devekut* is the key in the poet's journey. Her honest spiritual limbo is nothing short of remarkable. By learning to recognize the ebb and flow of faith, the poet nuances the soul's yearning to stay connected to its source amidst the throes of mystical vertigo.

[10.] Psalm 116:11.

[11.] Harold Bloom, *Anxiety of Influence* (New York: Oxford University Press, 1997), 19-49.

CHAPTER XII

REBIRTHING *DEVEKUT* FROM DARKNESS TO LIGHT

HAVIVA PEDAYA'S "GENTLY PLEASE," "THE GOLDEN MOLTEN STREAM," "SUN-SPACE," "CRACK THE SUN," AND "MAJESTY MANACLED"

If human consciousness is marked by its yearning to reunite with its disrupted primal unity within the divine, then how does the human self reflect this yearning? This yearning is constantly occluded and neutralized through language. In a world where language accentuates opposition through dichotomies—dark and light, good and evil, masculine and feminine—the task of the poet through the poem is to explore that lost unity of word and experience. Although such oppositions appear to demarcate mundane existence, the language of the poem offers the possibility of returning through those very oppositions to the lost primal unity of divine-human consciousness. Such a *coincidentia oppositorium* or a "coincidence of opposites" allows for the rebirthing of self otherwise disconnected from this primal unity.[1]

This desire for rebirthing self through a diversity of experiences is felt most strongly in the poetry of Haviva Pedaya. [2] Her unique poetry—mystical to the point of alchemical—transforms darkness into light. It is precisely from the beginnings of darkness that light shines forth in Haviva's poetry, positioning it at the interstices of contemporary Hebrew cultures of Israel. While perhaps less known through her Iraqi mystical lineage as granddaughter of the renowned mystic and dream interpreter, R. Yehudah Ftayya (1859-1942), Haviva's poetry is hailed as visionary by novelists like Amos Oz and sung by rock artists like

---

[1] On *coincidentia oppositorium* as *akhdut ha'shave*, see Gershom Scholem, *Origins of the Kabbalah*, trans. R. J. Z. Werblowsky (Princeton University Press: Princeton 1987), 312.

[2] This theme of rebirthing of redemption in Pedaya has been explored elsewhere; see Aubrey L. Glazer, "Rebirthing Redemption: Hermeneutics of *gilgul* from *Beit Lehem Yehudah* into Pedaya's Poetry," *Kabbalah: Journal for the Study of Jewish Mystical Texts* 11 (2004): 49-83.

Meir Banai and Barry Sokoroff.[3] Pedaya's foray into the renassiance of liturgical poetry in Israel known as *piyyut*, most notably through her performance-based group dedicated to reviving Judeo-Iraqi music with the *Yonat Rekhokim Ensemble,* allows her poetics to hover between categories—whether religious and secular, ultra-nationalist and spiritualist, popular and esoteric—as this strong voice of poetry in all its lyrical hybridity emerges.

A hermeneutical alchemy is at play in the poems that follow. By way of transforming their beginnings from darkness to emanations of light, a sealed desire is liberated back into the words of this first poem:

כ״ח.

אָנָא בְּרֹךְ

אָנָא בְּכֹחַ

תַּתִּיר נַפְשִׁי צְרוּרָה

אָנָא גַעְגּוּעִים וְהָמְיָה

דְּרוּשִׁים לִי יוֹתֵר מִן הַקַּיָּם

שֶׁאֶכְסֹף

וּכְלוּם לֹא יָבוֹא

אֲבָל שֶׁלֹּא אַפְסִיק לְבַקֵּשׁ

אָנָא הַחֲזֵר בִּי מִלִּים שֶׁנָּתַתָּ בִּי פַּעַם טְהוֹרוֹת

וְאֹמַר

אָנָא רַחֵם

הַיּוֹם הַיּוֹם וְלֹא מָחָר

אָנָא בַּשֵּׂר שֶׁגַּם אִם אֶתְמַהְמַהּ

בּוֹא אָבוֹא

וּבַדְּבָרִים עַצְמִי אָתֵּן אֲנָא

זְכֹר אוֹתִי

עַל אֲשֶׁר אִחַלְתִּיךְ לִי וְלֹא

עַל אֲשֶׁר אָדָם אֲנִי וָמֵת

עַל אֲשֶׁר קִירוֹת הַגּוּף נֶפֶשׁ מַכָּה

רוֹצָה תֵּעָקֵר

מַכָּה עַצְמָהּ צוֹוַחַת

אָנָא בָּרוּךְ

אָנָא בָּרֵךְ אֲנָא

הֲבֵן אוֹתִי שֶׁאֲנִי עֲרִירִית

שֶׁאֵין לִי לְמִי לְגַלּוֹת מַחֲלָתִי

---

3.   See Glazer, "Rebirthing Redemption," 60-61.

שֶׁלֹּא הֲבַנְתִּי בַּזְּמַן שֶׁגוּפִי הוּא אֲנִי
וּכְשֶׁהֲבַנְתִּי לֹא יָדַעְתִּי נַפְשִׁי
לֹא מָצָאתִי מוֹצָא לַבֶּכִי כִּי יַכֶּה
כִּי אֵין
אָנָּא הָבֵן אוֹתִי שֶׁאֲנִי צְרִיכָה קְצָת זְמַן
לַחֲשֹׁב אֶת סִכּוּיֵי הַפְּרִיחָה
אִם יֵשָׁם עוֹד
וְשֶׁאֲנִי מֵאֵימָה נוֹבֶלֶת
וּבֹקֶר לְבֹקֶר מְקִיאָה
וְלַיְלָה לְלַיְלָה יְאַיֵּם גַּעַת
וְדַעַת שְׁאוֹל לַשְׁאוֹל יַגִּיעַ
וְאֵין לִי סִכּוּי עוֹד לִבְרֹא מִלִּים בְּצַלְמִי וּבְדָמִי
וְלָתֵת בָּהֶן נְשָׁמָה
אַחַת שָׁאַלְתִּי אוֹתָהּ אֲבַקֵּשׁ
שֶׁבְתְּךָ בִּי תִּתֵּן בִּי נְשָׁמָה
אַחַת בָּכִיתִי בְּזָכְרִי אוֹתִי
שֶׁאָז כְּשֶׁהִתְפַּלַּלְתִּי מְאוּם לֹא חָסַרְתִּי
וְעַתָּה שֶׁכֻּלּוֹם לֹא אֹבֶה
הַכֹּל בִּי נִרְמָס אָנָּא חֹן אוֹתִי וְרַחֵם
בְּרֶכֶם יְמֵי טָהֲרֵם
כְּבַת גַּדְלָם בּוֹכָה עָלַי בָּבַת
אָנָּא אִם תּוּכַל

XXVIII.

O, Gently please
forcefully please
release my bound soul
please I need longing and sighing
more than what exists
may I yearn
and nothing come
but may I not stop asking
please give me words you once gave me pure
and I will say
please have pity
today today and not tomorrow
please declare that even if I tarry
I will surely come
and I will place myself in words please

remember me
for having wished for me and not
for my being dead
for a soul's striking the body's walls
wishing to be uprooted
striking itself crying
please blessed one
please bless please
understand me for I am barren
for I have no one to whom to reveal my sickness
for I did not understand in time that my body is me
and when I understood I did not know my soul
I found no outlet for my weeping when it strikes
as there is no-thing
please understand me for I need some time
to calculate the chances of flowering
whether more devastation will come
and I wither from terror
and vomit every morning
and every night threatens touch
and netherworld intuition reaches such knowing below
and I have no more chance of creating worlds in my image and blood
and giving them spirit
one word I desired, after it shall I seek
your dwelling in me your en-souling me
one thing I cried when I remembered myself
for then when I prayed I lacked nothing
and now that I desire nothing
everything is trampled within me so please be gracious to me and pity
bless my days purify them
raise them like a daughter crying over the apple of her eye
O, if you can please[4]

While Pedaya's poem may appear untitled by numbering it as the twenty eighth poem in her debut collection, she numerologically alludes to the very alchemical power [ko"ah=28] of *Ana b'Koah*. To access that hidden point of inner illumination or "sun-space" the poet draws upon mystical

---

4. Haviva Pedaya, *Mi-teva Stuma (From a Sealed Ark)* (Am Oved: Tel Aviv, 2002), 73-74; I have consulted with the translations of Harvey Bock and Peter Cole.

gnosis—drawn from esoteric traditions as well as from direct personal experiences. This depth of knowing is embedded in the ancient mystical poem, called, *Ana b'Koah*. Once concealed within the inner chambers of amulets for fertility and exorcism, this theurgic poem is attributed to the first-second centuries sage, R. Nehunya ben Hakanah. His magical poem, *Ana b'Koah,* is a forty-two letter divine name often inscribed within amulets to overcome death through "an aura of superlativer sanctity and awe" as encapsulated in the acrostic of sevenfold lines of six words.[5] This transformative matrix has been transmitted through generations, preserving the structural form while imbuing it with new words of poetry as evinced by other Iraqi mystics.[6] So notice how the poem of Pedaya follows in this alchemical trajectory, somewhat swerving the inherited poetic structuralism through the power of her free verse plea. That plea is to restore the power of language to rebirth redemption as she enters into a *devekut* of darkness—both somatic and creative—bringing forth light.

Although the poet desires to begin within the traditional word forms of the inherited mystical prayer, *Ana b'Koah,* from the beginning her desire rapidly exceeds the poetic form: "O, Gently please/forcefully please/release my bound soul." Splitting open the linearity of tradition, embodied by R. Yehudah Ftayya's desire to "open sealed words/of swallowed souls" [*va-eftakh teivot setumot*] are Pedaya's concentric poetic pleas. [7] She beckons with the source of all creative desire to ensure that the ensuing alchemy take place gently. Notwithstanding the immensely transformative power of *Ana b'Koah*'s alchemy of words, the poet hopes her reconstitution of self will emerge intact with a remnant of her incessant desire that brought her to this experience of *devekut* in the first place.

But as the poem progresses and reaches the twenty eighth line, the expectation is growing that something will be revealed or pointed to that is transformative. Yet at this very point, Pedaya seals up the alchemical amulet

---

5.   Joshua Trachtenberg, *Jewish Magic and Superstition* (Philadelphia: University of Pennsylvania Press, 2004), 90, 95, 174.

6.   For example, see one such poetic transformation by another Iraqi mystic, *Ben Ish Hai,* with his rendition of *Ana b'Koach* as *Ana b'Hasadim Gedolim Ya'ir Tiferet Tzaddik,* see R. Yosef Hayyim (1832-1909), *Leshon Hakhamim* (Jerusalem: Yehudah Amrat Itakh Publications, 1957), 55-57.

7.   See Glazer, "Rebirthing Redemption," 60-61; Yehudah Ftayya, "*Zekhut Rachel,*" *Makhberet Asirai ha-Tiqvah* [Hebrew] (Jerusalem: Hazon Ftayya, 1987), 30.

of the poem she has opened by admitting that: "I found no outlet for my weeping when it strikes/as there is no-thing." This earnest, almost naïve admission at the heart of the poem raises questions about the experiential gaps intrinsic to the radical transcendence of monotheism. When the yearning to dissolve in the *devekut* of desire strikes, the poet returns to the words of tradition that can no longer contain that very desire. And the deeper she enters into the darkness of her desire, the more she encounters the no-thing that dwells in this heart of darkness. This mystical experience of aphophasis—*saying* through *unsaying* into negation—is precisely what allows the poet to find her voice and reconstitute her selfhood through the alchemy of the word. Although the poet has been strengthened by this encounter with the darkness of No-thing, a question lingers at the final verses of the poem: "and now that I desire nothing/everything is trampled within me so please be gracious to me and pity/bless my days purify them/raise them like a daughter crying over the apple of her eye/O, if you can please." Can the poet continue to write and insodoing give birth to poems in the afterglow of this alchemical moment of *devekut*? Is the poet still capable of drawing on these divine powers? Is the source of inspiration itself replenishable?

This lingering question of poetic inspiration and its longevity that comes from incessant desire for *devkeut* is a recurring theme in Pedaya's poetry. In returning to the wellspring of creativity, the poet must continually be ready to venture forth deeper into the darkness in order to transform it into the light of the word. That perennial quality to the journey of the poet is strongest in the following three poems, "Crack the sun," "Majesty manacled" and "Sun-space" which we now turn to.

The daily discipline of writing by opening anew the sealed words nestled in darkness happens through the cracking of light on the horizon, through the contradiction of opposites happening in this opening poem in *From A Sealed Word*:

א.

קְרַע שֶׁמֶשׁ וְהִיא אֲדָמָה

בְּתוֹךְ דְּמָעוֹת רַבּוֹת בְּזִיזָתָה
עֲשָׂאוּהָ כִּכְבָרָה

הַשָּׁמַיִם לוּחַ שָׁחוֹר

וּמִישֶׁהוּ רוֹשֵׁם

צְפוּיָה לְךָ הַתְחָלָה נִפְלָאָה

מְחַק שָׁמַיִם טְהוֹרִים פָּנֶיךָ דָּבָר

בָּם לֹא רָשׁוּם עַד

כְּדֵי כָּךְ נְקַיִּים לֹא קִנְאָה

לֹא אַהֲבָה

יוֹם יוֹם מִתְאַוָּה קְבוּרָתָהּ

בְּרִגְשָׁתְךָ פָּקְעָה

דְּגֵיהָ בְּמַעֲמַקַּיךְ נוֹשֵׁר זְהָבָם

קֶרַע קֶרַע לִבְּךָ בּוֹלְעָם

זוֹ בֵּזַּת הַיָּם[8]

I.

Crack the sun & she's reddening

Plundered in her many tears
punctured as a sieve

Black board sky
as someone inscribes
your wondrous start foreseen

Efface pure heavens, your face a word
in them, not inscribed till
the point of clarity neither dirge
nor love

Day by day desiring her setting, burial in the sea

In your passions split

---

8.   Haviva Pedaya, *Mi-teva stuma* (*From a Sealed World*) [Hebrew] (Am Oved: Tel Aviv, 2002), 5.

Her fish into his depths, peeling their gold
cra-cra-crack your heart swallowing them

This is the sea's plunder.[9]

The process of cracking through the dark night of the soul into the illumined daybreak of consciousness takes place here through the symbol of the sun at dawn. As the day breaks, one would expect that any loosening of the boundaries between sentient realms would be reconstituted with the ordering power of light. However, light here functions to expand rather than contract the realms above and below. As the goldfish are "peeling their gold" swimming from the ocean of water to light, there are the sounds of the crows cawing—a Hebrew homophone at once, tearing, happening and reading—that give wings to rays of sun, ultimately plummeting into the plunder of the sea. In the midst of an alchemical moment of *devekut*, why focus on this plunder?

This plunder—a combination of jewels, weapons and food—remains a timeless symbol of materiality gone awry. The plunder of the vanquished Egyptian army at the Red Sea was even greater than the plunder the Israelites took with them upon their exodus from Egypt. Each valuable collection of booty stolen and reappropriated from enemies *seems necessary* to sustain and empower the Children of Israel to make their way to the Promised Land—necessary for those of little faith in the power of divine redemption. [10] *What then*—decries the poet—*is the cost of redemption from darkness to light? From Egypt to Israel?* Pedaya is constantly struggling with balancing her desire for *devekut* and her responsibility for the *other* amidst the afterglow of the Promised Land's illumination that is the Israel her ancestors emigrated to and that today she continues to dwell in. While the Land of Israel may be holy, stepping in to settle it with plunder from Egypt and the Red Sea contaminates that untarnished spiritual desire. Such a sentiment of exile within her homeland is felt in other poems like "Rachel Corrie, *in memoriam*"[11] and "A Man Goes"[12] insofar as the price tag of Hebrew identity reveals all its woundedness in the Hebrew language

9.   Translation by Aubrey Glazer 2001, 2012.
10. *Yalkut Shimoni Bo* §12:67a; *Bashalach* § 234.
11. Haviva Pedaya, *uncollected.*
12. Haviva Pedaya, *D'yo Adam* (*Blood's Ink*) [Hebrew] (Tel Aviv: *Kibbutz haMeuchad*, 2009), 54-56.

itself. So here in the poem at hand, the source of illumination itself is ashamed, recalling Ibn Gabirol's lament, once her light source opens, she blushes: "Crack the sun & she's reddening/Plundered in her many tears." Those tears of the sun intertwine with the sorrow of the Red Sea, co-operating with the the angels to exterminate one group of humans while freeing another. Yet even the angels sing out in sorrow.

This overwhelming lament of the poet and the Zion she yearns for is reflected in this pathetic fallacy of the shamed sun burying herself in her tears, bleeding into the Red Sea. As the bodies wash up on the shore of the Red Sea writhing in their final agony, the Egyptians witness their own destruction amdist the victory of the Israelites. To see the suffering on the other side of the plunder—whether in Egypt, at the Red Sea, or on the streets and checkpoints of contemporary Israel/Palestine—remains the poet's calling. The interbeing of suffering that affects the spiritual eco-system is embodied by the poet in her lament for the Land of Israel. Initially there is the horrible possibility, in this poem, that the corpses of the *other* will remain unburied, so that a debate between the sea and the earth ensues over ultimate responsibility for burial. Each natural realm blames the other for the slaughter of this people, but ultimately the earth relents and agrees to swallow the corpses by way of recompense for Pharaoh's belated acknowledgement of the justice of his afflictions. The earth's hesitation is instructive here insofar as its crust recalls with horror being cursed for having sucked up Abel's blood after being slain by his brother.[13] That fear and horror of being cursed for remaining in her Holy Land swimming in the blood of the *other* inspires much of Pedaya's alchemical poetry as well as her prophetic impulse.

Such a shift away from the earth out to the limitless sea and upwards to the infinite sun can also be seen in the following poem:

מקום שמש

מָקוֹם שֶׁמֶשׁ זָבַח מְאוֹרָיו וַיִּבְעַר
מָקוֹם זָנַח קַרְנָיו וַיַּךְ סָלַע רֹאשׁוֹ רַךְ
מָקוֹם הֻתּוּר מָקוֹם הַכְּמִיהָה
מָקוֹם פָּשׁוּט מָקוֹם נוֹאָשׁ
מָקוֹם לִבִּי שָׁאַף זָרַח

---

13. For example, see Louis Ginzberg, "Destruction of the Egyptians," *Legends of the Jews*, 1

Sun-space

Sun-space sacrificed its light & 'twas blazing
a space that abandoned its horn-light, & 'twas beating stone, tender-head
a space of complacence, a space of yearning
a simple space, a frantic space
a space my heart inhaled, shone[14]

The place of yearning is for an "intelligence of the heart [that] connotes a simultaneous knowing and loving by means of imaging." Embodied as the "Sun-space" it "glows in the center of our being and radiates outward, magnanimous, paternal, encouraging." It appears to be an external symbol that is really an inner, *imaginal* light. The poet's "Sun-space" is that primal space of few words that opens to taste the timelessness of the divine that dwells within every human heart. Standing as the coincidence of opposites as: "a space of complacence, a space of yearning/a simple space, a frantic space," this "Sun-space" is the spiritual organ of the heart. It is only in connecting the illumined center of the heart—the splendorous mystical sphere known as *Tiferet*—with the "tender-head" that the hand is able to bring forth the poem.

Behind the more elevated and dynamic symbol of the sun lies its earthly counterpart, embodied in the symbolic form of the king. Given the preponderance of the king as a symbol of illumination and majesty within Jewish mysticism and liturgy, once again it is the poet-as-alchemist who returns to those hackneyed words to attempt a transformation of their darkest denotations into the light of an innovative connotation:

ט"ו.

מֶלֶךְ אָסוּר יָפְיֵךְ
מֶלֶךְ אֲבָרִים אֲבָרִים
מֶלֶךְ נִכְבָּל
מֶלֶךְ לֹא אַחֲרַיִךְ בִּכְיִי
מֶלֶךְ מוֹשְׁכֵנִי מֶלֶךְ נָרוּצָה
אֵיכָה מִתּוֹכִי בָא
אֵיכָה נֶחְבָּא

---

14. Haviva Pedaya, *Motzah haNefesh* (*AnimaBirthing*) [Hebrew] (Am Oved: Tel Aviv, 2002), 24; translation by Aubrey Glazer 2005, 2012.

אֹמַר לְךָ דָּבָר

לֹא יָדַעְתִּי דָּבָר

וְכָל שֶׁיָּדַעְתִּי כְּאַיִן

כִּי כָּל זֶה הָיָה לִפְנֵי שֶׁעַיִן רְאִיתִיךְ

בְּעַיִן

מֶלֶךְ אַיֵּה מֶלֶךְ הִנֵּה

וְחֹשֶׁךְ מַה לְּךָ יוֹצֵר וְאַהֲבָה מַה לְּךָ בּוֹצֵר

הַתֵּר הַתֵּר

אַתָּה מְיַסֵּר[15]

XV.

Majesty manacled in Your beauty

King limbs upon limbs

King fettered

Majesty my tears are not for You

Majesty draws me, King shall we follow

from where within me are you coming

where are you hidden

a word shall I say to you

a word I knew not

& all I knew as no-thing

for this was all before any eye could see you

in the eye

Majesty O where, King here

& what's darkness to you, O Illuminator, & what's love to you, O Reaper

unbind unbind

tormenting you.[16]

Struggling with the majestic symbol of the monarchic within the theosophic spheres relates to the poet's earlier yearning for her "Sun-space" of *Tiferet*. Too often that yearning is eclipsed by this majesty of this rootedness in *Malkhut* that is "manacled" and "fettered." While the poet begins tapping into her desire by returning to the words of traditional

---

15. Haviva Pedaya, *Mi-teva stuma*, 44.
16. Translation by Aubrey Glazer 2001-2003, 2012.

liturgy with the "King," her desire for the limitless nature of this majesty exceeds the delimited symbol of any king.

The poet's desire for *devekut*, seeking to dissolve into her "Sun-space" will not be satiated by a reified, patriarchal symbol that keeps her at the distance of a servant. Rather, the poet is yearning to enter into his innermost chamber, as evinced in another poem called, "The King": "O King, bring me into your chamber/for days I've been expecting/and nothing have I seen." [17] It is in gap of "no-thing" between desire and reality where the poet feels her exile most strongly. Yearning for the King of Kings dwelling in the heart of her "Sun-space" where inner illumination shines, the poet prays: "Majesty O where, King here/& what's darkness to you, O Illuminator, & what's love to you, O Reaper/unbind unbind/tormenting you." A prayerful poem hovering between darkness and light must call on the powers of the King as Illuminator of light and Reaper of death. It is in the alchemy of her prayerful poetry that Pedaya draws these opposing powers into a coincidence that brings deeper unification.

Pedaya's poetry transforms the dark night of the soul into the light of her sun-space. It is precisely from the beginnings of darkness that light shines forth in the sealed words of Pedaya's poetry. As a Hebrew poet whose desire for *devekut* in word and experience is insatiable, Pedaya tears open the language of traditional forms in both the Jewish mysticism and Judeo-Iraqi liturgy of her upbringing to enter into more personal and embodied relation with an intimate transcendence. Such a unique poetry—mystical to the point of alchemical—while retaining its primal roots in song, positions her poetry to be dancing over the divide of contemporary Hebrew cultures of Israel to rebirth its nascent redemption.

---

[17]. Haviva Pedaya, *D'yo Adam*, 58.

CHAPTER XIII

CODA
GROSS, SUBTLE AND SECRET MOMENTS OF
DEVEKUT

Between vertigo and exactitude, between the strange and the familiar, between *other* and *self* as encountered in this contemporary Kabbalistic Hebrew Poetry, there has been a crossing-over of conundrums, cataclysms and conjunctions. Processing the constellation of experiences, this journey has been oscillating through subtle degrees of *devekut* in Jewish mysticism, common to Hasidic spiritual practice, namely: (1) exteriorized fervor; (2) interiorized stillness; (3) enrapturing ascent. Entranced by this oscillating dance of *devekut*—reaching *but not reaching*, hovering *but not hovering*, touching *but not touching*—an impulse has been pulsating more rapidly and more deeply. It is experience of that impulse of mystical vertigo which has been articulated most strongly through the language of some of the contemporary Kabbalistic Hebrew Poetry presented here in this study.

In truth, such categorization of degrees can never escape its heuristic limitations—place holders in an eternal dance. Whether these degrees of *devekut* are mapped from: (1) the instinctual, lower-mind/moving center; (2) to the heart-mind/brain center; (3) to the integral, higher-mind/mind-heart center;[1] or whether these degrees are categorized as: (1) Gross [*hitzoni*]; (2) Subtle [*emtza'i*]; (3) Secret [*penimi*];[2] one constant remains—the longing to connect the secret, mind-heart center with the subtle, brain center through the gross, moving center. This subtle process of the soul touching the fullness of its divine origins, as I have argued here, is itself undergoing transformation in the contemporary twenty-first century cultural matrices of Israel and its Hebrew sub-cultures—both devotional and poetic.

[1.] Mohammad H. Tamdgidi and J. Walter, *Gurdjieff and Hypnosis: A Hermeneutic Study* (New York: Palgrave Macmillan, 2009), 81n1.

[2.] R. Yitzhaq Maier Morgenstern, *YaM haHokhmah* (Jerusalem: Mechon YaM haHokhmah, 5771/2011), 642-4.

This journey began nestled deep within the hybrid networks of *haredi* worlds of Israel today, through the lens of a remarkable exemplar of devotional Hebrew sub-cultures—R. Yitzhaq Maier Morgenstern. The innovative side of his thinking continues to influence the devotional praxis of *devekut,* both inside and outside these contemporary Hebrew sub-cultures. Mystical apperception through *devekut,* for Morgenstern, expands beyond a mystical-magical charisma and hypernomian spiritual practice. Rather it is Morgenstern's hybridized mystical subjectivity that provides a matrix for rethinking the lived practice of the ever-pulsating devotional life of *devekut.*

Reflecting further on this alternate constellation of *devekut*—as translated through the non-dualist lexicon of Sri Aurobindo[3]—allows Morgenstern's innovation to come into clearer relief. These moments of Gross [*hitzon*], Subtle [*emtza'i*], Secret [*penimi*] touching allow for a different perspective on *devekeut.* (1) The Gross level [*hitzon*] traces the contour of topology[4] as vessel where the restoration [*tiqqun*] takes place, whereas in the Secret level [*penimi*] there is no change, and thus no restoration possible. (2) The Subtle level [*emtza'i*] sparkles to influence how the Gross level [*hitzon*] is manifesting as it seeks to integrate the Gross [*hitzon*] with the Secret [*penimi*] levels. Such integration is possible once there is a unification of the Gross [*hitzon*] with the Secret [*penimi*] levels. (3) Light from the Secret level [*penimi*] is so integrated it can be considered causal as it then emanates into the Gross level [*hitzon*]. This is where the capacity to transform and evolve what appears as manifestation becomes a spiritual reality.[5]

Looking at apperception through another ray of the speculum allows for an enriching exploration of contemporary Jewish mysticisms, beyond the mystical treatise and other textual boundaries. In dancing over the divide of those boundaries, in the second chapter the case was made for contemporary Jewish Mysticism and its need for poetry. Poetry is the contemporary record of intimate mystical apperception. Although Admiel

---

3. Sri Aurobindo Ghose, *The Life Divine* (Wilmot: Lotus Light Publications, 1990), 274.

4. Emmanuel de Saint Aubert, *Vers Une Ontologie Indirecte: Sources et enjeux critiques de l'appel à l'ontologie chez Merleau-Ponty,* "Topologie de la chair et topologie de l'être" (Paris: Vrin, 2006), 221-251.

5. Ibid., 274; see also, Morgenstern, *YaM haHokhmah* (5771/2011), 642-643 n. 2.

Kosman's poem, "Our God," nears its integral turn, such a turning towards non-dual consciousness still needs to let go of any binary distinction between the "god that's broken, & the *gurnesht,* no-thing," and the absolute infinite. By contrast, through a deep diaphaneity, Avraham ben Yitzhak's "When Nights Grow White" conveys how a new "spirit from eternity blows," perceiving the soul awakening to its integral origin in the whole. As an intimate record of mystical apperception, such poetry attunes the individual to the concretion of the spiritual, opening each and every soul to ~~touching~~ God.

Another constellation emerges in reading diachronically through the ensuing chapters—disconnection as connection, rupture as rectification. The explosive and disorienting *dissemiNation* of *devekut* of the third chapter challenges how cultural mosaics within Israel by necessity connect deeper amidst its phantasmagoric fusion in Agi Mishol's poems "Woman Martyr" & "Transistor *Muezzin.*" The descent into darkness continues by another degree in the ninth chapter through the parables and prayers of love and rape in Tamar Elad-Appelbaum's "Psalms for Jerusalem." *Devekut,* amidst the ruptures within dualism, opens both women's poetry to a depth of the female and a flow of the feminine self otherwise untouched.

Darkness and its descent for the sake of ascent through many degrees simultaneously take place in the tenth chapter throughout Yonadav Kaploun's epic cycles "Scent of Darkness" & "A Window of Opportunity." While these cycles are linked through their shared spatio-temporal rupture marked on the Seventeenth of Tammuz, the poet opens before the reader a masterful journey. As the yearning for *devekut* deepens, the poet accesses at once diverse degrees; from Gross [*hitzoni*] to Subtle [*emtza'i*] to Causal [*penimi*] levels. A synesthetic dissolution from Gross [*hitzoni*] to Subtle [*emtza'i*] *devekut* is at play in "Scent of Darkness" while "A Window of Opportunity " returns to present day Israel by fluttering between Gross [*hitzoni*] and Causal [*penimi*] degrees of *devekut.*

Once these spatio-temporal ruptures cause a fissure within normative dualistic thinking and living, then contrition follows within the soul. Otherwise sealed off, in the fourth chapter there is a pathway of return open to *devekut* through Binyamin Shevili's cycle "Contrition." As the heart and mind are opened from closure, poetry in the eighth chapter cycles outside/in further by disentangling intuitive time from eternal time in Binyamin Shevili's "HomosexuELity" with *(Hit)Devekut* as *durée* of the godlover. While *Devekut* can be ruptured through time, it can also be rectified through time.

Yet another constellation emerges by moving synchronically through the fifth, sixth and seventh chapters. By questioning whether there is duplicity in *devekut*, Schulamith Hava Halevy's poems "Strange Fire" & "Impregnation's Secret" open secrecy. Her poetry of coercion and impregnation reveals a concealed non-dual mystical apperception. A doubling of secrecy oscillates whereby transmigration is an embodied secret and impregnation is an ensouled secret. Only when existence continues to dance—oscillating between embodiment and ensoulment—can the opening of secrecy reveal redemption. Getting caught in this dance is only possible with the aid of Infinity Catchers. To sense *devekut* as a web of thinking, Shai Tubaly reveals this path through the sixth chapter with his poems "Infinity Catchers," "Come Here," and "I Came to God." Emerging from naked nets quivering, that oceanic feeling of *devekut* abounds. Through the seventh chapter there is a descent for the sake of ascent into an auto-erotic cosmogeny as *devekut* to divine self. While God is in the process of rebirthing as self through Haya Esther's epic poem, *My Flesh Speaks G!d*, by the eighth chapter any lingering sense of unity is once again cracked open through the contrition of the soul.

A coda within this coda are the eleventh and twelfth chapters, each revealing something daring—the centrality of indeterminacy and sacred doubt surrounding *devekut*.[6] Both in Zelda Schneerson Mishkovsky's "On that night" as well as in several of Haviva Pedaya's poems that confront the No-thing at the heart of *devekut*, it becomes a kind of religious obligation to return to a spiritual moment when the poet almost vows to touch God. In their inimitable ways, both mystical and mundane, Zelda and Pedaya each dare to confront the lingering doubt ingrained on the underside of *devekut*.

From the depth of *devekut* experiences, the poet sees that there is always a level beyond the tension of any oscillation. The poet sees that the highest level of realization is not discernible—*devekut* does not simply rest in the nature of the mind or not. The point of the integral

---

6. To be explored in a forthcoming study.

level of diaphaneity is that the individual is not compelled to be in one particular level or degree of *devekut*; namely, the poet is neither removed from phenomena nor subject to their influence. The poet of *devekut* is no longer reactive, no longer identifying with those reactions, lest she obstruct integration. *Devekut* thus oscillates between a palpable state of blissful energy motivating one's devotion [*Rachel*] and a non-palpable state motivated by a selfless devotion to connect [*Leah*].[7] But there is a level beyond alternation which is the level of the flow of Pure Compassion [*Attik Yomin/Arikh Anpin*]. In Hebrew poetry, as in all strong poetry, there is no love more supreme.

How fitting then to spiral back through the opening network of *haredi* sub-cultures of Jerusalem—from the *Ge'ulah* neighborhood, where Zelda could envision from one end of the universe to the other, to the *Tel Arza* neighborhood, where Morgenstern continues thinking, practicing, writing, and guiding a hybridized spiritual elite to be entranced into *devekut*. Whether the yearning calls out from the depths or from the straits, that subtle touch is always nearby, the secret already embodied. As with all strong poets, these Hebrew poets merely dance this longing—to connect the *secret*, mind-heart center with the *subtle*, brain center through the *gross*, moving center—homewards through mystical vertigo.

---

7. Morgenstern, *YaM haHokhmah* (5771/2011), 656.

AFTERWORD

To Pray After Praying/To Dance With No Feet

Raise a tent of shelter now
though every thread is torn
Dance me to the end of love

Leonard Cohen

Jacques Derrida once wrote, "So, when this break, this interruption happens in the everyday life, on the exceptional moment of prayer, we are going back to the name, to the name of the name, a nameless name, or a placeless place... We don't simply address someone, we pray to someone—God if you want, some unique one, to allow us to pray... It's praying after the prayer—*prier après la prière*—which is the prayer before the prayer, the prayer for the prayer."[1]

It strikes me that these words serve well as a summation of the philosophical-theological reflections proffered in Aubrey L. Glazer's *Mystical Vertigo: Contemporary Hebrew Poetry; Dancing Over the Divide.* Apart from the immensely important significance of studying several contemporary Hebrew poets in light of the kabbalistic tradition, an effort that has the potential to transform both disciplines, this is a book that seeks in its deepest crevices to pray for the possibility of praying, to pray after all the statutory prayers have been uttered, a retrieval of the prayer before prayer, the poem within the poem that is the silence preceding and succeeding all speech. To elucidate this promise of prayer, which disseminates through the book like the light refracted and fragmented

---

[1]. David Shapiro, Michal Govrin, and Jacques Derrida, *Body of Prayer* (New York: Cooper Union for the Advancement of Science and Art, 2001), 61-63.

through a crystal prism, let me begin with the expression "mystical vertigo." Glazer has been especially influenced in this regard by the statement of Alain Badiou, "dance is governed by the perpetual renewal of the relation between vertigo and exactitude."[2] More specifically, Glazer appropriates Badiou's locution to depict the nature of the mystical experience of nondual consciousness, the state of conjunction (*devekut*) with the infinite, which he links phenomenologically to ~~touching~~.

We will return to the matter of touching later, and particularly the implication of the author's penchant to cross out the word each time it is written, but first we must ponder the relation between vertigo and exactitude. How are we to think about this juxtaposition? On the most basic level, vertigo is a condition of dizziness brought about by a feeling of motion while one is in fact stationary. There is, however, a profounder meaning to be elicited from this movement at a standstill, the motion of immobility, the touching that is no-touching. Let us attend to the precise title of Badiou's essay, "Dance as a Metaphor for Thought." Badiou, of course, is in conversation with Nietzsche, who famously said that the noble education should consist not only of learning how to dance with one's feet, but with ideas, words, and the pen. Elsewhere he wrote that dance instantiates the speculative ideal, and hence the determination of the philosopher is measured by the desire to be a good dancer. It should come as no surprise, accordingly, that the prophet of the new dawn of humanity, Zarathustra, described himself as possessing "dancing mad feet." Finally, and perhaps most tellingly, in another aphorism, he confessed—perhaps with tongue and cheek—that he could only believe in a God who dances. I would humbly submit that we should only trust thinkers whose thought is a form of dancing, the brightening glance, to paraphrase Yeats, wherein we cannot know the dancer from the dance.

Simply put, to embark upon the path of thought set forth in *Mystical Vertigo*, one must take hold of the movement of dance. But how does one take hold of movement? Is it not the case, as Michel Henry put it, that *the thought of movement is not movement.*[3] Surely this should be the case with

---

2.   Alain Badiou, *Handbook of Inaesthetics*, translated by Alberto Toscano (Stanford: Stanford University Press, 2005), 70.
3.   Michel Henry, *Philosophy and Phenomenology of the Body*, translated by Girard Etzkorn (The Hague: Martinus Nijhoff, 1975), 61.

a phenomenon like dancing, which is quintessentially movement. Perhaps the singularity of dance makes it impossible to speak about it, leading one invariably to the tautological judgment, *to dance one must simply dance.*

And yet, in the course of time, dance has served as an apt metaphor to depict the life of the mind and the creative endeavor of the human spirit. Let us listen more carefully to Badiou. Nietzsche's metaphor of dance for thought is related to several other critical images: the flight of the bird, the overflowing of the fountain, the innocence of the child, and the intangibility of the air.[4] To think of thought as a form of dance, one must combine all of these characteristics to invoke an intensification of movement that is like the wheel that turns itself, a circle revolving in space free of all gravity and constraint, the "mobility that is firmly fastened to itself, a mobility that is not inscribed within an external determination, but instead moves without detaching itself from its own center."[5] Exteriority and interiority are no longer a viable distinction, for within the circle there is nothing peripheral that is not central and nothing central that is not peripheral. Thinking that is worthy to be thought is a vertical movement stretching—indeed leaping—toward its proper height rooted in the ground whence it originates. The leap requires spontaneity and discipline, a liberating of the body that is concurrently a control of the body. In Badiou's formulation: "Dance offers a metaphor for a light and subtle thought precisely because it shows the restraint immanent to movement and thereby opposes itself to the spontaneous vulgarity of the body."[6]

Translating Nietzsche into his own philosophical idiom, Badiou notes that dance provides the metaphor "for the fact that every genuine thought depends upon an event. An event is precisely what remains undecided between the taking place and the non-place—in the guise of an emergence that is indiscernible from its own disappearance... The event 'itself' is never anything besides its own disappearance." To be sure, we have no choice but to affix names to events, but these names are naught but inscriptions placed "as if at the gilded edge of loss." The dance itself, by contrast, points

---

[4].   Badiou, *Handbook of Inaesthetics*, 57-58.
[5].   Ibid., 59.
[6].   Ibid., 60.

toward thought as event before it has received a name, "at the extreme edge of its veritable disappearance, without the shelter of the name."[7]

Glazer cites these words of Badiou to depict his own notion of the immersion in the divine nothingness, the place and non-place of mystical apperception. The language of the mystic and poet alike is engendered from the unification or incorporation in the indifferent oneness of the infinite, the nihilating nonground where nothing and something are conjoined, the space of utter annihilation in relation to which everything is affirmed in its negation and negated in its affirmation. Mystical discourse and poetic utterance may be marked in Badiou's terminology as the event that appears in its disappearance, oscillating between the presence of absence and the absence of presence, the emanation of light through its withdrawal, the occlusion of nonbeing that is the manifestation of being. From this language is woven the garment that is the name of the unnameable and unknowable essence that permeates and yet escapes all beings, the groundlessness above time and space that is the elemental ground of the temporal-spatial world, the pleromatic vacuum that is neither something nor nothing, but the not-being that continually comes to be in the ephemeral shadow-play of being, the void wherein everything possible is actual because what is actual is nothing but the possible, the sheltering-concealing wherein the real is what appears to be real, the clearing in relation to which being is no longer distinguishable from nothing, the matrix within which all beings are revealed and concealed in the nihilation of their being.

As I have discussed elsewhere,[8] according to Yitzhaq Maier Morgenstern, a key figure who has informed Glazer's orientation, the goal of mystical piety is to ascend to this nothingness where emanator and emanated are conjoined. From this point, which is no point at all, the nonlocality of the pointless, one is absorbed in the infinite. Epistemically, being attached to this spot propagates the awareness that unification is discriminated through division, that identity is envisaged against the foreground of heterogeneity. This is identified, moreover, as the true intent of prayer, which is illumined

---

7. Ibid., 61.

8. Elliot R. Wolfson, *A Dream Interpreted within a Dream: Oneiropoiesis and the Prism of Imagination* (New York: Zone Books, 2011), 229-235. I have taken the liberty to repeat some of that analysis here.

by being compared to a dream that guides one contemplatively on the path that peaks with being bound to the light of *Keter*, the dark luminescence, where opposites converge in their opposition. Analogous to the dream, prayer draws one upward to the summit of the *scala contemplativa*, the place of the *coincidentia oppositorum*, where limitlessness and limitedness intersect and collude in the identity of their (in)difference, where nothing becomes something and something nothing.

The lowest rung of prayer involves the worshipper imagining a reciprocal relation to a transcendent other. However, as one mystically enlightened comes to understand, both the self of the former and the icon of the latter are products of an egocentric consciousness programmed instinctually to perceive reality from the standpoint of individual needs (at its best coalescing in the altruistic obligation to maximize the good for the greatest number). The psychological inclination translates theologically into the inexorable need to confabulate the divine in human terms. When conjured theistically, prayer ensnares one inescapably in a trap of metaphoricity, and hence, the face of the other, presumed to be incapable of representation, is shrouded anthropomorphically and anthropopathically. Even if the image of the face is meant to intimate an alterity that cannot be known or named, the "trace of *illeity*," in Levinas's telling terminology, the mind is still coerced to construct an image of the imageless. The acme of the ascent is an atheological showing, the apophatic venturing beyond the theopoetic need to configure the transcendent. But the route to this disfiguration, the facing of the face that necessarily cannot be faced, the contemplation of the meta/figure, the inessential essence that is (non)human, is through the veil of the divine anthropos/human imagination.

The ultimate purpose of worship, on this score, is to return language to the nothingness of infinity. Liturgical words lose their referential meaning, for in the infinite unity there is no other to be addressed dialogically, and, consequently, the mystical vertigo gives way to an apophasis in which the temptation to portray God in human terms and the human in divine terms is overcome. Let us recall here the following words of Meister Eckhart describing the ideal of detachment (*abegescheidenheit*) that brings about the kenotic state of releasement (*gelâzenheit*), which eliminates the dialogical distance between human and divine that makes prayer itself possible: "I say that purity in detachment does not know how to pray, because if someone prays he asks God to get something for him, or he asks God to take something away from him. But a heart in detachment asks for nothing, nor has it anything of which it would gladly be free. So it is free of all prayer, and its prayer is nothing else than for uniformity with God... And as the soul attains this, it loses its name and it draws God into itself, so that in itself it becomes nothing, as the sun draws up the red dawn into itself so that it becomes nothing. Nothing else will bring man to this except pure detachment."[9]

Eckhart has poignantly articulated the experience that Glazer refers to by the paradoxical phrase "touching and not-touching." Of the different senses, the phenomenality of touch is distinctive, insofar as the interior and the exterior are not only contiguous but inseparable. In the touching that is no-touching, we advance even beyond this coincidence of subject and object, for there is nothing more to touch, not even nothing, and hence we are restored to the language before language, the name before the name, the event that is before any nominal fixation,[10] where being is crossed out, in Heideggerian terms, or placed under erasure in Derrida's translation.

"In dance," writes Badiou, "there is therefore something that is prior to time, something that is pre-temporal. It is this pre-temporal element that will be *played out* in space. Dance is what suspends time within space."[11] Cast in Jewish eschatological terms, the pre-temporal may also be demarcated as the post-temporal, the messianic time that is the timeless moment, which cannot transpire temporally and therefore must always be capable of occurring (in)temporally. The messianic task imparted to the Jew—at once the source of elation and tragedy, the hope against hope, desiring the impossible possibility, that is, the possibility that escapes the very domain of the possible—portends the need to wait temporally for what cannot take place in time but which is nevertheless constitutive of the very nature of time, the advent of the (non)event, the occurrence of what cannot occur save in the nonoccurrence of its occurrence. Messianic

9. *Meister Eckhart: The Essential Sermons, Commentaries, Treatises, and Defense*, translation and introduction by Edmund Colledge, O.S.A., and Bernard McGinn, preface by Houston Smith (New York: Paulist, 1981), 292.

10. Badiou, *Handbook of Inaesthetics*, 61.

11. Ibid., 61-62 (emphasis in original).

anticipation hinges on the paradox of preparing for the future that is already present as the present that is always future, the *tomorrow that is now precisely because it is now tomorrow*.[12] To live in that space where time is suspended, it may be necessary to journey beyond the poetic, leaping backward to see ahead, envisioning the visibility of the invisible rendered invisible in its visibility, expecting the past and recollecting the future. To occasion this leap, we will need to learn to dance again, albeit without feet, as the seventh beggar in the famous tale of Nahman of Bratslav. Just as that beggar was compelled to come by not-coming, so we are bound to pray by not-praying, praying the prayer before and after there is any prayer, praying for the possibility to pray. In this precarious moment of spiritual impoverishment, that alone should suffice.

Elliot R. Wolfson
New York University

---

[12] For fuller discussion, see Elliot R. Wolfson, *Open Secret: Postmessianic Messianism and the Mystical Revision of Menaḥem Mendel Schneerson* (New York: Columbia University Press, 2009), 265-300.

BIBLIOGRAPHY

Abram, David. *The Spell of the Sensuous: Perception and Language in a More-Than-Human-World.* New York: Vintage Books, 1996.

Abrams, Daniel. "A Neglected Talmudic Reference to Maase Merkava." *Frankfurter Judaistische Beiträge* 26, 1999.

Adler, Rachel. "And Not To Be Silent: Toward Inclusive Worship," in *Engendering Judaism: An Inclusive Theology and Ethics.* Philadelphia: Jewish Publication Society, 1998.

al-Jerrahi al-Halveti, Shaikh Tosun Bayrak. *Inspirations: On the Path of Blame Shaikh Badruddin of Simawna.* Vermont: Threshold Sufi Classics, 1993.

Amuyel, Jill. "There Is Also a Different Love." *Dimui* vol. 10. Jerusalem, 1996.

Aranya, Swami Hariharananda. *Yoga Philosophy of Patanjali.* Albany: SUNY Press, 1981.

Aurobindo, Sri. "Indeterminates, Cosmic Determinations and the Indeterminable," in *The Life Divine.* Twin Lakes, WI: Lotus Press, 1990.

_____. *The Human Cycle, Ideal of Human Unity, War and Self Determination.* Pondicherry: Lotus Press, 1970.

Badiou, Alain. *Handbook of Inaesthetics*, trans. A. Toscano. Stanford: Stanford University Press, 2005.

Balakian, A. *André Breton, Magus of Surrealism*. New York: Oxford University Press, 1971.

Barthes, Roland. *Le Plaisir du Texte*. Paris: Éditions de Seuil, 1982.

Bar-Yosef, Hamutal. "An Introduction to Mysticism in Modern Hebrew Literature," in *Kabbalah: Journal for the Study of Jewish Mystical Texts* 11 (2004).

_____. *Mysticism in 20th Century Hebrew Literature*. Boston: Academic Studies Press, 2010.

Battersby, Christine. *The Phenomenal Woman: Feminist Metaphysics and the Patterns of Identity*. New York: Routledge, 1998.

Benjamin, Walter. "Unpacking My Library," Selcted Writings 1931-1934. Cambridge: Belknap, 2004.

ben Pazi, Hanoch. "Rebuilding the Feminine in Lévinas' Talmudic Readings," *Journal of Jewish Thought and Philosophy*, 12, 3 (2003).

ben Shlomo, Yosef. *Doctrine of Divinity in R. Moshe Cordovero*. Jerusalem: Mossad Biailik, 1965.

ben Yitzhak, Avraham. *Collected Poems*, trans. Peter Cole. Jerusalem: Ibis Editions, 2003.

Bergson, Henri. *Duration and Simultaneity*, trans. Leon Jacobson. Indianapolis: Bobbs-Merrill, 1965.

Betty, L. Stafford. "Towards a Reconciliation of Mysticism and Dualism." *Religious Studies* 14 (1978).

Bhabha, Homi K. *The Location of Culture*. London: Routledge Classics, 1994.

————. "Unpacking My Library...Again," in *The Post-Colonial Question: Common Skies/Divided Horizons*, ed. I. Chambers and L. Curti. London: Routledge, 1996.

Bialik, Haim. *Letters of Haim Nahman Bialik, vol. II, 1906-1923*, ed. P. Lachover. Tel Aviv: 1938.

Bloch, C. and A. Bloch. *The Song of Songs: The World's First Great Love Poem*. New York: The Modern Library, 1995.

Bloom, Harold. *Walt Whitman: Modern Critical Views*. New York: Chelsea House Publishers, 2007.

————. *Anxiety of Influence*. New York: Oxford University Press, 1997.

Boutang, Pierre. *Ontologie du Sécret*. Paris: PUF, 1973.

Boyarin, Daniel. *Border Lines: The Partition of Judaeo-Christianity*. Philadelphia: University of Pennsylvania Press, 2006.

Boyle, Marjorie O'Rourke. *Senses of Touch: Human Dignity and Deformity*. Leiden: Brill, 1998.

Brunton, Paul. *The Hidden Teaching beyond Yoga*. New York: Weiser Books, 1984.

————. *The Quest of the Overself*. New York: Random House, 2003.

Bucke, R. M. *Cosmic Consciousness: A Study in the Evolution of the Human Mind*. Secaucus, N.J.: Citadel Press, 1989.

Bucke, Richard M. *Cosmic Consciousness: A Classic Investigation of the Development of Man's Mystic Relation to the Infinite*. New York: E. P. Dutton, 1969.

Carus, Titus Lucretius. *On The Nature of Things,* Book III. Bohn's Classical Library, trans. R. J. S. Watson. London: George Bells & Sons, 1893.

Cassuto, Umberto. *The Documentary Hypothesis: Eight Lectures*, trans. I. Abrahams. Jerusalem: The Magnes Press, Hebrew University, 1961.

Celan, Paul. *The Meridian: Final Version-Drafts-Materials*, trans. P. Jorris. Stanford: Stanford University Press, 2001.

Chittick, William C. *Ibn al-'Arabi's Metaphysics of Imagination: The Sufi Path of Knowledge*. New York: SUNY Press, 1989.

Corbin, Henri. "*L'Imago Templi* face aux norms profanes," *Temple et Contemplation*. Paris: Flammarion, 1980.

Davies, Paul. *About Time: Einstein's Unfinished Revolution*. New York: Simon & Schuster, 1996.

de Beauvoir, Simone. *Le Deuxième Sexe*. Paris: Gallimard, 1976.

de Certeau, Michel. *L'Absent de l'Histoire*. Paris: Mame, 1973.

_____. "The Arts of Dying," in *Heterologies: Discourse on the Other*, trans. B. Massumi. Minneapolis: University of Minnesota, 1986.

de Saint Aubert, Emmanuel. "Vers Une Ontologie Indirecte: Sources et enjeux critiques de l'appel à l'ontologie chez Merleau-Ponty," in *Topologie de la chair et topologie de l'être*. Paris: Vrin, 2006.

Derrida, Jacques. *Of Grammatology*, trans. G. C. Spivak. Baltimore: Johns Hopkins University Press, 1974.

Eilberg-Schwartz, Howard. *God's Phallus: And Other Problems for Men and Monotheism*. New York: Beacon Press, 1995.

Eisenstadt, S. N. "Martin Buber in the Postmodern Age," *Society* 34, May/June (1997).

Elad-Appelbaum, Tamar. "At Nights Your Faith Is Greater." *Mashiv haRuah* 24, Fall (2007).

Elior, Rachel. "HaBaD: The Contemplative Ascent to God," in *Jewish Spirituality II*. New York: Crossroad, 1987.

Esther, Haya. *My Flesh Speaks G!d* . Jerusalem: Carmel, 2001.

Fishbane, Michael A., "Transcendental Consciousness and Stillness in the Mystical Theology of R. Yehudah Arieh Leib of Gur," in *Sabbath—Idea, History, Reality*, ed. Gerald G. Blidstein. 2004.

Foucault, Michel. *The History of Sexuality*, 3 vols. New York Vintage Books, 1990.

Fox, Harry. "Poethics: How Every Jew is a Poet," in *Contemporary Hebrew Mystical Poetry*. New York: Edwin Mellen Press, 2009.

Friedman, Maurice. "Martin Buber and Asia." *Philosophy East and West* 26, 1976.

Friedman, Richard Elliott. *The Bible With Sources Revealed: A New View Into the Five Books of Moses*. New York: Harper Collins, 2003.

Frymer-Kensky, Tikva. *In The Wake of the Goddesses: Women, Culture, and the Biblical Transformation of Pagan Myth*. New York: Free Press, 1992.

Garb, Jonathan. *The Chosen Will Become Herds: Studies in Twentieth Century Kabbalah*, trans. Y. Berkovits-Murciano. New Haven: Yale University Press, 2009.

_____. *"Ramah gevohah me'od shel intensiviot ruhanit,"* *Eretz aheret* no. 41 (2008).

_____. "Mystical and Spiritual Discourse in the Contemporary Ashkenazi Haredi Worlds," *Journal of Modern Jewish Studies* 9 (2010).

_____. "The Modernization of Kabbalah: A Case Study," *Modern Judaism* 30 (2010).

_____. "The Spiritual-Mystical Renaissance in the Contemporary Haredi World," paper presented at the conference *Kabbalah and Contemporary Spiritual Revival: Historical, Sociological and Cultural Perspectives*, The Israel Science Foundation and The Goren-Goldstein Center for Jewish Thought, Ben Gurion University, 2008.

Gebser, Jean. *The Ever-Present Origin,* trans. N. Barstad and A. Mickunas. Athens, Ohio: Ohio University Press, 1985.

Geertz, Clifford. *The Interpretation of Cultures.* New York: Basic Books, 1973.

Giller, Pinhas. *Shalom Shar'abi and the Kabbalists of Beit El.* Oxford: Oxford University Press, 2008.

Glazer, Aubrey L. "Imaginal Journeying to Istanbul, *Mon Amour*: Devotional Sociabilities in Beshtian Hasidism and Turkish-Sufism," in *Pillar of Prayer*, trans. M. Kallus. Louisville, KY: Fons Vitae, 2011.

_____. *A New Physiognomy of Jewish Thinking: Critical Theory after Adorno as Applied to Jewish Thought.* New York: Continuum Press, 2011.

_____. "Durée, Devekuth, & Re-embracing the Godlover: Involution of Unio Mystica via Collocative HomosexuELity," in *Vixens Disturbing Vineyards: Embarrassment & Embracement of Scriptures*, Festschrift in Honor of Harry Fox leBeit Yoreh. Boston: Academic Studies Press, 2010.

_____*Contemporary Hebrew Mystical Poetry: How It Redeems Jewish Thinking.* New York: Edwin Mellen Press, 2009.

Godzich, Wlad. "The Further Possibility of Knowledge," in *Heterologies: Discourse on the Other*, trans. B. Massumi, *Theory and History of Literature*, vol. 17. Minneapolis: University of Minnesota Press, 1986.

Gold, Nili. "'Merciful Father Abraham': the mystical poetry of Binyamin Shvili," in *Religious Perspectives in Modern Muslim and Jewish Literatures*, ed. G. Abramson and H. Kilpatrick. London: Rutledge, 2006.

Goldberg, Leah. *Encounter with a Poet*. Tel Aviv: Sifriat Poalim, 1988.

Goldman, Mordechai. "Solitude of the Writer." *Haaretz*, May 8, 1998.

Goodman, Hananya, ed., *Between Jerusalem and Benares: Comparative Studies in Judaism and Hinduism*. Albany: SUNY Press, 1994.

Gopin, Marc. *Between Eden and Armageddon: The Future of World Religions, Violence, and Peacemaking*. New York: Oxford University Press, 2000.

Green, Art. *The Language of Truth: The Torah Commentary of the Sefat Emet/Rabbi Yehudah Leib Alter of Ger*. Philadelphia: Jewish Publication Society, 1998.

Gruenwald, Ithamar. "The Jewish Esoteric Literature in the Time of the Mishnah and Talmud." *Immanuel* 4 (1974).

Halevy, Schulamith Chava. *Inner Castle: Poems about Being and Being Coerced*. Jerusalem: 'Eked Publications, 1998.

_____. *Breath Sign*. Jerusalem: Carmel, 2003.

_____. *Être Poete dans un Pays Ravagé par la Guerre*. Foi & Vie: 33e Cahiers d'Etudes Juives, n. 5, trans. G. Toledano & D. Banon. 2005.

Harvey, Warren Zev. "New and unexpected problems facing 21st-century Jewish philosophy." *Studia Judaica* 11-12 (2004).

_____. "The Term '*hitdabbekut*' in Crescas' Definition of Time." *Jewish Quarterly Review* 71, 1 (1980).

Hillel, Yaakov Moshe. *Sefer Ahavat Shalom*. Jerusalem: Mechon Ahavat Shalom, 2002.

Hobbes, Thomas. *Leviathan*. Cambridge: Cambridge University Press, 1904.

Huss, Boaz, Marco Pusi, and Kocku von Stuckrad, ed. *Kabbalah and Modernity*. Leiden: Brill, 2010.

_____. "The Mystification of the Kabbalah and the Modern Construction of Jewish Mysticism," trans. Elana Lutsky, *BGU Review* 2 (2008).

_____. "The New Age of Kabbalah: Contemporary Kabbalah, the New Age and Postmodern Spirituality," *Journal of Modern Jewish Studies* 6 (2007).

Idel, Moshe. "Martin Buber and Gershom Scholem on Hasidism," in *Old Worlds, New Mirrors: On Jewish Mysticism and Twentieth-Century Thought*. Philadelphia: University of Pennsylvania Press, 2010.

_____. "Universalization and Integration: Two Conceptions of Mystical Union in Jewish Mysticism," in *Mystical Union in Judaism, Christianity and Islam: An Ecumenical Dialogue*, ed. M. Idel and B. McGinn. New York: Continuum Press, 1989.

_____. "*Hitbodedut* as concentration in ecstatic Kabbalah," in *Jewish Spirituality: From the Bible through the Middle Ages, vol. I*. New York: Crossroads, 1986.

_____. "Mystical Techniques," in *Essential Papers on Kabbalah*, ed. L. Fine. New York: NYU Press, 1995.

Kallus, Menahem. "Pneumatic Mystical Possession and the Eschatology of the Soul in Lurianic Kabbalah," *Spirit Possession in Judaism*, ed. M. Goldish. Detroit: Wayne State University Press, 2003.

Kaplan, Aryeh. *Innerspace: Introduction to Kabbalah, Meditation, and Prophecy*, ed. A. Sutton. Jerusalem: Moznaim Publications, 1991.

Kaploun, Yonadav. *You Are Still Writing*. Jerusalem: Keter Publications 2004.

Katz, Nathan. "The Hindu-Jewish Encounter and the Future," in *The Fifty-Eighth Century: A Jewish Renewal Sourcebook*, ed. S. Weiner. Northvale, N.J.: Jason Aronson Press, 1996.

_____. "Buddhist-Jewish Relations throughout the Ages and in the Future." *Journal of Indo-Judaic Studies* 10 (2009).

_____. "How the Hindu-Jewish Encounter Reconfigures Interreligious Dialogue." *Shofar* 16, 1 (1997).

Keckeis, Jean. "In memoriam Jean Gebser," in *The Ever-Present Origin*. Athens, Ohio: Ohio University Press, 1985.

Kimmelman, Reuven. "*Unetane Tokef* as a midrashic poem," *The Experience of Jewish Liturgu. Studies dedicated to Menahem Schmeltzer*, ed. D. Reed Blank. Leiden: Brill, 2011.

Kook, Avraham. *Shemoneh kevatzim mi-ktav kodsho*, 2 vols. Jerusalem: n.p., 2005.

Kosman, Admiel. *Proscribed Prayers: Seventy-One New Poems*. Tel Aviv: HaKibbutz Hameuchad, 2007.

Krassen, Moshe Aaron. *The True and the Real: Neo-Hasidic Reflections on the Nature of Reality*. Sha'arey Gan Eden, 2005.

Lacan, Jacques. *The Seminar of Jacques Lacan*, vol. 20, trans. Jacques-Alain Miller. New York: Norton, 1988.

Lévinas, Emmanuel. *Temps et L'Autre*. Paris: PUF, 1948.

Levine, Renée. *Women in Spanish Crypto-Judaism, 1492-1520*. Waltham, Mass.: Brandeis University, Ph.D. Dissertation, 1983.

Lévi-Strauss, Claude. *The Savage Mind*. Chicago: University of Chicago Press, 1966.

Lozynsky, A. *Richard Maurice Bucke, Medical Mystic: Letters of Dr. Bucke to Walt Whitman and His Friends*. Detroit: Wayne State University Press, 1977.

Luzzatto, Moses Hayyim. *Sod haYiḥud: Siddur Ramḥal*. Jerusalem: Ramḥal Institute, 2007.

Maffesoli, Michel. *The Time of the Tribes: The Decline of Individualism in Mass Society*. London: Sages Publications, 1996.

Magid, Shaul. "Leviticus: The Sin of Becoming a Woman: Male Homosexuality and the Castration Complex," in *From Metaphysics to Midrash: Myth, History and the Interpretation of Scripture in Lurianic Kabbalah*. Bloomington: Indiana University Press, 2008.

Mann, Barbara. "Hovering at a Low Altitude: Dahlia Ravikovitch," in *Reading Hebrew Literature: Critical Discussions of Six Modern Texts*, ed. A. L. Mintz. Hanover: University Press of New England, 2003.

Mark, Zvi. "Review of Jonathan Garb, *The Chosen Will Become Herds*, in *Studies in Twentieth-Century Kabbalah*," *Kabbalah: A Journal of Mystical Texts* 17 (2008).

Matt, Daniel C. *Zohar*. Pritzker Edition, vol. 3. Stanford: Stanford University Press, 2006.

Meschonnic, Henri. *Critique du rythme*. Paris: Verdier, 1982.

_____. *Jona et le signifiant errant*. Paris: Gallimard, 1981.
Mehlberg, Henry. *Time, Causality, and the Quantum Theory: Studies in the Philosophy of Science*, ed. Robert S. Cohen. Boston: Kluwer, 1980.

Meir, Jonathan. *Imagined Hasidism: Satire, Reality, and Concept of the Book in the Anti-Hasidic Writing of Joseph Perl/Sefer Megale Temirin*. Ph.D. dissertation, Hebrew University of Jerusalem, 2010.

_____. "The Imagined Decline of Kabbalah: The Kabbalistic Yeshiva Sha'ar ha-Shamayim and Kabbalah in Jerusalem in the Beginning of the Twentieth Century," in Huss et al., eds., *Kabbalah and Modernity*.

_____. "Mikhael Levi Rodkinson—Between Hasidism and Haskalah", *Kabbalah: A Journal for the Study of Jewish Mystical Texts* 18 (2008).

_____. "The Revealed and the Revealed within the Concealed: On the Opposition to the 'Followers' of Rabbi Yehuda Ashlag and the Dissemination of Esoteric Literature," in *Kabbalah: A Journal for the Study of Jewish Mystical Texts* 16 (2007).

_____. "Wrestling with the Esoteric: Hillel Zeitlin, Yehoshua Zeitlin, and Kabbalah in the Land of Israel," in *Judaism, Topics, Fragments, Faces, Identities: Jubilee Volume in Honor of Professor Rivka Horowitz*, ed. Ephraim Meir and Haviva Pedaya. Beer Sheva: Ben Gurion University, 2007.

_____. "Lights and Vessels: A New Inquiry into the 'Circle' of Rav Kook and the Editors of His Works." *Kabbalah: A Journal for the Study of Jewish Mystical Texts* 13 (2005).

Meltzer, Yoram. "Looking at the World and Finding Himself" . *Ma'ariv: Literature & Books*. 2010.

Miron, Dan. "Afterword: The Comic Sybil," in *The New and Selected Works of Agi Mishol*. Tel Aviv: Hakibbutz Hameuchad/Bialik Press, 2003.

Mishkovsky, Zelda Schneerson. *The Poetry of Zelda*. Tel Aviv: HaKibbutz Hameuchad, 1985.

Mishol, Agi. *Look There: New and Selected Poems*, trans. Lisa Katz. Minnesota: Graywolf Press, 2006.

Morgenstern, Yitzhaq Maier. *Yam ha-ḥokhmah*. Jerusalem: Mechon Yam ha-hokhmah 2010.

_____. *De'i ḥokhmah le-nafshekha: Siḥot kodesh*. Jerusalem: Mechon Yam ha-ḥokhmah 2006.

_____. *She'airith Ya'akov: Hiddushim v'Beurim 'al Massechet Megillah*. Jerusalem: Mechon Yam ha-ḥokhmah 1999.

Mor-Hayyim, Adina. "Poetry Arousing Conventions," *Maariv:* Literature Supplement 1990.

Morris, Benny. *Righteous Victims: A History of the Zionist-Arab Conflict 1881–2001*. New York: Vintage Books, 1999.

_____. *The Birth of the Palestinian Refugee Problem Revisited*. Cambridge: Cambridge University Press, 2004.

Nagid, Hayyim. "Erotica and Mysticism," *Yediot Ahronot*, Sabbath Supplement 1992.

Novinsky, Anita Waigort. "Marranos and Marranism: A New Approach," *Jewish Studies* 40 (2000).

Or, Amir. "The Way to Mecca," *Ha'Aretz*, April 9, 1993.

Pachter, Mordechai. *Roots of Faith and Devekut: Studies in the History of Kabbalistic Ideas*, vol. 10, ed. Daniel Abrams. Los Angeles: Cherub Press, 2004.

Pöggeler, Otto. "West-East Dialogue: Heidegger and Lao-Tzu," in *Heidegger and Asian Thought*, ed. G. Parkes. Honolulu, Hawaii: University of Hawaii Press, 1987.

Ram, Uri. *Israeli Society: Critical Perspectives* . Tel Aviv: Breirot Publications, 1993.

Rayfield, Donald. *Reader's Encyclopedia of Eastern European Literature*, ed. Robert B. Pynsent and S. I. Kanikova. New York: HarperCollins, 1993.

Ritter, H. "Abū Yazīd (Bāyazīd) Tayfūr B. Īsā B. Surūshān al-Bistāmī," in *Encyclopaedia of Islam*, Second Edition, ed. P. Bearman, T. Bianquis, C.E. Bosworth, E. van Donzel, and W.P. Heinrichs. Leiden: Brill, 2009.

Sarna, Nahum. *The JPS Commentary to Genesis*. Philadelphia: JPS, 1989.

Saxe, Len, and Barry I. Chazan. *Ten Days of Birthright Israel: A Journey in Young Adult Identity*. Waltham, MA: Brandeis University Press, 2008.

Schäfer, Peter. *The Hidden and Manifest God: Some Major Themes in Early Jewish Mysticism*, trans. A. Pomerance. Albany: SUNY Press, 1992.

Scharfstein, Ben-Ami. "How to Justify Reductive Explanation of Myths: Mystical Experience," in *Ineffability: The Failure of Words in Philosophy and Religion*. Albany, New York: SUNY Press, 1993.

Schiffman, Lawrence H. and Michael D. Swartz, "Hebrew and Aramaic Incantation Texts from the Cairo Genizah: Selected Texts from Taylor-Schecter Box K1," in *Semitic Texts and Studies 1*. Sheffield, England: Sheffield Academic Press, 1992.

Schimmel, Annemarie. *Mystical Dimensions of Islam*. Chapel Hill, North Carolina: University of North Carolina Press, 1975.

Scholem, Gershom. *The Messianic Idea in Judaism*. New York: Schocken Press, 1971.

_____. *On the Mystical Shape of the Godhead: Basic Concepts in the Kabbalah*, trans. J. Chipman. New York: Schocken Books, 1991.

_____. "Religious Authority and Mysticism," in *On the Kabbalah and its Symbolism*, trans. R. Manheim. New York: Schocken Books, 1965.

_____. "Reflections on the Possibility of Jewish Mysticism in Our Time," in *On the Possibility of Jewish Mysticism in Our Time and Other Essays,* trans. J. Chipman. Philadelphia: JPS, 1997.

Schrag, Calvin O. *The Self after Postmodernity.* New Haven: Yale University Press, 1997.

Schwartz, Seth. *Were the Jews a Mediterranean Society? Reciprocity and Solidarity in Ancient Judaism.* Princeton: Princeton University Press, 2010.

Segal, Miryam. *A New Sound in Hebrew Poetry: Poetics, Politics, Accent.* Bloomington: Indiana University Press, 2010.

Segev, Tom. *The Seventh Million*, trans. H. Watzman. New York: Hill & Wang, 1993.

Sered, Susan Starr. *Women as Ritual Experts: The Religious Lives of Elderly Jewish Women in Jerusalem.* New York: Oxford University Press, 1992.

Shevili, Binyamin. "Contrition," *Carmel*, vol. 13, Jerusalem, 2010.

_____. *Poems of Yearning for Mecca.* Tel Aviv: Tamuz Publications, 1992.

_____. *Poems of the Grand Tourist.* Tel Aviv: Schocken, 1999.

_____. *A New Dictionary of Afflictions.* Tel Aviv: Schocken, 2004.

Shohat, Ella. "The 'Postcolonial' in *Translation: Reading Said in Hebrew*," in *Paradoxical Citizenship: Essays on Edward Said*, ed. S. Nagy-Zekimi. London: Lexington Books, 2006.

Sommer, Benjamin D. *The Bodies of God and the World of Ancient Israel.* Cambridge: Cambridge University Press, 2011.

Subtelny, Maria Eva. "The Tale of the Four Sages Who Entered the Pardes: A Talmudic Enigma from a Persian Perspective." *Jewish Studies Quarterly* 11 (2004).

Tamdgidi, Mohammad H., and J. Walter. *Gurdjieff and Hypnosis: A Hermeneutic Study.* New York: Palgrave Macmillan, 2009.

Thomson, William Irwin. *Coming into Being: Artifacts and Texts in the Evolution of Consciousness.* New York: St. Martin's Press, 1996.

Tigay, Jeffrey. *The JPS Commentary to Deuteronomy.* Philadelphia: JPS, 1989.

Joshua Trachtenberg, *Jewish Magic and Superstition.* Philadelphia: University of Pennsylvania Press, 2004.

Tsur, Reuven. *On the Shore of Nothingness: A Study in Cognitive Poetics.* Exeter: Imprint Academic, 2003.

Tzipor, Beni. "Novel: Books that Disjoint," *Ha'Aretz: Culture & Literature,* December 30, 2005.

Uffenheimer, Rivka Schatz. *Quietistic Elements in Eighteenth-Century Hasidic Thought.* Jerusalem: Magnes Press, 1968.

Walbridge, John. "Suhrawardi and Illumination," in *The Cambridge Companion to Arabic Philosophy,* ed. Peter Adamson, Richard C. Taylor. Cambridge: Cambridge University Press, 2005.

Wasserstrom, Steven M. *Religion after Religion: Gershom Scholem, Mircea Eliade, and Henri Corbin at Eranos.* Princeton: Princeton University Press, 1999.

Weinfeld, Moshe. "Feminine Features in the Imagery of God in Israel: The Sacred Marriage and the Sacred Tree." *Vetus Testamentum* 46, 4 (1996).

Wesling, Donald, and Tadeusz Sławek. *Literary Voice: The Calling of Jonah.* New York: SUNY Press, 1995.

Wexler, Philip. *Mystical Interactions: Sociology, Jewish Mysticism, and Education.* Los Angeles: Cherub Press, 2007.

Wilber, Ken. *The One Two Three of God.* Boulder, CO: Sounds True, 2006.

_____. *Integral Spirituality: A Startling New Role for Religion in the Modern and Postmodern World.* Boston: Shambala Press, 2007.

Wolfson, Elliot R. *A Dream Interpreted Within a Dream: Oneiropoiesis and the Prism of Imagination.* New York: Zone Books, 2011.

_____. *Language, Eros, Being: Kabbalistic Hermeneutics and Poetic Imagination.* New York: Fordham University Press, 2005.

_____ "Occultation of the Feminine and the Body of Secrecy in Medieval Kabbalah," in *Rending the Veil.* New York: NYU Press, 1999.

_____. *Open Secret: Postmessianic Messianism and the Mystical Revision of Menahem Mendel Schneerson.* New York: Columbia University Press, 2009.

_____. "Secrecy, Modesty, and the Feminine: Kabbalistic Traces in the Thought of Levinas." *Journal of Jewish Thought and Philosophy* 14 (2006).

_____. *Through a Speculum That Shines.* Princeton: Princeton University Press, 1997.

_____. *Venturing Beyond: Law and Morality in Kabbalistic Mysticism.* New York: Oxford University Press, 2006.

Wright, Robert. *The Evolution of God.* New York: Little, Brown & Co, 2009.

Yoffe, A. B. *Leah Goldberg: A Memoir*. Jerusalem: Tserikover, 1984.

Zevit, Ziony. "The Names of Israelite Gods," in *The Religions of Ancient Israel: A Synthesis of Parallactic Approaches*. New York: Continuum, 2001.

Zinger, Moshe. "What is a Jewish Poem?" *Ha'Aretz*, May 21, 1993.

Zisquit, Linda. *The Defiant Muse: Hebrew Feminist Poems From Antiquity to Present*. New York: The Feminist Press at CUNY, 1999.

INDEX

A

Abraham Heschel of Apt 110n.37

Abrahams, I. 73n.7

Abram, David

   The Spell of the Sensuous: Perception and Language in a More-Than-Human-World 214n.9-12, 224n.20

Abrams, Daniel 46n.99, 120n.4, 138n.61

Abramson, G.

   Religious Perspectives in Modern Muslim and Jewish Literatures 95n.8-9

Abu Yazid of Bistam 107n.32

Adamson, Peter and Taylor, Richard C.

   The Cambridge Companion to Arabic Philosophy 108n.32

Adler, Rachel

   Engendering Judaism: An Inclusive Theology and Ethics 172n.43

al-Jerrahi al-Halveti, Shaikh Tosun Bayrak

   Inspirations: On the Path of Blame Shaikh Badruddin of Simawna 112n.50

Adorno, Theodor W. 36n.68

   Negative Dialectics 124n.22

Agnon, Shmuel Yosef (Agnon, Shai) 96

   Till here 96n.11

   Yesterday, Day Before 96n.10

Albo, Joseph, Rabbi 109n.35

Alfassa, Mira 31

Alkabetz, Shlomo haLevi, Rabbi 185

Alterman, Nathan 86-91

   Ir Ha'yonah (The Dove City) 89

   Late Afternoon in the Market 86, 89

Amuyel, Jill 95n.7, 96n.11-13, 96n.15, 110n.40, 187n.31

Ana b'Koah 253-254

   forty-two letter divine name 254

*a*perspectival 38, 75, 78-79

apophasis 21, 271

Aran, Gideon 29n.38, 29n.41-43, 34n.59, 34n.64, 41n.84, 55n.136, 70n.195, 129

Aranya, Swami Hariharananda

   Yoga Philosophy of Patanjali 59n.155

Ashlag, Yehuda, Rabbi 43n.91, 141n.84

Ashton, E. B. 124n.22

Aurobindo, Sri 31, 31n.50, 199n.52, 263

   Indeterminates, Cosmic Determinations and the Indeterminable 31n.50

   The Life Divine 263n.3

   The Human Cycle, Ideal of Human Unity, War and Self Determination 199n.52

B

Ba'al Shem Tov (Besht) 62-64, 63n.167, 111

Badiou, Alain 22n.6, 39, 39n.79, 268-270, 268n.2, 269n.4-6, 272n.10-11

   Dance as a Metaphor for Thought 39n.79

   Handbook of Inaesthetics 269n.4-6, 272n.10-11

Balakian, A.

   André Breton, Magus of Surrealism 155n.4

Banai, Meir 251

Banon, D. 121n.13

Barnai, Jacob 142n.79

Barstad, N. 38n.74

Barthes, Roland 155, 155n.5, 175, 175n.51

   Le Plaisir du Texte 155n.5

   Roland Barthes par Roland Barthes 175n.51

Bar-Yosef, Hamutal 46n.104, 47n.206, 240n.3

   Mysticism in 20th Century Hebrew Literature 46n.104

   On Zelda's Poetry [Hebrew] 240n.3

Barzel, Hillel 240n.3
Battersby, Christine 200, 200n.1-2, 209n.16
 The Phenomenal Woman: Feminist Metaphysics and the Patterns of Identity 200n.1-2, 209n.16
Becker, Hans-Jürgen 142n.78
Begin, Menahem 212
Benayhu, Meir 120n.7
Benjamin, Walter 92, 93n.14
 Unpacking My Library 93n.14
ben Pazi, Hanoch 179n.9
ben Shlomo, Yosef 96n.10
 Doctrine of Divinity in R. Moshe Cordovero 96n.10
ben Yitzhak, Avraham (Avraham Sonne) 71, 71n.1,72, 77-78, 79n.28, 80n.29, 264
 Collected Poems 71n.1, 79n.28
 Psalm 71n.1, 79n.28, 80n.29
 When Nights Grow White 78, 264
Beauvoir, Simone de
 Le Deuxième Sexe 179n.8
Bergson, Henri 178-179
 Durée et simultanéité a propos de la théorie d'Einstein 178n.2
 Duration and Simultaneity 178n.2
Beshtian Hasidism 28n.33, 49-50, 61, 69
Betty, L . Stafford
 Towards a Reconciliation of Mysticism and Dualism 24n.14
Berkovits-Murciano, Y. 26n.22
Bhabha, Homi K. 81, 81n.1, 84, 88, 92n.12,
 The Location of Culture 81n.1
Bialik, Haim N. 77n.21, 89n.11, 171, 171n.41, 188, 198, 198n.47
 Letters of Haim Nahman Bialik 77n.21
Biderman, S.
 Myths and Fictions 25n.14
Bilu, Yoram 22n.4
birthing (*leidah*) 139-140, 143, 143n.88,165
Blake, William 31n.49, 157
Bland, Debra Reed
 The Experience of Jewish Liturgu. Studies dedicated to Menahem Schmeltzer 238n.26
Blidstein, Gerald G. 48n.108
Bloch, C. and Bloch, A. 83n.5
 The Song of Songs: The World's First Great Love Poem 83n.5

Bloom, Harold 31n.49, 123n.19, 154n.3, 157n.14, 160n.25-27, 161n.28, 162, 175
 How to Read and Why 158n.21
 Walt Whitman: Modern Critical Views 160n.25-27, 161n.28
 Anxiety of Influence 249n.11
Block, Harvey 179, 253n.4
Boertien, Maas 84n.7
Boulanger, Pier-Pascale 149n.3
Boutang, Pierre 121n.12
 Ontologie du Sécret 121n.12
Boyarin, Daniel 34-35n.62
 Border Lines: The Partition of Judaeo-Christianity 35n.62
 Carnal Israel: Reading Sex in Talmudic Culture 187n.33
Boyle, Marjorie O 'Rourke 67n.186
 Senses of Touch: Human Dignity and Deformity 67n.186
Bratzlaver Hasidism 48-49, 68-69
Breton, André 155n.4
brokenness (*Zebrukhenkeit*) 66, 110, 111n.43, 152
Brunton, Paul 43n.90
 The Hidden Teaching beyond Yoga 43n.90
 The Quest of the Overself 43n.90
Buber, Martin 30, 30n.45-46, 30n.48, 31, 34, 44n.93
Bucke, Richard M. 31n.49, 154n.3, 156, 156n.10-11, 157, 157n.12-15
 Cosmic Consciousness: A Classic Investigation of the Development of Man's Mystic Relation to the Infinite 156n.10-11, 157n.12-13
 Cosmic Consciousness: A Study in the Evolution of the Human Mind 31n.49, 157n.14
Burroughs, William S. 180n.3
Butler, Judith 187n.27

C
Carpenter, Edward 31n.49, 157
Carus, Titus Lucretius (Lucretius) 207
 On The Nature of Things 207n.13
Cassuto, Umberto 73n.7, 74n.10-11, 74n.14
 The Documentary Hypothesis: Eight Lectures 73n.7, 74n.11, 74.14
Celan, Paul 224

The Meridian: Final Version-Drafts-Materials 224n.16-17

Certeau, Michel de 85n.8, 145, 145n.1, 149
L'Absent de l'Histoire 85n.8

character, good [*khuluq*] 112

chiasmic 213-214, 223, 225

Chipman, J. 154n.2, 156n.9

Chittick, William C.
Ibn al-'Arabi's Metaphysics of Imagination: The Sufi Path of Knowledge 112n.54-55

chivalry (*futuwwa*) 112

Christianity 22n.5, 35n.62, 123-124, 198

classical Kabbalah 31, 37n.70, 42, 49, 50, 57, 61, 65n.182, 69, 96, 109, 120n.6, 123

Cohen, Eliaz 201

Cohen, Leonard 267

Cohen, Martin, A. 134n.50

coitus (*zivvug*) 124, 143

Cole, Peter 71n.1, 79n.28, 253n.4

collocation (*tzeruf 'otiyot*) 171, 171n.41, 173-174, 187-188, 191-192, 194, 198

communion and interpenetration 63

congenital darkness of the poem 224-225, 236

conjunction of the heart (*devekut di-reu'ta de-libba*) 28

consciousness
expansive consciousness 39
filling divine consciousness (*melo kol ha-aretz kevodo*) 47
first-/second-tier consciousness 38
simple consciousness 156
unitive consciousness 38-39, 51, 60n.156, 62-65, 94, 119

contraction (*tzimtzum*) 143

contrition [*haratah*] 94, 97,109-112, 118

Cosmic Consciousness 31n.49, 156, 156n.10-11, 157, 157n.14, 175-176

cosmogenesis 155, 159

cosmogonic 154, 158-159

cosmogony 159-160, 172, 176
auto-erotic cosmogony 160, 172, 176

Corbin, Henri 30, 30n.44, 227n.21

Cordovero, Moshe, Rabbi 37n.70, 65n.182, 96n.10, 240n.3

cosmic I, cosmological self 31n.49, 156-157, 161-163, 165-166, 173, 175-176

Crane, Hart 180n.13

Crescas, Hasdai 179, 179n.6, 186n.24

crypto-Jews (*Anusim, Marranos, Conversos*) 121, 123-124, 130, 130n.35, 130n.38-39, 133-134, 134n.46-50, 135n.51-53, 139n.67-68, 142n.79

D

daemonic real Me 161-162, 175-176

Darbandi, A. 194n.42

Dasein, the locus of being 149

Davis, D. 194n.42

Davies, Paul
About Time: Einstein's Unfinished Revolution 183n.18-19

death of God 23

Deluze, Gilles and Guattari Félix 173n.45
Kafka: Toward a Minor Literature 173n.45

demonstrative language ("that") 247-248

demise of the human subject 23

Derrida, Jacques 36, 36n.67, 267, 267n.1, 272
De la grammatologie (Of Grammatology) 36n.67

Devekut-Tiferet 51, 260
Memory of Awe-*Hod* 51
Memory of Love-*Netzah* 51
Memory of *Devekut-Yesod* 51, 57

devotional cultures 40, 45, 47, 68, 118, 121

devolutionary force (*me'akev*) 37

devotional life of 42, 42n.87, 43, 50, 52, 54, 69, 263

Diaphanous Divinity 73, 77, 224

Dimui, multidisciplinary journal 95n.7, 187n.31, 201

divine personae or *parsufim* 57, 57n.151

Dowling, David
Chasing the White Whale: The Moby-Dick Marathon; Or, What Melville Means Today 149n.2

Dov Ber of Lubavitch, Rabbi (Mittler Rebbe) 62, 62n.165, 64

dual mystical apperception 24

duplicity in 119, 265

durée of the godlover 177, 182, 199, 265

Durie, Robin 178n.2
Duration and Simultaneity: Bergson and the Einsteinian Universe 178n.2

E

East or West 24, 26

Eckhart, Meister 271-272, 272n.9
  The Essential Sermons, Commentaries, Treatises, and Defense 272n.9

Eilberg-Schwartz, Howard
  God's Phallus: And Other Problems for Men and Monotheism 21 n.1

Eisenstadt, S. N. 44n.93

Elad-Appelbaum, Tamar 200-202, 204n.6, 207n.12, 264
  At Nights Your Faith Is Greater 207, 207n.12, 208
  Mashiv haRuah 202n.5, 204n.6
  Psalms for Jerusalem 200, 264
  Remember what Amalek did to you 203-205

Eliade, Mircea 30, 30n.44

Elior, Rachel 27n.26

embodiment 63, 107, 124, 138, 139n.67, 144, 154-155, 160-161, 165-167, 169, 171-173, 175-176, 209, 223, 237, 265

enrapturing ascent in oscillating integration of *Keter* 47,64-66, 68, 94, 262

erasure (*makha*) 27-28, 36, 39, 138, 141, 272

Erlanger, Moshe 48

Eros/Thanatos 92
  auto-erotic 154-155, 158-160, 172, 176, 265
  dibbuk haverim or a mystical camaraderie 194, 194n.43, 196
  godlovers 180, 183, 186, 199
  homo-erotic imaginalities 179-180, 182, 186, 191
  homosexual relations 179, 179n.11, 180, 186, 191
  real homosexuELity 33n.86, 177, 187, 191
  true Homo-eroticism 186-187

eruption 39, 125, 185

encircling pleroma of divine consciousness (*sovev kol almin*) 47

enrapturing ascent 47, 64-66, 68, 94, 262

ethical manuals 46

Etzkorn, Gerard 268n.3

evolution of consciousness –from Mental to Integral 79

exterior (*hisoniyut*) 47

exteriority of descent in *Binah* 62

exteriorized fervor; 47 , 63-65, 68, 94, 262

Ezekiel, A. D. (Abraham David Salman Hai Ezekiel) 31

F

faith ('*emunah*) 46, 84, 130, 207-209, 241, 249, 257

Falk, Marcia
  The Spectacular Difference: Selected Poems of Zelda 240n.3

Farid al Din Atar
  The Conference of the Birds 194n.42

female, sex, gender 108, 134, 139n.67, 141n.77, 158, 170-171, 194, 197-198, 200-203, 206, 209, 264

Feminine Minor Persona [*Nuqbah de-Zeir Anpin*] 57n.151

Festugière, R.P. 139n.64

Fine, Lawrence 180n.12

Fishbaine, Eitan P. 124n.21, 180n.12
  As Light Before Dawn: The Inner World of a Medieval Kabbalist 124n.21

Fishbane, Michael A.
  Biblical Myth and Rabbinic Mythmaking 124n.22
  Sabbath — Idea, History, Reality 48n.108

fivefold turnings of consciousness (*Bewusterdungs Prozess)* 72

flesh 213-214, 223-225, 228, 239

Foucault, Michel
  Histoire de la Sexualité (The History of Sexuality) 187n.28

Fox, Harry 57n.149, 162n.30, 174n.47

Freud, Sigmund 21 n.2

Friedman, Maurice 30n.45,

Friedman, Mordechai A.
  Jewish Marriage in Palestine — A Cairo Geniza Study: Marriage Contracts according to the Custom of Eretz Israel 170n.40

Friedman, Richard Elliot
  The Bible With Sources Revealed: A New View Into the Five Books of Moses 74n.10

Frymer-Kensky, Tikva 137n.59, 142n.80
  In The Wake of the Goddesses: Women, Culture, and the Biblical Transformation of Pagan Myth 137n.59

Ftayya Yehudah R. 250, 250n.2, 254, 254n.7

G

Gadamer Hans-Georg 25.14

Garb, Jonathan 21n.3, 22n.4, 26n.22, 32n.55, 33n.56,, 35n.65-66, 41, 41n.84, 42n.85-86, 43n.89, 43n.91, 43n.94, 43n.96, 48n.109-110, 49n.111, 50n.115, 52n.121, 55n.134, 59n.155, 60n.158, 67, 68n.189,
The Chosen Will Become Herds: Studies in Twentieth Century Kabbalah 26n.22, 32n.55, 33n.56, 35n.65-66, 41n.84, 43n.96, 48n.110, 68n.189-190
Shamanic Trance in Modern Kabbalah 21 n.3

Gebser, Jean 38, 38n.74, 71-72, 72n.5, 74n.12, 75n.15-18
The Ever-Present Origin 38n.74-76, 74n.12, 75n.15-18

Geertz, Clifford
The Interpretation of Cultures 45n.95

Giller, Pinhas
Shalom Shar'abi and the Kabbalists of Beit El 49n.112

Gimello, Robert M. 31n.52

Ginsburg, Allen
The Book of Martyrdom and Artifice: First Journals and Poems 1937-1952 180n.13

Ginsburgh, Yitzhak, Rabbi 41n.84, 70n.195, 211, 211n.3, 212

Ginzbeg, Louis 258n.13

Godzich, Wlad 85n.9

Golan, Galia 200n.3

Gold, Nili 95n.8-9

Goldberg, Leah 77n.22, 158,158n.21, 159n.22
Encounter with a Poet 77n.22

Goldish, M.
Spirit Possession in Judaism 45n.94, 123n.20

Goldman, Mordechai 95n.4, 111n.44

Goldreich, A. 159n.

Goldstein Baruch 41n.84, 211

Goodman, Hananya
Between Jerusalem and Benares: Comparative Studies in Judaism and Hinduism 27n.26

Gopin, Marc
Between Eden and Armageddon: The Future of World Religions,Violence, and Peacemaking 41n.84

Green, Art 35n.65, 48n.108
The Language of Truth: The Torah Commentary of the Sefat Emet/Rabbi Yehudah Leib Alter of Gur 48n.108

Greenstein, Edward L. 155n.6

Gruenwald, Ithamar 120n.4

Guenther, Lisa
The Gift of the Other: Levinas and the Politics of Reproduction 179n.9

Gurer Hasidism 48-49, 68-69

Guttari, Felix 173n.45

Gwiazda, Piotr K.
James Merrill and W.H. Auden: Homosexuality and Poetic Influence 180n.13

H

Halevy, Schulamith Hava 120-124, 125n.24, 129, 131n.40, 132-133, 133n.42-45, 1137n.55, 140n.69-70, 143, 148, 265
Inner Castle: Poems about Being and Being Coerced 121, 121n.10, 123-124, 130, 131n.40
Breath Sign 121, 121n.11, 123-124, 136n.54, 140n.71
Être Poete dans un Pays Ravagé par la Guerre 121n.13-16
A Place in Time 122, 122n.17
Impregnation's Secret 135-137, 265
Creation (according to woman) 140n.71
Mending 140n.72
Ot Hevel [The Sign of Abel] 124n.23
15th of Av, Mylopotamos 126, 126n.25
Strange Fire 130, 131n.40, 265

Hammer, Jill 128n.30

haredi (ultra-Orthodox) 29, 33, 34n.59, 35n.65, 40, 41n.84, 42, 45n.96, 48, 49n.111, 52, 54, 58, 60, 68-69, 263, 266
cultural regeneration of 44n.93, 48

harmonization (*hishtavu'ut*) 37

Harvey, Warren Zev 179, 179n.5-6, 186n.24

Hasan-Rokem, Galit 158n.21

Hasidic networks 42

Haya Esther (Godlevsky) 154-155, 160-161, 172, 175, 265
My Flesh Speaks G!d 154 n.1, 160-161, 161n.29, 163-170, 172n.42, 173n.44, 175n.49, 176, 176n.52, 265

Hayyim, Yosef, Rabbi 254n.6
  Leshon Hakhamim 254n.6
Heidegger, Martin 25n.14, 26n.23, 27n.27, 272
henology (theologically unique) 145-146, 152-153
Henry, Michel 268
  Philosophy and Phenomenology of the Body 268n.3
Herrero-Brasas, Juan A.
  Walt Whitman's Mystical Ethics of Comradeship: Homosexuality and the Marginality of Friendship at the Crossroads of Modernity 180n.13
Herzl, Theodor 55n.135, 225
Hesiod 129n.32
Hess, Tamar 158n.21
heterology (mystically altered as *other*) 145-146, 152-153
  heterological tradition 85
Hever, Hanna
  Producing the Modern Hebrew Canon: Nation Building and Minority Discourse 158n.21
Hick, John H. 31n.52
Higgens, Elford
  Hebrew Idolatry and Superstition: Its Place in Folk-Lore 137n.56, 137n.58
hylic self, seed (instinct, urges, and bodily sensations) 160, 162-163,166, 169, 172-173, 175-176
Hobbes, Thomas 240n.2
Hoeller, Stephan A.
  Jung and the Lost Gospels: Insights into the Dead Sea Scrolls and the Nag Hammadi Library 162n.31
holiness (*Hokhmah*) 33n.56, 55, 64-65, 158, 185
  interiority of ascent in *Hokhmah* 62
  interiorized stillness through the calm of *Hokhmah* 47, 65, 68, 94, 262
holistic 80
Holocaust (*Shoah*) 41, 72, 83, 87, 155, 178, 224, 226
Homer 129n.32
Homiletical writings 46
"Homosexu*EL*ity" 36n.68, 177, 182n.15, 187, 191, 265
Horner, Thimas, M.
  Jonathan Loved David: Homosexuality in

Biblical Times 187n.32
Horowitz, Israel 109n.36
Huss, Boaz 26n.22, 31, 41, 49n.111, 50n.115
  Kabbalah and Modernity 22n.5, 29n.38, 30n.49, 31n.51, 41n.84
hybridized
  subjectivity 32, 32n.53, 43, 148, 263
  thinking 42, 59
hypernomian 42, 58, 58n.154, 186, 198, 263

I
Idel, Moshe 22n.5, 30n.46, 30n.48, 45, 46n.98, 63n.169, 183n.16-17, 247n.8
  Kabbalah and Eros 183n.17
  Studies in Ecstatic Kabbalah 183n.16
  Universalization and Integration: Two Conceptions of Mystical Union in Jewish Mysticism 22 n.5, 63n.169
immersion into mystical union 37-29, 47-48, 63, 66, 199, 270
impregnation (*'ibbur*) 123-125, 137-138, 142-144, 265
inscription 39-40, 173, 269
integrating factor (*yishuv ha-da'at*) 37
interworld 56, 185, 239
*in*volution 36, 36n.68, 38, 58n.154, 62, 69, 71, 146, 180, 182n.15, 186-187, 199
involutionary force (*redifah*) 37
Isaac ben Samuel of Acre, Rabbi 123n.21
Islam 53, 88, 94, 102n.22, 103n.24, 106, 107n.32, 108n.32, 113n.57
Israel, communities in
  Bethlehem 87, 90
  Bezalel Institute 156
  Gal Einai Institute 211
  Gush Emunim 35n.66, 55n.136, 211
  Kfar Mordechai in Gedera 87
  Kuntillet 'Arjud 142, 142n.80
  Mercaz haRav Kook Central Yeshiva 211
  Nekuda Judea, Samaria and Gaza (YES"HA) 201
  Od Yosef Hai, Yitzhar 211
  Poria Ilit, Galilee 121
  Rafah Plain, south Gaza Strip, Sinai Penninsula 211-212
  Ramle 145
  Yemin Moshe 95

J

Jacobson, Leon 178n.2

Jerusalem's *haredi* (ultra-Orthodox) neighborhoods in Israel
Tel Arza 48, 54, 266
Geulah 54, 266

jouissance *(sha'ashua)* 39, 66, 121, 143,155, 163, 165

Jorris, P. 224n.16

joy *(semaikhim)* 39

K

Kabbalah and theosophy 31
Intuitive Kabbalah 30, 31n.49, 154, 157, 157n.14

Kahane, Meir, Rabbi 212

Kallus, Menahem 28n.33, 63n.166, 123n.20

Kaplan, Aryeh
Innerspace: Introduction to Kabbalah, Meditation, and Prophecy 65n.182

Kaploun, Yonadav 201, 210-212, 210n.1, 214, 223, 223n.13, 228, 235-237, 264
You Are Still Writing 235n.23
Scent of Darkness 215-223, 223n.13, 236, 264
A Window of Opportunity 215, 228-237, 264

kataphasis 21

Katz, Lisa 87n.10

Katz, Nathan 27n.26,

Katz, Steven T.
Language Epistemology, and Mysticism 31-32n.52

Kaufman, Shirley
The Defiant Muse: Hebrew Feminist Poems 158n.21

Kedar, Mira 201

Keckeis, Jean 72n.4-6

Kerouac, Jack 180n.13

kevutzah (kvutza) 44, 44n.93

kibbutz 44, 44n.93

Kimmelman, Reuven 185n.22, 238n.26

Klein, Shmuel 201

Kook, Avraham Yitzhak, Rav 32-33n.56-57, 35n.66, 41n.84, 211
Orot ha-Kodesh 32n.56
Fragments of Light 68n.191
Shemoneh kevatzim mi-ktav kodsho 35n.66

Kook, Tzvi Yehuda, Rabbi 35n.66, 211

Kosman, Admiel 71-72, 75-76, 76n.19, 77, 156, 264
Proscribed Prayers: Seventy-One New Poems 76n.19
Eloheinu [Our God] 75-76, 76n.19, 77, 264

Krassen, Moshe Aaron 43n.90, 111n.43

Kravel-Tovi, Michel 22n.4

Kronfeld, Hanna 173, 173n.45
On the Margins of Modernism 173n.45

L

Lacan, Jacques 187n.27

Lachover, P.
Letters of Haim Nahman Bialik 77n.21

Lao-Tzu 26n.23

Leah and Rachel 57, 57n.151, 59, 266

Lehrman, Shmuel 201

Lévinas, Emmanuel 120n.6, 179, 179n.9-10, 271
Temps et L'Autre 179n.7

Levine, Renée 134n.46, 135n.52, 139n.67-68, 142n.79
Women in Spanish Crypto-Judaism, 1492-1520 134n.46, 135n.52, 139n.67-68, 142n.79

Lévi-Strauss, Claude
The Savage Mind 34n.61

Liebes, Yehudah 159n.24

Limitless as *Ein Sof* or *Tathagata* 28

loss, gilded side of (gilded edge of loss) 22, 39-40, 269

Lozynsky, A.
Richard Maurice Bucke, Medical Mystic: Letters of Dr. Bucke to Walt Whitman and His Friends 31n.49, 157n.14

Lubavitcher Hasidism 48-49, 54, 68-69

Lucretius (Titus Lucretius Carus) 207, 207n.13
On The Nature of Things 207n.13

Luhrman, T. M.
When God Talks Back: Understanding the American Evangelical Relationship with God 21 n.4

Luria, Isaac, Rabbi 57n.149, 120n.7-8

Luria, Zippora 201

Lutsky, Elana 26n.22, 41n.84

Luzzatto, Moses Hayyim (Ramhal) 109n.36, 111n.45

M

Maffesoli, Michel
  The Time of the Tribes: The Decline of Individualism in Mass Society 44n.93
Magid, Shaul ix-xii, 57n.149, 186n.26, 192n.40
Mahayana Buddhism 27-28
Manheim, R. 31n.49, 157n.15, 158n.17
manifest and non-manifest 56, 65-66, 69, 239
Mann, Barbara 158n.20
Mark, Zvi 35n.65, 45n.96, 48n.110, 68n.189
Martin, Robert K.
  The Homosexual Tradition in American Poetry 180n.13
martyr, woman (Shaheedaa) 81, 85-89, 264
Maruvan, Abdullah ibn (Muhammad ibn Abdullah ibn Mihran Dinawari) 103, 103n.24, 114, 114n.58, 115
Mashiv haRuah (Return the Spirit), journal 201-202, 204n.6, 207n.12
Massumi, B. 85n.9, 145n.1
Matt, Daniel C. 65n.182
maturity (gadlut) 143
Mayama, Alain
  Emmanuel Levinas' Conceptual Affinities with Liberation Theology 179n.10
McGinn, Bernard 22n.5, 272n.9
Mehlberg, Henry
  Time, Causality, and the Quantum Theory: Studies in the Philosophy of Science 178n.3-4, 181n.14
Meir, Jonathan 33n.56, 41n.84, 49n.112
  Imagined Hasidism: Satire, Reality, and Concept of the Book in the Anti-Hasidic Writing of Joseph Perl/Sefer Megale Temirin 41n.84
Meir, Ephraim
  Judaism, Topics, Fragments, Faces, Identities: Jubilee Volume in Honor of Professor Rivka Horowitz 41 n.84
Meltzer, Yoram 95n.1
mending the feminine (tiqun denuqbe) 140, 143
meontological mysticism 27-28
Merleau-Ponty, Maurice 213, 213n.5-8, 239, 263n.4
  Le Visible et L'Invisible 213n.5-8
Meroz, Ronit 159n.24
Merrill, James 180n.13

Meschonnic, Henri 146, 149, 149n.3, 150n.9-10
  Critique du rythme 149n.5, 150n.9-10
  Jona et le signifiant errant 149n.3
Mickunas, A. 38n.74
Miller, Jacques-Alain 187n.27
minor persona [Zeir Anpin] 57n.151
Mintz A. L.
  Reading Hebrew Literature: Critical Discussions of Six Modern Texts 158n.20
Miron, Dan 89, 89n.11 210, 210n.1, 212n.4, 223, 223n.14, 228, 236n.24
Mirsky, Yehudah
  An Intellectual and Spiritual Biography of Rabbi Avraham Yitzhaq Ha-Cohen Kook from 1865 to 1904 33n.56
Mishkovsky, Zelda Schneersohn (Zelda) 240-242, 244, 247-249 265-266
  The Poetry of Zelda 242n.5
  On That Night 241-247, 265
Mishol, Agi 81-85, 87-91, 87n.10, 89n.11, 92n.12, 93, 264
  Look There: New and Selected Poems 87n.10
  The Transistor Muezzin 81, 85, 91-92, 92n.12, 264
  Shaheeda [Woman Martyr] 81, 85, 87n.10, 88-89, 93 264
Miura, Isshu
  The Zen Koan: Its history and use in Rinzai Zen 240n.1
moments, Gross [hitzon], Subtle [emtza'i] and Secret [penimi] 262-264
Mor-Hayyim, Adina 95n.3
Morgenstern, Yitzhaq Maier, Rabbi 22-23, 34n.59, 37n.72, 40, 42, 42n.86-87, 43, 48-70, 72, 94, 148, 196n.45, 198n.50, 262n.2, 263, 266, 270
  Yam ha-hokhmah 37n.72, 38n.73, 39n.77-78, 40n.83, 43n.91, 47n.106-107, 50n.114, 52n.122, 53n.124-126, 53n.128-129, 55n.132, 56n.137-144, 57n.145-148, 57n.150, 58n.152-154, 59n.155, 60n.156-157, 60n.159, 61n.160-162, 62n.163-164, 63n.166-170, 64n.171, 64n.173-176, 65n.177, 65n.179-180, 66n.183-185, 68n.192, 69n.193, 262n.2, 263n.5, 266n.7

De'i ḥokhmah le-nafshekha: Siḥot kodesh
50n.116-117, 54n.131, 55n.133
*She'airith Ya'akov: Hiddushim v'Beurim
'al Massechet Megillah* 55n.134-136
Mor-Hayyim, Adina 95n.3
Morris, Benny
*Righteous Victims: A History of the Zionist-
Arab Conflict 1881–2001* 29n.40
*The Birth of the Palestinian Refugee
Problem Revisited* 29n.40
Morse, Carl
*Gay & Lesbian Poetry in Our Time: An
Anthology* 180n.13
moshav 44, 44n.93
mystical apperception 21, 23-24, 26-28,
31, 35, 38-43, 47, 50n.114, 51, 53-55,
59n.155, 62, 66, 69, 94, 112, 118, 124,
156, 200, 209-210, 263-264, 270
nondual 24, 27-29, 33n.56, 34, 34n.59, 35,
47, 53, 56, 58-61, 63, 68-72, 140, 143,
146, 155, 161, 172, 175, 180, 187, 189,
192, 194, 198,-199, 203, 206, 265

N

Nagy-Zekimi, S.
*Paradoxical Citizenship: Essays on Edward
Said* 30n.45
Nagid, Hayyim 95n.6
Nahman of Bratzlav, Rabbi 38n.73, 40n.83,
53, 65n.182, 110, 110n.41-42, 111,
Names of God, (*Eloheinu*, IntegrEL Divinity,
Elohim, YHVH, No-thing) 71, 73-80, 138,
142, 151-153, 167, 171, 204, 209, 255, 265
Nasrudin, Mullah 105n.26, 115, 115n.60
Natan of Nemirov, Rabbi 65n.182, 110n.42
national-religious [*da'ati le'umi*] 55, 201
negative energies (*Qelippot*) 53
Nietzsche, Friedrich 268-269
Ninian Smart, Roderick 32n.53
Nissinovitch, Yoram 201
Novinsky, Anita Waigort 130n.38-39,
134n.47-49, 135n.51, 135n.53

O

Odyssey, The 106n.27
oceanic feeling 21, 150, 265
Ocker, Varda Koch 240n.3, 247n.6

ontology of secrecy 124
Or, Amir 95n.5
oscillation 37-40, 50-51, 56-60, 62, 64-65, 119,
124, 144, 148, 185, 190-191, 237, 247, 265
Oz, Amos 250

P

Pachter, Mordechai 46
*Roots of Faith and Devekut: Studies in the
History of Kabbalistic Ideas* 46n.99-102
Parkes, Graham
Heidegger and Asian Thought 26n.23
Parsons, William B.
*The Enigma of the Oceanic Feeling:
Revisioning The Psychoanalytic Theory of
Mysticism* 21. n.2
Passover *Haggadah* 247-248
Patanjali 59n.155, 60
Pedaya Haviva 41n.84, 123n.19, 250-251,
253-261, 265
A Man Goes 257
Crack the sun 255-257
D'yo Adam (Blood's Ink) 257n.12,
261n.17
Gently please 250-253
Majesty manacled 259-261
Mi-teva Stuma (From a Sealed Word)
251-253, 253n.4, 255, 256n.8, 260n.15
Motzah haNefesh (AnimaBirthing)
259n.14
Rachel Corrie, in memoriam 257
Sun-Space 250, 258-261
Petchnik, Nahum 201
Pinhas-Cohen, Hava 201
pleasant plants (*nitaina'amanim*) 139,143
pneumatic realm (spiritual) 162-163, 166,
169, 172-173, 175-176
Pomerance, A. 21 n.1
Pöggeler, Otto 26n.23
Poortman, J. J.
*Vehicles of consciousness: the concept of hylic
pluralism (Och⁻ema)* 162n.31
postmodernity 23, 25-26, 33n.58, 33n.66
praeligio(n) 75
Pure Compassion (*Attik Yomin/Arikh Anpin*)
266
purification (*Binah*) 64-65

Pusi, Marco 22n.5, 30n.49
Pynsent, Robert B.
    Reader's Encyclopedia of Eastern European
    Literature 102n.21

R
Rabbinical High Court (Beit Din Tzedek) 58
Rabia Al-'Adawiyya (Rabia of Basra) 114, 114n.59
Ram, Uri
    Israeli Society: Critical Perspectives 29n.40
Ramhal (Luzzatto, Moses Hayyim) 43n.91,
    109n.34
racing and restraining 66
Rayfield, Donald 102n.21
Raz-Krakotzkin, Amnon 32n.54, 33n.57
reaching but not reaching (mate ve-lo matai)
    21, 23, 36, 262
rebirthing from darkness to light 250
religion (Halakhah) 57, 59, 148
returning
    to deeper consciousness of intimacy in
    the divine (teshuvah) 109-110
    to primordial 122-123, 227
Robinson, James M. 162n.30
Rimbaud, Arthur 31n.49, 157
Ritter, H. 108n.32
Rodkinson, Mikhael Levi 41n.84
Rolland, Romain 21n.2
Rumi, Jelaludin 101, 101n.19, 114-116

S
Saadia haGaon, Rabbi 109n.34
Sabbath 48, 52, 79, 87-90, 134n.46, 135,
    184-185
Sadeh, Pinhas 96, 187, 198, 198n.47
    Tavas Zehavi: Mivhar Shirai Bialik 198n.47
Said, Edward 30n.45
Saint Aubert, Emmanuel de 263n.4
Sarna, Nahum 73n.9,
    The JPS Commentary to Genesis 73n.9
Sasak, Ruth Fuller 240n.1
Schäfer, Peter
    The Hidden and Manifest God: Some Major
    Themes in Early Jewish Mysticism 21 n.1
Scharfstein, Ben-Ami
    Ineffability: The Failure of Words in
    Philosophy and Religion 25n.14

Scheindlin, Raymond
    Wine, Women, and Death: Medieval
    Hebrew Poems on the Good Life 188n.34
Schiffman, Lawrence, F. 141n.75-77
Schimmel, Annemarie 102, 102n.22, 113,
    113n.57
Schneerson, Menahem Mendel, Rabbi
    27n.28, 54, 58n.154, 119n.1, 241,
    273n.12
Schneersohn Menahem Mendel (Tzemach
    Tzedek) 62n.165, 241
Scholem, Gershom 22n.5, 22n.5, 30, 30n.44,
    30n.46-48, 31, 31n.49, , 33n.57, 34, 45,
    65, 65n.178, 69, 96, 96n.10, 154, 154n.3,
    156n.9, 157, 157n.14-15, 158, 165n.35,
    183n.16, 250n.1
    Major Trends in Jewish Mysticism 183n.16
    On the possibility of Jewish Mysticism
    in Our Time & Other Essays 154n.2,
    157n.16, 158n.18-19
    On the Mystical Shape of the Godhead:
    Basic Concepts in the Kabbalah 165n.35
    Origins of the Kabbalah 250n.1
    Reflections on Jewish Mysticism 156n.9
Schrag, Calvin O. 23-25, 33n.58, 35n.66, 45
    The Self after Postmodernity 23n.8-9,
    25n.15-20, 26n.21, 26n.23-25, 33n.58,
    35n.66
Schwartz, Seth
    Were the Jews a Mediterranean Society?
    Reciprocity and Solidarity in
    Ancient Judaism 82n.2-3
secular [hiloni] 29, 32, 32n.56, 34, 43, 67,
    156, 158, 199, 201, 251
Sefirot (spheres of divine consciousness)
    Awe-Gevurah 51
    Love-Hesed 51
    Grounding-Malkhut 51, 57, 60, 260
Segal, Miryam
    A New Sound in Hebrew Poetry: Poetics,
    Politics, Accent 164n.34, 201n.4
Segev, Tom
    The Seventh Million 29n.40
sensible 213-214, 223-226, 228, 235
sensitive 214, 223-224, 228
sentient 71, 213, 235
separation (nesirah) 143, 191, 249

Sered, Susan Starr
  Women as Ritual Experts: The Religious Lives of Elderly Jewish Women in Jerusalem 141n.76
Shabbetai Tzvi 111
Shaikh Tosun Bayrak al-Jerrahi al-Halveti 112n.50-53
Shalom Shar'abi, Rabbi (RaSHa"SH) 49, 69, 109n.36
Shekhinah as Neighboring Divine Presence 52
Shekhinah's exile 130, 133
Sheleg, Bambi 201
Shevili, Binyamin 94-96, 96n. 10-11, 101n.20-21, 102n.22, 106n.27, 109-117, 181-199, 264-265
  A New Dictionary of Afflictions 177n.1, 185n.20
  Exile poems of the secret circle 194-195, 195n.44
  Harata (Contrition) 97, 97n.18, 113, 116-117, 264
  Homosexbird 193
  Homosexudeath 197
  Homosexy 190
  Poems of the Grand Tourist 96n.14, 189n.36, 190n.37, 191n.38, 192n.39, 193n.41, 197n.46, 198n.49
  Shirai Ga'aguim L'Mecca (Songs of Longing for Mecca) 96, 96n.13, 110
shimmering of cultures (*tzahtzahot*) 42n.88, 44, 67-70
Shiur Qomah 165
Shneur Zalman of Lyadi, Rabbi (Alter Rebbe, Ba'al ha-Tanya) 61, 64, 64n.172, 110, 110n.38, 111n.43, 175.n.50, 241, 247n.7
Shohat, Ella 30n.45
Slater, Jonathan 67n.187
Sławek, Tadeusz 149n.4, 149n.6-7, 150n.8
socio-psychological "communion" 45, 69
Sokoroff, Barry 251
Sommer, Benjamin D.
  The Bodies of God and the World of Ancient Israel 21 n.1
Song of Songs 81, 82n.4
soul ascent (*aliyat ha-neshamah*) 63
Soul, levels of
  libidinal-soul *(nefesh)* 160

pneumatic-soul (*neshamah*) 160
spirit-soul *(ruah)* 160
unified-soul (*yehidah*) 160
vital-soul (*hayah*) 160
spirals of existence 80
spiritual evolutions [*tiqqun*] 110
spiritual self 43, 61
spirituality (*Kabbalah*) 58-59, 148
Sprinzak, Ehud
  Brother Against Brother: Violence and Extremism in Israeli Politics to the Rabin Assassination 211n.3
Spivak, G. C. 36n.37
Stace, Walter T. 32n.53
Stambaugh, Joan 27n.27
Stoeber, Michael 32n.53,
Stone, Ira 35n.65
subjectivity 23-24, 31-35, 43, 47, 50n.115, 58n.154, 62, 67, 70-71, 113, 148, 171, 263
Subtelny, Maria Eva 37n.70
Sutbosky, Daniel (Daniel Ben Yosef) 95
Swartz, Michael, D. 141n.75-77
synesthetic dissolution 210, 264
systematic theosophies 46

T
Tagore, Rabindranath 30
Takatka, Andaleeb 87-88, 89
Tamdgidi, Mohammad
  Gurdjieff and Hypnosis: A Hermeneutic Study 262n.1
Thomson, William Irwin
  Coming into Being: Artifacts and Texts in the Evolution of Consciousness 49n.111, 74n.13
Tigay, Jeffrey 74n.10
Trachtenberg, Joshua 254n.5
  Jewish Magic and Superstition 254n.5
Toledano, G. 121n.13
Toscano, Alberto 22n.6, 268n.2
Trace (*sous rature*), *reshimu* 36, 39, 51, 63
trans-haredi 32, 43, 50, 50n.115, 68, 71-72
transition of a soul to different psychic state (*'ibbur*) 123, 123n.20, 137
transmigration (*gilgul*) 123-124, 123n.19 144, 194, 250n.2, 265
transversality 25

Tsur, Reuven 46
   *On the Shore of Nothingness: A Study in
   Cognitive Poetics* 46n.103
Tubali, Shai 145-146, 148 151n.11, 152n.12,
   153, 265
   Come Here 152-153, 265
   Infinity Catchers 146-148, 151n.11, 265
   I Walked to God 151, 265
Tzaddok haCohen Rabinowitz of Lublin, Rabbi
   22n.7, 39-40n.80, 71n.2, 79n.27, 110n.37
   Kuntrus et le-okhel 39-40n.80
Tzemach Tzedek see Schneersohn, Menahem
   Mendel
Tzipor, Beni 95n.2

U
Uffenheimer, Rivka Schatz
   *Quietistic Elements in Eighteenth-Century
   Hasidic Thought* 55n.135
unknowing 38, 66, 116

V
vertigo and exactitude 22, 35, 37, 39, 262, 268
Vilna Gaon 43n.91, 69
Vital, Hayyim 37n.70, 57n.151, 61, 63n.166,
   109n.36, 120n.7-8, 143n.82-91

W
Walbridge, John 108n.32
Wallach, Yona 241
Walter J. 262n.1
Wasserstrom, Steven M.
   *Religion after Religion: Gershom Scholem, Mircea
   Eliade, and Henri Corbin at Eranos* 30n.44
Watzman, H. 29n.40
Weiner S.
   *The Fifty-Eighth Century: A Jewish Renewal
   Sourcebook* 27n.26
Weinfeld, Moshe 139n.62, 142n.80
Wainright, William 32n.53
Werblowsky R. J. Z . 250n.1
Wesling, Donald, and Tadeusz Sławek
   Literary Voice: The Calling of Jonah
   149n.4, 149n.6-7, 150n.8
Wexler, Philip
   *Mystical Interactions: Sociology, Jewish
   Mysticism, and Education* 44n.93, 45n.94

Whitman, Walt 31n.49, 154n.3, 155n.4, 157,
   157n.14-15, 160n.25-27, 180n.13
Wilber, Ken
   The One Two Three of God 45n.97
   *Integral Spirituality: A Startling New Role
   for Religion in the Modern and
   Postmodern World* 49n.111
Wisse, Frederik 162n.30
Wisse, Ruth
   *The Modern Jewish Canon: A Journey
   through Language and Culture* 158n.21
Wittgenstein, Ludwig 36n.68, 248, 248n.9
Wolfson, Elliot R. 21 n.1, 22n.5, 27-28,
   36n.67, 37n.70, 42n.86, 54n.130,
   58n.154, 69, 119n.1, 120n.6, 138n.61,
   159n.23, 179n.11, 185n.22, 198n.50,
   227n.21, 267-273
   *A Dream Interpreted Within a Dream:
   Oneiropoiesis and the Prism of
   Imagination* 42n.87, 270n.8, 273n.12
   Circle in the Square 179n.11
   *Language, Eros, Being: Kabbalistic
   Hermeneutics and Poetic Imagination*
   22n.5, 179n.11, 185n.22
   *Open Secret: Postmessianic Messianism and
   the Mystical Revision of Menahem Mendel
   Schneerson* 27n.28-31, 28n.32, 28n.34-
   37, 36n.67, 54n.130, 58n.154, 119n.1
   Seminar in Lurianic Kabbalah 120n.8
   Through a Speculum That Shines 21 n.1,
   179n.11
   *Venturing Beyond: Law and Morality in
   Kabbalistic Mysticism* 42n.88, 58n.154
World of Emanation (*Aztilut*) 65
World of Points (*Olam ha-Nequdim*) 57n.151
World of Unification (*Olam ha-Atzilut*)
   57n.151
Worlds of consciousness 66
Wortzman, Elyssa N. 123n.18, 137n.57
Wright, Robert 73n.10
   The Evolution of God 73n.10

Y
Yehuda Arieh Leib Alter of Ger, Rabbi
   48n.108
Yitzchak Isaac Yehudah Yechiel Safrin of
   Komarno (Komarno Rebbe) 43n.91, 49, 61

Yoffe, A. B.
  Leah Goldberg: A Memoir 158n.21, 159n.22
Yonat Rekhokim Ensemble 251
Yovel, Yirmiyahu
  The Marranos: Split Identity and Emerging Modernity 130n.35-37
youth (*qatnut*) 143

Z

Zaehner, Robert C. 32n.53
Zaka volunteers/*Zihuy Korbanot Ason* 34n.59
Ze'ev Wolf of Zhitomir, Rabbi 110n.37
Zeitlin, Hillel 41n.84
Zeitlin, Yehoshua 41n.84
Zelda (see Mishkovsky, Zelda Schneersohn)
Zevit, Ziony
  The Religions of Ancient Israel: A Synthesis of Parallactic Approaches 138n.62, 139n.63, 139n.66
Zilberberg, Tzvi Maier, Rabbi 48
Zinger, Moshe 95n.6
Zion 52-58, 202, 225, 234, 258,
  Axis Mundi 213
  Daughters of Jerusalem 56-57
  Festival of Water Drawing 56
  Eretz Yisrael 84, 110n.41, 170n.40

Fifteenth of Av (Tu B'Av) 56, 127-130
Garden of Eden 93, 151-152
German Zionists 30
Holy of Holies 56, 133
I.D.F. 77, 94, 96, 145, 212
Ithaca of Jerusalem 117
Middle Eastern nation-state
Minoritization 81-85, 90-91, 93
Mount Sinai 212
Ninth of Av 128-130, 212
Orientalism 30, 32, 32n.54, 69,
post-Zionism 29, 32, 49-50, 55n.135, 61
physicality of Zion and Jerusalem 54
Seventeenth of Tammuz 212-214, 223-224, 235, 264
Six Day War, 1967 121, 212
Song of Ascents 223, 227
Sons of Zion 56-57
State of Israel 32, 83, 155, 178, 201, 224
Temple Mount 54-55
Third Temple 55, 55n.136, 56
Western Wall 53, 53n.124, 53n.126, 132
Zionist/anti-Zionist 29, 55n.135
Zisquit, Linda
  The Defiant Muse: Hebrew Feminist Poems From Antiquity to Present 92n.12, 158n.21

SHORT BIO

Aubrey L. Glazer is an independent scholar with a Ph.D. in Hebrew Hermeneutics (University of Toronto, June 2005) who also serves as rabbi at the Jewish Community Center of Harrison, New York. His book correlating Jewish Mysticism and Hebrew Poetry, called *Contemporary Hebrew Mystical Poetry: How it Redeems Jewish Thinking* (Edwin Mellen Press, 2009), has been awarded the Adele Mellen Prize for its distinguished contribution to scholarship. His most recent book is *A New Physiognomy of Jewish Thinking: Critical Theory After Adorno as Applied to Jewish Thought* (Continuum Press, 2011).

CPSIA information can be obtained at www.ICGtesting.com
Printed in the USA
BVOW02s1348211013

334245BV00004B/29/P

9 781618 113757